2008

Attack of the Monster Movie Makers

Attack of the
Monster Movie Makers

Interviews with 20 Genre Giants

by TOM WEAVER

RESEARCH ASSOCIATES:
MICHAEL AND JOHN BRUNAS

McFarland & Company, Inc., Publishers
Jefferson, North Carolina, and London

British Library Cataloguing-in-Publication data are available

Library of Congress Cataloguing-in-Publication Data

Attack of the monster movie makers : interviews with 20 genre giants /
by Tom Weaver
    p. cm.
    Includes bibliographical references and index.
    ISBN 0-7864-0018-8 (lib. bdg. : 50# alk. paper) ∞
    1. Science fiction films — History and criticism. 2. Horror films —
History and criticism. 3. Motion picture actors and actresses —
Interviews. 4. Motion picture producers and directors — Interviews.
5. Screenwriters — Interviews. I. Weaver, Tom, 1958–
PN1995.9.S26A94 1994
791.43'615 — dc20   94-124
                                              CIP

Manufactured in the United States of America

McFarland & Company, Inc., Publishers
  Box 611, Jefferson, North Carolina 28640

Dedicated to

EDWARD BERNDS

—the writer/director who gave me
my first-ever interview, and who made
it so much fun that I caught "the fever."

Preface

History is only a confused heap of facts.
—Earl of Chesterfield (1694–1773)

On that fairly accurate note, we're off together on another trip down Memory Lane—the memories of the stars, writers, producers and directors of the old horror and science fiction movies.

When I started on this kick several years ago, in some ways I had the field largely to myself; in fact, I wasn't at all sure I'd be able to find a magazine that would be interested in the sort of people I wanted to interview. Sure, from time to time there would be a chat with some well-known old-time movie maker or star in the occasional sci-fi or horror mag, but I wanted to be the *first* person to talk to the Richard E. Cunhas and the Susan Cabots and the Reginald LeBorgs—not the five-hundred-and-first guy to elicit the same old, dog-tired reminiscences out of, say, Roger Corman or Christopher Lee. It was *Fangoria* magazine, under the editorship of Dave Everitt, that took me aboard and enabled me to make a go of my newest hobby; and I'm still writing for that magazine (now in the capable hands of fearless leader Tony Timpone) a dozen years later. I've had a lot of great times interviewing some of my favorite stars and made a lot of new friends in those 12 years and I don't intend ever to forget that initially it was *Fango* which made it all possible. Nor do I intend to overlook the other magazines that have let me chat with film-makers, air my opinions and spew my bile, most notably *Starlog* and its equally fearless commander-in-chief Dave McDonnell, whose affection for the old-time character players equals (surpasses?) my own.

Now *Scarlet Street, Cult Movies, Psychotronic* and several others have joined in the fray, sprinters in the race-against-time to put onto paper the memories of the old pros who might otherwise take their colorful tales to the next world (where, I'd like to think, interviewers like us have celestial counterparts scribbling away right now!). New to the next world since last we got together (in the pages of *Science Fiction Stars and Horror Heroes*, 1991) is that book's interviewee Robert Shayne, the no-nonsense Inspector Henderson of television's *Adventures of Superman,* who died December 2, 1992, at a reported age of 92. (Phyllis Coates tells me she's certain he was even older.)

vii

Slowed down during the final years of his life by poor health and failing eyesight, Shayne still remained a popular convention regular, and even appeared as a blind newspaper vendor in episodes of the 1990-91 television series *The Flash*. During the half-century or so he spent in front of the cameras, Shayne worked in countless television episodes as well as approximately 100 movies — including four which are missing from his filmography in *Science Fiction Stars*: *See Uncle Sol* (Educational short, 1937), *The Meadville Patriot* (Associated Filmmakers/Astor, 1944), *Sea of Lost Ships* (Republic, 1953) and *Revolt in the Big House* (Allied Artists, 1958). Even toward the end, Shayne never let his health problems get in the way of communicating with fans; in fact, on *very* short acquaintance, he invited me to stay at his home whenever "work" (interviewing) brought me out to California. (I never stayed with him, but I was flattered by the offer.) Shayne was the kind of nice old guy the world is quickly running out of.

Writer Robb White *(House on Haunted Hill, The Tingler),* also featured in *Science Fiction Stars,* passed away while that book was in the final stages of production. This time around the same thing has happened to one of the all-time great actors (and, from every account, one of the all-time great people), Vincent Price. I never interviewed Price one-on-one; I knew I could hit him with a lot of questions that few if any interviewers had posed to him before, but he was so often interviewed by horror film fans that I could never bring myself to hound him. (Also, toward the end he gave every impression that he was finding his *too*-close identification with horror flicks demeaning — which it *was*.) Now that it's too late, that decision is shaping up to be one of my biggest regrets associated with this hobby.

Table of Contents

Acknowledgments

This companion volume to my earlier *Interviews with B Science Fiction and Horror Movie Makers* (1988) and *Science Fiction Stars and Horror Heroes* (1991) could not have been written without the generous assistance of many of the same people who have helped me in the past: Sincere thanks go to Mark Martucci, Paul and Donna Parla, Dennis Daniel, Mary Runser, Kevin Marrazzo, Glenn Damato, Don Leifert, Jon Weaver, Alex Lugones, Richard Valley, Joe and Jeff Indusi, Bandit, Carl and Debbie Del Vecchio, *Fangoria's* Tony Timpone and *Starlog's* David McDonnell (as well as all the other kind folks down at Starlog Publications; you know who you are), Tom Johnson, Greg Luce, Greg Mank, Gary Svehla and the whole FANEX crew, Ruth Brunas, Edward Bernds, Bernard Glasser, Rich Scrivani, John Antosiewicz, John Foster, Alex Gordon, Richard Gordon, Joe Dante and Joe Kane. Special thanks to my indefatigable filmography co-compilers John Cocchi and Jack Dukesbery, the best (and most detail-conscious) in the business.

Thanks also (as always) to all of my new interviewees; to the writers of the occasional angry letter (keep 'em coming!); to Research Associates John and Mike Brunas (the best in the world); and to the readership of loyal sci-fi/horror fans which has helped me turn a parttime hobby (documenting schlock horror's history) into a fulltime racket.

Abridged versions of the interviews featured in *Attack of the Monster Movie Makers* originally appeared in the following magazines: *Merry Anders:* "Time Traveler," *Starlog Spectacular* #2, July, 1991; *Charles Bennett:* "The Oldest Working Screenwriter Explains It All," *Starlog* #193, August, 1993; *Ben Chapman:* "Creature King," *Starlog* #180, July, 1992; *Herman Cohen:* "How to Make a Teenage Monster Movie," *Fangoria* #109, January, 1992, "Field Trips to Terror," *Fangoria* #110, March, 1992, and "Crime & Crimson," *Fangoria* #111, April, 1992; *Robert Day:* "Director of Apemen," *Starlog* #164, March, 1991; *Susan Hart:* "The Bride of AIP," *Fangoria* #108, November, 1991; *Candace Hilligoss:* "Her Life Was a Carnival," *Fangoria* #118, November, 1992; *Rose Hobart:* "An Outspoken Interview with Rose Hobart," *Filmfax* #29, October/November, 1991; *Betsy Jones-Moreland:* "The Saga of the Corman Actress," *Fangoria* #126, September, 1993; *Jacques Marquette:* "Killer Brains & Giant Women," *Starlog* #187, February, 1993; *Cameron*

Mitchell: "Cameron's Closet," *Fangoria* #103, June, 1991; *Ed Nelson:* "Full Nelson," *Fangoria* #104, July, 1991; *William Phipps:* "Tales from the Phipps Dimension," *Starlog* #172, November, 1991; *Vincent Price:* "Priceless," *Fangoria* #100, March, 1991; *Ann Robinson:* "In Martian Combat," *Starlog* #195, October, 1993; *Harry Spalding:* "Friend to the Fly," *Starlog Yearbook* #10, 1992; *Kenneth Tobey:* "His Favorite Things," *Fangoria* #124, July, 1993; *Lupita Tovar:* "Bitten in Spanish," *Fangoria* #119, December, 1992.

*I never did anything, in the twenty years I spent in the industry,
where I didn't have at least a bathing suit or covering of some sort.
Never did any semi-nudity or R-rated or X-rated or anything like that.
And maybe that's why I'm out of the industry!*

Merry Anders

ANOTHER IN THE LONG LINE of 1950s starlets who made their mark in SF and horror, green-eyed blond Merry Anders' genre career has truly run the gamut, from the medieval fantasy *Beauty and the Beast* to the futuristic *The Time Travelers* and the *Star Trek*-like *Women of the Prehistoric Planet;* from a frothy haunted house comedy like *Tickle Me* to the openly sadistic *Legacy of Blood* and *The Hypnotic Eye*. Long (and happily) retired from the industry, she treasures the memory of her 20 years in pictures and looks back (with the type of encyclopedic film-buff's memory interviewers encounter too seldom!) at a unique career in *cinemacabre*.

Born in Chicago, Merry Anders (real name: Merry Helen Anderson) practically grew up in local bijous watching films and their accompanying stage shows with her movie-crazy mother and grandmother. The family relocated to Los Angeles in 1949 and, while attending John Burroughs Junior High School, Merry made the acquaintance of Rita LeRoy, an old-time film actress who convinced her to take a modeling course. Later, to help her with her modeling, she took dramatic lessons at the Ben Bard Playhouse and was "spotted" by a 20th Century–Fox talent scout in a Playhouse stage presentation. After several years at Fox, Anders turned freelancer, working in television as well as starring in a string of modestly budgeted Western, science fiction and horror films.

According to your publicity, you were "discovered" by a Fox talent scout while taking dramatics lessons at the Ben Bard Playhouse.

That's right. As luck would have it, there was a lady talent scout in the audience the night that we gave our presentation [*Little Women,* with Anders as Beth] for the parents and friends. Her name was Irma Bermudez and she was the secretary to Ivan Kahn, who was the head of talent scouts at Fox. I didn't know anything about it; I went back to school, and one day the following week, I got a phone call from Mrs. Ben Bard: "Did you contact Fox?" I said, "Did I contact *who?*" —I was that naive *[laughs]*! She said, "Darling, didn't you check the green room? There was a note in there for you to call Twentieth Century–Fox." So I called Fox, Ivan Kahn's office, and made an appointment to see them. And everybody I knew tried to discourage me from going! The high school drama teacher said, "I'll give you the part of Emily in *Our Town* if you'll give up this phony movie business"; Rita LeRoy said, "Merry, they see three hundred fifty girls a week, all far more beautiful and slim and talented and decorative than you. Don't waste your time." But I didn't care. I went out there and they gave me six months of free drama lessons and made a screen test at the end of the six months. After I made the screen test, they said, "Call back in ten days."

So I waited the ten days, not even thinking of hassling these people. At the end of the ten days, Irma Bermudez called me and said *[in a cold tone of voice]*, "They're running your screen test at four-thirty this afternoon, *if* you're

Previous page: **Merry Anders, during her early 1950s stint as a 20th Century–Fox starlet, strikes a pose at Santa Monica's Deauville Beach Club.**

interested. Would you like to see it?" Well, of *course* we wanted to see it—how exciting! My mother and I went over to Fox, and Irma was extremely cold. She had been such a wonderful friend that I couldn't quite understand it; Mother said to me, "You better find out why she's so upset." So I asked Irma, and she said, "Well, you didn't call back!" I said, "You told me to call back in ten days." Irma said, "Don't be silly! *Every*body calls, *every* day. To find out which producers and directors have seen the screen test, and how they voted." I said, "Do you mean to tell me that all the producers and directors at this studio have seen this test?"—I was flabbergasted, because I didn't know anything about the industry. Irma said, "By the way, the head of casting is going to see it with you, and then they want you to go and sign a seven-year contract immediately following."

What was your first film?

Wait Till the Sun Shines, Nellie [1952], which was produced by Georgie Jessel and directed by Henry King, who scared the living daylights out of all of us, he was so cross. I had a scene where I was to be married in the movie, and Henry King came up to me and said *[growling]*, "Why don't you smile?! You look like you're going to the gallows!" So I smiled, but the tears were welling up in my eyes, I was so scared.

One film at Fox that I was involved in—that never got made—was very interesting. They spent a lot of money and gathered together some very fine technicians for a movie that they were going to call *First of April*, with "talking" animals. We went in and prerecorded the lines and then they were going to go out and photograph animals moving their mouths so the lines could be dubbed in. I did the voice of a French poodle and spoke French—which was taught to me over a weekend by Natasha Lytess, who was Marilyn Monroe's drama coach. I also did the part of an old nag; I was supposed to be the mother of Kathleen Crowley, who played a filly. And Warren Stevens played First of April, who was a racehorse. But they never could get the animals to work out quite right and that was a shame, because we had all spent an awful lot of hours in that dubbing room.

You were at Fox for about three years.

Right. But everybody else at the studio either had more aggressive agents or were better prepared; they were all getting their nice raises. I was only up to one hundred twenty-five dollars a week, which meant a take-home paycheck of fifty-seven dollars and ten cents, and I was staying at that rate. So I went in to see Lou Schreiber, who was right under [production chief] Darryl Zanuck, and I said, "Mr. Schreiber, if I don't get my raise this time, I'd like my release." He said, "Do you think you're worth more money?" I don't know what made me say it, but I said, "If I am, I better get out and start making it; and if I'm not, I better get out of the industry." He said, "That's a very

Horror and science fiction films were a specialty for Merry Anders, who turned a love affair with motion pictures into a busy B-movie career.

good answer." Well, they let me know their decision two weeks later: They dropped my option. And I cried for three days and three nights, thinking I'd made the biggest mistake of my life *[laughs]*!

Then, after Fox, a lot of TV, including as a regular on a show called Trouble with Father.

It was very difficult working with [stars] Stu Erwin and June Collyer. They were married, and they had wanted their daughter Judy to play the part. So they were not too thrilled with *me [laughs]*! Incidentally, there was another beautiful young lady who was far more talented than I, that interviewed for the part of Joyce Erwin, and didn't get it. Possibly because she was much more assertive and would not have been as cooperative. Her name was Natalie Wood.

Your first horror film, The Hypnotic Eye, *was a bit ahead of its time in its gruesomeness.*

I enjoyed working on *The Hypnotic Eye*. That's when I worked with Jacques Bergerac for the first time, and through Jacques I was able to meet his brother Michel, who was later to become the head of the Revlon Company. Jacques thought it would be an ideal situation for me to meet Michel — Jacques was playing Cupid *[laughs]*. Jacques and his wife Dorothy Malone were going over to Michel's for dinner, and Jacques said that Michel would like very much to call me and have me over, too. I took a cab over to Michel's home, which was in the Hollywood Hills, and the four of us sat down to a very lovely dinner. That was the only time I ever saw Dorothy Malone — a charming woman and an incredible lady. I was in such awe of her I couldn't relax the whole evening long.

I think I was starstruck all my life. I was in the industry for twenty years and I don't think I ever stopped being starstruck.

Did you enjoy working with Bergerac and Allison Hayes in Hypnotic Eye*?*

Bergerac was adorable, he was a handsome and charming man, very agreeable and very helpful. I remember him asking for suggestions from people, he wanted everything to be right. And he was very personable and charismatic on the screen. I didn't work in that many scenes with Allison Hayes, but I felt she was a very fine performer and a very agreeable person. I worked more with Marcia Henderson and I liked Marcia very much.

How were you levitated in Hypnotic Eye*?*

A metal T square–type brace was fitted under the shoulder blades of my back and under my hips. I had a rod that hooked onto the heels of my shoes. Then it was all strung with wires. I wore a dress that was two sizes too large for me, to cover up the brace and everything. It was incredibly well-designed. But there was no head support, so of course I went out with a very stiff neck after about four hours of filming *[laughs]*! It was a very interesting experience!

Who did your acid-face makeup?

The sulfuric acid burns were done by a genius by the name of Emile LaVigne. He was just absolutely incredible, the way he had everything pre-planned. What he used for the puffiness and the torn skin effect was cotton puffs. They were flattened out and applied to my skin with collodion. On top of that he put permanent papers [for hair setting] — he'd taken those and torn them, so there were rough edges, and placed them on top of the cotton pads with the collodion. Then he lifted the rough edges, so that it gave the effect of severe burns. It took three hours to do my face and my arms, up to my elbows, and I'm very grateful that we were able to do all of those scenes in one day, so that I didn't have to go around scaring everybody *[laughs]*. It was a lonely lunch hour!

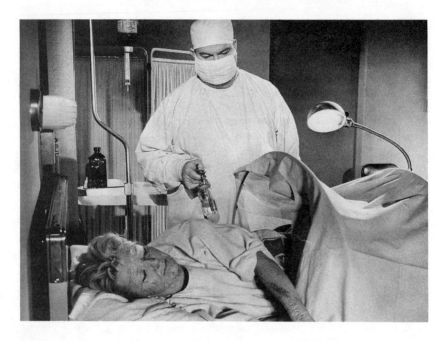

Talk about a run of bad luck: Not only is Anders' *Hypnotic Eye* character self-mutilated, her doctor turns out to be "The Great Impostor" Fred Demara!

You had another interesting co-star in Hypnotic Eye, *Fred Demara, "The Great Impostor."*

Fred Demara was a man who made a career out of assuming the identities of others—a schoolteacher, a prison warden, a surgeon, whatever—without any qualifications or formal education in any of those fields! He played my doctor in *The Hypnotic Eye,* and he was the kindest and gentlest man; I don't know how in the world he could have created so many different personalities and been that unnoticeable. He was just a phenomenal man, and a darling when they introduced me. He didn't seem terribly assertive, he was very shy and very quiet and soft-spoken. I just couldn't believe that he was "The Great Impostor," and that he had performed surgery and all these incredible things!

I count myself lucky to have been in *The Hypnotic Eye* because the producer was Ben Schwalb, and I worked with him in later movies; he called me in for the Elvis Presley movie *Tickle Me,* and if I hadn't worked with Ben Schwalb in *The Hypnotic Eye,* I don't think I would have ever had the opportunity to work with Elvis Presley. Ben was just a wonderful man to work for, he was very tasteful and a terrific gentleman—which you didn't run into too often in the industry *[laughs]*! He treated his people extremely well.

Why do you play such a minor role in Beauty and the Beast?

I interviewed for the part of Beauty, but [producer] Edward Small and [director] Edward Cahn didn't feel that I was particularly right for the part. They had selected Mark Damon for the male lead, and I don't think physically we worked well together as romantic leads. So Mr. Small made a very wise decision in selecting me for the aunt instead. It was a joy for me because I got the opportunity of working with Michael Pate, someone I had admired in films for such a long time. Michael was just delightful. He had so much Shakespearean background that he was giving me a lot of help; he suggested we do it with a very cultured accent, *à la* Shakespearean drama. The idea was just wonderful, and I enjoyed working on that very, very much.

Joyce Taylor ended up playing Beauty to Mark Damon's Beast.
Joyce Taylor I thought did a very fine job. She had just done *Atlantis, the Lost Continent* for George Pal, and I'm not sure that she was ready for smaller budgeted films *[laughs]*! I had worked on quite a few of them and had done some live TV, so I knew the importance of being cooperative; no temperament is allowed when you get on this type of picture. They don't have the money to put up with temper tantrums on the set!

Next was House of the Damned, *a good haunted house–type horror film with some of its "monsters" played by real-life sideshow performers.*
House of the Damned was for a director by the name of Maury Dexter; I did four films for him for [producer] Bob Lippert, and I liked working with Maury tremendously. He pretty much gave you your own way, he gave you a lot of leeway. And he had a wonderful sense of humor, and always had an excellent crew, fun people to work with, so that there wasn't much pressure on his sets. Maury went on later to work with Michael Landon on *Little House on the Prairie* and *Highway to Heaven.*

What can you remember about the circus performers [The Legless Man and The Legless Girl] that were in House of the Damned?
I enjoyed very much working with John Gilmore and Freda Pushnick. They mentioned having been with Barnum and Bailey — Freda and Johnny had toured with them and everything else. They had had quite interesting lives, I'm sure. Freda was just a torso — she had no legs or arms. She was so sweet, so dear. She had (I believe it was) her mom with her on the set of *House of the Damned,* and I got a chance to talk to them, just briefly, which I enjoyed. Johnny Gilmore's body was not formed beyond his chest, and he was able to "walk" around using his hands as feet. He was fully maneuverable; was capable of anything and everything; did not use a wheelchair; and he had the most incredibly beautiful hands, with long, tapered fingers. And a good sense of humor — an impish sense of humor, and the kind of beautiful, radiant smile that you see so rarely! He was a dickens, a delight to work with. I

Anders and Ronald Foster have understandable reservations about entering the *House of the Damned*.

corresponded with both of them after the picture was finished: Freda's mother had to write for her, but Johnny Gilmore had the most beautiful handwriting in the world. We corresponded for one or two years, and I was kind of sorry that I lost touch with them.

If you can stop and look beyond handicaps (or handi*capable*, if you will), you get to find out so often that there's a terrific personality with a lot of intelligence behind it.

You also had Ayllene Gibbons in House of the Damned, *as the Fat Woman.*

Ayllene was a wonderful woman to work with — she handled her lines extremely well and I thought she was quite good in the part. She gave the pathetic we're-so-lost-and-we-need-help effect. I've seen her in things since and thought she was fun. And then of course we also had a rather tall actor by the name of Richard Kiel, who went on to great fame as Jaws, the steel-toothed James Bond menace!

How did you become involved with The Time Travelers?

I had worked with [director] Ib Melchior before, when I did a picture called *The Case of Patty Smith* [1962] for Leo Handel. Ib was the associate producer on that one. That's where I first met Ib, so when *The Time Travelers* came up, he remembered me and decided that he wanted to use me. Ib was always very encouraging, very helpful. There were certain things that he wanted done a certain way, and he didn't say, "Damn it, do it *my* way," he said, "Let's try it *this* way," or "Let me give you some thoughts on this." He was a wonderful director.

So you enjoyed working on Time Travelers?

That was the movie that I probably enjoyed making the most. There were so many good people on that, such good performers; I just loved working with everybody. Preston Foster was a delight; he brought his guitar down on the set and he played all sorts of songs. Preston had written a song called *Two-Shillelagh O'Sullivan [laughs]* and he played it on the set. I told him I was crazy about it, and he gave me the sheet music and a record of it *[laughs]*! Dennis Patrick, who played the villain in *The Time Travelers,* had learned some Irish street dancing, and he was doing clog dancing on the set as Preston played the guitar and sang! And John Hoyt was fun to work with, too, because he had such a dry wit. It was a fun group to work with, which takes an awful lot of the pressure and the stress out of working on long, difficult scenes.

Was Philip Carey as "difficult" as some of his co-workers have indicated?

No, I liked Philip. He did have kind of a grand attitude and an aura about him, but I got a big kick out of working with him. He had an amazing amount of dignity in spite of the fact that he had a commercial for Granny Goose Potato Chips running at the time *[laughs]*. We did our best not to remind him or call him Granny Goose on the set.

Where were some of the places The Time Travelers *was shot?*

We worked at the Cathay Studio, a little soundstage down on Pico near Fairfax, and at a soundstage over in Glendale. Cathay was where we shot the scenes of the main auditorium in the "future" scenes, and also the scenes in the "present day" time travel laboratory; the cave sequences were done at

Preston Foster keeps co-stars Joan Woodbury and Merry Anders smiling between takes on *The Time Travelers*.

that little soundstage over in Glendale. We worked at the Pisgah Crater and Lava Flow, a lava field forty miles east of Barstow; we flew up there and did a day's location. There was a group of basketball players (they played the "mutants") chasing us across the field there, and we were told to wear shoes that we didn't care a great deal about because they would get cut up by the lava rock, which was razor-sharp. We had to run and run and of course I was huffing and puffing, but Philip Carey and Preston Foster were doing just fine. Of course *[laughs]*, their legs were longer than mine! And then some of the film was done on the U.S.C. campus. For a movie that was filmed in so many different locations, I think it came together amazingly well.

We were filming at the Cathay Studio the day that John F. Kennedy was assassinated. I had a little transistor radio and they announced over the air that he had been shot. We all gathered together for a moment of prayer, which I felt was unique because there isn't too much emotion or religion on a set. It was something that we were all quite devastated by. But work went on after that: We were behind schedule and we had certain schedules that had to be fulfilled on certain sets.

Part of the charm of Time Travelers *is knowing that many of the special effects were achieved on the soundstage, without optical work.*

David Hewitt was an unbelievable talent. He did the special effects, all of the miniatures, and all of the actual magician's illusions that are used as special effects throughout the picture. For instance, he devised the table that allowed them to remove the head of the android and replace it—that was quite a technique. Having been suspended by wires for *The Hypnotic Eye,* I know what's involved in lowering your head but keeping your body horizontal—you go home with a very stiff neck *[laughs]*! I think some of the things that he did were absolutely marvelous.

Any anecdotes about the film's android actors?

Their masks were very hot, because they were made out of a flexible rubber. And they were a little upset over the fact that some of them had to go home to their wives with shaven chests *[laughs]*! Some of 'em had to have their chests shaved almost every day, because their chest hair growth was very much like their beards. And then they also wore little pasties, so that they looked more like androids than humans. But they couldn't have anything except smooth skin on them if they were going to be playing androids.

How about the big battle scene at the end of the film?

It was amazing that it looked as active as it did, because there were not that many people on the set. It was a "cast of thousands" that was performed by probably a cast of *[laughs]*—dozens!

Any recollections about your semi-nude "ray bath" scene?

That was such a riot. I had the cutest little bikini bathing suit that I wore behind that screen and I was covered from head to toe, every inch of bare skin, with body makeup, but I felt like I looked nuder than anybody else in the scene *[laughs]*! And the other girls in the scene *were* topless—I began to wonder what kind of a movie I was doing! And I could never understand the significance of the scene, except that maybe it was necessary to make my character a little more human—a little less crisp and dried and dull. Uncanny as it sounds, we had one scene with Philip Carey saying the word *damn,* which was cut out of the movie the first times *The Time Travelers* was shown on TV, but the nude ray bath scene was left in, which made me very uncomfortable *[laughs]*!

I never did anything, in the twenty years I spent in the industry, where I didn't have at least a bathing suit or covering of some sort. Never did any semi-nudity or R-rated or X-rated or anything like that. And maybe that's why I'm *out* of the industry *[laughs]*!

What do you remember about Peter Strudwick, who played the malformed Deviant?

Oh, a delightful man, with a glib, cute sense of humor. He was a scientist in real life, and very gifted, and he had been born this way: He was born without his feet fully formed, and his hands had like talons for fingers. He was very agile, and handled it beautifully. He was just comfortable to work with and very professional for his first movie. He worked for the Rand Corporation, in their think tank in Santa Monica. At the cast party he told me that he was being teased unmercifully by his fellow workers at Rand, because he was a "big movie star" who had risen to fame from a laboratory.

You also got all your scientific equipment from Burroughs, right?

The scientific equipment we used in our "time travel" laboratory *was* provided by Burroughs. It was used for the first U.S. manned flight into space [Alan Shepard] — it helped plan that flight and also to track the John Glenn flight. It was apparently taken out of storage for *The Time Travelers,* and I don't know whether it was deep-sixed afterwards or what. We had a Burroughs representative on the set, so that they were able to make sure that we were using the vernacular correctly. At the time we did the movie, photon and ion drives were so new that the script had to be cleared before Ib Melchior could utilize some of these phrases. He had written about things that were so far into the future that they were just barely declassified. Ib was very exact in his research, and all this made it very interesting to work with. We were working with things that were actual, and gaining an education. I had no idea, with some of these things, what he was even talking about! I'm only now beginning to realize how new and how progressive Ib was in his research, and it just amazes me. He had a phenomenal background, but I didn't know any of this at the time I worked with him.

Have you been in touch with him in recent years?

Just recently, my husband and I were invited to his home for *koldt bord* — a "cold table," a Danish smorgasbord type of thing. Ib served herring which he'd prepared, salmon roe — Ib's a wonderful cook, and it was just incredible. Dennis Patrick was there with his lovely wife [actress Barbara Cason], Les Tremayne and his wife, Leo Handel and his lovely lady, Ib and his wife Cleo (a very elegant, wonderfully artistic, gifted woman). There were about ten people there, and they were the most interesting, well-educated, charming people I'd met in a long time.

What do you think of The Time Travelers *today?*

I probably see more substance in it today than I did back then. I felt very happy that the picture turned out as well as it did; I don't know whether it was accepted as much as I really expected it to be, because I thought it was really well thought out and well written, well photographed and well directed. A lot of people worked awfully hard to make it a good movie. They were agreeable and amiable, all professionals, and I think that's what made it turn out that well.

You also were in that haunted house comedy with Elvis Presley, Tickle Me.

To me, that young man was an absolute darling, down to earth and comfortable to be around. I brought my mother and my ten-year-old daughter down to the set, and Elvis Presley came down, pulled up a director's chair next to my mother and sat and talked to her for about forty-five minutes about how much he loved his mother and how great he thought it was that she came with me. And then he picked my daughter Tina up in his arms and took her around and showed her the set and talked with her for fifteen, twenty minutes. Tina was an absolute fan of the Beatles at the time *[laughs]*, but he broke through this because he was so kind and such a perfect gentleman.

Any memories of Women of the Prehistoric Planet?

Just that there were so many nice people to work with on that one; I wish I had been on the movie longer, because I really enjoyed the few days that I had on the set. I enjoyed working with Wendell Corey, because I'd been a fan of his for a long time. He had a very sarcastic wit and he'd say little things under his breath that would crack everybody up. He was concerned about the fact that his costume was so tight that if he bent over, he would rip his pants *[laughs]*! John Agar was so nice and Keith Larsen was just a darling to be around. But the thing that really impressed me about *Women of the Prehistoric Planet* was this one particular young man who was in it. I kept saying to myself, "God, that guy is so well-built and he has such a good presence on-screen!" Now, years later, I watch the film again on television and I darn near fell off the couch, because it was Robert Ito, who went on to star with Jack Klugman in the TV series *Quincy*—one of my all-time favorites! And all the years I'd been watching *Quincy,* I didn't realize he was the one I admired so much on *Women of the Prehistoric Planet*!

Your last feature was a "murder-in-the-mansion" horror film, Legacy of Blood.

That's one I hope will only run in the wee small hours of the morning *[laughs]*, although it was an exceptional experience because it had people in it like John Carradine, John Russell of *Lawman,* John Smith of *Laramie,* Faith Domergue, Jeff Morrow, Dick Davalos—some really capable people. The producer was a charming gentleman from Aruba named Ben Rombouts who had been in a very serious accident. Ben had been in the hospital, in a full body cast, for months, and he had some incredible doctors. And he wanted to make a movie so badly that he talked all of these doctors into backing this movie *[laughs]*! Ben and the director had us rehearse for six weeks before we ever put anything on film; we'd gather in a circle and do a read-around and talk about scenes and how important it was that they tied in logically. But when the film was edited together, it lost all the sense of what we had worked with on the rehearsing script; I almost felt like some of the scenes were out of sequence. I don't know whether it was the fault of the editor or if it was just running too long. I am so sorry that it never really made the money it was supposed to.

Where was Legacy of Blood *shot?*

We filmed that at the Van Valkenberg estate in Pasadena, which was the house that was used for the exterior of Wayne Manor on [TV's] *Batman*. We were one of the first filming companies to work inside there. We filmed on the grounds, too, and there was one scene that I had to do which involved wading into a fish pond with live goldfish that were six to eight inches long — very mucky, murky water — at twelve-thirty in the morning, which thrilled me. But it was a very dramatic scene and it was apparently very important to the plot. I knelt down into the water and skinned both knees, so we had to cover those with makeup because it was in the days of wearing short skirts. So for two or three days we covered my skinned knees with lots of makeup, and we kept filming *[laughs]*!

The day after the fish pond scene, Mrs. Van Valkenberg came up and she was watching one of the scenes that was being filmed. I was sitting in one of the bedrooms and she came in and sat down and she said, "I understand that one of the actresses on this film waded into the fish pond." I said, "Yes, that was me." She said, "Did they ask you if you could swim?" "No, they told me it was only hip-deep." And she said, "Oh, my dear, the thing is *bottomless!*" *[Laughs.]* She said, "If you'd moved over about two feet, you'd have gone down over your head!" Ah, the joys of being an actress *[laughs]*!

Did you get a chance to meet John Carradine on Legacy of Blood*?*

No, I didn't work the day that he did. But I have to tell you that, from what I heard from John Russell and Faith Domergue, who were on the set that day, the man came in letter-perfect with his dialogue. He did the scene two or three times, not because he wasn't right on target, but because of different mechanical difficulties. He knew every line in the script, never held up production and was just an absolutely consummate professional. I've only heard that about two or three people that I've worked with in the industry. Another great horror star that I worked with was Lon Chaney, Jr., who was in a Western

I did called *Young Fury* [1965]. A darling, kind, gentle man ... who I think possibly wanted to seek the approval of his father, and who maybe never quite did receive the assurance from his dad that he was doing well. Maybe I understood him a little bit better than other people might because I never felt that I really had the approval of my father until I left the movie industry and got a regular job *[laughs]*! So I think I felt a kinship with Chaney.

Any regrets, looking back at a career that maybe wasn't all it should have been?

The only regret that I might have was that I wasn't able to climb out of my shell and trust my directors more, and allow myself to be more free in what I did. I held back because I was insecure most of my life. That probably sounds crazy coming from someone who spent so much of their life out on the screen portraying roles. But I was always hiding behind the characters. (I feel more secure about myself today.) But once I left the industry, I enjoyed having a steady job and that I didn't have to worry about someone saying, "You've got to lose ten pounds!" or "You've got to change your hair color!" or "I don't like the way you do your makeup!"

When people think of Merry Anders, they think of TV and what used to be called B movies. Is that okay?

I worked a great deal because I loved working with the people. I could spend seventeen hours a day on a set, stand until my feet hurt, and be so tired I'd think I was practically catatonic. Then I'd go home and climb into the tub and wash off the makeup, set my hair if it was one of those low-budget films where they didn't have a hair dresser—and go to sleep looking forward to going to work the next day. It was a wonderful experience, a wonderful twenty years. I loved the industry.

MERRY ANDERS FILMOGRAPHY

Wait Till the Sun Shines, Nellie (20th Century–Fox, 1952)
Les Miserables (20th Century–Fox, 1952)
Belles on Their Toes (20th Century–Fox, 1952)
The Farmer Takes a Wife (20th Century–Fox, 1953)
How to Marry a Millionaire (20th Century–Fox, 1953)
Titanic (20th Century–Fox, 1953)
Three Coins in the Fountain (20th Century–Fox, 1954)
Princess of the Nile (20th Century–Fox, 1954)
Phffft! (Columbia, 1954)
All That Heaven Allows (Universal, 1955)
Hear Me Good (Paramount, 1957)
No Time to Be Young (Columbia, 1957)
Calypso Heat Wave (Columbia, 1957)

Escape from San Quentin (Columbia, 1957)
Death in Small Doses (Allied Artists, 1957)
The Night Runner (Universal, 1957)
Desk Set (20th Century–Fox, 1957)
The Dalton Girls (United Artists, 1957)
Violent Road (Warners, 1958)
Spring Affair (George Bagnall Associates, 1960)
Five Bold Women (Citation Films, 1960)
The Hypnotic Eye (Allied Artists, 1960)
Walking Target (United Artists, 1960)
Young Jesse James (20th Century–Fox, 1960)
When the Clock Strikes (United Artists, 1961)
Secret of Deep Harbor (United Artists, 1961)
The Police Dog Story (United Artists, 1961)
20,000 Eyes (20th Century–Fox, 1961)
The Gambler Wore a Gun (United Artists, 1961)
The Case of Patty Smith (The Shame of Patty Smith) (Impact Films/Ellis Gordon/
  Topaz, 1962)
Air Patrol (20th Century–Fox, 1962)
Beauty and the Beast (United Artists, 1963)
Police Nurse (20th Century–Fox, 1963)
House of the Damned (20th Century–Fox, 1963)
The Quick Gun (Columbia, 1964)
A Tiger Walks (Buena Vista, 1964)
FBI Code 98 (Warners, 1964)
The Time Travelers (AIP, 1964)
Raiders from Beneath the Sea (20th Century–Fox, 1964)
Young Fury (Paramount, 1965)
Tickle Me (Allied Artists, 1965)
Women of the Prehistoric Planet (Realart, 1966)
Airport (Universal, 1970)
Legacy of Blood (Blood Legacy) (Universal Entertainment, 1973)

*I've been a writer all my life, ever since I gave up
acting in nineteen twenty-six. That's what I live for. If I couldn't
write, I wouldn't want to live.*

Charles Bennett

THE OLDEST EMPLOYED SCREENWRITER IN THE WORLD, Charles Bennett has had an amazingly wide-ranging writing career: It has reached from the mid–1920s (when he began to find success as a playwright in his native England) to the present day, and has included hall-of-fame titles like *The Man Who Knew Too Much* and *The 39 Steps* along with colorful exploitation items like *Voyage to the Bottom of the Sea* and *War-Gods of the Deep*.

Born just before the century turned (August 2, 1899), Bennett made his acting debut as a child in 1911, fought in France during World War I while still a teen and resumed his acting career after the war's end. In 1926 he dropped acting to concentrate on being a playwright, later turning one of his most famous plays, *Blackmail,* into a screenplay for production under the direction of Alfred Hitchcock. The affiliation with "Hitch" continued into the early 1940s, by which time both Bennett and the director were working in Hollywood. In the 1950s, Bennett began a long association with producer/director Irwin Allen, working on Allen's movies (*The Story of Mankind, The Lost World,* etc.) as well as on his TV series *Voyage to the Bottom of the Sea* and *Land of the Giants*; amidst these assignments he also penned the horror classic *Curse of the Demon,* based on Montague James' short story *Casting the Runes*. At 94, he's still writing, still razor-sharp, and always ready to share his candid memories of the highs — and occasional lows — of his remarkable life in the writing profession.

I know you must be regularly courted by interviewers who want to hear about your Hitchcock films and your other classics. How often do you hear from someone like me, who wants to know about The Secret of the Loch *and* War-Gods of the Deep?

[Laughs.] I never hear from anybody about those at all! As far as I'm concerned, they're forgotten. Certainly *The Secret of the Loch* is one that I thought no one could possibly remember — that was nineteen thirty-three, I think!

According to the credits, you co-wrote that with someone named Billy Bristow.

No, actually, she didn't do a damn thing, but she *was* around and I did do some pictures with her. So I think I gave her credit, yes. The picture was my idea. What had happened was, the Loch Ness Monster was just starting to hit the London newspapers and I decided that there might be a film in it. This was mid-winter, nineteen thirty-three. I got my car out and I drove to the Highlands of Scotland. I'll never forget passing over the pass of Glen Coe, a very wild pass in the Highlands, with this great drop on one side and the car skidding all over the place! Anyway, I got to Loch Ness, to Fort Augustus, where the monks were reporting that they had seen the monster. I got hold of the head of the monastery and I said to him, "I understand you saw the monster." He said, "Oh, yes, yes, yes, it was here this morning." "Oh, fine,"

Previous page: "[Writing is] what I live for," says still-active screenwriter Charles Bennett, now 94.

I said, "where is it *now?*" He said, "It's gone up the Loch. Go up there." So
I drove up the Loch about fifteen miles to Urquart and I found the pier master
of this broken-down pier; he was an old gentleman, I remember. I said to
him, "Well, where's the monster? I understand it's around here." And the old
gentleman said, "Oh, yes, yes, yes, it was here this morning. But it's gone back
to see the monks down there!" *[Laughs.]* So I couldn't find the monster!

The other thing I remember is that by that time I'd been struck by the
utter loneliness of the Loch—not a soul anywhere! I decided to go along the
road on the south side of the Loch, a narrow road with weird little bridges.
I followed it around looking for the monster, hoping to spot it. I didn't find
the monster but I found a pub, and there inside were about ten newspaper-
men, some from Glasgow, some from Edinburgh and two or three from London. And I found the most beautiful Scotch whiskey in the world *[laughs]*!
(*So* beautiful that when I came to California years later, I used to import this
Scotch whiskey!) So at least *some*thing came of this trip!

After that, you wrote the film.

Yes, and it was terrible. I saw it again recently—I thought the picture
needed cutting like hell and it was out-of-date. I was amateurish, I was a
beginner then. But it's *amusing.* We used a lizard or something like that as
the monster, and I suppose the picture made a certain amount of money—it
was cheaply made. It was mainly shot at Twickenwood Studios and Loch Ness.
A famous actor in those days, Seymour Hicks, played the lead and Milton
Rosner directed it. This was at a time when the British government was saying
that a certain amount of programs *had* to be made in Britain, so the American
companies were financing cheap British pictures—we called them "pound-a-
footers," meaning you made the pictures for one pound per foot of film. Then
they were put in as second features to very important pictures. *Secret of the
Loch* was made under those circumstances. It was a six-reel picture, I think,
running about sixty-five or seventy-five minutes.

Do you believe in the Loch Ness Monster?

Oh, of course I do! I think too many people have seen it *not* to believe
in it. It's been seen by thousands of people now. I wouldn't say that I necessarily believed in it at the time I wrote that crappy picture about it *[laughs]*, but
I believe in it now!

What do you recall about writing The Clairvoyant?

Maurice Elvey directed it, and I think the producer must have been
Michael Balcon of Gaumont-British. It was made as a Gainsborough Picture,
but Gainsborough and Gaumont-British were the same company in those
days. Whereas Gainsborough had its studios in Islington, the Gaumont-
British studios were in Shepherd's Bush. I suppose I came up with the idea for

The Clairvoyant. I remember they said that they'd got Claude Rains coming over to do a picture for them, and they could also get the *King Kong* woman, what was her name?, Fay Wray. They had a lot of writers trying to come up with ideas, and I came up with the idea which they used: A "clairvoyant" who made predictions, but the events only happened *because* the guy had prophesied them. I was told to go ahead and write the story and screenplay, so I did.

According to the credits, it was based on a novel by Ernest Lothar.
     I never read it. I never *heard* of it! But that sometimes happens: Often they would put the name of an author of a novel [on a picture] after the screenplay was finished, after the picture was finished. That happened with me with Cecil B. DeMille, on a picture called *Unconquered* [1947] with Paulette Goddard. When it was finished, it was "from a novel." And the novel was actually written from *my* screenplay! My screenplay wasn't written from the novel, the novel was written from my screenplay! But people thought it gave a picture more importance, to *say* that it was from a novel.

Your co-writer on Clairvoyant *was Bryan Edgar Wallace.*
     Yeah, he was a . . . useless character. He was only there because he happened to be the son of Edgar Wallace. He couldn't write, he hadn't an idea in his head. I was happy with the picture when it came out; I haven't seen it for a long, long time now *[laughs]*!
     One other thing I remember about *The Clairvoyant* is that I fell in love with the woman who was playing the second part, Jane Baxter. This is a funny story! I was doing what is sometimes called "writing just ahead of the cameras": I was in the studio, and the assistant director would come up and say, "Have you got any more pages?" He'd take them down to Maurice Elvey, the director, and they'd shoot them. One day, Claude Rains came up to my office and said, "By the way, Charles, have you noticed this girl who's playing the second part?" I said, "Yes, she's quite lovely." He said, "I only ask because she keeps on saying, 'That writer up there, he's so good-looking, I can't put him out of my mind.'" I thought, "*This* is very interesting!" So I went down to the set, met Jane Baxter, and we became very close friends. After the picture was over, one night we were having dinner on the lawn at the big hotel in Bray, and she said, "Do you know, Charles, how I met you?" I told her what had happened. She said, "No, it wasn't quite like that. Claude Rains used to come up to me every day and say, 'Have you noticed this writer? He can't put you out of his mind. . .!'" Rains was a practical joker *[laughs]*! He was on his way back to America on the *Normandie* and we sent a telegram to him that night, thanking him very much.

Who brought you to Hollywood? Some sources say it was Universal, others say David O. Selznick.

Universal brought me over in nineteen thirty-seven. I'd done, by that time, seven pictures for Hitchcock. Universal put me under contract for much more money than I was getting in England, so I couldn't turn it down. I came across, but it was about a year later that Universal was running low on funds and I dropped out of my contract and went to work for David Selznick, writing a picture for Janet Gaynor [*The Young in Heart*, 1938]. One night we were having an all-night conference on the thing, and Selznick said to me, "Charles, it's been suggested to me that I should bring over one of two English directors. One is named Alfred Hitchcock and the other is named Robert Stevenson. You've worked with both of them, who should I bring?" I said, "Bring them both!" *[Laughs.]* So, you see, it wasn't David Selznick who brought me over, but *I* brought *Hitchcock* over!

Another one of your early Hollywood films, They Dare Not Love *[1941], was directed by James Whale.*
    James Whale didn't direct that film, strangely enough. He was thrown out after the first week, and Charles Vidor directed it—and *hated* it. (I didn't like it, either, quite frankly; I don't consider it one of my good pictures.) I had great respect for James Whale, I thought he was an extremely fine director, but he had [trouble from] Harry Cohn—the most revolting character in the world, with a foul tongue all the time. Cohn was head of the Columbia studios and he took a dislike to James Whale immediately, and threw him out after the first week.

How and when did you hook up with Irwin Allen?
    I'd been directing a lot of television *for* Hollywood in England. When I came back, Irving Cummings was going to produce a picture called *Where Danger Lives* [1950] with Robert Mitchum and Claude Rains, and I was asked to write it. Irwin Allen knew somebody who worked for Howard Hughes, and Howard Hughes owned RKO, so somehow it was finagled into him being associate producer. Once the picture was made, after that, every picture he made (until *The Poseiden Adventure*) I wrote. I was his favorite writer. I couldn't stand him, he was a dreadful man, with the most horrible swollen head and everything. He always took other people's credits and things like that; he never wrote a damn thing himself, but he always put his name on pictures if he could.

Well, that takes care of my next question. I was going to ask if you two were friends!
    Nobody could ever be a personal friend of his. But he had tremendous respect for me, and he never dared to cross me in any way. In fact, I remember a case at Twentieth Century–Fox when I actually threw him out of my office— and he was the producer, you know *[laughs]*! I said, "Get out of here. Get *out,*

you're stopping me working." And he had to take it, because he knew that I could write and he couldn't. He was a horrible man. So there was no real personal relationship, no. He'd come to my house for drinks occasionally, yes, but then, so did many other people.

Whatever his failings, he was loyal to certain actors; the same ones turn up in a lot of his early movies.
     Like Peter Lorre and people like that? Well, yes, when an actor was as good as Peter, naturally you'd employ him whenever you possibly could! It was as simple as that. But Irwin couldn't always get the actors he wanted. For example, I wrote the original screenplay of *Voyage to the Bottom of the Sea*, which later turned into a very successful television series. We had wonderful actors in it, but none of 'em ever played again for Irwin Allen except for Peter Lorre. Because they didn't like Irwin Allen. Joan Fontaine was one of the people that was in it, and she couldn't *stand* him *[laughs]*!

After writing these movies for Allen, did you visit the sets at all?
     Oh, yes. I was usually in the studio [at 20th Century–Fox], because if he was shooting one picture that I had written, I'd be writing the next one at the same time. I had my own offices there.

Without wishing to dredge up too many painful memories, what can I ask you about Warners' The Story of Mankind?
     That dreadful picture! I came back, again, from England and Irwin Allen implored me to work on that thing. I didn't realize quite how dreadful it was going to be, I didn't realize when I was starting off that it was really going to be just a collection of snippets from old pictures and things like that. It was dreadful, I hated the picture. But I'm a writer, I wrote it, I was being paid quite handsomely, so that was it.

Did it follow the book it was supposedly based on?
     Certainly not! In fact, I never read the book—and I don't think Allen did, either *[laughs]*!

Vincent Price?
     Oh, he was a very dear friend of mine, I was awfully fond of him. I had him in seven different movies and he's always been, to me, a fine, fine actor. But I don't know that he enjoyed playing the Devil in *The Story of Mankind*; I don't think *anybody* enjoyed any *part* of it. I know Ronald Colman hated it and I don't think Vincent Price liked it, either. No, nobody liked it, it was just a revolting picture and it should never have been made. And it was much too long. I remember the sneak preview at a theater in the Valley, and the wretched Jack Warner (who owned Warner Brothers) was there. At the end,

Montague James' *Casting the Runes* **was the inspiration for Bennett, who had his own ideas about casting the movie.**

we all went and talked about it around a table in a pub, and I said, "It's got to be cut. This is no good in its present form." Jack Warner said, "Oh, let's just put it out." And all his yes-men said, "Yes, Jack's right, let's put it out." So they did.

The worst scenes were the ones with the Marx Brothers.

They were just given their heads. Nobody wrote the stuff, they were just told to do it themselves and that was it; the basic idea of Groucho Marx's segment was the sale of Manhattan by the Indians.

Were any of the historical vignettes to your liking? Do you have anything nice to say about The Story of Mankind?

I have nothing to say in its favor at all *[laughs]*!

How did you become involved with Night of the Demon *[U.S. title:* Curse of the Demon*]*?

I read the short story *Casting the Runes* by the late Montague James and I loved it, I thought to myself, "There's a movie in this." So I arranged with the James estate (with his wife, who lived in Africa) to buy the rights myself. I bought the rights and then I wrote my own screenplay. My screenplay was extremely good—my original title was *The Bewitched*. Actually, it turned into a very sad situation: I was in London directing the *Monte Cristo* TV series for Edward Small, and I was just about to leave to come back to Hollywood. I was leaving Thirty-nine Hill Street, which is just off Berkeley Square, and Hal Chester (who was a little producing man) was waiting in the foyer as I came by. He said, "Look, I can set this picture up with Columbia Pictures. Will you just give me your signature now?" I was on my way to catch a plane and like a fool, I signed it. When I got back to Hollywood, two days later I learned that RKO had given the okay for my screenplay to be shot, exactly as I wanted to make it, with *me* directing my own screenplay. But it was too late, I'd signed this paper on the way out to my plane, I'd signed it away.

Reportedly Robert Taylor and Dick Powell were both interested in starring at one point.
     Robert Taylor certainly wanted to do it. In fact, it was his right hand man (whose name I now forget) who had set it up in my absence with RKO. Dick Powell also was very, very interested and talked to me about it a tremendous lot. But we never quite got down to a contract.

In the picture's main titles, you share the writing credit with Hal Chester.
     Oh, no, I didn't *share* it at all, he just put his name on. He was in England, I was in America, there was nothing I could do about it. Hal Chester didn't do it any good, but I thought the James story and my screenplay were so good that he couldn't *entirely* ruin it! He did mess up the script, but never mind about that [*laughs*]!

Dana Andrews mentioned that Chester even tried to interfere in the directing.
     [*Laughs.*] I'm sure he did!

In your original screenplay, were you faithful to the James story?
     I tried to be, yes, but you *can't* be faithful entirely to a story like that. The fundamental idea was the guy being passed the runes, and then having to pass them *back* in order to avoid his coming death. That was the original story and from that I built my screenplay. [The movie makers] put in a monster to look at, which made me very angry. I preferred that the audience should have to *imagine* the horror that was after this man, instead of *seeing* it. Hal Chester made quite a few *bad* changes, and they cut out some beautiful things, too.

What did you think of the special effects involving the demon?
     They were not bad; considering how many years ago it was, they were pretty good.

The cast was also good.

Dana Andrews they had trouble with, but he was a good actor. For the Niall MacGinnis part, I wanted Francis L. Sullivan; he would have been better, *much* better. But MacGinnis gave a . . . *competent* performance, let me put it that way. The *idiot* thing that happened was that when it came to Columbia in Hollywood, they said, "Oh, we can't use [the title] *Night of the Demon* because it'll be mixed up with *Night of the Iguana*." So they called it *Curse of the Demon*. I hated that title because it made it a B picture immediately, a title like that.

Did you ever meet director Jacques Tourneur?

I knew him very well and I was awfully fond of him. He was a very good director. But he got involved in some dreadful, *dreadful* picture which I should never have had anything to do with, *War-Gods of the Deep*. It was simply horrid, the worst thing I was ever involved in, I think. Jacques, the poor devil, got the blame for it, but actually he was not to blame at all. I had written a good script, and [while it was in production] I was asked to go to England to make alterations. The wretched American International Pictures came up with a lousy offer which my agent turned down, so they put on some other writer who *completely* annihilated the thing. It was dreadful, I should have taken my name off it. At any rate, poor, poor, *poor* Jacques got the blame—and he blamed *me* for not coming over *[laughs]*! But he was a great friend of mine.

But AIP did ask you to go to England and do some rewriting on War-Gods?

They wanted to send me to England, yes, but they wouldn't pay me any money. Their idea of money was absolutely so trivial that it would have *cost* me money to go *[laughs]*!

AIP credited War-Gods *to Edgar Allan Poe, but to me it was very Jules Verne.*

Oh, Christ, do we—*[laughs]*—do we *have* to talk about that film? Can't we forget it ever *existed*? It was supposed to be based on a tiny Poe poem; they said, "Can you take this and make it into a story?" Which I did—I did a pretty good story, as a matter of fact. And it was completely ruined when it came to a matter of my *not* going to England and protecting my own screenplay. Jacques Tourneur did a good job himself with an impossible script. The writer who did rework it put a chicken into the movie, as one of the main characters—oh, God, that was *awful*! That was stolen directly from *Journey to the Center of the Earth*, which was made by Twentieth Century–Fox. In *Journey*, it was a goose. But the chicken in *War-Gods*, that had nothing to do with me, thank you!

Who came up with the idea for the nineteen sixty The Lost World?

It was as simple as the fact that somebody suggested to Irwin that he should make *The Lost World*. He liked the idea of prehistoric monsters and things like that, so he asked me to write the script.

Did you reread the Arthur Conan Doyle novel?

Oh, I knew the novel by heart; I know *all* Conan Doyle's stuff by heart, I *loved* him. I knew him personally: I was playing Dr. Watson in *Sherlock Holmes in the Speckled Band* at a theater in Paris. I was only twenty-four at the time, and Conan Doyle was in front. He came 'round after the performance and said that I was the finest Watson he'd ever seen. So I must have been a pretty good actor at the age of twenty-four *[laughs]*! Of course, I never told that to Nigel Bruce, who played it so often with Basil Rathbone!

Allen hired one of the most famous stop-motion animators for The Lost World, *Willis O'Brien—and then Allen went ahead and used lizards in the film.*

I don't remember that. Quite frankly, I never went near that set, as far as I can remember. But there was no question of animation, no, the whole thing was special effects [with the lizards]—the Twentieth Century–Fox people were pretty good at that sort of thing.

These Irwin Allen pictures like The Lost World *got some bad reviews at the time, but audiences must have liked them.*

Oh, audiences *loved* them. And, to be frank, they *didn't* get bad reviews at all, ever—or, at least, I can't seem to remember bad reviews for them. (Not that I really bother much about reviews.)

What did you think of Claude Rains as Prof. Challenger?

He was wonderful—always. Claude Rains was always superb, whatever he did. I think Claude Rains was one of the best actors the world ever knew. I had him in seven different movies.

Some fans were disappointed that your Lost World *didn't end up with the dinosaur loose in London, the way the original silent* Lost World *did.*

Oh, God, we didn't do that, because the Conan Doyle *novel* doesn't end that way. The silent film ended with *that*? Then I guess I never saw it! *Our* ending was the escape of the people *from* the "lost world." I thought ours was a competent show; I didn't think it was very *good*, I didn't think it was very *bad*. It was *good enough*, let's put it that way.

Was Voyage to the Bottom of the Sea *your idea?*

Irwin's girlfriend had said, "Why not a movie about a big submarine?", and he told me that this was a good idea for a movie. So I wrote the story of it, and then I wrote the screenplay. It was as simple as that.

Inadvisably making its home in a pool of boiling lava, a fin-backed lizard rises to menace the stars of Bennett's *The Lost World*.

The Voyage *script involved a lot of scientific plot points. Is science a hobby of yours?*

I researched it a certain amount. It certainly wasn't a hobby, no; I'm not interested in science at all. I've spent my life writing all sorts of pictures, and many of them have entailed doing a lot of research.

In general, would you know as you were writing an Irwin Allen movie who would be playing the various roles?

I usually made suggestions myself; for instance, on *The Lost World*, it was I who suggested Claude Rains. And, yes, in all the films I used to suggest the cast, because I was working very closely with Irwin — my office was very close to his. Walter Pidgeon was excellent in *Voyage to the Bottom of the Sea*; he was my suggestion, too. Peter Lorre, and Joan Fontaine, also. And she *hated* it, and she blamed *me* for it! She was one of my closest friends, we used to ride horses together all the time, things like that. She was in my movie *Ivy* [1947] which Sam Wood directed at Universal, I adored her and she adored me, too. But she said she hated the part [in *Voyage*], and didn't like the picture.

Joan Fontaine (seen here with Walter Pidgeon) "hated *Voyage to the Bottom of the Sea,* and she blames me for it!" remembers Bennett.

Did you visit the sets of Voyage?

Oh, yes, I was in and out pretty frequently, particularly since Joan Fontaine was in it. And I also adored Peter Lorre. I had him in seven movies, and that's a lot of movies. The first time he was in a movie of mine was *The Man Who Knew Too Much* [1934]. He was an adorable, very kind, very gentle, very sweet man. Like Boris Karloff, another "very gentle monster." I was very fond of him.

Curt Siodmak told me Lorre was "a sadistic son of a bitch—liked to look at operations."

That's not true! Peter was a kind, very pleasant person with a big sense of humor, very delightful. I remember a funny thing about Peter, on *The Man Who Knew Too Much*. We had a secretary who was named Joan Harrison, and she had come down from Oxford. She was *supposed* to speak French very well, and Peter Lorre couldn't speak English but he *could* speak French and a smattering of English. So Hitch said to Joan, "Look, go and explain the scenes to Peter in French, so he'll understand them." So Joan did: She went to Peter, talked a lot of French to him, he listened very beautifully. And at the end of it he said, very kindly, "Please ... I do not understand ... speak English!" Her French was so bad, he had a better chance of understanding in English *[laughs]*!

You later worked on the Voyage to the Bottom of the Sea *TV show.*

I did a lot of them; I did about eight, when I had nothing better to do. I did 'em for the sake of the money *[laughs]*. I think I also did one or two of the series, oh, what was it called, *Giant Men*? What the hell was the name of that? Oh, yes, *Land of the Giants*, I did one or two of those. I also did one *Time Tunnel*, but I've forgotten what it was about.

How about Lost in Space?

That was my idea, but I never wrote anything for it. After we'd done *Voyage to the Bottom of the Sea*, I came up with the idea of a space picture — people were starting to go up into space then. I suggested to Irwin that *Lost in Space* would be a good idea for a movie. Well, I went off somewhere else, and Irwin stole the idea — instead of making it into a movie, he stole the idea and made a television series of it. It was as simple as that!

One TV show that you'd have been ideal for was Alfred Hitchcock Presents — *and you never wrote for them once.*

I never *wanted* to, quite frankly. I was a great, great friend of Hitch's and I preferred to remain a great friend, instead of getting mixed up with that particular show. Partly because the producer had been our secretary for so long, Joan Harrison. I couldn't *bear* the thought of working under my own secretary *[laughs]*!

In one of the Hitchcock biographies, it says that you called Psycho *"the work of a sadistic son of a bitch."*

I said that to Hitchcock's face. I was having drinks with him at his home in Bel-Air and I said that he was a sadistic son of a bitch. He said, "Charles, why do you say that?" I said, "Well, look at *Psycho*, look at that bathroom scene." He said, "Charles, you've lost your sense of humor." I said, "What are you talking about?" He said, "I didn't film that for drama, I filmed it for *comedy*, I wanted the audience to *laugh*." What do you know about that?! Amazing! According to Hitch, he shot it for comedy!

Another actor who turned up in some of your Irwin Allen movies was Sir Cedric Hardwicke.

Oh, Cedric I adored, I was very fond of him. He played in a lot of my movies and he was a very, very close friend of mine always. And a very good actor indeed. I had him in the last picture I did for Irwin, which was *Five Weeks in a Balloon* [1962], and he was in half a dozen more of my pictures.

He starred in your King Solomon's Mines *in nineteen thirty-seven.*

I didn't really write that. My name was on it, but actually I took myself off it because I objected to having a woman going with the men. I was a fan of Rider Haggard and *King Solomon's Mines,* and in it the four main characters were men. I objected to having a woman coming along, looking as if she had just walked out of a beauty parlor. It was a damn silly idea. So I took myself off.

Anna Lee did a good job of playing the role.

Yes, she did, but, hell, it was wrong. The idea of dragging a woman across the desert...!

What's going on with the remake of Blackmail *that you recently wrote?*

The script is finished, and it's a very good script. It's now a question of finding the right cast. Making a picture in Hollywood now is a very difficult problem, because (no matter how much money you're putting into it) you've still got to get the right cast, and you sometimes find the actors you want aren't available for eighteen months or something like that. And then, if you get the actor you want, you find the *director* isn't available! It's a complicated business, not like it used to be fifty years ago when the actors and the directors were all under contract to the studios like MGM and Warner Brothers, and did what they were told.

And how is your autobiography coming along?

Fine, I'm about halfway finished, but this last week I've been in hospital over my damn injured leg. And that irritates me very much, because every day I feel I'm missing doing something. Either on the autobiography, or on a *new* screenplay which I am writing.

Are you going to keep on writing?

Yes, yes! As long as I possibly can, I will. I've been a writer all my life, ever since I gave up acting in nineteen twenty-six. That's what I live for. If I couldn't write, I wouldn't want to live.

*My conception, when I sat down and read the script
and discussed it with Jack Arnold, was, "Hey, this is
simply Beauty and the Beast." The Gill Man is really
a nice person, it's simply that he's in love with the
girl and just kills people that get in his way!*

Ben Chapman

MENTION THE *CREATURE FROM THE BLACK LAGOON* and deep-dyed science fiction buffs think of Ricou Browning, the amazing swimmer who played the modern merman in the underwater scenes, and who has frequently shared with fans his memories of working in this classic 1950s adventure. This, however, is only half the story. In the movie's on-land scenes, shot at Universal while Browning and the second unit were working in Florida's Wakulla Springs, the man in the foam rubber suit was Tahitian Ben Chapman, a low-profile Universal contractee who steps forward now for the first time to share *his* memories of playing the quintessential 1950s movie monster.

Chapman was born in Oakland, California, while his Tahitian parents were on a trip to the United States. He was raised in Tahiti, relocated to the United States in 1940 and went to school in the Bay Area of San Francisco. Working as a Tahitian dancer in nightclubs led to his first movie job, a bit in MGM's *Pagan Love Song* (1950); other small film roles followed before Korean War duty temporarily sidetracked his career. Talent scouts from Universal-International "discovered" Chapman upon his return, and for a year he became a U-I stock player—and, at 6'5", an ideal choice for *Creature*'s finny title role.

Was your dancing career your first brush with show business?

No, I've been around show business a long time. If you remember *Mutiny on the Bounty* [1935] with Clark Gable and Franchot Tone, the chief in there, Hitihiti, was played by my uncle William Bainbridge. He had appeared in a lot of other pictures: *Tabu* [1931], *White Shadows in the South Seas* [1928], quite a few more. I also had a cousin that I used to come down and visit, [actor] Jon Hall, who starred in a lot of pictures with Maria Montez, *The Hurricane* [1937] with Dorothy Lamour, on and on. His real name was Charles Locher, and he changed it to Jon Hall because we had an uncle named James Norman Hall, who was one-half of the [Charles] Nordhoff and Hall team that wrote [the novels] *Mutiny on the Bounty, The Hurricane* and a few others. In taking a stage name, he wanted to honor our mutual uncle. He couldn't take *that* name, because James Hall had that name, and he didn't want Jim or Jimmy Hall. So he took J-o-n, which is Scandinavian for James, and there was born Jon Hall. So I've been around show business, even in my youth.

Was English your first language?

I've always known four languages—fluent French, Tahitian, English and, in my youth, Chinese. In Tahiti, I spoke English at home, French at school, and Tahitian and Chinese in the streets. That was Tahiti in the thirties, when the South Pacific was really charming.

And your first movie role was in Pagan Love Song.

Previous page: Ben Chapman takes pride in "bringing life" to the greatest fifties movie monster, the *Creature from the Black Lagoon.*

That's right. I was hired on as a dancer; Robert Alton, who was a dance director, was also directing the movie. We got along famously, and he gave me an additional small part, as Rita Moreno's boyfriend. Then I went on to do a few other things at MGM. I was about to do *Bird of Paradise* [1951] at Twentieth Century–Fox when along came the Korean War and I was called up into the service. I went on to serve in the Marine Corps in Korea, going from the Inch'ŏn landing until I was sent home a year later. After I got back, I ended up a stock player at Universal-International.

How did you come to be under contract there?

I was appearing at a nightclub in Hollywood called the Islander Room, located at the Hollywood Roosevelt Hotel. My dancing partner was Tani Marsh; this was an all–Polynesian revue, by the way. A producer named Will Cowan came in one night, and asked us if we would appear in a Universal musical featurette which would be starring Pinky Lee, Mamie Van Doren, Lisa Gaye and the Miss Universe Girls. And I did do the short; it was called *Hawaiian Nights* [1954], and I played a young Polynesian chieftain in there. Later, I was asked to go under contract as a stock player.

How did you get the job as the Creature?

At Universal, there was a woman named Jonny Rennick who was head of casting, especially for wranglers and stunt men. We were talking one day and she said, "Benny, have you heard about this *Black Lagoon* picture they're going to make? Have they considered you at all?" I told her they hadn't approached me, and she said, "You're the only person who's right for it on this lot!" She knew I was a diver, a swimmer, etc., etc. —I had all the qualifications to portray the Gill Man. So eventually we went off and met with a group of people to talk about this; one of 'em, of course, was [director] Jack Arnold, another was [producer] William Alland, and then also a few other people. We sat down and talked, and they told me what would be involved; Jonny really went to bat for me, she told 'em, "This guy here *is* actually part fish!" *[Laughs.]*

How much were you paid to play the part?

I was making (I think) one hundred twenty-five dollars a week as a stock actor at Universal, but since *Creature* involved diving and swimming and a few stunts, I told 'em I was going to need a little bit more money. We settled on three hundred dollars a week.

The next stop, then, was the makeup department.

Right. I'd report in to makeup every day: plaster of Paris impressions of my body, testing various pieces and so on. It was tedious, but I enjoyed it. The suit was literally built right onto my body, to make sure that everything fit properly. This kind of caused me a problem, because I had to be careful not to gain or lose weight. If I lost weight, the suit would crinkle all over, and if I gained, or course, I'd have trouble getting into it.

Did you see any of the rejected Gill Man costume designs?

Yes, they did come up with different designs, different prototypes; the Creature went through all different "looks" before they settled on what is to-day the Gill Man. I was very fortunate to be there to watch the designs. A lot of days I didn't *have* to be at the studio, but I would come in just to hang around. Jack Kevan was most responsible for the costume, but Bud Westmore got most of the credit because he was the head of the makeup department.

Was the costume claustrophobic at all?

No—well, at least not for *me* it wasn't. It fit perfect, it was like part of my body, my skin. I *would* heat up, because I had a body stocking on and then the foam rubber outfit over it. In a situation like that, your pores cannot breathe, and when that starts to happen, boy, you're in trouble.

So how did you contend with the overheating?

On days when we worked on sound stages, what they would do was set up hoses, and there was someone there I could go to between takes and say, "Hey, do me a favor, hose me off." Because once you were into that suit, there was no taking it off! On the back lot, I would just stay in the lake to keep cool.

Ricou Browning's problem was trying to stay warm.

Oh, hey, I had *that* problem, too, during one scene that I did in the water at night. Let me tell you, it was freezing. And I do mean *freezing,* up in the hills, in the back lot there. I just had to get in the water and do it, but of course they had hot soup, they had heaters, hoses that would pump warm water. And I got off *easy* compared to Richard Carlson and Richard Denning—they were in the water just like I was, but they didn't have a foam rubber suit on, they were in their bathing suits! But we all survived; if you're a true actor, you're a trouper, and that's what you get paid for. I was getting three hundred dollars a week, which in nineteen fifty-three was a *lot* of money.

If you look at the film, you'll see that Ricou's stuff was kind of . . . I'm not going to say *easy,* but it was a little bit more simple. Swim this way, swim that way; that great water ballet scene where he comes up underneath the girl; the scenes where the guys are shooting at him. There wasn't that much. Play-ing the Creature on land involved a lot more work.

Did you have any ideas of your own for the character?

My conception, when I sat down and read the script and discussed it with Jack Arnold, was, "Hey, this is simply Beauty and the Beast." The Gill Man

In his other vocation (Tahitian dancer), Chapman hulas with partner Lorraine Harris. Today he deals in Hawaiian real estate.

is really a nice person *[laughs]*, it's simply that he's in love with the girl and just kills people that get in his way! Jack and I worked together a bit to try to bring life to the Creature, rather than just make him a cardboard cartoon. We each had a few opinions, and we worked together on the character. This is what lent the picture some of its success, our taking this seriously and "breathing life" into the Gill Man and showing that he had feelings. For one thing, Jack wanted the Creature *not* to just stalk around, *clomp, clomp, clomp.*

He told me, "I want him to *glide*; he glides in the water, and also on *land*." You can see it especially in one scene where there's a shot of the Gill Man's feet walking across the deck of the *Rita*: The soles never come off of the deck, or if they *do*, never more than a fraction of an inch. It kind of gives it that "Moon-walk" look that Michael Jackson made famous *[laughs]*. We were doing the same thing, but walking *forward*. It was very hard to walk without picking your feet up, so Jack Arnold thought up the idea of putting lead in the bottom of the boots in certain walking scenes. That was a good reminder for me not to lift my feet.

The toughest acting to do is when you cannot allow the people to see your facial expressions, and there's no dialogue. So I had to do it all with body language, and try to get this idea over to the audience — "Hey, I'm in love with this girl and I simply want to take her away, down to my cavern, and live happily ever after." That was the whole idea of *Creature from the Black Lagoon*.

What was entailed in getting into the Creature outfit?

First of all, there was a one-piece body stocking that I would have to slip into, like thermal underwear, or like the tutus ballet dancers wear. I'd stand there, and my two or three attendants would put it on me. They'd slip the legs on first, inch 'em up little by little so that every last bit of material fit into each crevice of my legs. Then onto the torso, and the arms. The [Gill Man] body and the [upper] arm and leg pieces were glued to this body stocking.

After that, the rest was pretty easy. I'd slip on the boots, which came up to my calves. They zipped up from the bottom, then a fin would snap closed over the zipper. The same thing for the hands; the zippers were on the sides of the gloves, then fins would snap over *them*. These gloves then snapped onto the body suit itself so that it would look like it was all one piece. The last thing was the helmet, which had a zipper also through the back. A fin covered the zipper there, too. Wherever you see fins, whether they're on the body suit, the gloves, the boots or the back of the helmet, they're there to conceal zippers. It might take, on the average, two hours to get in and out of it.

Did you do all this in the makeup room or at the lake location?

Normally in the makeup room, in the main part of the studio. They would get me into the complete costume — complete, that is, except for the helmet. Then I would go down the stairs and onto one of those little trams that they used to use to transport actors to and from the sets. I would have to stand up on the tram — in fact, I could *never* sit down once I was in the suit. They would put the helmet on me on the set itself. And once I was in that outfit, I'd stand anywhere between twelve to fourteen hours a day. I'd come in at seven o'clock in the morning and go home at ten o'clock at night, but the total amount of time I'd spend in front of the camera on a given day might be a matter of an hour, or it might be a matter of minutes.

Was vision a problem for you like it was for Ricou Browning?

There were different sets of eyes for different situations. The eyes of the Gill Man popped out, like contact lenses. For closeups, we had eyes that were "complete," that looked like regular eyes. These eyes I really could not see through, and they would have to direct me with lights. Somebody would stand off to a side or behind me with a flashlight; they'd ask me if I could see the light, and if I could, they told me, "Okay, just follow the light." For medium shots, I'd wear eyes that had pin holes in 'em; my visibility then was limited but quite clear. Then, of course, in the long shots, they would simply take out an eighth-of-an-inch hole, the size of the pupil itself, so I could see quite well. It all depended on how far away I was from the camera.

Do you remember any other costume-related problems?

Lunch time. I'd take the helmet, the boots and the gloves off, get onto a tram and go in for lunch. They had for me what they call a "stand-up" chair: It looks like a chaise lounge, except it stands straight up and has arm rests on it. I'd get into that, and there would be a very high table for me to eat off of.

Could you swim well with the suit on?

It was a *great* suit to swim in, because it had large fins for the feet and for the hands. By the way, if you look closely at some of the scenes, you'll notice that the "claws" on the webbed hands bend and flutter in the air; they're not real hard, like regular nails. It was very hard for me to grab something, and not spoil the illusion that they were real nails. For instance, in the scene where my arm comes up out of the water and I claw the bank, I had to be careful not to put too much pressure on them.

Do you remember stuntman Al Wyatt doubling for you in the fire scene?

Sure. I knew Al, he used to double for Rock Hudson. I came down to the set that day they were going to shoot it; Al had on the asbestos suit and they were getting ready to set him ablaze. But as they were setting up, I got called away. Actually, that's really *me* in that suit: Whit Bissell hit me with the lantern, and then it looks as though I'm on fire. But if you look very closely, you can see that that is a superimposed fire. It was Al Wyatt who was on fire, and somehow they were able to superimpose the flames over me.

Any mishaps or accidents while playing the Creature?

No, never. The only "stunt" that I had was when I grabbed Julie Adams and dove with her off the bow of the boat. Actually, that was Julie's stunt double [Polly Burson]. In falling off the boat with her, I rolled so that I broke her fall when we hit the water. I didn't want her to get hurt; I had this big padded suit on, so there was no way *I* could get hurt there.

The closest thing I came to having a mishap was during the fight scene on the beach with Bernie Gozier. He was supposed to swing at me with his

As Julie Adams watches, Chapman (unsuccessfully) tries to block Bernie Gozier's machete attack.

machete, and I was going to counter by grabbing his hand. We rehearsed it, and I told him he was going to have to help me; with the helmet on, I couldn't see that well. Well, he came down with the machete, I reached up and I missed his hand — and *bang,* right on top of my head. Of course, the blade was dull and the top of the helmet was quite thick, so there was no damage.

That was one of your best scenes on the beach there.

As I was walking out of the cave onto the beach, Jack Arnold told me to do no "acting" other than to just extend my arms forward; he wanted no animation on my part, he said it would be more eerie his way. After the Gill Man passes out on the beach, Richard Denning starts clubbing him with the rifle; actually he was hitting a gunny sack full of some kind of material.

Do you remember clunking Julie Adams' head against the cave wall in the grotto scene?

Yeah, I do. The cave set was very dimly lit, as you can see, and very narrow for two people to try to get through—especially with one carrying the other! The cave walls looked like rock, but they were made of plaster—but, still, it was very hard, like a wall. It was just one of those things: I was wearing the "medium" eyes, trying to carry her through there, when all of a sudden, *clunk*! And she let out a yelp, let me tell you—she saw stars!

How did the pulsating gills work?

Rubber tubes came into the back of the helmet, through the dorsal fin, and ran into the gills, where there were little "balloons" or air pockets. On the other end of the hose, there was somebody sitting off-camera with a little hand pump. We coordinated and worked together to create the effect. I would open my mouth and gasp at the same time that he would pump the gills; that way, it looked like the gasping was what made the gills flare out. It was just a matter of timing.

How did all the cast members get along?

Doing *Creature from the Black Lagoon*, we grew to be a family. Richard Carlson was a fine man, intelligent, a phi beta kappa man (I believe) from the University of Minnesota. Whit Bissell, nice man, also. Richard Denning—boy, talk about a handsome guy! He was married to Evelyn Ankers at the time. And Nestor Paiva was a great, gritty character actor; I mean, who could say anything bad about him? And Julie Adams was charming, too. All these people were just great, very professional.

And Jack Arnold?

Oh, Jack Arnold, too—he was a little tough at the beginning, but once we settled our differences about how to play the character, he turned out to be a sweetheart to work with. He made a lot of good movies, especially *It Came from Outer Space*—that's another classic right there. Directing-wise, he was *not* a tyrant, he would ask actors for input. Then he would give *his* input. Shake all the inputs together, and what came out was a successful movie called *Creature from the Black Lagoon*.

The Creature became quite a story on the lot; my God, did it! I was

Beauty (Julie Adams) looks none too happy about the romantic advances of her Beast (Chapman).

visited just about every day: Universal stars would bring guests onto the lot and say, "Let's drive out to the back lot and see the Creature." Someone would phone ahead and say that (for instance) Rock Hudson or Tony Curtis was bringing people back to see us. They'd have me swim out to the middle of the lake, and I would float there with just the top of the helmet and the eyes showing. I would look until I'd see them arrive, then I'd go underwater and come bursting up out of the water like a porpoise, then back under again. It would be tough for the people to get a good look at me. Then I would swim in towards them with just the eyes and the top of the head showing. I'd swim in this way, getting as close to shore as I could—of course it's becoming shallower and shallower. I'd swim in to where it was about a foot and a half deep and then all of a sudden I would stand right up and RRROOOAAARRR! Some of the guests would just about wet their pants *[laughs]*!

You also appeared as the Creature on TV's Colgate Comedy Hour *with Abbott and Costello and Glenn Strange, who played Frankenstein.*
    I remember standing around backstage with Glenn Strange and, being a buff of thriller movies, I knew that he had played Frankenstein. So I asked him

about that and we talked about it, and he asked me about the Creature. We talked about our careers in general and horror films particularly; he told me how he liked working with Boris Karloff. General chitchat about our careers — and hoping that we would go on to bigger and better things!

Why don't you get a screen credit on Creature*?*

The reason for this was a guy named Jack Smith. He was head of publicity at the time, and it was his idea not to credit either Ricou or myself. He wanted to give the illusion that Universal had actually gone to South America, to the Amazon, to the Black Lagoon, and captured a creature that they later named the Gill Man. He didn't want the audience to see in the credits that the Creature was a guy in a suit; he wanted 'em to *look* for that credit, *not* find it, and say to themselves, "They didn't say who played the Creature. They must've got a *real* one." That was [Universal's] thinking. I didn't go along with it; I mean, don't underestimate people, they're not so stupid that they'd believe this was a real monster *[laughs]*.

Was William Alland on the set much?

Yeah, Bill Alland used to come out. This was nineteen fifty-three, the time of the McCarthy hunt-for-the-Reds, looking for Communists. There were stories going around that Alland was a Communist, and everybody kind of poked fun. I don't know if he was ever officially accused or not; as far as I was concerned, he was a fine man. But evidently he didn't care for *me,* because I wasn't even considered when it came time to do the second Creature picture. I hope this doesn't sound like I'm letting my ego run away with me, but I thought I did a hell of a job on *Creature* and why *wouldn't* they have me on the second? But, hey, it was their movie.

Maybe it was because you weren't under contract to Universal anymore when the second one was made.

That's right, I was gone by then, but I did come back to talk to them about doing the second one and they said, "No, we're going to go with somebody else." That was the end of that—I've never been one to cry over spilled milk. Tom Hennesy played the Creature throughout *Revenge of the Creature* [the on-land scenes]. John Lamb was hired to play the Creature in some scenes, too; Johnny and I were very dear friends. If I remember correctly, John told me they still had my old Gill Man suits and they were trying to find guys that would fit into 'em. John and I were built exactly the same — same height, same weight, same measurements.

Why were you dropped by Universal?

There were one hundred twenty of us under contract to Universal, and a *lot* of us were let go; they came to us and said, "Hey, you have no talent."

Well, if that was the way they felt, that was okay with me. Our name for Universal in those days was "The Factory," because it actually *was* a factory for actors. One hundred twenty of us were under contract, and everybody was going to different classes, whether it be dancing or elocution or acting or fencing — God, they had classes for *everything!* Of course, these were the great days of Hollywood.

What did you think of the Creature *sequels?*
They were so bad, Universal should have burned the film on 'em. Well, *Revenge of the Creature* was *f-a-i-r,* but the dumbest one was *The Creature Walks Among Us,* which was terrible. Burning his gills off, and putting him into a suit...!

Have you ever played any other monsters in movies?
Back in the seventies, when Lee Majors was doing his *Six Million Dollar Man* [TV] show, they did a segment here [in Hawaii], and I portrayed one of the men from outer space.

Do you take pride in having played one of the most popular movie monsters?
[Emphatically.] Yes — *very* much so. Even to this day, whenever I mention *Creature from the Black Lagoon,* there's always somebody who'll say, "God Almighty, what a great movie!" — which gives me pride. I enjoyed the experience very much, I had a lot of fun. Especially on the back lot, when we were out at the lake. Between shots, I was out there swimmin' around and having a great old time!

Did you realize at the time that these Creature films would become classics?
Well, I don't know about "these" films. Even if I had done [*Revenge* and *Creature Walks*], if they had been done as badly as they were — which I'm sure they would have been, because who am I? — I wouldn't have taken pride in 'em. (Don't get me wrong, I would *like* to have done the trilogy and be able to say I played all the Creatures.) But at the time, we just thought it was another movie, and it never entered my head that it would become a classic such as your *Frankensteins,* your *Draculas,* your *Wolf Mans,* your *Mummys.*
Universal Studios was very famous for their thriller/chillers, and if you look at all of them closely, you can find their secret. Back in the twenties, Lon Chaney, Sr., made movies like *The Phantom of the Opera, The Hunchback of Notre Dame.* Then of course came the thirties, Boris Karloff doing *Frankenstein,* Bela Lugosi *Dracula.* We get now into the forties and there's Lon Chaney, Jr., doing the Wolf Man and the Mummy. Then, the fifties — science fiction. And in nineteen fifty-three, they decided they were going to do another thriller, and they were going to do this one in three-D. This was *Creature from the Black Lagoon.*
So if you look back at all of the thrillers that Universal Pictures made,

The Phantom, The Hunchback, Frankenstein, Dracula, The Mummy, and of course *Creature*: They were all very successful. And why? If you'll think about it, they're all Beauty and the Beast. The Phantom was in love with the girl; the Hunchback loved his Esmeralda; the Mummy had his Princess. They would never hurt the girl, only the people that got in their way. And the Gill Man was the same type of monster character. After that, of course, movies changed; Universal changed; stories changed; people's attitudes changed; and now the studios are not coming out with the quality thrillers they made before. Now it's all blood and gore. But in the old days, these Universal Pictures were all well done, and the best of 'em were all Beauty and the Beast. And *my* pride is that I was the original Creature from the Black Lagoon.

BEN CHAPMAN FILMOGRAPHY

Pagan Love Song (MGM, 1950)
Hawaiian Nights (Universal short, 1954)
Creature from the Black Lagoon (Universal, 1954)
Ma and Pa Kettle at Waikiki (Universal, 1955)

Chapman also appeared in a few of the Johnny Weissmuller *Jungle Jim* movies. On TV his credits include *Playhouse 90, Adventures in Paradise, Hawaiian Eye, Follow the Sun* and *Hawaii Five-O.* Clips of Chapman as the Gill Man are featured in *Fade to Black* (American Cinema, 1980) and *It Came from Hollywood* (Paramount, 1982).

I've always believed that, in making a horror picture, you gotta give the audience something to laugh at before you hit 'em.

Herman Cohen

I WAS A TEENAGE WEREWOLF. Or a *Teenage Frankenstein*. *How to Make a Monster*. *Horrors of the Black Museum*. There are very few 1950s horror films that are as well remembered as these near-legendary titles, and they represent only the proverbial tip of the iceberg in the amazing career of writer-producer Herman Cohen. The Detroit-born Cohen made his first films (including *Bride of the Gorilla*) during the early 1950s during his association with Realart Pictures honcho Jack Broder, and he continued to specialize in horror right on up through the 1970s; today he operates (with partner Didier Chatelain) Cobra Media, which also leans heavily toward the horrific in its roster of titles. In his first-ever truly comprehensive career interview, Cohen looks back over his years of filmmaking and divulges the deepest secrets behind some of exploitation's greatest horror hits.

What was your first job in the movie business?

My motion picture career began at our local cinema, the Dexter Theater in Detroit, as a gofer when I was about eleven, twelve years old. I started out by helping the janitor after school to get free passes for my family and me. Then the manager hired me to watch the exit doors on Saturday matinees, so nobody'd sneak in *[laughs]*! And when they were short an usher, and I was about thirteen years old, they put me in a uniform and tried to pin it down and what have you, because it was for somebody sixteen or seventeen. Then I went downtown to the big Fox Theater, which was *the* theater of Detroit, and I got a job as an usher there. Then I was made chief of service, then assistant manager.

Did your parents encourage your showbiz bug?

No, my parents really had nothing to do with it, and there was nobody in my family that was in showbiz, *per se*. While at school, I used to put on all the plays and I was in the glee club and choir, I acted (I played Tom Sawyer!), all kinds of things. I was captain of the monitors, captain of the safety patrol—anything in the way of extracurricular activities, I did. And once I was thirteen, I worked seven nights a week at the theater—after school I had to dash to Hebrew school for an hour, and then the theater was my life until late every night. I was picked up by the state labor board twice for working underage. One of my oldest sisters helped me write a letter to the State Labor Commissioner, John H. Thorpe, to ask for a special permit when I was fourteen. I wrote that this was going to be my career; I knew it even at that age. In fact, there was an interview with me in my high school paper when I was a junior, saying I was going to go to Hollywood and get into production.

Anyway, I wrote this John H. Thorpe for a special permit, saying in my

Previous page: As a producer for American International Pictures, Herman Cohen created a star (Michael Landon)—and a fear-film legacy not easily forgotten—starting with 1957's *I Was a Teenage Werewolf.*

letter, "Would you rather I be a member of a local drug store gang, or work in a theater where I am protected by the manager?", "This is going to be my career," all that jazz. I heard nothing. Then about three weeks later, the principal of our school said there was a car and a driver waiting to take me downtown to the Superintendent of the Board of Education in Detroit—he wanted to see me. They drove me downtown, and there was John H. Thorpe, the Secretary of Labor, who was down from Lansing—he wanted to meet the kid that wrote this letter! To make a long story short, he gave me a special permit to work to ten p.m. (Of course, once I got *that*, I worked till midnight!)

You could work in a factory or a sweatshop at fourteen, but you could not work in a theater, you had to be sixteen. Well, by the time I was sixteen, I was *managing* the place!

So you've been a movie fan all your life.

Oh, yes—I spent seven nights a week in a theater! And when I was a gofer for the operators in the projection booth, they taught me everything about the projection. In fact, one operator drank a lot, and I remember that many times I used to get up on a chair and make the changeovers for him on nights when he was drinking too much *[laughs]*.

Were horror films your favorite type of film while growing up?

I had no favorite type of film; if the picture was good, I loved it. Including horror. As a kid, I always loved horror, and I used to scare my sister and kid brother going home from the theater!

How did you land your first job in Hollywood?

When I got out of the Marine Corps in nineteen forty-nine, I started working for Columbia Pictures, as sales manager in their Detroit branch. I didn't want to stay there in Detroit, but my mother wasn't too well at the time. When my mother passed away, then there was nothing holding me in Detroit, and that's when I came out to California. I got a job in the Columbia publicity department from Lou Smith, who I had been in touch with for years.

You produced your first films for Jack Broder's company.

Jack Broder owned theaters in Detroit, but I had never met him. But now that I was out in Hollywood, I was told by many people, "Gee, you ought to look Jack up," because he was an ex–Detroiter. He was the head of Realart Pictures, which was the company that had bought the Universal library. Then Jack Broder decided to go into production, and he was looking for an assistant, someone who would work very cheap. I went and had an interview with him, and he hired me. And that's how I got to work for him.

Anthony Eisley, who acted in one of Broder's pictures in the '60s, said that for a guy who made pictures, Broder knew amazingly little about them.

It's true. With all respect to Jack, Jack had money, and loved the business. When I was his assistant, it gave me an opportunity to learn all facets of the making of pictures. I got a lot of titles from Jack, instead of money [laughs]—I was vice-president of Jack Broder Productions, this, that and what have you, all at a very young age.

Do you remember what your duties entailed?
Yes—*everything [laughs]*! Including, when Jack and his wife Bea would go out of town, moving into their house and taking care of their kids! Mind you, it didn't bother me, 'cause he lived at Eight Ten North Camden, which was a beautiful house in Beverly Hills with a swimming pool and a basketball court and everything. They had a black nanny and they had a black cook, but when he and Bea would go away, Jack wanted someone else to be there, too, to supervise the kids and just to be there in case of any problem. So he would ask me, and I didn't mind it because, when I did that, I would call up my friends and invite 'em to come over to go swimming. I played like it was my house! The cook would call to me, "Herman! What do yo' want me to make fo' yo' friends fo' lunch?" And she'd make whatever I asked for [laughs]! So I wasn't getting paid anything, but I was always hoping that Jack would go out of town!

You were "assistant to the producer" on Broder's Bride of the Gorilla.
During the making of *Bride of the Gorilla* was the big *menage à trois* with Franchot Tone and Barbara Payton and Tom Neal. Barbara and I became good friends, and—well, what can I say? Even in those days, Barbara Payton, who was a gorgeous gal, was one step away from working Sunset Boulevard. And she was a bit strange—she thought she was a cat, and always wanted to play "cat" with me 'cause I was a young, handsome kid then. She would confide in me. At that time she had Franchot going (because of his money) and Tom Neal (because he was an animal!). We shot *Bride of the Gorilla* at the old Sam Goldwyn Studios, and I remember the gate calling one day to say that Tom Neal was there. And Franchot Tone was in Barbara's dressing room! So I had to keep the two of them from meeting!

This was before their big fight?
Right, the fight took place after the picture was finished. But she was toying and playing with both of them during that time. Raymond Burr was also in the picture and he was a great guy, and Lon Chaney, too. I worked with Lon Chaney not only in *Bride of the Gorilla* but in *The Bushwhackers* [1952] and in *Battles of Chief Pontiac* [1952], which we shot in Rapid City, South Dakota. Lon Chaney was a wonderful man—he loved the business, he loved the outdoors. In fact, when we did *Battles of Chief Pontiac,* he refused to sleep in the hotel, he wanted to sleep with the Sioux Indians when we went on loca-

tion. We had to put up a tent for him and he slept in it, out on the location. In fact, right where Kevin Costner shot his film *Dances with Wolves* [1990]. I have fond recollections of Lon. He *was* Lennie in *Of Mice and Men,* just a big, overgrown puppy and a hell of a nice guy.

Was Curt Siodmak, the director of Bride of the Gorilla, *a good director?*
    He was from Europe — a very serious man — and when he did *Bride of the Gorilla,* he thought he was doing *Gone with the Wind*! He was very serious about everything. He was the brother of Robert Siodmak, a big director, and I genuinely think he thought he was doing a big, *big* picture. He had a very thick accent, and, of course, to him I was "the kid" — "Hey, kid," "Listen, kid . . ." But he did do a good job on the picture, for what it was — we made it with spit. Of course, William Beaudine, who directed *Bela Lugosi Meets a Brooklyn Gorilla* for Broder, was one of the all-time terrific directors; he must have done one hundred pictures at Monogram and Allied Artists alone. He was such a pro, he was unbelievable; I learned a great deal from Bill Beaudine. A real no-nonsense guy from the old school.

You were associate producer of Brooklyn Gorilla.
    "Associate producer" was just another title; actually, what I was doing was learning how to produce. On *Bela Lugosi Meets a Brooklyn Gorilla,* the guy that got producer credit, Maurice Duke, had two young guys that looked like Dean Martin and Jerry Lewis [Duke Mitchell and Sammy Petrillo] under contract, and that's why he got producer credit. I actually made the picture. And, oh, I hated it — I thought it was just a ridiculous idea. And Bill Beaudine hated the picture as much as I did; to him it was just a job. He said he did so much crap at Monogram and Allied Artists, that it didn't matter if he did another one! But Jack Broder, who knew Martin and Lewis, thought it was funny. We shot that at General Service Studios and our offices were right next door to Lucille Ball and Desi Arnaz, who were just starting *I Love Lucy.*

What do you remember about Lugosi?
    He was very, very sick. He was an old man and not well, and his wife and son were on the set all the time, the wife giving him shots in the dressing room. I don't know what the hell she was giving him; at that time, I didn't know anything about drugs. But I *did* see syringes occasionally in the dressing room. Lugosi was a nice old guy, and he was happy just to be working. His wife and son would go over his lines with him, he was there when he was sup-posed to be — but it was sort of like he was "out of it." They brought him there, they told him what to do, he did it for the money — that's my recollection of Bela Lugosi. You couldn't have a personal relationship with him, or a personal conversation, because the minute he was through shooting anything on the sound stage, they would whisk him back to his dressing room.

Didn't Broder get in trouble, ripping off Martin and Lewis?
    Oh, yes, we had trouble with Paramount and Hal Wallis. In fact, Jerry
Lewis came over from Paramount to talk to Jack about it.

Did you think Mitchell and Petrillo were any good?
    No, I thought they were a couple of rip-offs. And that's what the picture
was, a cheap rip-off picture, and *[laughs]* I was embarrassed making it!
However, in those days, I'd take credit on anything. With Jack Broder, I got
credit on *Two Dollar Bettor* [1951], which was a good little picture with John
Litel and Marie Windsor; *The Basketball Fix* [1951], another good picture,
with Marshall Thompson, Vanessa Brown, John Ireland; *The Bushwhackers,*
which was a hell of a good Western, with Ireland, Wayne Morris (remember
him?!), Dorothy Malone, Lon Chaney; and *Battles of Chief Pontiac* with Lex
Barker, Helen Westcott and Chaney, again. I think that was it, 'cause that was
about the time I left Jack to form my own company.

What did James Nicholson do for Jack Broder?
    That was when I first met James Nicholson. Jim owned the Academy
Theater on Hollywood Boulevard, and at one point he became very ill. He had
to go to the hospital for a long period of time, and when he came out of the
hospital, he had lost his theater. Jim was a devastated man. At one time, Jim
had been the manager in one of Jack Broder's L.A. theaters, and so Jack, who
liked Jim, introduced us and said to me, "Herman, can't we use him in the
company? He's terrific at advertising and publicity." I said sure. So Jim worked
virtually as my assistant at that time—he worked in advertising in our offices
during that period. And when I left Broder, Jim stayed and was promoted.

What did you have to do with the British film Ghost Ship?
    That was one of the pictures I handled after I formed my first company.
I met Nat Cohen, who was one of the heads of Anglo Amalgamated Films
in England, and we formed a company to do some cheap pictures in London.
(Nat was not a relative, by the way.) I would own 'em in certain territories [the
Western Hemisphere] and they would own 'em in the rest [the Eastern
Hemisphere]. The pictures involved were *Ghost Ship, Undercover Agent*
[1953] and a couple more. I made a deal with Lippert Pictures, and they
distributed these things for me here in the States. Then I told Nat, "Look,
why don't I bring an American star over to London for the next picture? We'll
get more money for it." Nat thought that was a good idea. He was hot,
publicity-wise, for Phyllis Kirk, who was in *House of Wax* with Vincent
Price—at that time, that was a big picture. So I signed Phyllis Kirk and I produced the picture, which was called *River Beat* [1954]. Bet you never heard
of that one.

The first picture you produced stateside was Target Earth.

Target Earth started with me buying a short story called *Deadly City* — in fact, Jim Nicholson was with me when I found the magazine with the story in it at a newsstand on North Las Palmas. Jim took the story and started writing a treatment for it, and I bought the treatment from Jim, I think for two hundred fifty dollars. I changed the title to *Target Earth,* and then I developed the script with a writer named Bill Raynor.

Then I maneuvered to get a deal for financing, and two guys who were really nice to me were Harold Mirisch and Steve Broidy at Allied Artists. I was a young whippersnapper, in my early twenties, and I called up wanting to make an appointment with these guys — and they *saw* me! They read my first draft script, they liked it, I gave 'em the budget (which was under one hundred thousand dollars) and they said, "If you can get somebody to put up the balance of the financing, we'll put in X-amount of money." I flew to New York and got the head of DeLuxe Labs, Alan Friedman, to put up the money for the print order. And that's how I got the financing on my first independent picture. It really was something — everybody marveled that I put the damn thing together.

Then you got a film editor, Sherman Rose, to direct it for you.

Sherman Rose was "Pop" Sherman's nephew — Harry "Pop" Sherman, who produced all the *Hopalong Cassidy* Westerns. Sherman Rose practically grew up on a sound stage. He and his wife Kathleen worked a couple of the Jack Broder pictures, and I also met him at Columbia, socially. (And Kathleen Rose won an Academy Award for sound effects editor a few years ago, I want you to know. She's a great sound effects editor, one of the tops in the industry.) So I hired Sherman Rose to direct — that was his first directing job.

Where did you shoot Target Earth?

We shot at Kling Studios — Charlie Chaplin Studios — which is now A&M. And also we were on location all over the place. We shot on weekends without permits . . . my garage . . . you name it. We shot on the empty streets of L.A. early in the morning on four or five weekends, to get the scenes of the evacuated city. A friend of mine was a cop with the L.A.P.D., and he came with us one early Sunday morning in his uniform. (We didn't have any permits. We could've got in real trouble.) We cleared the streets in downtown L.A. The only problem we had was that there was a Catholic church right across from where we were shooting. There were no people on the street, we were shooting and then all of a sudden the church doors swung open and the people came piling out *[laughs]*! "Oh, God! Stop the cameras!" We forgot that they were all in there!

You had a good cast in Richard Denning, Kathleen Crowley and Virginia Grey.

It was a wonderful little family; they cooperated like crazy. They worked early Sunday mornings where we "stole" shots on the city streets, so on and so forth. Sherman Rose and I went out there, not with our crew, but with a hand camera, an Eymo, and shot it ourselves. Then we put in the sound afterwards.

How many robots did you have in that film?
  We attacked L.A. with one robot *[laughs]*! David Koehler was a special effects guy that I've occasionally worked with, and he built the thing in my garage. (*Very* economically!) I also let Dave Koehler have several other jobs on the picture. The guy who wore the robot suit was my gorilla in *Bride of the Gorilla* and *Bela Lugosi Meets a Brooklyn Gorilla*, Steve Calvert; the first time I met him, he was a bartender at Ciro's on Sunset Strip. He just recently passed away.

Did the picture end up costing one hundred thousand dollars?
  We did come in under budget; in fact, the Chemical Bank of New York gave money back to both Allied Artists and DeLuxe when we came in under budget. I think *Target Earth* cost about eighty-five thousand dollars. It took about a week as far as actual shooting, but then we did a lot of post-production. All the shots of Denning and Kathleen and Virginia and Richard Reeves on the streets and everything else, that was done in post-production.

Shortly after Target Earth, *you produced a number of pictures for United Artists.*
  [Producer] Leonard Goldstein and his twin brother Bob had made a deal with United Artists to produce some pictures; Bob Jacks was also involved because at that time he was Darryl Zanuck's son-in-law. Anyway, Leonard died and Max Youngstein, who was head of production at the time, needed a producer very badly. He had seen *Target Earth* and another picture of mine, *Magnificent Roughnecks* [1956], and he'd seen the budgets. Robert Blumofe, who was an executive at UA, said, "Max, you ought to talk to this kid Herman Cohen." So Youngstein interviewed me, and to make a long story short, he signed a deal with me to produce four pictures for UA that Leonard Goldstein was supposed to produce. They were *The Brass Legend* [1956] with Hugh O'Brian, which was a Western; *Dance with Me, Henry* [1956], Abbott and Costello's last picture; *Fury at Showdown* [1957] with John Derek; and *Crime of Passion* [1957] with Barbara Stanwyck, Sterling Hayden, Raymond Burr and Virginia Grey. *Crime of Passion* got great reviews—some people said it was the best Stanwyck picture since *Double Indemnity* [1944] and all that. And it died—didn't do *any* business! I hadn't picked the stories, I was just under contract to produce 'em, but I felt terrible. So at the end of those four pictures, I wanted to go back to my own company.
  It was during this time that Jim Nicholson left Jack Broder to form his own company. Roger Corman had produced a film called *The Fast and the*

Furious [1954] with Dorothy Malone and John Ireland, and gave it to Jim to release if he could get the franchise holders throughout the country. And Jim formed a company at that time called American Releasing Corporation.

Which later became AIP.
Right. Jim wanted me to be his partner — Sam Arkoff would have never been around if I had been Jim's partner! 'Cause Jim and I were close personal friends, even after I left Broder. Jim told me his ideas and this and that, and I said, "Jim, I can't come with you" — this was while I was in the midst of making those four pictures for UA. "But anything you need," I told him, "my secretary, my staff and I will help you." In fact, we did all his mimeographing and everything else at my offices!
Jim got an office at Six-two-two-three Selma in Hollywood, a one-room little office, and in another one-room little office was this attorney with a big fat cigar, Sam Arkoff. That's where Jim met Sam, in this building on Selma — Sam had a law office there. Jim told me that this attorney Arkoff said that if he got a piece of the company, he would do the contracts for 'em. That's how Jim and Sam got together.

And you were in a position to work with them once Crime of Passion *went bust.*
When *Crime of Passion* did not do business, I said, "Shit, I gotta do something quick to make some money." And Jim was asking me, "Herm, can you do a picture for us?" That's when I thought of doing a teenage werewolf picture; I felt that for a fledgling company which was trying to get the teenage market, it could be ideal. I came up with the title *Teenage Werewolf*, and Jim Nicholson added *I Was a*. And that's how I got involved with *I Was a Teenage Werewolf*.

Was Nicholson one to help creatively once a picture was underway?
The only thing Jim had anything to do with was the advertising campaign. He had nothing to do with the script whatsoever, or with the making of the picture — I wrote it with Aben Kandel. Aben was one of my dearest friends, and we worked very well together. To play the Teenage Werewolf, I signed Michael Landon to Herman Cohen Productions — and not just for one picture, I had him under personal contract for a multiple deal. But I released him to do *Bonanza*. I could have sold the contract, but I just ripped it up.

Two other actors who supposedly were up for the Werewolf role were Scott Marlowe and John Ashley.
Scott Marlowe was, but in the auditions and what have you, I felt that Michael Landon was the best. Landon was a hell of an actor, and he did a damn good audition. John Ashley was never up for *Teenage Werewolf*.

He says he was, and that you gave him a part in How to Make a Monster *as a sort of consolation prize.*
That's a lot of crap, I never even heard of him at that time. John was a kid who came out here from Oklahoma with a lot of money—his [foster] father was a very wealthy doctor. Jim Nicholson was going to use John in one of the AIP pictures, but it didn't work out. So when I was doing *How to Make a Monster* and it had a musical number scene, Jim said, "Herm, maybe you can use this John Ashley"—because AIP had committed themselves to use him in *some*thing. Jim sent John over to my office; I liked him and we rehearsed him, and that's how he was in *How to Make a Monster.* John was a nice guy, but he was never up for *Teenage Werewolf.*

Do you think Landon did a good job?
Oh, he was marvelous. At that time, he was living in one room with this gal Dodie, who he later married, and with her kid from a previous marriage. And they had about five or six cats in this one room! When I signed him, I took him to the Ranch Market, which was open twenty-four hours a day in those days, we went through there and I bought him whatever he thought he could use to eat. I got a big hug and a kiss in the parking lot when I drove him home, because he had no money at that time—he was broke, he was in tough shape.

And you got along with him well throughout the picture?
We got along great; long after the picture was finished, he used to come across to visit me at Raleigh Studios when they shot *Bonanza* at Paramount. We were very close friends until I went to London to do *Horrors of the Black Museum.* I was spending a great deal of time in London and he was busy at *Bonanza,* and we sort of drifted apart. These things happen.

Did he do all of his own stunts in the film?
He sure did. In fact, we thought he had almost killed himself in that gym scene, when he ran after Dawn Richards and jumped right into the bunch of iron chairs. That was Michael. It's funny, but when he had that makeup on, he said he felt like he *was* a werewolf. He was excellent. There was nothing he didn't do that we wanted him to do; in fact, he always wanted to do more.

Was he wearing a mask or makeup?
It was actually makeup, but there were a couple of appliances on the side. Philip Scheer was a makeup guy who used to work at Universal—that's why I hired him, because he knew about the old Wolf Man and Frankenstein makeups and what have you. He was like an assistant in those days there at Universal.

Gene Fowler, Jr., directed Teenage Werewolf.
When I was going to do *Teenage Werewolf,* I thought of Sherman Rose.

Michael Landon (notice the glove) takes on director Gene Fowler, Jr.'s, dog Anna in the exploitation classic *I Was a Teenage Werewolf.*

But throughout those years, he was going through a problem within himself, and he was having a problem with his marriage to Kate; I had to do a lot of directing on *Target Earth* myself. I gave him *Magnificent Roughnecks* reluctantly, and I did a lot of directing on *that,* too. He was a very shy guy, and his wife was pushing him, pushing him all the time to direct instead of cut. (He was a hell of a film editor.) Gene Fowler, Jr., and his wife Marge were very close friends of mine, and Gene Fowler wanted to direct—he hadn't directed any features before, he was a film editor. And I didn't know whether I should trust Sherman with *Teenage Werewolf* or not. So I looked at some of the stuff that Gene Fowler had cut, we sat and we talked, and to make a long story short, I hired him as the director.

Gene Fowler's wife Marge is an Academy Award film editor, by the way. I was the first producer in Hollywood to start hiring so many women for the cutting room. You've heard of Verna Fields? She was vice-president at Universal, in charge of post-production for years. I gave her her first jobs, as the assistant sound effects editor on my four pictures for UA. These people, Kate and Sherman Rose and Marge and Gene Fowler and Verna Fields and I — we were all close personal friends in those days.

Why did Aben Kandel use pseudonyms in writing these early pictures for you?

Aben and I wrote the scripts together and used a joint pseudonym. The reason for that is, Aben at that time was doing a couple of big things at MGM and Warners, so therefore he couldn't use his own name. But I didn't feel happy taking solo screenplay credit. So we decided not to use our real names. In fact, I almost did not use *my* real name as the producer of *I Was a Teenage Werewolf,* because after doing *Crime of Passion* and *Dance with Me, Henry* and the other pictures at UA, it seemed like a big step down. Friends of mine, like Harry Cohn's nephew Bobby Cohn, were saying, "Jesus, you're not gonna use your own name on *I Was a Teenage Werewolf,* are you? Herm, you'll be *ruined*!" So I started thinking, "Gee, maybe I better *not*!"; I was thinking of using [the pseudonym] "Ralph Thornton" as the writer *and* the producer. Then all of a sudden, Jack Benny, Bob Hope and various other comedians got ahold of the title and they started making fun of it. We started getting calls from *Time* magazine and *Look* magazine, and they wanted to talk to the producer of *I Was a Teenage Werewolf.* My secretary Donna Heydt (who was the wife of Louis Jean Heydt, the actor) said, "Herman, what do I tell 'em?" Well, when *Time* and *Look* and *Life* started calling for the producer, I decided that the producer was going to be Herman Cohen.

Did you get along well with Whit Bissell?

He was terrific in *Teenage Werewolf,* and *I Was a Teenage Frankenstein,* too. I just recently saw him at the Motion Picture Home; he and Aben Kandel are both out there and I had lunch with 'em a couple weeks ago. [Kandel died 1/28/93.] Whit Bissell is in great shape still. Whit was terrific to work with, a great gentleman. And even now, at the Motion Picture Home, *what* a nice guy! He's a class man: you ought to see how he is with the other older people at the Home. He even does their shopping across the street at the drug store for 'em.

Was I Was a Teenage Werewolf *called* Blood of the Werewolf *at any time?*

[Emphatically.] Never. In reference books, I've seen that and a couple other names for it, too. It was titled *Teenage Werewolf* from the beginning — I still have the original script. Jim Nicholson worked on the advertising campaign himself, came up and showed me a great ad on *I Was a Teenage Werewolf* and I said, "Jim, that's genius." We made the picture for under one hundred fifty thousand dollars and it grossed over two million dollars in the first two weeks.

Where was Teenage Werewolf *shot?*
We did a lot of it at Ziv in West Hollywood, where I had offices at the time. The high school was just a block away. The woods and all that were Bronson Canyon.

Were you on the set much?
All the time. I'm on the sets of *all* my pictures, *all* the time. If I'm not on the set, then my associate or my assistant or somebody is there, so if anything happens where they need me, they can call me and get me on there right away.

And that's why you're in a lot of these pictures, in bit parts?
[Laughs.] No, that was just for fun — a lot of the producers and directors do that. Sometimes I forget which pictures I'm in.

Teenage Werewolf *has an excellent music score by Paul Dunlap.*
Paul was a very underrated composer. I used Paul in a lot of pictures; in fact, prior to *Werewolf*, Paul did *Target Earth, Crime of Passion* and lots more for me. I got along with him very well because I'm very involved in music and with all my music composers. Paul would have been a hell of a top composer, but he was always involved with ex-wives and alimony, and he always had to work. So he would take anything that came his way. In my opinion, that really hurt him. He was also Sam Fuller's favorite composer.
Speaking of composers, I gave Elmer Bernstein one of his first pictures: He did *Battles of Chief Pontiac* when I was with Jack Broder. I met Elmer Bernstein at Schwab's Drug Store. I was having breakfast there and a friend came over and said, "Herm, I want you to meet this new young composer from New York," blah, blah, blah. We met, we talked and he wanted to know if I could someday come up to his place in Laurel Canyon and listen to some of his music. Which I did, and I was very impressed. So I introduced him to Jack Broder. Elmer's a very short guy — five feet five inches, five feet six inches or something. Jack was a very small man, too, but Elmer was even shorter than Jack! And I'll never forget Jack, with his hand in his pants (he always put his right hand in his pants as he was talking), saying to me with his little Yiddish accent, "Herman vhere did you find this *kid*? He's a *kid*!" I told him, "Jack, we

can get him very cheap," and he got all excited: "*Cheap*?! How much for the score?" Elmer did a hell of a score for us for *Battles of Chief Pontiac*.

Did you see the Highway to Heaven *TV episode where Michael Landon did his takeoff on* Teenage Werewolf?

Yes, I did, because we okayed it and sold them the piece of film that they used. I thought it was fun. I don't know what the ratings were like on that particular episode, but I think they were very high because I believe it was repeated several times.

Did you have a multiple picture deal with AIP?

No, it was just picture by picture, I never signed a multiple picture deal. Believe me, if one of my pictures had dropped dead, Jim and his people, which at that time was Sam Arkoff and Joe Moritz and so on, would have said, "Herm, we're not gonna do any more pictures with you!"

Sam Arkoff tells the story that a big Texas exhibitor asked for two new AIP horror pictures on Labor Day, and that I Was a Teenage Frankenstein *and* Blood of Dracula *were ready for him by Thanksgiving.*

That's true. *Werewolf* did terrific—in fact, the big Interstate circuit in Texas kicked it off and it just did great. I made personal appearances in Dallas and Houston and Austin. Bob O'Donnell [the head of Interstate] said to me, "If we can get another picture like this, I'll give you the Thanksgiving date." So in discussing this with Jim Nicholson, I said, "What if I did *I Was a Teenage Frankenstein*?" and Jim said, "Great!" I came up with the original story and got Aben in with me on the screenplay. And then Jim said, "Herm, if you've got a second feature to go back-to-back with *Frankenstein*, we'll have the whole program! We won't have to share it with one of the majors." So that's when I came up with *Blood of Dracula,* and we shot the two virtually back-to-back. O'Donnell gave us Thanksgiving in the entire circuit, with the kickoff at the Majestic in Dallas.

Herbert L. Strock directed the pair of 'em.

Herb was directing some Ziv TV shows at the time—*Highway Patrol*s with Brod Crawford, a West Point show, so on and so forth. He was on the lot and I met him, and I felt that he was a director that I could get along with and work with. He was fast and quick, and that was what we needed—these were budget pictures.

Teenage Frankenstein *doesn't go over nearly as well as* Teenage Werewolf.

Both *Frankenstein* and *Blood of Dracula* were written and put in front of the camera in only four weeks, in order to make that Thanksgiving date. And there was a shortage of money at the time. So I had to really, really cut down.

So you made Teenage Frankenstein *very indoorsy to reduce costs.*

And *Blood of Dracula,* too. Well, we got out of the house a *little* on *Blood of Dracula*—although it was just outside on the lawn *[laughs]*!

On Teenage Frankenstein, *where did you shoot the scenes with the alligator?*

At Ziv, which is where we shot the whole thing. Actually, that's quite a story. We got the alligator from the Buena Park Alligator Farm, and it was an alligator that they had brought in from Texas. There it was owned by a guy that owned a roadside inn in a small town outside of Dallas. He would hire a waitress who had no family, he would swing with her and what have you, and then when he got tired of her, he would throw her in a pool in his basement where he had this alligator! That alligator had killed about *seven women*! This is a true story! And when I needed an alligator in *I Was a Teenage Frankenstein,* that's the one they sent me!

You shot that conclusion in color, which was very novel.

At that time, I thought that was quite inventive. We couldn't afford to make the picture in color, so I came up with that idea, and I talked Jim Nicholson into letting me spend a few extra bucks.

Did you think Gary Conway did a good job in Teenage Frankenstein?

He sure did—he did a *very* good job. In fact, *I* changed his name to Gary Conway. His name was Gareth Carmody, and I thought that was just too classy. I sat down with his mother and father, who were schoolteachers who came to meet the producer, and we changed his name to Gary Conway. Again, it was Philip Scheer doing the makeup; it was an appliance, in about four parts.

Do you stand by that Frankenstein makeup today, despite all the criticism it's gotten?

[Contemptuously.] Of course! Criticism never bothered me—I couldn't care less. Critics have to write something.

Didn't you ever run into problems with the censors on these older pictures?

Oh, sure we did! There were things that we had to cut out, but I can't recall what they were; it was a give-and-take situation. A wonderful guy named Geoffrey Shurlock used to be the head of the MPAA out here on the West Coast. He was head of it for twenty-five years, and of course everything had to be submitted to him—scripts in advance, and then the rough cuts when the pictures were done. Geoffrey and I became pretty good friends.

Take a look at my pictures. In my horror films, I never went for the *Texas Chainsaw Massacre* type of blood and guts and tearing stomachs out and what have you. Most of my horror I did with sound effects and music. You *thought* you were seeing what you were *not* seeing.

I thought I saw a smashed and bloody disembodied leg and hand in Teenage Frankenstein.

Oh, yes, but that wasn't really horror. I used to tell Geoffrey Shurlock, "Come on, Geoff, I'm doing this in good taste" *[laughs],* and I sold him on it. I had a lot of fights with his staff, so I always had to finish everything with him directly.

Why doesn't Whit Bissell try for a British accent when he's playing a British Dr. Frankenstein?

Actually, it depends upon the ear of the listener. Even today, when I talk to him at the Motion Picture Home, he sounds English to me. I spent the equivalent of fifteen years in England, and it depends what part of England you're from. He didn't have to talk like a Cockney or like the Royal Family to be "British." In the later pictures that I did with Michael Gough, I would try to have Michael talk "mid–Atlantic," so it wouldn't be too British — even though he *was* British!

At the end of Teenage Frankenstein, *there are crates in Whit Bissell's lab addressed to One-thirteen Wardour Street, London. Was that an in-joke reference to Hammer Films, which was headquartered there?*

No — that was the address of *my* office, which was in the same building! Nat Cohen and Stuart Levy, who were my partners in England, had the fourth floor at One-thirteen and Hammer had the sixth floor. Jimmy Carreras, the head of Hammer Films, was a wonderful friend of mine.

Six of your films had a teenager manipulated or transformed into a monster by an evil adult. What was it about that formula that you went back to it so often?

I have always felt that most teenagers think that adults — their parents, or their teachers, anyone that was older and that had authority — were the culprits in their lives. I know *I* felt that way when I was a teenager, and in talking to many teenagers, I found out that that was how *they* felt. (And even today — it hasn't changed, you know.) And so, in doing pictures primarily for the teenage audience, I thought that this theme would strike them just right.

And in some of your early pictures, you even had the songs and the comedy moments for the teenage audience.

I've always believed that, in making a horror picture, you gotta give the audience something to laugh at before you hit 'em.

Blood of Dracula *was also shot at Ziv.*

And also at a house I rented, someplace in Beverly Hills — that was the school in the picture. AIP didn't have its own studios or soundstages. When I

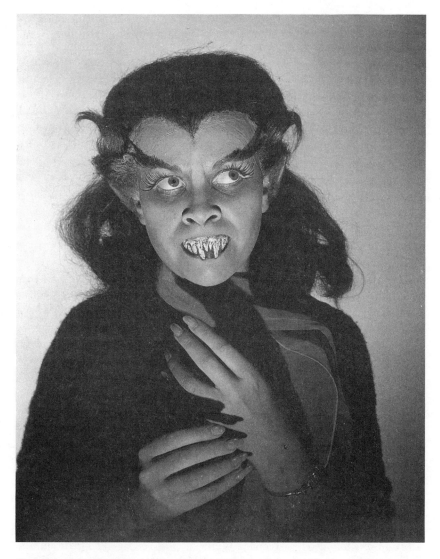

Vampiric girl student Sandra Harrison seemed more interested in Type A than straight A's in Cohen's *Blood of Dracula.*

did *How to Make a Monster,* I put up the sign that said AMERICAN INTERNA-TIONAL STUDIOS over the gate, but that's actually Ziv. In fact *[laughs],* they left the sign up long after the picture was over, so Jim and Sam would bring people to Ziv all the time, as though it was *their* studio!

How did you go about rounding up the teenage casts of these movies?

We'd just put a call out to agents, and they submitted various young actors and actresses. I auditioned those that I thought I wanted to audition, and that's how I'd pick the casts. It's the way I pick any cast for any film.

Herbert Strock told me you had reservations about having Sandra Harrison play the lead in Blood of Dracula.

Well, I didn't have reservations about her originally, 'cause if I did, I wouldn't have signed her as the lead! But she was a pain in the ass once we got started.

When the Film Forum Theater in New York City recently scheduled Blood of Dracula, *she called the theater frantically begging them not to show it.*

Once I signed her, she suddenly thought she was Joan Crawford—which she *wasn't [laughs]*! As far as her acting went, though, she was fine. I wasn't that excited about the picture itself, personally, but it was going to be the second feature to *I Was a Teenage Frankenstein* and I had to get it done and get everything ready before Thanksgiving, for the opening in Texas. So I don't take pride in a lot of things that I did with *Blood of Dracula* because I had to slam-bang-rush it out.

Louise Lewis was good in Blood of Dracula, *as the evil teacher.*

Wasn't she? I had used her earlier as the principal in *I Was a Teenage Werewolf*; in fact, that's why I used her in *Blood of Dracula*, because she was so good in that first small part.

Why did you invoke the Dracula name in the title? Why not I Was a Teenage Vampire?

Because I thought *Blood of Dracula* was a damn good title. In fact, Jimmy Carreras tried to get me to change it *[laughs]*! He called me from London and he said *[growling]*, "How dare you use *Dracula*! *Dracula*'s *my* title!" I said, "What do you mean, *your* title? Did you forget about Universal? How about *this* picture and *that* picture? What are you givin' me this shit for, Jim?" *[Laughs.]*

A two-in-one follow-up to Teenage Werewolf *and* Teenage Frankenstein *was a great idea. Who came up with* How to Make a Monster?

That was completely my idea. Many a night I would leave the studio late, and at that time you didn't have good security like we do now. Now we have so many guards they bump into each other *[laughs]*! But at that time, studios used to be very dark at night—a light here, a light there. And I thought to myself, "Gee, what a great spot to do a horror film." There were several studios at that time that were being taken over by conglomerates, so I thought that would be a good plot for it. I knocked out the original story and I hired Aben Kandel to do the screenplay with me.

Gary Conway (fifth from left), Robert H. Harris, Cohen and werewolf Gary Clarke join a colorful lineup of dress extras. Behind the scenes on *How to Make a Monster.*

Why Gary Clarke instead of Michael Landon as the Teenage Werewolf?

I was very pissed off at Landon, because I wanted him to do *How to Make a Monster* and he wouldn't. Michael got a lot of teasing for doing *Teenage Werewolf,* from all the young actors in that period. We had a whole group that used to meet at the Cock 'n' Bull for Sunday brunch: Natalie Wood and Robert Wagner, Jeffrey Hunter, Tab Hunter, Edd "Kookie" Byrnes and the gal that married him, Asa Maynor—it was a real fun crowd. Anyway, when *Teenage Werewolf* first came out, Michael was ribbed like crazy, because at that time they all wanted to be Serious Actors. When I approached Michael with *How to Make a Monster,* I certainly felt, for starting his career and getting him all this publicity, that he should have done it for me. And he didn't *want* to do it! So, like I said, I became pissed off at him at the time. But then, of course, everything got smoothed over; I was at his adopted son Mark's *bar mitzvah* a couple of years later and everything else.

So Gary Clarke took over as the Teenage Werewolf.

Gary Clarke had the same slight, thin build as Landon, and the same contour of the head. So Phil Scheer was able to do the same makeup that he did for *Teenage Werewolf* on Gary Clarke. Clarke did all right, he was very cooperative, and of course Gary Conway was, too. And Robert H. Harris, who played the crazy makeup artist, was a dream. A marvelous Broadway actor and a wonderful man personally; I wish I had had more things for him to do. I had seen him in a picture where he wore real thick glasses and he was playing a crazy guy who liked to start fires. I said to myself, "Who *is* that guy?" and I waited for the cast of characters at the end and got his name. And when I was about to do *How to Make a Monster,* I called him in.

Any anecdotes about the fire scene?

It was tough to do, and we had to do it in one take. Going from black and white to color at the end of *Teenage Frankenstein* had worked so well that I decided to do it again: When Harris takes the two boys into his home in *How to Make a Monster,* I went to color again, from there to the end of the picture, about ten minutes. I thought the flames and the burning of the masks—all of Harris' "children" on the walls—would look better in color, which it did. That ending was talked about by a lot of critics.

Were the two studio executives in How to Make a Monster *meant to make Hollywood insiders think of Nicholson and Arkoff?*

No. In fact, let me tell you something: I never thought of Sam Arkoff in any way, shape or form in those days. He had nothing to do with the making of the pictures. The fact that I went to AIP was because of my relationship with Jim Nicholson.

And now a big step up, with Horrors of the Black Museum.

As I told you before, I had a very good contact with Nat Cohen and Stuart Levy of Anglo Amalgamated Films of England, where I did my first co-production, *River Beat.* Because of my contact with Cohen and Levy, I was virtually the agent that sold AIP pictures to Anglo Amalgamated, for release in the United Kingdom; and I was the first one to take Jim Nicholson and Sam Arkoff to London, to introduce 'em to Cohen and Levy.

Anyway, I was reading a group of articles in the *Sunday Parade* about Scotland Yard's Black Museum. I went to London, and while I was there, a friend of mine that knew an inspector at Scotland Yard got me a special pass to go through the Black Museum. (They won't let the public go through it unless you're a V.I.P., a police officer or something like that.) From that, I wrote the original treatment of *Horrors of the Black Museum;* then Aben and I did the screenplay. I got Nat Cohen and Stuart Levy to agree to put up fifty percent of the financing of the picture, then I got Jim Nicholson and AIP to agree to put up fifty percent. That's how I got the financing to make the picture.

Black Museum *was the first color/CinemaScope picture for AIP.*

I told Jim, "Hey, it's time for AIP to do a bigger picture. You can't keep doing these small pictures." In fact, it was right after *Black Museum* that they gave Roger Corman the okay to do his Edgar Allan Poes, because of the success

A highpoint of 1950s film horror: The shocking spiked-binoculars scene from *Horrors of the Black Museum*. (Pictured: Dorinda Stevens.)

of *Horrors of the Black Museum*. That's when AIP started going for bigger budgets.

Some sources list the producer of Black Museum *as Jack Greenwood.*

At that time, when an American did a film in England, we had to hire a British subject as a producer, plus other Brits, to qualify for a British subsidy. That's another reason why I was able to talk [AIP] into spending more money on the picture, because I was going to make it under British Eady. Therefore, Jack Greenwood was my "associate producer." Only in the United Kingdom prints did Jack Greenwood get producer credit, and I was the executive producer. Jack Greenwood was a hell of a nice guy, by the way, and I used him on a lot of pictures as my British counterpart.

How did you hook up with Michael Gough?

I saw him in a British film, in a small part; I think it was Hammer's *Horror of Dracula*. Now, initially, I wanted to hire Vincent Price to star in *Horrors of the Black Museum,* but we couldn't afford Price at that time. There were other people I was thinking about, too, like Orson Welles. Anyway, under British Eady, you're allowed to bring X-number of Americans in, but Nat

Cohen said, "Herm, why can't you use a British actor? If you bring an American over, we're gonna have to house him at the Dorchester, give him per diem, this and that. And there are so many British actors that can play this kind of role!" I remembered Michael Gough, I made a dinner date with him, we sat and we talked and I just flipped over him personally. He's a marvelous man, a wonderful person. That's how he ended up in *Black Museum*.

His bravura performances in your horror films won him lots of new fans.
       I was so pleased when he won the Tony in New York [for *Bedroom Farce*] a few years ago. We're in touch all the time, although he hasn't worked for me since *Trog* with Joan Crawford.

The binoculars scene in Black Museum *still shocks today.*
       You really don't see anything happen in that scene. After the girl screams, "My eyes! My eyes!" as the blood drips through her fingers, we then cut to a closeup of the binoculars on the carpet, with the needles extended. But you don't see it happen, you have to visualize it.

Whose idea was the binoculars scene?
       Every instrument of murder in *Black Museum* was from an actual murder and is in Scotland Yard's Black Museum. The murder with the binoculars happened in the thirties, in Kent, which is outside of London. A young stable boy who was very much in love with his master's daughter was fired for having sex with her in the stables. And she would have nothing to do with him after that. When the Royal Ascot meet started the following year, she received through the mail a pair of binoculars, mailed from the Paddington Post Office. She took them to the window, she focused them, and the needles penetrated through her eyes and killed her. The stable boy was found, was tried and was hung. And those binoculars are in the Black Museum in Scotland Yard. The ice tongs, the portable guillotine [the other murder implements in *Black Museum*] — people don't realize it, but these were actual murders in England.

I thought America had the market cornered on outlandish murders.
       Oh, no, no. The kinkiest murders are done in England *[laughs]*!
       Ruth Pologe, who handled the publicity for *Black Museum* in New York, came up with the idea for me to bring the spiked binoculars over from England, and then at the airport in New York say that they were lost! She said, "That would hit the wire services and the front pages of all the papers!" So we did — of course, these weren't the *real* Black Museum binoculars, they were the binoculars that we had made for the film, but they were just as deadly. (In fact, I still have 'em today, under lock and key!) So that was the gimmick:

We suddenly "misplaced" them at the airport when I came from London, and we made the papers and everything. In fact, the assistant D.A. called me at the Hampshire House to talk to me about this, 'cause he had figured out that it was a stunt. (Of course, I never admitted it!)

You had a top-flight director of photography in Desmond Dickinson.

He was a real class cinematographer, and also a wonderful guy — we just got along terrific. That's why I used him so often.

And how about the director of Black Museum, *Arthur Crabtree?*

A nice Englishman. I needed a director who was English because we did the picture under the British Eady, but I wanted a director who was not going to be *too* British, who was not going to be in my way too much and who would do what I wanted done. Arthur Crabtree had just done *Fiend Without a Face* with Marshall Thompson, and on the basis of that, I interviewed him. The price was right and the old guy needed a job, and I hired him. And he was exactly what I wanted and needed as a good craftsman.

Why have you never tried directing?

Because I learned at a very early age that you can't do everything. I *have* directed, like on *A Study in Terror* when my director suddenly disappeared *[laughs]* — I've done it quite a few times during my career. However, I was head of my company and a real hands-on line producer, plus also head of the second largest theater in the world, the Fox Theater in Detroit, and other things that I was involved in. To be a director, you have to give one hundred percent of your attention, so I always just hired directors that I could work with.

How much did you have to do with the thirteen-minute prologue AIP tacked onto Black Museum?

That was Jim Nicholson's, not mine, and we did not use it anyplace but the U.S.A. Jim was looking for another gimmick, and he came up with HypnoVista. When Jim told me what he was writing and working on, I was reluctant to permit it to be tagged on, but I let Jim talk me into it; he said, "Herm, if it's really *that* bad, we'll take it off." We tested it in a few theaters and the audience went for it like crazy, hokey as it was. It helped make the picture a success, I guess, 'cause people were looking for gimmicks at that time. But when the picture was released on television in this country, we had to take it off because it *does* hypnotize some people. I saw it again recently and it *is* interesting, but my executive vice-president Didier Chatelain said, "Oh, God, is that corny!"

Right now, Martin Scorsese, Steven Spielberg and George Lucas are donating forty pictures to the Museum of Modern Art in New York, and Marty Scorsese has contacted me to tell me that he and the boys want *Horrors of the*

Black Museum as one of the pictures. They said they grew up on it and just loved it, and they thought there were a lot of inventive things done in the film. (Martin Scorsese said that, as far as he was concerned, that binoculars scene was one of the greatest scenes of any picture *[laughs]*!) In fact, Marty just talked to me the other day, because they're going over the negative in order to get a top print, and they've decided they're going to leave the Hypno-Vista business off, and go right into the picture after the main titles.

What was the rationale behind the horror-comedy The Headless Ghost? *It's not a funny picture.*

No, you're right, it isn't; I never liked that picture. While I was making *Black Museum* and we were near the end of shooting, Jim Nicholson called me from Hollywood and he was all excited about *Black Museum* even though he hadn't seen any of it—and *wouldn't* see it, until I brought it back from London. (In those days, he and Sam didn't spend the money to come across, and if they did, I wouldn't have shown 'em anything anyway!) Jim said, "Gee, if we only had a second feature..." I was awfully busy with *Black Museum* and with planning some other future projects, but he kept after me: "Herm, look, if you can knock out a second feature in black and white, just to go with *Black Museum,* we'll get the whole program from RKO, from Loew's, from Texas," blah, blah, blah. I told him I'd see what I could come up with.

I started thinking, "What the hell can I do?", and I thought maybe I should do a comedy. So Aben Kandel and I wrote this picture *The Headless Ghost* where these teenagers meet up with a ghost in a British castle. I got great publicity for using Richard Lyon in one of the leads—Louella Parsons gave us a headline story—because he was Bebe Daniels and Ben Lyon's son, who was acting in London. I met him and he needed a job badly, so we hired him. We knocked out that picture very, very fast; that's why the running time is so short, like sixty-five minutes. The director, Peter Graham Scott, was a film editor in London who always wanted to direct, and I needed somebody to do a fast job under my guidance. In fact, we started *Headless Ghost* as I was still finishing *Black Museum,* editing and cutting it. But I honestly don't recall too much else about this picture, it was so bad.

Was any of it shot on your Black Museum *sets?*

They were shot at the same studio, *Headless Ghost* in black and white and *Black Museum* in color, so we *did* reuse some of the sets after we redressed 'em. Then we also had to build some other sets, plus we went on location to an actual castle.

How often do you watch your old pictures?

I really don't, unless I happen to catch one at somebody's house. I haven't seen some of these pictures in twenty-five years. I don't have time to run yesteryear.

Around this same time, you announced you were going to produce Aladdin and the Giant *in London and in Europe, in Technicolor and CinemaScope.*

Originally, I was going to do that for AIP, but then it got put aside. I've brought it out many times since then—we almost made it for Warner Brothers, almost made it for E.M.I. in England. I've come so close on *Aladdin and the Giant* a half a dozen times, but I just never was able to put the picture together.

What did you have to do with Circus of Horrors?

I was involved in that through Nat Cohen. I had quite a bit to do with it—picking Anton Diffring and other things like that. I didn't get a credit—I didn't ask for one—but I was the executive in charge, representing the money, representing Nat Cohen and Stuart Levy, and I owned a piece of the picture. I was out on the set but it wasn't like it was one of my own personal pictures. I had a lot of respect for Julian Wintle, who got the screen credit as producer. Julian was a very classy producer for Rank who had his offices at Pinewood, he was quite a British gent but he did not know horror. So Nat Cohen asked me to be a part of the picture.

Next came Konga, *which you also made in England.*

Nat and Stuart Levy were so excited about the business that *Black Museum* did in England and in Europe (it was a very big hit there), they said, "Herm, can you do another exploitation type of picture?" Well, I had always flipped over *King Kong* and *Mighty Joe Young* and all that, so I came up with *Konga* and Aben and I started writing the script.

Konga *involved a lot more special effects than any of your other pictures.*

We did a tremendous amount of special effects with Rank Labs. I supervised them myself, all these special effects. For the scenes where Konga's a giant, the head of special effects at Rank Labs, a wonderfully clever guy named Victor Marguetti, developed a traveling matte technique that employed yellow sodium lights; *Konga* was the first picture that they used it on. Some of the special effects of Konga, when he's big, are really good, rock steady. *Konga* only cost about five hundred thousand dollars, in color, but the effects were so good that people thought the picture cost millions.

How long did it take to supervise the effects on Konga?

Eighteen months—over a year and a half to get those bloody special effects done perfect. It just went on and on and on, 'cause it was trial and error. AIP was after me constantly—"Where's the picture? When are we gonna get the picture?" They didn't realize how much fucking work was involved, 'cause they never used special effects at that time.

Herman Cohen—a giant of the horror/exploitation picture business, *and* on the miniature lab set for *Konga*.

The closest AIP came to special effects pictures prior to Konga *were the Bert I. Gordon jobs.*

    Yes, but *Konga* was in color, and that's a whole different bag of beans. To have Konga hold Michael Gough, what I had to do there was matte five different scenes on one frame.

I assumed that you had built a giant ape arm.

    Are you kidding? We didn't have money to build a giant *putz* at that time *[laughs]*!

You also had the actor in the ape suit on miniature sets, just as he was starting to grow.

    For a cheap picture, those miniature sets that we built were pretty good. I worked my ass off; in fact, I don't think I ever worked harder on a picture than I did on *Konga*. And don't forget those giant plants that we had in the greenhouse scene. My art director Wilfred Arnold and I did a lot of research on all those plants—I had to go to all kinds of places with him, in the Kew Gardens, here and there. They were based on actual carnivorous plants. We had them made at Shepperton Studios. But it was exciting to do this on spit. We had to use a lot of ingenuity in place of money. Luckily, I had an enthusiastic crew with me.

I almost got thrown out of England 'cause of *Konga*. Once Konga grew into the giant ape, I needed to shoot the streets of London near the Embankment. Jack Greenwood and [production manager] Jim O'Connolly told me, "Herm, we can't get permission. The Metropolitan Police will shut us down." I was also told that you can't bribe an English bobby; unlike in New York, Chicago, Detroit or L.A., it won't work. So I had to take things in hand. I went to meet the inspector in charge of the precinct in Croyden, which is the jurisdiction of the Embankment area. I sat and visited with him for a long time, talked about all different subjects, on and on. Then we got to talking about television, and he said, "Oh, I wish I could afford a color television set." That was my opening—I went out and bought him a color television set, and I had it sent to his home. And suddenly I got permission to shoot on the streets in London! The thing that I *didn't* mention to him was that, at the finale, all hell was going to break loose—that we were going to shoot sub-machine guns, bazookas, etc., etc. I purposely didn't tell him this *[laughs]*!

It's always easier to get forgiveness than permission.
    That's what I figured! We had permission to shoot from twelve midnight until five in the morning, each night for four or five nights. And on the last night, the night when we were going to shoot the finale, who should come out but the inspector, to have biscuits and a cup of tea with me and see how everything was going! I said, "Gee, it's awfully late for you to be up, it's like two o'clock in the morning." I wanted to get rid of him, I knew what was coming up! I did get rid of him, but there were also a couple of sergeants that were with me all the time—I didn't tell *them* what was going to happen, either!
    Anyway, comes the final scene and we blaze away: I had told all my people, "Have the trucks ready, 'cause when we're done, we gotta split!" Which we did! Well, the nine-nine-nine [emergency number] got something like three hundred phone calls—people thought London was being invaded *[laughs]*! This was only fifteen years or so after World War II, and they were still worried. I had a lot of apologies to make—a *lot*. There were a few old women that claimed that the excitement affected their health, all kinds of shit. The Metropolitan Police gave me the addresses of the ones that were threatening to go to the Consul and what have you, and I had to go visit each of them in person and charm the bejesus out of them, which I did, fortunately. Jack Greenwood, Jim O'Connolly and I went and bought like twenty boxes of chocolates, which are terribly expensive in England, flowers, all sorts of crap for them. They took the candy and the flowers and kissed me goodbye *[laughs]*!

With a title like Konga, *people started making comparisons to* King Kong—
    —which was *fine*, which was what I *wanted*! We paid RKO so that we could use in our ads the line, NOT SINCE KING KONG . . . HAS THE SCREEN THUNDERED TO SUCH MIGHTY EXCITEMENT! I paid RKO because I didn't want

them to think we were stealing it; we paid 'em twenty-five thousand dollars so there would not be any lawsuit.

After Konga, *you came back to Hollywood and made* Black Zoo.

That was an original idea of mine, and then I hired Aben Kandel to work with me and we did the script together. I built the zoo right here at Raleigh Studio [formerly Producers Studio] on North Bronson—the entire zoo that you saw in that picture was an interior set. (We have one of the largest sound-stages in town here on our lot.) We built the entire zoo exterior here on the soundstages so we could contain the animals. As a for-instance, when at the beginning you see the girl walking down the street, that actually was a public street. But when she gets attacked by the tiger, those were bushes we put up on the soundstage, because we had to control the tiger.

You must have an animal anecdote or two.

Well, one of our lions escaped during the shooting of the picture, and we had front page headlines in all the papers! Everybody said I must have done it as a publicity stunt, but it actually happened. A full-grown American mountain lion named Chico, three hundred pounds, broke loose and dashed out through a door. We immediately removed the cast and crew from the set, and someone was broadcasting warnings over loudspeakers for all the various studio personnel to take cover—this all happened just before lunch, and everybody was told to stay in their offices. The police were called and they sur-rounded the studio, and there was also a helicopter announcing over a speaker, telling the children at the nearby schools to get off the playgrounds and back inside the buildings! More than fifty police officers with their cars blocked off streets and were searching for him. And the lion's owner, Ralph Helfer, was asking 'em *not* to shoot the thing. This went on for an hour or two before they recaptured him—he had squeezed himself into a sub-basement under the soundstage, down through an electrician's crawl-hole in the stage floor. And he was scared stiff, the poor thing. Well *[laughs]*, at least we got a lot of free publicity out of it!

Did all these animals come from Ralph Helfer?

Yes. In searching for someone to provide the animals, I heard about him through other animal handlers. He was using a new technique for training wild cats for films, where they never used a whip, never did any beating. It was all through kindness and love and what have you. I went out to his animal training ranch, way out in the Valley in Saugus. I was there for hours with a couple of my staff, and I was so impressed with what he showed me that I signed him. We worked together on the script and we worked together with the animals. We had several African lions and lionesses, a tiger, a black panther, several cheetahs, a Himalayan black bear, oh, a whole menagerie.

How did your actors like working with the animals?

Some were afraid of them. But Michael Gough, who I brought here from London to do the film, loved animals, and the animals took to him beautifully. And I must say they took to me also. But we had to be very careful on *Black Zoo* (and on *Konga*, too, because that had chimps in it): When I interviewed any female in the picture, I had to ask when they had their periods. And right away, they shouted, "*What?!*" But if an animal smells blood, chimps especially, there can be trouble.

I've read that Michael Gough was bitten by the tiger.

No, I don't remember that; that sounds like a phony publicity release. However, a trainer *was* attacked by Zamba, one of our lions. One of the new young trainers was bringing Zamba from his cage to the soundstage to work in a scene, and when you bring an animal from place to place, you must have some meat in your hand. And you should walk *next* to him, never in *front* of him. This trainer was late in bringing Zamba out to the soundstage, and he was pissed off that Zamba didn't want to go. I was standing talking on the phone near the door, and I could see that Zamba did not want to go any further. That was when the trainer did a really stupid thing: He got in front of Zamba and said, "God damn it, *come here!*" and he started pulling on the rope. And Zamba *leaped*. Knocked him on his ass. The trainer put his arm up, and Zamba took a big bite. I was just a few feet away from Zamba, and I screamed for Ralph Helfer. Zamba stopped after he bit him—he realized what he'd done—and the trainer didn't move. Of course, Ralph and the other trainers came running like crazy and they lassoed Zamba. (Even Ralph didn't want to go near him, 'cause Zamba had blood dripping from his mouth.) The guy had to have seventy stitches. We calmed Zamba down, talked to him, brought him some food, and then he was fine. And I've got to hand it to Michael Gough: Two hours later, Michael was working with him in a scene.

You also did a lot of publicity with the cats.

First we were on the Johnny Carson show, when Carson was doing his show in New York. I brought Zamba and a tiger named Patrina to New York on American Airlines, and, of course, the animal trainers, four of them, two to an animal. I checked the animals into a suite at the Edison Hotel; I was staying at the Hampshire House myself, but for publicity purposes, we made like I was staying with the animals. (I have pictures of the lion standing at the registration desk, putting his paw print in the book like he was checking in.) This was all great publicity. Then I had two premieres, one in New York and another at my Fox Theater in Detroit. (In Detroit, they stayed at the Statler Hilton Hotel.) We built cages in the lobby of the Fox Theater and we had 'em there for three or four days.

Herman Cohen and one of the feline stars of *Black Zoo* amuse themselves between takes. (Notice that Cohen is *losing*.)

Did the cats enjoy all this?

Patrina the tiger was spooked coming on TV for interviews, spooked by the lights and the audience. We had to be very careful with Patrina. And Zamba — let's face it, if he turned his head the wrong way and you were there, he'd break your jaw. And they wanted *me* to pose for pictures with my head next to his and what have you! There was a big full-page ad we took in *Variety* that showed me with Zamba, and a caption, "Herman Cohen with Zamba. (Please note: Herman Cohen is on the right.)" *[Laughs.]*

Were you happy with the way Black Zoo *came out?*

Oh, very happy. It was a beautiful picture to make, because of the wild cats, and it was a very unusual film. I didn't like the title, but Allied Artists did. I didn't like it because I felt that people wouldn't know what *Black Zoo* was — the title doesn't really convey much. So because *Horrors of the Black Museum* had been so successful, in some territories I had Allied Artists put out some alternate ads in which *Black Zoo* was called *Horrors of the Black Zoo*. That's when our grosses jumped considerably. And it ended up being very successful.

Why did you stop making pictures for AIP after Konga?

Sam Arkoff told me, "We're not gonna make partnership deals anymore.

We'll give you a small piece of the profits, and a salary." That's when AIP was really in the black and doing great, because of the pictures that Roger Corman and I did for 'em. (And they told Roger the same thing at that time—"No more fifty-fifty!") And that's when I told Sam, "Goodbye!" *[Laughs.]*

What's the story on A Study in Terror?

I made a deal with two English distributors, Michael Klinger and Tony Tenser, who were talking about doing a Sherlock Holmes picture at the same time I wanted to do one. So we decided we'd do one together, and that I would make the film. Klinger and Tenser would have the United Kingdom and certain other territories to distribute it in, and I'd have the rest of the world. Then I in turn made a deal with Columbia Pictures, to be my partner in it. That's how *A Study in Terror* was put together.

Producer credit goes to someone named Henry Lester.

The Conan Doyle estate appointed Lester, who had to get a credit on the film. He was the representative to see that we didn't do anything in the script that would injure the Sir Arthur Conan Doyle name.

Study in Terror *did have an excellent script.*

Yes, it was very, very good. Donald and Derek Ford get screen credit for the writing but they *didn't* write it, although the idea of combining Holmes and Jack the Ripper was theirs. Michael Klinger and Tony Tenser had signed them for "their" Sherlock Holmes movie, but they didn't execute their script properly and I didn't like it. I hired Harry Craig, a writer that Adrian Conan Doyle [Arthur's son] and Henry Lester liked very much. He worked closely with me and James Hill, the director, on the final screenplay, which was based on the original story and screenplay by Donald and Derek Ford. Harry Craig didn't want a credit on *A Study in Terror* because he was doing a big picture for Columbia at that time.

Did Henry Lester or Adrian Conan Doyle pitch in creatively at all?

Not Adrian; Adrian just visited with his wife and friends for tea and lunch occasionally. But Henry Lester and I discussed many, many facets, and there were many things we wanted to do that he would say, "Oh, no, *no, no,* Sherlock Holmes wouldn't *do* that!"

You mentioned before that you had to take over the direction one day.

Yes, I did, because Jim Hill had a habit of disappearing. He was a nice guy, but weird—strange. Nobody could get close to him. And he was always fidgety and very nervous. In fact, I talked to Carl Foreman about this and he said, "Yes, Hill disappeared on *Born Free* [1966], too!" And nobody knew where he went or what he did! So the assistant director had a tough time keeping tabs on him. Now, here we had this big fire scene upstairs in the pub, and we were all set for it. The special effects were ready, the fire department was standing by and everything else, and we had to be out of that stage that night — this was Shepperton Studios in London. That's when the a.d. came up to me and said, "Herm, I can't find Jim Hill!"

"Can't find the director?! Chrissakes, it's four-thirty in the afternoon!" And the a.d. said, "Well, he's disappeared!" I said, "Okay, *I'll* direct the scene." So we put the red light on, locked the doors, and I did the scene in one take — the whole bloody thing. As the firemen were putting out the fire, Jim Hill came back in and said, "I'm ready to—. Hey, what happened?!" I said, "We've already done the scene! Where in hell have *you* been? *Where* do you disappear, goddamn it?!" Well, believe me, he never left after that! He was so embarrassed, because the crew and everybody was laughing at him.

Did Study *have a bigger budget than some of your other British horror films?*

Oh, yes, it did, because of Columbia coming in with me. John Neville was marvelous as Sherlock Holmes, a fine actor; at that time he was running a theater in Nottingham. I had Donald Houston, Robert Morley, Anthony Quayle, Georgia Brown, Adrienne Corri—some top actors. I cast it myself, and I was very lucky to get the people that I did.

You sound pleased with A Study in Terror.

I was *very* pleased with the film. In fact, it turned out so well that Stanley Schneider, the president of Columbia Pictures, used *A Study in Terror* to show the studio what kind of a film could be made on a low budget. He ran it a half a dozen times for new young executives. (Which, by the way, Mike Frankovich was not too happy about. Mike was head of production in Hollywood, and he didn't like the fact that Schneider was showing *A Study in Terror*, which was not made in Frankovich's jurisdiction.) And I have a book on all the Sherlock Holmes movies that says *A Study in Terror* was the best Holmes movie which was ever made. But again, as with *Black Zoo*, I was not pleased with the title. Columbia insisted on *A Study in Terror*; I hated it. They wanted it because Sir Arthur Conan Doyle had written a book called *A Study in Scarlet*, but I didn't like the word "study" in there; I felt that the teenagers would think it would be like extra homework! Columbia fought me, and I had to go along with them in the end. My title was *Fog*, a nice, simple, one-word title.

Then Columbia went and . . . *[laughs]* fucked me up again! The big hit on TV at that time was *Batman*, so the head of advertising, Robert Ferguson, wanted to sell *A Study in Terror* almost like a comedy. On one of the one-sheets, he had POW, BIFF, CRUNCH, BANG, and HERE COMES THE ORIGINAL CAPED CRUSADER — which I didn't like at *all*! I wanted to sell it as horror, and so we had a big fight about the advertising. We did our own campaign for the

United Kingdom, France, Italy—Columbia had nothing to do with the picture there—and it was a much bigger hit over there than it was here.

I thought A Study in Terror *was crying out for a sequel. Were you ever tempted to do another Holmes picture?*
    In those days, I never thought of doing sequels. I always wanted to do something different, something new. Several people did make Holmes pictures in the years following *A Study in Terror*; in fact, one which I have not seen called *Murder by Decree* [1979] prompted several people to call me or write me, telling me that the script was practically stolen from *Study in Terror*. And they even stole some of my cast—they had Anthony Quayle, and another actor, Frank Finlay, playing the same inspector he played in *my* picture!

How did you come to meet Joan Crawford, the star of Berserk *and* Trog?
    I wanted to try to pitch the lead in *Berserk* to Joan Crawford, because I felt that Joan would be perfect for the picture. Joan was a very close friend of Leo Jaffe, the president of Columbia Pictures at that time, and I asked Leo if he would introduce me to her. He was the one who made the introduction, and that's when I became friends with Joan Crawford.

In writing Berserk, *were you thinking back to how well* Circus of Horrors *came out?*
    No, that had no effect on it, I just felt that the circus would be a good backdrop for a horror story. I made a deal with the Billy Smart Circus in England, to use their circus in the film. We shot at Shepperton Studios, then we also shot at night at the circus, after the place was closed, for about two weeks.

Today Joan Crawford has the off-screen reputation that she does because of Mommie Dearest, *the book and the movie. What kind of lady did* you *find her to be?*
    Fascinating. Exciting. In spite of her sipping hundred-proof vodka, she was very professional with me, and would never take a drink unless I okayed it. She always knew her lines and she was always on time. She would come in very early in the morning, like six-thirty, and she loved to cook: She made breakfast for her hairdresser, for her costumer, for "her team." She was strong-willed, she was tough—but, tough as she was, at the drop of a hat, she could be reduced to tears.

For her age, she looks great in Berserk.
    Doesn't she? And doesn't she look great in the leotard? Edith Head designed that leotard for her as a favor.

Cohen and star Joan Crawford with the circus performers from *Berserk*. (Left to right, skeleton man Ted Lune, bearded lady Golda Casimir, Cohen, Crawford, strongman Milton Reid; front and center, vertically challenged George Claydon.)

Crawford's biographies say she was a lonely lady during this period.

Oh, yes, Joan was a very lonely lady, but we became very close friends, from the time of *Berserk* until she died. We went out a lot, in London and New York and here in L.A., in the years after I met her on *Berserk*.

She was taught everything at MGM, and one thing that she was taught there was that the producer is the boss. She always went to the producer if she had any problems, with the director or with any member of the cast or crew. As an example, one morning she called me, about two o'clock a.m. — woke me up out of a sound sleep — asking, "Herm, you have your script with you?" As if I go to bed with my script *[laughs]*! She said, "Go get your script! I'm working on tomorrow's scenes and you're sleeping!" I got the script, and she started in, "Now, on page blah, blah, blah," and she wanted to talk about it because, as I said, she was lonely. She would stay up late at night, sipping her vodka, going over her lines for the next day.

Then she said to me, "What time are you leaving for the studio tomorrow morning?" — we were shooting at Shepperton at the time. "Look, why don't you leave around five-thirty and pick me up?" I said, "Well, what's wrong with *your* car?" "Oh, there's something wrong with the car," she said. That was all b.s. It turned out that one of our prop men had to have all his teeth extracted, and she sent her Rolls-Royce over to pick him up — take him to the dentist —

wait for him—and take him home. Then she had it go to a Jewish restaurant in Soho called Isow's, where a lot of members of the industry would always go, and pick him up some chicken soup and bring it to his house! That's why she didn't have a car that day! So I had to call my driver, wake *him* up, and have him pick *her* up at five-thirty in the morning. She didn't tell me until after all this happened—in fact, it was the *prop man* who told me what Joan had done. But she was always doing this kind of stuff—

None of which you'll find in Mommie Dearest.

Right. Christina [Crawford] doesn't mention the nice things that Joan always did, especially for the crew. She was always very close to the crew, and knew all of them by their first names. When we were doing *Berserk,* Christina married Harvey Medlinsky, who was a director, and Joan gave Christina a check for five thousand dollars, told her to enjoy herself—I was right there at the time. And she gave her a big dinner party at Les Ambassadeurs, which was *the* restaurant club in London. *None* of this is covered in *Mommie Dearest.* (Harvey was married to Christina for about six years, and he said he never heard Christina tell *one* of these awful stories. It was her *second* husband who got her to write this book—they were broke and needed the money and what have you.) Joan ended up leaving Christina and [Joan's] son Chris out of her will, and that was a big mistake. Her attorneys should have advised her to leave them, say one thousand dollars, so they could not contest the will. (They *both* contested the will.) She was closer to her twins, the two girls, than she was to Christina or Chris. Joan had a lot of problems with Chris.

Did she seem to enjoy horror movies? She did What Ever Happened to Baby Jane?, *then two each for* William Castle *and for you.*

With Joan and with Bette Davis, they never looked at these pictures as horror films—not even *Berserk.* Joan just looked at it as a drama with some horrific moments. You had to be very careful—anyone who is a star never wants to feel they're going into a horror picture. You never use the word "horror" in front of them. In fact, the original title was *Circus of Blood,* and she hated that title. Fortunately, we came up with the title *Berserk,* which everybody loved.

Why *did* she do these pictures? Mainly she wanted to be Joan Crawford, mainly she just wanted to work. She was intrigued by the fact that *Berserk* was going to be shot in London, because she loved London and the Brits loved *her.* And in England, she was still the Joan Crawford of yesteryear, she wasn't "the old gal" there.

Were you pleased with the job she did in the picture?

Oh, yes. After she agreed to do the picture, of course we did a lot of changes on the script to make it fit her, and we had a lot of meetings prior to bringing her to London and shooting the picture. She was very much caught up in the idea of the story. Knowing what kind of a big star she was, I did not want to diminish her stature in any way. Joan always thought of yesteryear, so I assigned her a Rolls-Royce with a chauffeur. Even though it stretched the budget, I did whatever I could to make her realize that she was still Joan Crawford. She was revered in England, and we got great publicity there, not only from the tabloids but also *The London Times, The Sunday Times* and *The Observer.* Everybody did stories on her while we were shooting the picture.

Were you happy with the way Berserk *came out?*
    [*Laughs.*] I've never been happy with the way *any* of my pictures have come out. I always want to do something over again. But *Berserk* was a huge hit — a very big success. In fact, we were one of the two top grossers for Columbia Pictures that year. But you keep asking me if I was "happy" with various pictures. We had pictures to make, we made the pictures, we did the best we could with the budgets we had, and there you are. That's the most you can do on a film.

Let me rephrase, then. Which of your horror movies were you least un*happy with? Is that a fair question?*
    Well, it's a fair question, but there's no answer. Although, because it was period, and because I had a lot of fun with the research on Sherlock Holmes and Jack the Ripper, I enjoyed *A Study in Terror.* The most successful box office–wise was *Berserk* and then *Trog.*

So Trog *was also a nice experience, working with Crawford again?*
    A great experience. *Trog* was based on an original story by Peter Bryan and John Gilling that I had bought, and then Aben and I wrote the screenplay. I changed the professor from a man to a woman; because we were so successful with *Berserk,* I wanted to do another picture with Joan. Fortunately, we got the same apartment for Joan that she had had during *Berserk* — Columbia Pictures owned this huge apartment at the Grosvenor House on Park Lane, and we rented it for Joan for *Trog.* Which was great, because she knew the whole staff — the maids, the waiters, everybody. It was like old home week. Joan also had a maid called "Mamacita," who went with her wherever she went.

Did Trog *cost as much as* Berserk *did?*
    Trog cost *more* than *Berserk.* Between *Berserk* and *Trog,* I did *Crooks and Coronets* [1969] for Warner Brothers — Telly Savalas, Dame Edith Evans, Warren Oates, Cesar Romero, Harry H. Corbett — and that was a big picture. Then we did *Trog* for Warners. We shot at Bray, and also out on the English moors. The cave interiors were built at the studio.

Director Freddie Francis and producer Cohen flank the prehistoric star (Joe Cornelius) of 1970's *Trog*.

One Crawford bio says Trog's *budget was so low that portable dressing rooms were not sent on location, and that Crawford huddled in a car parked on the moors.*

Untrue. She had a huge caravan—and I have reason to remember that well! We were out on location and it was quite chilly out, and I was told by my assistant that Joan was deathly ill in her caravan. I had my car take me there immediately, I went in to see her and she was saying *[huffing and puffing]*, "Oh, Herm ... oh! ... get me a doctor ... I can't work..." I told her I'd do it, and I turned to run out. On these caravans, the door is low, and I ran and smashed my head against the top of the door [frame]—knocked myself for a loop! Joan jumped up and yelled, "Oh, Herman, Herman, darling! Come here, lie down!" She got a cold compress for my head—"You rest! I'll work!"—and within an hour, she was on the set! She forgot that she was sick, now that she was taking care of *me*!

Did Freddie Francis do a good job for you as director?

Of course. Freddie had done some horror pictures for Hammer and for Max Rosenberg and Milton Subotsky, and he was a terrific director of photography—he just won an Academy Award for *Glory* [1989]. In asking him to do *Trog,* knowing what he had done, I felt that Freddie was right for it. Then when he read the script, and heard that we were going to have Joan, he wanted very much to do it.

During the making of *Trog,* I brought my three sisters over from the States, and Joan Crawford just took to them like they were *her* sisters. She gave a dinner party for 'em at Les Ambassadeurs, had a couple brunches, on and on. Joan was always "The Movie Star." There was many a Sunday when it was raining and cold in London, and a group of us from the film was going to go to a movie matinee. Joan said, "I'd love to see that picture," and I said, "Come on!" She said, "Oh, no, no, I'd have to get dressed." "No, you don't, just put a pair of slacks on." And she said, "I would *never* go out in a pair of slacks!" In other words, she *was* Joan Crawford. She just hated the young female stars that would go out on the street like they just got up. Whenever you saw Joan, *you saw* Joan Crawford. She wouldn't even dash to a movie with dark sunglasses on!

And her drinking was never a problem?

Well, on *Trog,* her drinking was worse than it was when we were doing *Berserk.* I had to reprimand her a few times for drinking without asking. (She had a huge frosted glass that said PEPSI-COLA — but inside was hundred-proof vodka!) In fact, when she arrived to do *Berserk* as well as *Trog,* she arrived with four cases of hundred-proof vodka, 'cause you can't get hundred-proof vodka in England. And when she arrived in both instances, she had something like forty pieces of luggage, and she had to arrange for Pepsi-Cola to send two trucks to meet the plane and pick it all up. These were *huge* cases, that she and "Mamacita" had packed themselves! And Joan knew where *every*thing was, she was *that* organized. Now, I guarantee you that she didn't open seventy-five percent of these cases while she was in England, but obviously felt that she had to have 'em all there.

She also had me come to New York and pick out from her own wardrobe what she should wear in these pictures — because she owned a big piece of both pictures, she didn't want us to spend any extra money on wardrobe. In her penthouse in New York, on East Seventy-ninth, she had a huge room, like a two-story room, with a ladder, and in it she kept all her clothes! And she knew where everything was, everything was catalogued! So we picked costumes out of there for both films.

And Trog *was a big hit again.*

It was *very* successful. Both *Berserk* and *Trog* came in under budget, on schedule, and again I say that Joan was very professional. When I hear stories today of Kim Basinger and some of the other young stars, I say, "Thank God for people like Joan Crawford and Bette Davis, all the old pros."

What can you tell me about Craze, *with Jack Palance?*

We had a very good cast in that: Palance, Trevor Howard, Diana Dors, Dame Edith Evans, Hugh Griffith. Jack Palance and I got along very well, but

Jack Palance and Cohen behind the scenes on the English-made *Craze* (a.k.a. *The Infernal Idol*).

everyone else was afraid of Jack—he has that aura about him. Freddie Francis was scared stiff of him, and any time a problem came up with Jack, Freddie called me immediately. The gals that were in the picture were scared, too, Suzy Kendall and Julie Ege. Jack had a sex scene with Julie Ege, and he got carried away and grabbed her so hard, one of her breasts started bleeding! I got him a flat right near my flat in London, and I remember that he loved Chinese food. I never ate so much Chinese food in my life, because virtually every night I had to find another Chinese restaurant for him! But as far as his work was concerned, he was very professional and he always knew what he was doing. And he's quite a thinker; you had to explain a lot of things to him, because he wanted to understand what the character was supposed to be doing, this and that. (By the way, he let me know from the beginning, when I first met him here in Hollywood before I signed him, that, "It's Jack *Pal*-ance like *balance,* and don't call me Pa-*lance!"* He let me know that very quick!)

Supposedly you, Francis, and Palance-like-in-balance were all going to do another film together, but it got called off when Craze *didn't do well.*

No, not true at all. *Craze* did *very* well. But the thing with *Craze* was that I had a deal with National General for release in the U.S.A., and National General was sold to Warner Brothers. So the release was held up because Warner Brothers. had the pick of what films they wanted to release from what National General owned. They finally did pick *Craze,* but it took a long time.

Today you're busy with your new company, Cobra Media.

The reason I formed Cobra Media was because the ancillary markets were becoming very big, and we were getting (to put it bluntly) *screwed* by various companies on the reports and moneys and what have you. We formed Cobra Media in eighty-two and we've had some very successful pictures, *Crocodile,* for instance. And we've also been successful with a picture called *Watch Me When I Kill,* another horrific film, and a number of other biggies. We're putting together a package of films right now for the ancillary markets—for cable, for video, for pay-per-view.

Do you get much of a chance to be a hands-on producer these days?

Not recently, except on pictures we've reedited, put music in, etc. I've paid my dues, and certainly I don't want to work for some company as a producer. However, we *are* working on two screenplays right now that I'm very excited about. One is really horror, and the other sort of leans toward horror. I will be producing these together with Didier Chatelain, my partner.

Are you going to be writing your autobiography soon?

Not right away, because I might be doing those two horror films soon. But after that, what I've been thinking I might do is write a book like Roger Corman did, on all my horror films to date.

In making your AIP horror movies, did you suspect that in thirty or forty years they'd still have fans, and that some of them would be playing at the Museum of Modern Art?

No, never. Never once. Never *thought* of it! But, let's face it, as long as there are new electronic devices being invented, who knows where our pictures are going to end up? I think it goes without saying that I'm very, very pleased.

If we'd have had more money, of course we would probably have been more elaborate with everything! That's the interesting thing that happens with these low-budget movies—that's why, so often, directors make their best movies when they don't have that much money. They have to use their imaginations instead.

Robert Day

THEY'RE SORELY MISSED IN THIS NEW ERA of film school hotshots, but years ago some of the best of what movies and TV had to offer was served up by journeymen directors. Their job wasn't to blow their own horns, to outshine their stars or to consciously work at building up an *auteur* reputation; they merely toiled at their chosen trade, bouncing from film to TV, from genre to genre and sometimes even from country to country.

Emblematic of this dying breed, globe-trotting Robert Day has directed numerous features and countless TV episodes since he broke into the business a half a century ago. Day worked his way up from clapper boy to camera operator to full-fledged lensman in his native England before giving directing a shot in the mid–1950s. His first film as director, the black-comic *The Green Man* (1957) for the writer-producer team of Launder and Gilliat, garnered fine reviews and a classic notoriety, and using this as a starting point Day went on to become one of the industry's busier directors. He relocated to Hollywood in the 1960s and now has moved again, from the smog of L.A. north to Washington, but Day still keeps his hand in, returning for the occasional directing assignment. Long-wed to actress Dorothy Provine, Day takes a self-effacing view of much of his work in films, but his output—which includes such well-crafted thrillers as *The Haunted Strangler, First Man into Space, Corridors of Blood* and the best-ever Tarzan film *Tarzan the Magnificent*—will continue to belie his modest appraisals.

How did you get hooked up with Amalgamated Pictures, producers of The Haunted Strangler?

That was through a guy named John Croydon. Amalgamated was run by three people: there was Croydon, there was an American involved, Chuck Vetter from New York—I don't know *what* happened to him!—and there was Richard Gordon, an English guy who lived in New York. We didn't see much of him, I think he was a sort of front man arranging the finance and the distribution more than anything else. John Croydon was the guy who asked me to make *The Haunted Strangler* with Boris Karloff. I guess they'd seen what I'd done already and liked it, and figured that I could probably bring it in on budget.

What kind of budget did you work with?

Oh, very little. Certainly not more than one hundred thousand pounds.

Where was Amalgamated headquartered?

We had an office at Walton Studios, which is where *The Haunted Strangler* was shot. We shot our interiors inside the studio and our exteriors on their back lot. *The Haunted Strangler* was my first film for them, then came *First Man into Space,* which we made not in a studio but in a house in Hampstead. And finally *Corridors of Blood,* with Boris Karloff again.

Previous page: **One of American television's busiest directors in the '70s, director Robert Day remembers well the early days of low-budget British sci-fi and horror films.**

Boris Karloff has had enough of asylum maid Jessica Cairns' off-key singing in a gripping scene from Day's *The Haunted Strangler.*

What can you remember about working with Karloff?

I met him for the first time on *The Haunted Strangler,* and he was a wonderful, wonderful man. We were very close friends, and we used to eat together almost every weekend — he would come to my house or I would go to his. He lived at that time in Cadogan Square in London, where he had an apartment. I just can't say enough good things about him — he was kind, gentle, not a bit like any of the characters he's played in movies. I directed the two films with Karloff, *The Haunted Strangler* and *Corridors of Blood,* we became friends and remained friendly thereafter.

Did he seem to appreciate his better-than-average role in The Haunted Strangler?

I think he treated every character, every script with respect; I know that he was very much involved in the portrayal of the character in *The Haunted Strangler.* He didn't treat it just as another role, he was very, very deeply interested in what he was doing. We discussed the characterization for hours and hours, the way he should look and everything.

If the budget had allowed for more elaborate special effects, would you have wanted a more monstrous-looking Karloff?

I thought he was just right. He had a little makeup on but mostly it was

Boris Karloff gave one of his (few) good 1950s film performances in director Day's *The Haunted Strangler* **(British title:** *Grip of the Strangler***).**

just him, distorting his face. But if we'd have had more money, of course we would probably have been more elaborate with *everything [laughs]*! That's the interesting thing that happens with these low-budget movies—that's why, so often, directors make their best movies when they don't have that much money. They have to use their imaginations instead, and it works out very well so often.

The Haunted Strangler *has scenes of strong violence. Did Karloff voice any objections?*
    I wouldn't say that he enjoyed it, but I had no complaints from him!

John Croydon has complained about Karloff's too-melodramatic style, but if Karloff was too melodramatic in Haunted Strangler, *it was the fault of Croydon's script which called for it.*
    Right—exactly. Croydon was a little stuffy—in fact, he was a weird man,

really strange. When I first met him, we had lunch at a restaurant in London, and I remember his dirty fingernails! And that's what always stuck in my mind — isn't that weird? He was just strange, and kind of sly.

I just enjoyed *The Haunted Strangler* very much. I was very cognizant of the fact that we didn't have much money to make the movie, so we were cutting corners all the time. So often, when I wanted to make a reverse shot, I thought, "Well, I *can't* do that because I don't have the time." And then also I had John Croydon up my ass all the time, talking about the budget and the schedule and so on. But I was pleased with the way the film came out — I mean, under the circumstances, and for the cost.

Are you a fan of horror films?

I'm not really a fan of horror now — I think I used to be. But to me it is so disgusting now, with contemporary horror movies, that I just cannot watch them. People getting cut up and all the graphic violence — I just can't stand it! But I liked them back in the old days.

How did you enjoy working on First Man into Space?

That was all right, but again we were so hamstrung with the budget. We had just no money at all. And the script wasn't very good — *I* didn't think it was, anyway. Actually, we had hardly any script when we started shooting! Chuck Vetter and I would meet after shooting, and prepare the next day's shooting — write the dialogue and everything!

How did the actors like this hectic pace?

Actors are usually used to that kind of thing anyway. I'm not saying by any means that they like it, but it does happen and professional actors can cope. Marshall Thompson was an okay guy; I don't know where they got Marla Landi. I never heard of her before *First Man into Space* and I never heard of her again *[laughs]*! What she did in the film was okay; it wasn't much of a part, anyway.

Did you have any say in casting?

Oh, yes. Again, it was always within the confines of the budget with those people. I didn't cast Marshall Thompson, I think he came with the package, but I helped to cast the remaining roles.

Were you pleased with the monster costume?

It was made of some plastic material, and then touched up with makeup afterwards. It was okay.

What fans don't like about First Man *is the way it shifts gears in mid-picture, from sober semi-documentary to lurid monster movie.*

Marshall Thompson (right) watches his mutated brother (Bill Edwards) take his last breath in *First Man into Space* (shooting title: *Satellite of Blood*).

I think that, to a degree, that was some of John Croydon's influence again. I hated the monster anyway, I thought it was dumb. My feeling at the time was, I thought that somebody could come back out of space with an aberrated mind, rather than the costume. I put that idea forward, but most of the people involved wanted the horror. Which I thought was almost a caricature. It's not one of my favorite movies.

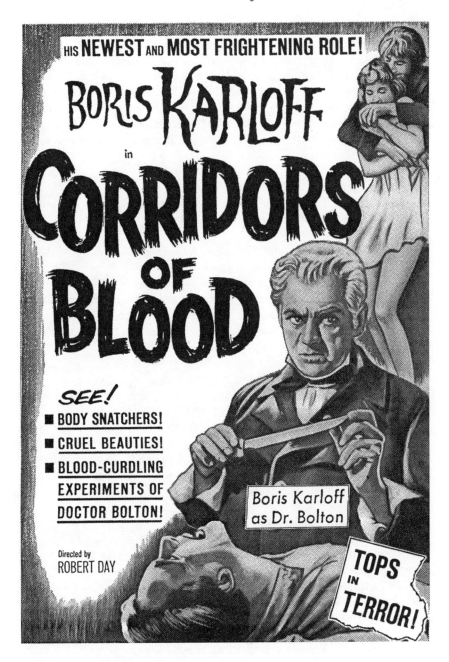

Day collaborated with Karloff a second time on *Corridors of Blood* (shooting title: *The Doctor from Seven Dials*), a historical drama with horrific flourishes.

Corridors of Blood *is another hybrid—a serious film about the discovery of anesthesia that suddenly detours into Grand Guignol.*

That's right, the same thing happened as in *First Man into Space,* where they wanted all this horror stuff again. By the time we got around to *Corridors of Blood,* we were shooting at the MGM British Studios in Boreham Wood, and we had a bit more money in the budget. How much more I have no idea, but I would think it was probably twice the budget of *The Haunted Strangler,* about two hunded thousand pounds. And the shooting schedule was a bit longer, about four weeks.

Any Karloff anecdotes on Corridors of Blood?

Well, he and I were deeply involved in characterization. I enjoyed it again, because of Karloff mainly.

Around this same time you also directed a fantasy/comedy called Bobbikins, *about a talking baby.*

That was a weird experience, from what I remember of it. The only thing I really remember about *Bobbikins* is that that baby drove me crazy all the time *[laughs]*! I would go home and think about what I could buy to attract his attention—I spent hours waving things and talking to him from behind the camera. It took all my energy!

How did you get interested in a career in the movies?

I've always been interested, ever since I saw my first movie. I just went from there! I remember that, even at just ten or eleven years old, I was determined that when the time came, I would get into the business. My father knew somebody at Warner Brothers in London and talked to them, and I got a job at Warner Brothers at Teddington, as a clapper boy. In the darkroom. Loading magazines and putting the numbers on scenes. That's how I started, and I went from there. That was nineteen-forty.

How did you climb the ladder to director of photography?

Just by hard work, I guess, and by having friends. Gradually I became an assistant cameraman, then a camera operator, and then on to photography. Then after being under contract to Warner Brothers for several years, I signed a contract with British Lion at Shepperton Studios, as a camera operator, and worked there for a long time. I worked with some good directors—I did a lot of work with Carol Reed, and Launder and Gilliat—I did *The Great Gilbert and Sullivan* [1953] and *The Constant Husband* [1955] with Rex Harrison for them. And then I didn't see them for a while and I went to Africa with Zoltan Korda to work on *Storm Over the Nile* [1956] and he kind of took a shine to me. I don't know if he was influential in talking to Launder and Gilliat subsequent to that, but when I went back to British Lion, Sidney Gilliat asked me if

I would like to direct a movie. I mean, it wasn't as sudden as *that,* but that was the bottom line. I said yeah, and then forgot all about it, really, because it was so outrageous. I went to the South Seas, to Western Samoa, working on a movie called *Pacific Destiny* [1956].

After I'd been there for two or three months, I got this cable from Sidney Gilliat saying they were about to make *The Green Man* and would I like to direct it? Of course I answered yes, but I was very sick. I had slipped on a reef and I cut my leg, got a tremendous cut which festered because of all the coral. Also, I was sharing a huge room with my assistant—they didn't have hotels there, it was like a huge government rest house that the whole crew was living in. My assistant and I had nothing to do in the evenings—there was just *nothing* in Apia—so we bought a couple of harmonicas and we used to play harmonicas in the evening. In bed, under the mosquito net! One night he was asleep and I was playing and I had a cigarette in my hand, too, and the next thing I knew I woke up and flames were all around me—I had set the whole thing alight! And I was covered in mosquito bites, I was awful. One became septic on my elbow and I had like a huge bag on my elbow with this damn infected mosquito bite! Anyway, to cut a long story short, that's how I arrived back in England—I'd lost many, many pounds and I was really in a bad state. But I guess the juices kept going, and the thought of directing *The Green Man* was a wonderful thought. Luckily, there was a long preparation time on the movie, so by the time we started I was in better shape *[laughs]*!

The Green Man *has a great reputation.*

It was tough, it was my first directing job. But it went well, and the reviews were excellent. Bosley Crowther in New York gave it a rave, and Pauline Kael loved it.

How did you get involved on Tarzan the Magnificent*?*

First Man into Space was running at a Leicester Square theater in Picadilly, [Tarzan producer] Sy Weintraub saw the movie and then contacted me to direct *Tarzan the Magnificent.* He came to my house in Roehampton, he and a second guy (I think he was an assistant director) and asked if I would be interested. I said, "Send me the script." So he did, and talked to my agent, and before I knew it I was in Africa!

They sent you the script? *I* thought *you* wrote it.

They sent me the original script, which I changed. I think that was my first time writing a screenplay.

Did you enjoy the opportunity of working on a Tarzan film?

It was okay. I was more interested in the action rather than Tarzan himself. Actually, this Tarzan phase is a period that I'm not that happy with in my career. I think it's just dumb, that's all. Especially what they did with him, making him talk—it's against the popular concept of Tarzan. But at that time, the business was really bad in England, and I guess those things came along when there was nothing else happening. It's not that I don't like them, I just wonder what the fuss is all about!

Maybe they were popular because Tarzan is such an immortal character.
I don't know—it's like any legend, I guess. Maybe one reason that Tarzan has perpetuated is because people like to think of somebody going back to basics and living in the jungle. The fundamental aspect appeals to them. It's almost primeval, you know.

Did you enjoy the location trip to Africa on Tarzan the Magnificent?
Yes, I enjoyed that. We shot *Tarzan the Magnificent* in Kenya. Part of the time we were based at Lake Nyvasha, which is a couple of hundred miles from Nairobi, and part of the time we were in Nairobi. Then we shot the waterfall scenes at a place called the Blue Posts, about two or three hours' drive from Nairobi.

Gordon Scott was your star in Tarzan the Magnificent.
He was all right. I remember one funny incident—well, *I* thought it was funny!—on the first day of shooting. Gordon Scott got out of this limousine that drove him to the location, they made him up and he started flexing his muscles and all that stuff. Then they gave him the bow and the arrows that he had to use. And then when we were ready to shoot, he took his shoes off and all of a sudden he was hopping around because the ground was so hot *[laughs]*! I can't begin to tell you how funny it was, to see this guy jumping around—*ouch, ooooch, ouch*—because he couldn't endure standing on the bare rock! I break up every time I think about it.

You also had John Carradine in Tarzan the Magnificent.
Oh, he was wonderful, just great. But there was his drinking, you know. When we got back to England, there were some extra scenes to do, and at Shepperton Studios we shot a scene of Carradine and the actors who played his sons wandering through the swamp. And he was drunk as a lord in that scene, and he was reciting Shakespeare during the rehearsals! But he was a great guy.

Many fans consider Tarzan the Magnificent *the best-ever Tarzan film.*
It makes me feel good that some people think that, yes. Naturally, I used to see the old Johnny Weissmuller Tarzan films when I was a kid; I thought they did a good job on those, and that Johnny Weissmuller was probably the

best Tarzan. That was a different era, of course; those early Weissmuller films were made at a time when we were just out of the silent period.

You shot Tarzan films all over the world. Did this create hardships, working in all these desolate locations?

Yeah, it did—it's not easy. You have to adapt to the surroundings and use the local talent—or what passes for it *[laughs]*! It was a lot cheaper, shooting in all these various places that we went to, especially at that time. And, of course, it was bringing new places to the screen, places that hadn't been seen in movies before. All the sound had to be added to these films after they were completed. We'd bring sound equipment along, because we had to get guide tracks, but we dubbed the whole movie, every time.

How about Jock Mahoney [Tarzan's Three Challenges] *as Tarzan?*

I thought Jock Mahoney did a good job but that he looked too old. He got pneumonia while on the picture. We carried on shooting, but, boy, was he sick! But Woody Strode did a good job playing the villain—he's great, isn't he? *Tarzan's Three Challenges* was shot in Thailand; we were in Bangkok, and in Chiang Mai, the northern province. We also shot in a sacred shrine, and that created all kinds of problems. Right at the last minute, they changed their minds and wouldn't let us photograph the monks, so we had to manufacture our *own* monks. We went into the town in Chiang Mai and got all the rickshaw drivers, we put bowls on their heads and cut their hair in a certain way, and used *them* as monks *[laughs]*!

Your next three Tarzan films featured Mike Henry.

We cast him in Los Angeles. We saw a lot of people looking for our new Tarzan, and I guess he came off best. The first film we did with Mike Henry was *Tarzan and the Valley of Gold,* which we shot in Mexico. The scenes in the ancient city were shot in Teotihuacán, which is a historic site, but we had problems. We got permission, but there again they reneged on the permission at the last minute and we had awful troubles day by day with the lawyers in shooting that. We went ahead somehow, I don't know how we did—I think Sy Weintraub was there in the background, talking to the lawyers all the time. They thought we were desecrating their holy ground by having Tarzan romping around there. It was hairy, but we got it done—although we did have to smuggle the film out! It was a great location.

The Mike Henry films are reviled by Tarzan purists—they say he isn't Tarzan, he's James Bond in a loincloth.

That was the trend at that time, the James Bond films and so on. And I must say I think I went along with it, too.

In these Tarzan films, much of your wild animal footage came from stock, right?

Yes, that's right. But when there was specific action with the animals, we'd have them on the sets. I remember that on one of the movies, *Tarzan and the Great River*, Mike Henry was bit by a monkey. We were in Brazil, we were working in a zoo in Rio and the scene called for Mike to be walking with a professor through the zoo and they come upon this chimp that Mike knew in Africa, that was now in captivity. The chimp came up to Mike, Mike embraced it, and as he embraced it, this chimp just bit his chin off! It was awful! We shot around Mike for a while, then I think the insurance took over.

Why are there no Janes in any of your Tarzan films?

I just don't know. I think it might have been because they wanted to keep him a free agent all the time, so he didn't have to return to that one nest.

Were you offered an opportunity to work on the Tarzan *TV series?*

I shot the pilot, with Ron Ely — that was shot in Rio as well. But I didn't work that show regularly. I'd had it up to my neck with Tarzan by then.

You also directed Hammer's remake of She *around this same time.*

That was my one and only time working with Hammer; they simply asked me to make the movie, although if you were to ask what made them think of me for it, I'd have to tell you that I just don't know. *She* was shot in London and Israel — all the desert scenes and the backgrounds for the special effects were all shot in Eilat, in Southern Israel, right on the ocean. The weather was right for it, anyway — it was hot, *boy*, was it hot! We were working in the Negev Desert.

Had you seen any of the earlier versions of She*? They date back to 1899!*

Yes, I did — I saw the one with Helen Gahagan [1935], and I saw one other one. I insisted on running them. I thought *I* did a better job *[laughs]*!

I'll tell you one interesting thing about *She*. While I was directing a movie called *Two Way Stretch* [1960] with Peter Sellers, Sellers was really involved with a guy called Morris Woodruff, who was a clairvoyant in London. And Sellers kept after me, saying, "You've got to go see Morris Woodruff." So eventually I did go to see him, and he told me some incredible things. He said that in a few years' time I would be making a movie written by a spiritualist; he said I would move to America; that I would be working for a producer with the initial W or M; and that I would marry a blonde and have a son in America. He told me all these things. Well, I made *She* in sixty-four which was written by Rider Haggard, who was a spiritualist; I'm living in America; I worked for both Sy Weintraub and for Quinn Martin, who brought me to America; I married Dorothy Provine in nineteen sixty-seven; and we have a son. Interesting, isn't it?

Day had to "watch the pennies again" while directing Hammer's remake of *She* (with Ursula Andress and Christopher Lee, pictured), but still feels that the film was superior to the more famous 1935 version.

Did that make you a believer?
  [Laughs.] No!

What can you tell us about the stars of She, *Peter Cushing and Christopher Lee?*
  Oh, I liked them very much, particularly Peter Cushing. He was a lovely man, just like Karloff. I also worked with him on *The Avengers*. Working with Ursula Andress was tough going at that time, because she hadn't had that much experience then. But it was okay.

She has a big-budget look—
  But did you know that that was made for two hundred forty thousand pounds? That was a fairly big budget film by Hammer standards, but we had to watch the pennies again.

Were you happy with the results on She?
  For what it was, yes. I understand it was a success at the box office.

You've also done plenty of "fantastic" television on both sides of the ocean, including The Avengers, The Invaders, Ghost Story *and* The Sixth Sense.

Oh, *The Avengers* was wonderful, I enjoyed it very much, enjoyed working with everybody there. *The Invaders* was fun, too; I felt the stories were quite good. That was a Quinn Martin show, and it was Quinn Martin who gave me my break in America. He'd seen my British movies and what I'd done on television, like *The Avengers,* and I signed a contract with him.

How does working in America differ from working in England, and around the world?
The industry is so cosmopolitan, wherever you go you meet the same kind of people. It's rather like the newspaper business—a reporter is a reporter is a reporter, anywhere. It's the same in the film industry.

Have you appeared in your own movies or TV shows?
Yeah, I was in *The Haunted Strangler*—I drove a horse-drawn cab. I was also in *Two Way Stretch,* and I played a scribe in a mini-series I did called *Peter and Paul* [1981]. There were more, but it's hard to remember.

Once in America, you immersed yourself in TV, and turned your back on features.
It's not that I turned my back on it, it's just that I was working so much in television I guess I got dubbed as a television director more than features. Right now we're living here in [the state of] Washington; Dorothy is from here, she was raised in Seattle. We used to come up here for vacations and I liked it so much I bought some property here, and when I couldn't stand Los Angeles anymore we moved up here, in nineteen eighty-one.

Are you happy with the work you've done in films and television?
Well, one is never really happy, one always wants to do better. I would like to do more good movies and good stories—I would like to read something that I want to do, a good story. Other than that I'm just at home enjoying myself, with my computer and my photographic darkroom. We just love it here.

*When somebody asked me to make a horror film, my first
reaction was, "Yes, but I want to do it differently."
I tried to "think around it," "think sideways," tried to
find a different approach to it. To make people who
were the way I was want to see it.*

Val Guest

ENGLAND'S HAMMER FILMS MAY BE MOST widely known today for their series of Dracula and Frankenstein snoozers, but in the days before Christopher Lee donned his vampire fangs and before Peter Cushing despoiled his first grave, the company leaned toward science fiction and produced its best three films: *The Quatermass Experiment* (U.S. title: *The Creeping Unknown*), *Quatermass II (Enemy from Space)* and *The Abominable Snowman (The Abominable Snowman of the Himalayas)*. All were based on television serials by writer Nigel Kneale and, just as importantly, all were adapted for the screen and directed by Val Guest, a reluctant dabbler in sci-fi whose remarkable aptitude made these films — and Guest himself — classic fan favorites. Returning to the genre in 1961, he added to his legendary canon what many consider his best-ever film, *The Day the Earth Caught Fire*.

Born in London in 1911, Guest began his career as an actor on the British stage and in early sound films. He ran the one-man London office of *The Hollywood Reporter* until an encounter with director Marcel Varnel led to a screenwriting job at Gainsborough Studios. Guest's directing career began in the early 1940s with a Ministry of Information short about the perils of sneezing(!), an inauspicious start to a lengthy roster of films which also includes (in the science fiction category) *Toomorrow*, *When Dinosaurs Ruled the Earth* and the wacky all-star spy spoof *Casino Royale*.

Your first entry into Hammer science fiction was The Quatermass Experiment *in 1954.*

And I very nearly didn't enter at all, because at first I wasn't going to make it. I wasn't interested. I think I was one of the very few people in the whole of England who hadn't seen the television series upon which it was based. [Hammer producer] Tony Hinds called me just as my wife Yolande [actress Yolande Donlan] and I were going on holiday to Tangier, and he said, "We want to do a film of *The Quatermass Experiment*. Would you like to make it?" I said, "Well, I don't know anything about it." He said, "Look, I'll let you have all the television scripts. I'll wrap them up for you, and you take 'em to Tangier with you and read 'em" — he wanted me to make *a* script out of it. So he met us at the airport and he gave us this great bundle of scripts, which I could well have done without on the plane *[laughs]*. In Tangier, I put it at the side of the bed, and it was there for a *week*. Yolande said to me one day, "What's this down here?" and I told her it was a science fiction thing Tony Hinds wanted me to do. She asked me, "Have you read it?" and I said, "No, no — that's not *me*, I'm no good for that sort of thing." And she said, "Well, *read* it. Since when have you been *ethereal*?" I couldn't answer that at all *[laughs]*, so I said, "All right, I'll read it."

Well, I read it — I *plowed* through it. I took it onto the beach with me, and I got absolutely hooked on it. I called Tony Hinds and I said that, yes, I'd do it. That's how I got onto *Quatermass*. Except for Yolande prodding me, I would never have done it.

Previous page: **Val Guest during his directing heyday.**

What made Hammer think of you for Quatermass?

I don't know. I'd done quite a lot of films for Hammer already and they kept coming to me now and then about all *sorts* of things.

Part of the money for the film came from an American producer named Robert Lippert.

[Laughs.] Robert Lippert was one of the — I don't want to say Poverty Row producers, but you know what I mean. He was one of the small independent producers working in Hollywood. Jimmy Carreras used to do quite a bit of work with Bob, and Bob used to give Jimmy [American] distribution of some kind in the early days of Hammer. Lippert was a nice enough guy and he had a girlfriend called Margia Dean who I was asked to put into the film. She was a sweet girl, but she couldn't act *[laughs]*. That's about all I know about Bob Lippert himself except that I think he made an *awful* lot of money one way or another, and if *he* did, I'm sure Jimmy Carreras did, too.

Are my ears playing tricks on me, or is Margia Dean over-dubbed throughout the whole film?

What probably happened was that she was not very understandable *and* the sound was bad, too. We did an awful lot of that film on location, and in those days Hammer didn't really have the power to stop Windsor Castle and everything, you know. We post-synched a lot of people, but the same voices.

What part of Quatermass Experiment *was shot in Windsor Castle?*

Not in the castle, in the city of Windsor. In the *shadow* of the castle, yes; in fact, we were about one hundred yards away when we shot the scene of Richard Wordsworth breaking into the pharmacy.

Was there American money in most of these early Hammer films?

Yes, there was. Jimmy Carreras was an incredible man. He would suddenly go to the art department and say, "Do me a picture with a dinosaur and a girl in its mouth," this, that and another. And the art department would come up with a great big, flamboyant poster. Then Jimmy would send it over to Lippert, or whoever he was working with at the time, and say, "How 'bout a picture about this?" And *that* was how he set up his pictures — he drew 'em out as posters. He did that for *One Million Years B.C.*, he did that for *When Dinosaurs Ruled the Earth* — *all* those things.

One of Lippert's associates, a writer named Richard Landau, gets screen credit for the Quatermass *script.*

Exactly what Dick Landau did was this: As we were working for the American market, when I had done my script, they would pass it to Dick and say, "If there's anything you want to Americanize, do it." So if I had put *got*, he would put *gotten*. It was things like that *[laughs]*—it was sheer nonsense! And *this* became a "co-script"! I can only tell you that on all the copies of the film that *I've* seen, my name is there [as screenwriter] and Landau's is not. But when we made it, I do remember either Mike Carreras or Tony Hinds saying, "Look, Dick Landau says that he ought to have his name on this. He's going to take it up with the Writers Guild." I said, "Oh, Christ, who cares? If it means that much to him, put his name on." I was told later that in America it only had Richard Landau's name on it.

Did you have any input on that first picture from Nigel Kneale?

Now, it's a strange thing about Nigel; I hear from all sorts of places that he's terribly unhappy about all his films. I don't know why that should be—maybe a hurt ego over the fact that some of his stuff had to be cut [to fit into a feature film running time]. For instance, when we did *The Abominable Snowman*, we let Nigel do the whole script. But, as I had to direct it, I had the final say on what happened. And I had to do all sorts of nips and tucks, because we could never have got away with it [the way Kneale wrote it]—people would have been up and out of the cinema. A brilliant writer, but one who writes stuff as though you were reading it in a book. An attention span, especially that of a science fiction audience, is *not* all that big *[laughs]*. So you have to make it a little bit more concise. And I don't think he was very happy with *that* film, either, even though he got sole credit on the screenplay.

But I really, honestly am sad about the situation with Nigel. He's a brilliant guy and he's had an enormous success with all these things—and he hates every minute of them. There's something rather twisted there, and it's sad that he doesn't enjoy the fruits of it all. I only met him a couple of times, that's all, and I can only vaguely remember what Nigel Kneale looked like.

If he disliked these films all that much, why did he keep going back to Hammer?

Money. *Money.*

Then he's got nobody to blame but himself if he doesn't like his subsequent Hammer films.

He seemed to have a chip on his shoulder, Nigel. See, at the beginning, he had a chip on his shoulder because he was not a screenplay writer and so they wouldn't let him write the screenplay. So therefore, automatically, everybody who was going to touch that piece of work was going to be a butcher.

In watching your Quatermass *films, we're struck by the overlapping dialogue, the realistic style—what directors and what films influenced you?*

I remember saying, when I told Tony Hinds I'd do *Quatermass Experiment,* "But only if I can do it *my way."* Tony said *[in a nervous voice],* "W-well, w-what's your way?" I told him, "I would like to shoot it as though a television company had said, 'Go on out and cover this story.'" And I must say, to Tony's credit, that he said that would be all right. I wanted it to look as though it was [filmed by] handheld cameras; we didn't *have* to frame somebody absolutely in the middle—make it *real.* That is how that happened.

Now, the person who had influenced me there was Elia Kazan, who when he made *Panic in the Streets* [1950] did virtually the same thing. I was terribly impressed with that. And I think that's the thing that put the germ into my head. I've used that technique on an awful lot of movies, not just science fiction.

That rapid dialogue just pulls you through the film.

I'm glad you think so, because that's what I was hoping would happen on that. To me, there's nothing worse than hearing question-and-answer, question-and-answer. Also, it gives you *pace.* I think an awful lot of British films lacked pace in the old days—that was *one* of our faults. We all learned these techniques as we *[laughs]* got older and older and older in the business!

Did your actors have problems with it?

At the beginning, yes, there were a few heels dug in. Once they realized what we were doing, once they'd been to the dailies the following day and *seen* what we were trying to get at, there wasn't a problem, no. They were rather excited about it.

Howard Hawks was one of the first filmmakers who liked to have overlapping dialogue in his films. Were you inspired by those?

No. I mean, I admire Howard Hawks' work, but it doesn't ring a bell with me. Another person who did it, of course, was Orson Welles. Where that [overlapping dialogue] came from for me was *not* from any director or anything, but from the fact that that is a great way to get pace. And if you are doing "reality," in reality *none* of us wait for someone to finish the complete sentence. That is all part of the *cinema verite,* the *rapportage,* whatever you want to call it. Making you feel *you're there.*

Much as I admire Alfred Hitchcock's thrillers, they always seem very over-rehearsed, whereas in Welles' films everything seems spontaneous because of the overlapping, fluid dialogue.

[Laughs.] Well, Hitch was always over-rehearsed. I worked with Hitch on *The Lady Vanishes* [1938] and things like that, because his office was next door to mine in the old Gainsborough Studios. We *all* used to work on each other's

films there. Hitch used to say, "Give me five 'gizmicks,'" and we would think up five particularly startling moments—"gizmicks" was his word for that. Then he'd say, "Now find me five *unbelievable* locations." And that is how he would start his films, by finding an unusual location and just these "bumps," as we used to call them. Then the script was developed to bring in these "bumps," the locations and everything. He used to really work very hard at that, and then Hitch would draw every single shot at the side in his script. And when he had done *that,* he would say, "Oh, shit, now I gotta make it." He *hated* making films. He *loved* preparing them, he loved getting right up to the first day of shooting, and then he'd have been thrilled if someone else would then take over. He was an extraordinary, fantastic man.

What did you do on Lady Vanishes?

What happened at Gainsborough was, there were four of us under contract as writers: There was Frank Launder, Sidney Gilliat, myself and a fellow called Marriott Edgar, who was *my* writing partner. And every script that came up there would go around. Frank and Sidney wrote the *Lady Vanishes* screenplay, and that screenplay was pushed onto us; and the comedies that Marriott Edgar and I wrote were pushed onto Frank and Sidney. We read each other's scripts and added and suggested and things. Then, on *Lady Vanishes,* I also spent a lot of time down on the set and everything.

Did more money go into Quatermass *than into a run-of-the-mill Hammer?*

I don't really think so, no. On these Hammers, there were never any locations to speak of, most of it was done on the lot at Bray Studios. Or there was an old, empty hotel next door where they'd make all the "spooky" things— they used that in a million films. We were all very tight for money on *Quatermass,* and I think that we had probably gone a *little* over because of weather problems, shooting in Windsor and at Whipsnade Zoo. (That was about twenty-five miles away—that's a big location for Hammer *[laughs]*!)

I remember on the next-to-last day of the shooting on *Quatermass,* my assistant came to me and said, "You know, you haven't got [actor] Jack Warner tomorrow, guv." I said, "Why?" He said, "Tony Hinds won't pay for him." I said, "But he's a main character!" Jack played the cop who was in charge of the investigation throughout the whole film, and now he wasn't going to be around for the denouement! The assistant said, "Well, Tony won't pay for him, he hasn't got the money to pay his daily [rate]." I said, "You write your star out because you haven't got the money to pay for the *last day's* shooting?! That's absolute nonsense. Call Jack Warner, on *my* authority, and tell Tony Hinds that *I* will pay for his last day out of my salary." And that's what happened. I *didn't* end up paying out of my salary, no, Tony picked it up, but I really had to threaten that. Otherwise we wouldn't have had the end of that story. It would have been played with bit players.

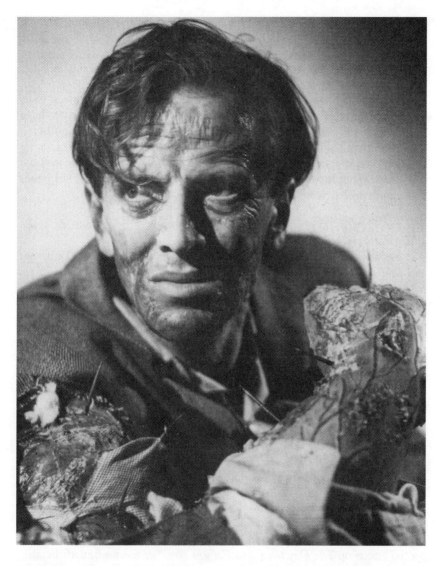

Richard Wordsworth's striking performance as the mutating astronaut was one of the main assets of Guest's *The Quatermass Experiment* (American title: *The Creeping Unknown*).

Would you say that Hinds was more interested in the money than the product?

Strange thing about Tony. Tony used to write an awful lot of those thrillers and horrors and things, under an assumed name. And he *loved* the business. But when he was producing, he was much more [money-minded].

(Also, *Quatermass* was *not* one of his stories.) It was just one of those things. But I was great friends with Tony long after that—we got over that little squabble.

Did you have much say in casting?
    Yes, I did. I had no say about the American stars who were given to us by the U.S. investors, but on the other people I did. In fact, I used to have a sort of a "rep" company that I used to use from one picture to another. I used to write little bits in for them in each film, and if they knew it was coming up, they'd try and keep themselves clear. We had some great people in those early days—people who became stars *over there*. Leo McKern and Sid James and people like that we'd keep busy.

Richard Wordsworth gives one of the best performances in Quatermass, *as the afflicted astronaut.*
    He was *very* good, yes. He came from the Royal Shakespeare Company, and that was his very first film. I thought he had the right gaunt face. And he never stopped laughing throughout the years afterwards, saying that his very first appearance in a film was his hands coming out the door from inside a rocket . . . pulling himself up . . . and getting twenty-three hoses worth of water right in his face *[laughs]*! That scene with the rocket was shot on the lot at Bray. The gnarled old tree that we propped the rocket up against is still there. And the little girl in *Quatermass* turned into Jane Asher, who nearly married Paul McCartney.

Do you remember your budget or schedule?
    Oh, nothing that Hammer ever did was much more than ninety thousand pounds. And the shooting was never more than about two, three weeks at the most.

What do you think of the special effects in Quatermass?
    I thought dear old Les Bowie, who we used to employ from picture to picture, was brilliant. He would do "everything for nothing," because he was told he *had* nothing *[laughs]*, and he really worked like mad. He later did my special effects on *The Day the Earth Caught Fire*. Les was a wonderful craftsman—he did it all, practically in his own garage, and never failed to come up with something.

Quatermass's *claim to fame is that it scared a boy to death in Illinois.*
    That was in the Guinness Book of World Records. I'd be interested to know what Nigel Kneale thinks of *that [laughs]*!

How big a hit was Quatermass?
    Very big—one of their biggest. In fact, it started them off on that bent.

The Creeping Unknown was the American title. The most wonderful title was the one they used in Germany, and I wish to *God* we had used it; there it was called *Shock*. When I found that out, I thought, "What a hell of a title!"

In growing up and being a movie buff, were you a fan of horror and science fiction movies?

I'd love to say yes, but *no* — not till Tony Hinds said, "Read *Quatermass*." I'm trying to think of all the things that I *had* seen and been taken by, but I can't honestly remember *any*. Maybe I'm missing one, but I can't remember any one that really stuck with me. I think that also is part of the reason why, when somebody asked me to make a horror film, my first reaction was, "Yes, but I want to do it *differently*." I tried to "think around it," "think sideways," tried to find a different approach to it. To make people who were the way *I* was want to see it.

You've made, what?, eighty-five films, and only a small handful are science fiction. And yet you may go down in the record books as "a sci-fi director." Is that all right with you?

[Emphatically.] Yes — *sure*! Why not? My God, just to "go down in the record books" is all right!

Next — obviously — came Quatermass II.

Everybody said to me — press, and people like yourselves — that *II* was far and away the best *Quatermass*. I didn't think so. I was very disappointed with *Quatermass II*. I didn't think it was a patch on the first one, because the first one had *freshness*. *Quatermass II*, I felt, was *reaching* somehow or other. But, it was very successful.

Did II *have a bigger budget?*

Yes, a little bigger budget. We were able to do more location work, and we had a *minutely* better schedule — I mean, probably another two days or something *[laughs]*! We drove down to the Shell Oil Refinery, where we shot a lot of that stuff. That was quite a long way away. That meant that the whole unit had to go down and be put up and paid location pay. The other locations were all based from Hammer, and you drove there in the morning and you drove back at night.

In nearly all the interviews we do, we hear how far imagination has to go to make up for the money that's not there.

Having no money means you have to use your head, that's all. The worst thing you can do, going into one of those, is think, "Well, this is a low-budget picture so they can't expect too much from us." That's *fatal*. You go into that picture saying *[through gritted teeth]*, "Nobody's going to say *this* was low-budget!", and you break your skull to try and overcome it. Everybody thinks up ideas that, if you had the lazy, easy advantage of just spending more dough, *no*body would have come up with.

Take [production designer] Bernie Robinson. I did a film with him called *Yesterday's Enemy* [1959], a war film set in the jungles of Burma, and we won an awful lot of awards with this. Our opening in London, at the Empire Cinema, was a big opening for the Burma Star Organization, Lord Louis Mountbatten was the guest of honor and everything. I sat next to Mountbatten during the showing, and he kept nudging me: "I know where you shot that and I *cannot* think where it was...!" Now, it was *all* shot at Shepperton or Bray, the whole thing! So this was that brilliant little man Bernie Robinson, who made a jungle on rolling trucks so that once the actors went through one part of the "jungle," we rolled our trucks and they were in an entirely *different* part! We built the swamp, the river, everything. And the Burma Star Organization and Lord Louis Mountbatten, who commanded over there, were absolutely convinced, not only that we were *there,* but that he knew exactly where we *were [laughs]*!

What arrangements did you have to make with Shell to shoot at their refinery? Did you shoot on days when they weren't working?

I honestly don't know, because that would have been the production department organizing that. I can't recall at any time having to hold up because of anything. It was a pretty empty place, as far as I can remember — there weren't an awful lot of people there. I think it ran itself, mostly.

One of the best scenes had that nosy investigator stumbling down from the top of the giant tank, covered with slime.

His name was Tom Chatto; he's become a well-known character actor in London, and his wife Ros is one of the top casting directors. I don't know what the hell kind of gunk they made up to smear all over Tom for that scene *[laughs]* — jelly, or something that looked like oil. He would come staggering down those steps, I'd say it was okay and my cameraman would say, "I'd like one more." And I'd say, "I'm sorry, Tom. One more." And *he'd* say, "Oh, shit...!" *[Laughs.]* He'd have to go all the way up the stairs again and be doused down again at the top while we cleaned the steps and the tank up!

Had you managed to catch the Quatermass II *serial on TV?*

No. It was far better that I didn't. Because then you're not bound by anything, you come in with a fresh eye. It's like an actor who's going to be in a new version of *A Streetcar Named Desire* going to see the Brando version. Absolutely fatal! Come in with a fresh approach. Or, again, if you're going to remake an old-time movie. I think it's quite fatal to go and see the original.

Tom Chatto, thoroughly "slimed" by the *Enemy from Space* (a.k.a. *Quatermass II*). According to Guest, the film "wasn't a patch on the first one."

How was Hammer thought of within the British film industry during that mid-1950s period?

Well, *my* feeling about Hammer was that it was one of the happiest "family" studios—I've never met anything like it ever again. You went into a family every morning. And that was a wonderful atmosphere. We *knew* that we had no money, we knew we had to make it look three times what it was costing, and we learned an awful lot of our trade through all that. We would be shooting in a small room and need to get a medium shot in there, and we'd have to get the cameraman to put his ass in the fireplace *[laughs]*! You learned what you could get away with and what you could make things look like. So it was fabulous. As far as the industry was concerned, I think that the industry looked down on Hammer a little. It was almost a laugh. They didn't do it with any derision, it was just like *[in a scoffing tone of voice]*, "Oh, well, it's a *Hammer*...!"

How did you like working with Brian Donlevy on these Quatermass *films?*
Oh, I got on with Brian fine. But so many stories have been concocted since, about how he was paralytic [drunk]. It's absolute *balls,* because he was *not* paralytic. He wasn't *stone cold sober,* either, but he was a pro and he knew his lines. There were times when he didn't know what the *story* was about, but he would say to me, "Give me a rundown up to here," I'd give it to him and he'd say, "Fine, fine." I never had any trouble with Brian, no.

Were you approached to do the third Quatermass film?
No.

What kind of a guy was James Carreras?
Jimmy was a fabulous character, no doubt about that—he had all the energy in the world. Enormous showman, terrific salesman. Didn't know anything about movies—didn't *profess* to know anything about movies. But he knew how to sell them and get 'em going. I was very fond of him. But he and his son Michael never got on—that was the sad thing about it. When Michael broke away [from Hammer], he swore that his father stopped him from getting jobs here and there. It was all very sad.

What do you recall about the proposed Hammer version of I Am Legend?
Mike Carreras was a buddy of mine then, and just becoming a producer around that time. Mike was one of the best producers I have ever worked for, because you knew that if you were out there on a lonely moor, that everything you needed was going to be there. You could rely on the guy completely and utterly. He did his homework.

Mike brought me the book *I Am Legend* one day and asked, "Do you think we'll ever get away with a film like this?" I said, "Let's try, let's see what we can do." The British censor *absolutely* said no, under no condition whatsoever would it be allowed. They then tried it on the American censor, and, of course, *no* again. It was completely blocked on both sides, unless great alterations were made. Now, I *think* Hammer had a script done, and that they tried the script out, and *again* they had terrible trouble. I don't know any more about *I Am Legend* than that, that we toyed with it at one time and that they were talking about having me direct it.

Hammer got into horror films much more than sci-fi. Were you ever asked to direct one of the Gothic thrillers?
No, not that I can recall. Somewhere along the line I might have been, because I was great chums with all of them and we used to spend weekends together *whatever* happened. I don't know if I'd have been very good at Gothic. I'd have started laughing, I think.

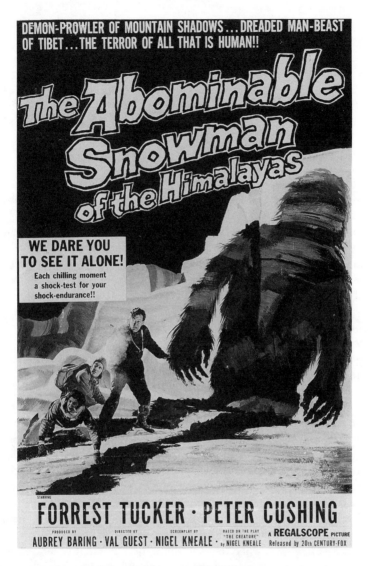

DEMON-PROWLER OF MOUNTAIN SHADOWS...DREADED MAN-BEAST OF TIBET...THE TERROR OF ALL THAT IS HUMAN!!

The Abominable Snowman of the Himalayas

WE DARE YOU TO SEE IT ALONE!
Each chilling moment a shock-test for your shock-endurance!!

STARRING
FORREST TUCKER · PETER CUSHING
PRODUCED BY   DIRECTED BY   SCREENPLAY BY   BASED ON THE PLAY   A **REGALSCOPE** PICTURE
AUBREY BARING · VAL GUEST · NIGEL KNEALE · "THE CREATURE" Released by 20th CENTURY-FOX
                                                          by NIGEL KNEALE

The best of the several 1950s films about the legendary Phantom of the Himalayas was Guest's suspenseful *The Abominable Snowman*.

Any memories of what led up to The Abominable Snowman*?*

No, just that it was something they sent to me; I think they sent me Nigel Kneale's script of it. I thought it was a very good idea, because there was so much going on [in the news] about the Abominable Snowman and there'd been so many people going up to the Himalayas: "Yes, we saw it," "No, we didn't." It was a topical thing, and I was very interested in doing that.

Were you under contract to Hammer?
No—*never.*

Where was Snowman *shot?*
I went out with doubles and a full unit for a couple of weeks, up into
the French Pyrenees, and we shot an awful lot of stuff up there. The rest was
done at Pinewood Studios, on one of their vast stages in which Bernie Robinson had done a complete snowscape.

*Your actors, Peter Cushing, Forrest Tucker and all—did any of them ever see
the light of day, or were all their "outdoor" scenes shot on soundstages?*
I don't think they went out anywhere at all. The Tibetan village was shot
out of doors—we built *that* for the film—but it was on the Bray lot. We had
some bloody good lighting cameramen down at Bray. Arthur Grant did so
many of my pictures—in fact, I took him *away* from Bray when I had my own
company. A wonderful little cameraman, very quick . . . *cheap [laughs].*
Now, when I say "cheap," what I mean is, he didn't demand five hundred arcs
and all that sort of thing.

*Did you have a lot of say in the photographing of your films, or did you leave
it to the directors of photography?*
No, I would leave it to the director of photography. Once we had decided
upon the mood we wanted to create on the thing, it was left entirely to him.

What can you tell us about Cushing and Tucker?
Oh, Pete is an old chum. There's a man with the most incredible sense
of humor. He'll be in the middle of a very dramatic scene—he's Shakespearean, he's everything—and at the end when you say *cut,* he'll suddenly
go into a "Knees Up, Mother Brown" dance! And have everybody on the set
in hysterics! He's nothing at all like you would expect. Wonderful, great, great
character. And he was mad about props—we used to call him "Props" Cushing. He would work it all out and *not* tell you anything about it until the take,
and then all these things would start happening. In that particular film,
Abominable Snowman, when they show him the Yeti's tooth, none of us had
any idea what was going to go on in that scene. But it sure went on! He took
a tape measure out, he scraped the tooth with a nail file, he came up with a
magnifying glass—all during the scene, talking the whole time. It was quite
hysterical.

He and Tucker were sort of an "odd couple" in that film.
They were complete, complete opposites. "Tuck" I made two pictures
with, *Snowman* and *Break in the Circle* [1957], and he was a great big . . .
schoolboy. In those days, he didn't have a drinking problem—or at least, if

he did, he didn't show it with us at all. He was a thorough pro, and I had no problems with him at all.

He really holds up his end in Snowman — *he's as good or better than Cushing.*
   He was very good. They used to kid each other a lot, Cushing and Tucker. Pete will kid anybody, and "Tuck" used to kid Peter Cushing. I remember we did a take and something went wrong, and I said we had to do it again. "Tuck" said, "Oh, Christ, that's the first time I've ever had to do a second take." And Cushing said, "Well, at least you're not a Method actor. They do it *seven* or *eight* times!" *[Laughs.]*

You went into the film intending not *to show the complete Snowman, correct?*
   Oh, absolutely. I refused positively to show the whole thing — I didn't want the audience to see the full figure, to see the full *anything.* I thought that people were liable to laugh. Let *them* think they've seen the whole thing, and just let's show bits of it. Which is what we did.

Are any of these sci-fi films you made favorite films of yours?
   Yes, *Quatermass* and *The Day the Earth Caught Fire.* But not the other science fictions, I'm afraid.

Were you never tempted to "go Hollywood" while you were in your prime, à la, say, a Hitchcock?
   No, not really. I mean, I'd been over here and shot bits and pieces of films that I had to finish for various people — things like *Killer Force* [1975] that I made in Southwest Africa. But there was far too much to do over there in England. Also, I was in a very lucky position: To be able to write and direct your own movies, that's a pretty good position to be in. And then, every so often, to also *produce* and write and direct is *also* good. That makes it a situation where there's nobody else to *blame* but you. So, no, I never thought of leaving.

Where did the idea for The Day the Earth Caught Fire *come from?*
   It was something that had been going around in my head for a long time, that gradually we were fucking up the whole planet. I had always been very interested in what we are liable to do to ourselves without realizing it. We can be an awful bore about this, talking about Greenpeace and this and that. It was like the old Campaign for Nuclear Disarmament marches and all of that — it becomes a bore. And I thought, there must be a way of getting that same story over without being a bore.
   I wrote out the idea in a treatment form about *eight years* before I made the movie. And every time I made a movie and [the producers] said, "What

do you want to do next?", I'd tell them my idea and they'd say *[disdainfully]*, "Oh, Christ! No one wants to know about the Bomb!" No one would ever let me do it. For eight years I kept on with that thing, and eventually I talked somebody into it: I finally got Sir Michael Balcon and a couple of other people at British Lion Films to say yes, but what I had to do was put up as collateral a film of mine called *Expresso Bongo* [1960], which had made a *lot* of money and got us a lot of awards one way or another.

Did Day the Earth Caught Fire *have the biggest budget of all the science fiction films that you'd done?*
      Do you know what that film cost to make? People just do not believe it. It cost us, in pounds sterling, just under two hundred thousand pounds, which at today's rate is four or five hundred thousand dollars. *Ludicrously* cheap.

This was made by your own company.
      Oh, yes, it was a Val Guest Production. The first Val Guest Production was *Penny Princess* [1951], which I made for Rank, with Yolande and Dirk Bogarde. Our company was Yolande, myself and an actor who was in all our films, a very close friend of ours called Reginald Beckwith — a wonderful comedy character. As we formed that film company, Yolande was in a play in London called *To Dorothy, a Son* — she and Richard Attenborough, just the two of them on stage all night. It was a knockout success and it was running for about two years. We were getting this company together and Dickie Attenborough kept saying, "*Can't* I come in this? *Can't* I come in with you?" And we said, "No, Dickie, it's just the three of us. Sorry." "Oh, well . . . I suppose one day I'll have my own company. . ." *[Laughs.]*

How did Wolf Mankowitz get involved on Day the Earth Caught Fire?
      Wolf's been a chum of ours for a long, long time; a very brilliant guy. He's a writer with *bite*; he will churn you out twenty pages which you can whittle down to three *brilliant* pages. An undisciplined writer, but he has everything going for him. And there are certain subjects that you instinctively know he would be absolutely right to come in on. I brought him in on various pictures I've done. He's living now in Santa Fe — he moved there a long time ago and he's teaching as a professor there and writing books and things.

Did you have scientific advisers and people like that helping you on the picture?
      Certain things that I wanted to know about, I asked certain people, yes, but I didn't have people working *with* me. What I did was, when I had the script, I would send it to (for instance) the weather people — I'd find somebody in a high weather office, and ask them to put me right if I'd used any wrong phrases. Or I would call somebody else and ask, "How long would it take an

ice cap melting to get to the Atlantic?" Things like that I would ask, but, no, I didn't have a technical adviser.

Your SF films give the impression that, if these crazy things did *begin to happen in real life, what we're seeing is how they would be handled.*
I'm glad to hear that, because that's what we tried very hard to do.

Was there American money invested in Day the Earth Caught Fire*?*
Not a penny, no. It was all English money. And I was able to cast it exactly as I wanted to without having to take star names, which would have killed it.

Where were some of the places you shot?
All around London. One thing we did was recreate at Shepperton Studios the office of the *Daily Express* [newspaper]. We had *so* many stills taken of that office, and I said to my art department and my set designer, "Make [our set] look like *that.*" We copied the *Daily Express* office absolutely, right down to the last piece of paper on the floor. I did three shots *only* of somebody walking down a passage in the real *Daily Express* building, and then we also shot in the entrance to the *Express* building.

We also shot in Fleet Street, and that was planned like a military operation. It *had* to be. To start with, we had to make it completely uninhabited. Fleet Street! We had to have boarded-up windows, dust, crap in the road, absolutely deserted, cars on the sidewalk left derelict — we had to do all that to make it look like the day before the end of the world. To do that in one of the busiest bloody streets in the world is not easy. So we planned it, and I must say the police were wonderful.

It was easy enough to get buildings to let us board 'em up (this was a Sunday), and to let us paste stuff on window panes to make 'em look cracked. What I told the police was, "I want no traffic; I want no cars parked on Fleet Street all the way from the *Express* office up to the law courts" — which has got to be a mile. They said, "We will have the street like that for you *for three minutes at a time.*" They put NO PARKING signs all the way down, on both sides of the street; they were on stands which could be kicked over. So there was nobody parked at all, except our "dead" vehicles.

We rehearsed everything with all the traffic and the busses and everything going — we rehearsed it absolutely up to the time we had to shoot. Then we told the two cops that we were ready to go. They were both on motorcycles, one on each side of the street. They blew a whistle, which stopped everything [all traffic] at the top. Then they drove off up Fleet Street, hell-bent for leather, kicking these NO PARKING signs down so that you couldn't see them, they were all flat on the ground. Following them was our prop truck with the back down, and three prop men in the back with shovels shoveling all the crap into the road that they could get in. And the moment they disappeared 'round the corner at the top, I said, "Action!" (We had two-and-a-half minutes by then.) And we got our scenes that way. The instant that the time was up, the police let the traffic through again.

The big action scene in the film is the water riot.
    We staged the entire thing *again* in the studio. I remember that an agent (who was also a chum) called me one day and said, "Look, there's an awfully nice actor who needs a job and has got to pay his rent and he's a good actor and—can you give him a bit when you do your water riot?" I said okay. He arrived down there, we paid him something like twenty-five pounds—and it was Michael Caine. So Michael was in all those riot scenes, too, but he was only there for a day, day and a half, something like that.

Did you stage that big peace demonstration in the film, or just take advantage of a real one?
    We did take advantage of a real one, and then we went on another Sunday when there was nothing happening, with our own little bit of crowd, for closeups. We matched all the wardrobe off the people who had been there before. Very much the same way as I used newsreel shots of floods and riots and all that, and "rebuilt" tiny pieces of those scenes in a studio with people with the same umbrellas and the same whatevers. It sounds awful to say this, but I did what Oliver Stone has just done in *JFK* [1991] *[laughs]*!

Speaking of JFK, wasn't he quite taken with Day the Earth Caught Fire?
    John Kennedy asked for his own copy of it, and he screened it for two hundred foreign correspondents in Washington. And they asked if I could talk Arthur Christiansen, who was editor at *The Daily Express* and who played himself in the film, into going over and speaking to them. "Chris" went over, but *I* couldn't—I wish I could have gone, but I was busy on another film at the time. Christiansen was a legendary character in Fleet Street. Half the people who saw the film said, "Oh, he's awful in there!", and the other half said, "What an unusual performance!" *[Laughs.]* Poor "Chris," we had a terrible time with him, because he wasn't an actor and he couldn't remember his lines. I had to do some terrific cutting in that office, when he's talking to all the reporters. But a lot of people thought it came off as being an unusual character. Yolande always says, "Oh, you *ruined* it, putting him in!"

Did he get much help or advice from the "pros" there?
    I can only tell you that Edward Judd was a real horror with him. Judd didn't help at all; in fact, he kept saying, "Oh, shit," and walking out, and *that* doesn't help a guy when he's forgetting his lines. But that was Eddie Judd, I'm afraid. Eddie was very good and *Day the Earth Caught Fire* was his big break and it got him a contract with Columbia, but he was such a pain

Doomsday looms closer for Edward Judd (and the rest of the Earth's population) in Guest's environmentally aware *The Day the Earth Caught Fire*.

in the ass to everybody. He had an enormous opinion of himself, and he was his own worst enemy. Columbia just loaned him out here and there and then let him go.

Good actor, though.

Very good. Well, I put him in there because I'd seen him in a TV thing and I thought he had enormous talent. I thought, what an unusual type to use and launch off.

Any special memories of leading lady Janet Munro?

I always knew Janet as a very good little performer, and she had just finished her contract with Disney. She kept saying to me, "Oh, I want to grow up. I don't want to be Disney. I want to do a grown-up part." And I said, "Well, this'll do it for you." And she said, "You've got to tell me how to grow up, and put it on that screen." In the Disney movies, they used to make her tie her boobs down for all her parts, to make it look like she had none. (We got *those* out, to start with *[laughs]*!) She had a very tragic end. Very nice girl.

Stupid question of the day: What was the weather really *like as you filmed scenes of all these actors broiling?*

Pressbook ad for *The Day the Earth Caught Fire.*

I can tell you that on the day that we shot in Battersea Park, with everybody sun bathing, it was about fifty-eight, sixty degrees at most. And everybody was *freezing* — in *bikinis*! We told them to keep their coats on until we were ready to shoot. That whole scene of Janet and Eddie Judd on the grass — it was very cold weather. On the other stuff, Fleet Street and things like that, it wasn't all that cold, but in the scene where it was supposed to be the hottest day of the century, it was a very cold day!

Tell your story about shooting the fog effects.

The day that we did all that fog in Battersea Park, we had every fog machine we could get from every studio, all 'round this vast park on the Thames. We had all these machines going, hundreds of extras — the whole idea was that this strange mist was coming up the Thames and covering the whole of London. When we were very near the end of the shooting, we were suddenly invaded by about three or four police cars; the cops came up and said, "You must stop this *immediately*!" What was happening was, just on the other side of the Thames was the Chelsea Flower Show, which the Queen was opening. And they had all this fog, pouring all over Her Majesty *[laughs]*! The policemen said, "You have no right to do this! You didn't say anything about all this fog!" So I said to my assistants, "Go and argue with them. Keep 'em arguing as long as you can." They went and argued with the cops, and really had a high heated argument, while we got on with what we had left. And we shot it, *in* the fog, while my guys were arguing. Finally I came out and said, "Well, all right, okay, we're sorry. We'll stop." But, of course, we had finished by then!

Did you have anything to do with the yellow tinting on the opening and closing scenes?

Yes, that was my idea, and it was written in the script. I *fought* against making the movie in color, I didn't want color, I thought color would kill it. But, I thought, what a difference it could make *if*, when the world is near its end, it is so hot that everything is this yellow shimmer. I thought that, if we could do the beginning and the end like that, it would make a difference. And they had terrible trouble doing it, because at that time, it was not all that easy to cut from color to black and white in a strip. They had to hand-tint the beginning and the end, and it became so expensive — we're talking about worldwide prints — that a lot of times they left it out.

The up-in-the-air ending was also terrific.

It was a terrible battle, getting them to agree to let me do that. I said, "You'll defeat the whole object of this film," and finally they let me do it, but then they said, "Well, can we have angels singing or something?" *[Laughs.]* I said I'd go that far, yes.

It was church bells, and that gave us the impression that the film seemed to be hinting—

—that maybe it was all right. But I refused to say *yes it was* or *no it wasn't.* I said, "All right, we'll give 'em a little feeling that *maybe...*"

Were you happy with all the special effects in the movie?

Yes. I mean, I can look at them and say, "Well, I'd have liked to have done this or that," but for what it was at that time, I thought Les Bowie did a very good job.

You wrote in films and filming *that you've never been happy with any picture once it was finished.*

Actually, that's not a complete quote. What I said was, I've never been completely happy with any film we ever made *because* you always sit and see so many other things you could have done. Which is quite normal, and doesn't mean that I'm *un*happy with a film. The day you sit at a film and think, "I could never have done anything better," I think you've had it.

Did all the positive reviews for Day the Earth Caught Fire *help your career?*

It would be nice to say yes, but I don't think so, no. I'll tell you what happened: Through my life, I have gone through a career where occasionally we've had, *oh,* a great big hit and wonderful press and everything, and you think, "Ah, now it's going to be easy." But it's not. All it does is that, for the *next* film, you can get in to see who you want to get in to see. Where, before you had done that, it's *tough* to get in to see who you want to see. It opens doors, but it doesn't make it any easier for you to make the pictures you want to make.

Was Day the Earth Caught Fire *profitable for you?*

Yes, it was, I'm glad to say. Universal released it in the U.S. and in England it was released by British Lion. Actually, Michael Balcon and Steven Pallos started their own distribution company, Pax Films, just for that picture, and then it went out through British Lion over there.

Do you have a favorite story about the making of Casino Royale?

[Laughs.] I could write a *book* on *Casino Royale!* It was an unbelievable experience in my life. I went on it under contract for eight weeks, and I was still under contract *nine months* later. [Producer] Charlie Feldman was a *mad-man.* There were days when you loved him and could hug him, and then other days you could *throttle* him! An extraordinary man, who would change his mind overnight—*during* the night, mostly—and call you at all hours.

They had bought a book called *Casino Royale,* which was a Bond book. *But,* when they went through it, they found that every single sequence in that book had been used in all the other Bond pictures. This was the only book that had "gotten away," the only one [Bond producers] "Cubby" Broccoli and Harry Saltzman didn't have. But they had used all the bits out of it, including the big card game!

You directed Woody Allen's segment.

Oh, yes—Woody and I sat down and wrote it all together. Then we took it all over to Charlie Feldman, who would go through it and send it back with all the gags cut out, having left all the buildups *[laughs]*! Woody would be in *tears,* Woody'd say, "How can a guy *do* this?", and I'd say, "Look, don't worry about it. Let him think he's cutting something. We can put 'em back when we shoot!" Which is exactly what we did. Woody has less confidence than anybody you would ever meet; you wouldn't think that, but it's so. You have to hold his hand and so on.

Did you work in collaboration with the other Casino Royale *directors?*

No, only to say, "Hey, don't use (such-and-such a star) Wednesday 'cause I need her!", that's all. It was a very strange set-up. At the beginning, it was just John Huston and me. One day, John said to me, "Is Feldman as mad as I think he is?" I said, "Oh, he's *madder!*" Huston said, "He's talking now about having a compendium of directors." I didn't know that *[laughs]*. "Oh, yes, it's not just us! There's a *compendium* coming along!" Then Charlie said to me he wanted a compendium of *stars* as well—a lot of stars, different segments and a compendium of directors. He gave me a script by Terry Sothern, a script by Ben Hecht, a script by Richard Maibaum—and he said, "Take all these away and see if you can get *one* out of 'em." It was an impossible job.

I ended up working on the film to the extent that Charlie said to me, "You've done so much on this, I'm going to give you a credit of your own: COORDINATING DIRECTOR: VAL GUEST." I said, "If you do that, I'll sue you." 'Cause people were going to say, "*This* is coordinated?!" *[Laughs.]*

Orson Welles was in the cast. What did he think of all this?

Orson Welles and Peter Sellers could not get on. And Orson Welles said one day, "Call me when that fucking amateur has finished." That gives you an idea of how they got on.

Was that your worst filmmaking experience in some ways?

Oh, no, not *worst,* I wouldn't say that. We had a lot of fun on it, and it taught you how to keep your head when all about you are losing theirs *[laughs]*. You have to be resilient.

Do you remember how you got involved on Hammer's When Dinosaurs Ruled the Earth?

It was a sorry day and I *do* remember it *[laughs]*. A lady called Aida Young was the producer of that; she used to be the production manager's assistant-cum-everything at Hammer. Aida called me at our little holiday pad in Malta and she asked, could she come over, would we be there? So she flew over and said, "Jimmy Carreras wants to do another dinosaur film." She brought over a few sheets of paper with ideas and things that matched up with the poster he'd sent to Hollywood. I thought it might be fun; I'd never done anything like that, so why not? I sat down and wrote a story. That's how I got involved, it was as easy as that. And I was *hoping* at that time that we could do it in Malta; then I could stay at my pad there and everything. But there were no mountains anywhere near there, and that didn't help! We shot it in the Canary Islands.

Maybe I'm not very good at working with a woman producer *[laughs]*. We didn't get on between us. After it was over, I was in on the editing, working with our editors as I always do, and then I went away onto another film and got on with my life. Then the editor called me up and said, "I don't like to tell you this, guv, *but...*" Aida Young had reedited the whole picture. But, what the hell, it's not as though we're talking about *Citizen Kane*! So I don't honestly know how it ended up, because I was too fed up with the whole thing to go and see it. I don't have much else to say about that, except I *loved* the animator, Jimmy Danforth—who I also believe was very unhappy with the film. But I thought we did rather well by him.

Was he unhappy as the picture was being made, or after it was all screwed up?
    Well, I don't think it *did* get "screwed up" for *him*; he was nominated for an Oscar for that picture! Brilliant little man. Whether he wanted to have more to say in the film or *what* his complaint was, I don't know.

Did you at least enjoy the making of the film in the Canary Islands?
    I enjoyed being in the Canary Islands because I love any location but, no, it wasn't a very scintillating company. As our star, we had a bimbo called Victoria Vetri, who was Miss Playboy or Miss Centerfold or something like that. She was a real nothing, and a very strange mixed-up lady, too. The rest of the cast were people I knew, like Pat Holt and Robin Hawdon—in fact, Robin Hawdon, who played the juvenile in it, played the office boy who died in *Day the Earth Caught Fire*. And he went on to become quite a good playwright.

Did Vetri give you a hard time?
    She never gave me a hard time, the only tough time was *taking* her. It was tough to take her. She was a ... nitwit.

I don't like to say this to your face, but when I tried to watch the film, it was impossible. It's grueling, it's so bad.
    It's awful, awful, awful. And they went and shot some more stuff, too.

Was that sort of prehistoric story even your "cup of tea"?

No, but like I said, I did it because I'd never done one and I wanted to try it. And, let me tell you, had I done that with Mike Carreras or even Tony Hinds, it would have been an entirely different picture. Absolutely. I would have gone in and said, "All right, let's try and get another angle on this — we've *seen* Raquel Welch. Now let's try and do something strange." But I couldn't, working under the auspices that I was. It was just sort of another *One Million Years B.C.*

Was creating a prehistoric lingo your idea?

Yes. I wish I hadn't thought of that. It was a sort of half-hearted attempt. It should have been followed by other things — which they didn't want to know about.

What can you tell us about your space musical Toomorrow?

That was a madhouse, with Harry Saltzman and Don Kirshner producing. They didn't talk to each other, they didn't like each other. It was an absolutely madhouse film, but it wasn't too bad a film — we launched Olivia Newton-John, who we found singing and playing a guitar in a nightclub. But there was so much going on behind-the-scenes during that film, with Kirshner wanting *this* and Harry saying, "Tell him you can't do it," all that sort of thing.

At the end of production, I was way over my contractual period — probably about six *months* over, and still working. Comes the time when the money's to be paid, Harry Saltzman says he doesn't have it. So *my* lawyer says, "Well, you better *find* it. Because the film is opening at the London Pavilion next week, and if you *don't* find it, we will enjoin the film so you can't open it." I allowed it to open, because I didn't want to stop it opening; it opened, and the following week I enjoined it; and it's been enjoined ever since *[laughs]*! The picture was not allowed to be shown until I was paid, and I was never paid.

My contract was with [a company] called Sweet Music, which was in Switzerland. And when we descended on Sweet Music, Sweet Music had nothing. What Harry had done was, he had put up his share of the Bond films to the Bank of Switzerland in exchange for money to back *Toomorrow*. But "Cubby" Broccoli, Harry's partner in the Bond films, and Harry had a contract which said that nobody else could be a partner in their Bond films. When "Cubby" found out that Harry had used them as collateral, they broke — that was the end of "Cubby" Broccoli and Harry Saltzman.

And now you're working on a remake of Day the Earth Caught Fire.

Winchester Films of England came to me about my proposed remake, and they had an idea of how to update it. I was very impressed, and I said I'd go along with them. At that time, I had Paramount, Warners and Twentieth

Currently living a chip shot away from a Palm Springs golf course, director Val Guest was England's most valuable contributor to the 1950s sci-fi/horror movie scene.

Century–Fox [vying for it]—*all* of them suddenly decided they wanted to remake the film. But it's much too nice down here in Palm Springs for me to be up there [in Los Angeles] arguing with all of them, so I leave this all to Winchester—they have done all the deals and things, and I just do the writing. We've done the first draft script, and brought it up to date. I don't want to say too much about what we've done on it, but it looks like we were slightly ahead of our time, because global warming is today a real concern.

You'll be directing?

Oh, no, no, I'm done with all that now. I've co-rewritten, and I'm co-producing.

Any closing comments? Proudest moments? Regrets?

Well, we've all got regrets about this, that and the other, but, yes, I'm happy, I think life has been very good to me. I think maybe I could have done more, and better, but I don't complain. I've had a very full life and a very interesting life. Somebody up there has been very good to me.

*It was at [our first] meeting that Jim Nicholson asked
me if I liked boats, and I said, "Well, yes, I love
boats." Had he asked me if I liked boa constrictors,
I would have said, "Oh, they're very nice!" He was
handsome, charming and the kindest man I'd ever met.*

Susan Hart

ACTRESS SUSAN HART STARRED (and showed off the type of figure that bikinis—even invisible ones—were invented for) in an assortment of horror and fantasy films in the 1960s. She debuted in the notorious *The Slime People* and later became a contract player at American International Pictures, where she was ideally (swim-)suited to her roles in way-out comedies like *Pajama Party, Dr. Goldfoot and the Bikini Machine* and the never-to-be-forgotten *The Ghost in the Invisible Bikini.* More importantly, she became the sweetHart—and later the wife—of the company's guiding light James H. Nicholson, and reigned as the First Lady of AIP during one of the more colorful eras in the history of horror, action and exploitation films.

Widowed but now happily remarried, her interests have shifted since the days when she was AIP's favorite Queen of Scream, first to country-western music (her 1981 "Is This a Disco or a Honky Tonk" made it to the Top 100) and now to ice skating, which she takes every bit as seriously as her earlier avocations. Taking a break from her daily ice routines, she gives us a rink-side seat as she reminisces about the films, the fun—and the intrigues—that were AIP.

How did you first become interested in pursuing an acting career?

I suppose my first step in that direction was going to the movies *[laughs]*! My mother gave me tap dancing lessons, ballet lessons, singing lessons, all the kinds of lessons that in those days mothers were prone to do to daughters that had naturally curly hair. I think I enjoyed all those things; I *asked* to do all those things. I wasn't enamored with school or schoolwork; these lessons seemed to put me in a happier mood. (I still do take lessons—right now, ice skating lessons.)

I had a relative by marriage who was in films in the late forties through the fifties. Her screen name was Noreen Nash. She was born and raised in Wenatchee and her brother was married to my sister. The first time I saw Noreen, I thought she was something from Heaven—she was probably the most beautiful girl that I had ever seen, and certainly that Wenatchee had ever produced. And I remember thinking, "Gee, does *every*body in the movies end up looking like that?" She was lovely—and she still is, by the way. So she was perhaps like an idol when I was a little girl. Of course, I didn't know that it took work and that one actually needed to *act* to be in the movies; as a seven- or eight-year-old, I just thought you had to be beautiful. So I remember meeting Noreen and thinking, "I would like to be in the movies like her."

We were spending the summers in Washington and winters in Southern California. I graduated high school—barely, as I recall *[laughs]*—and I worked at the telephone company in Palm Springs. One of my best girlfriends in those days worked at the *Desert Sun* newspaper. We saved up our money, working for maybe seven or eight months, and wound up with about nine hundred

Previous page: **She went from being Susan Neidhart of Wenatchee, Washington, to the First Lady of AIP: Lovely, leggy Susan Hart.**

dollars apiece to go to Hawaii—at that point, our dream was to go to Hawaii and learn to surf. (My big ambition was to be a great girl surfer.) We hung out with the beach boys and learned to surf—we spent about a month or so there. I came back to California, managed a dress shop for awhile, made enough money to go back to Hawaii and got a job in the International Marketplace, selling Hawaiian clothes. An agent named Morton Smith came into the shop one day and gave me his card, and told me that he was not only an agent but a photographer, too. He was doing a piece for *Playboy* on the Girls of Hawaii, and wanted to know if I would pose. I said, "Of course—as long as I don't have to take off my clothes." I told him that I loved to surf, so we went down to the beach at Waikiki the next day: I got on a surfboard and he took pictures from a catamaran. This was my first time in front of a professional camera-person, and the picture appeared in *Playboy*.

I stayed in Hawaii another month or so, and then came back to see my parents in California. I still had the agent's card, and decided at that point that, why not?, I'd give it a whirl. I had appeared in plays in Palm Springs, at the various playhouses and local community theaters and high school and so forth. I also sang on occasion, at weddings and, oh, various school things—I wasn't a very good singer, but maybe I was a little bit of a better actress because people thought I could sing. (I *was* a good actress—right?) I went in to see the agent and he was legitimate—he had an office on Sunset Boulevard and a small roster of clients. And that same day, I signed a year's contract with him representing me. I went out on an interview within about two weeks, and it was for a role on *The Joey Bishop Show*. It was about three lines, and I got it. That was my first job. Several others followed, always small roles for about a year—five lines here, three lines there. Then I worked myself up to maybe twelve lines *[laughs]*! *Laramie, 77 Sunset Strip, Cain's Hundred*—shows that were popular during those years.

This was all about the time of The Slime People.
   You had to remember *Slime People,* didn't you?

I'm afraid I have to rub your nose in that one for a little while—
   Oh, no, no, no—*The Slime People* was great fun! Bob Hutton had been a big star at Warner Brothers in the forties, he evidently wanted to direct a picture, and he had found a backer named Don Hansen who ran or owned a chain of dry cleaning establishments. (Don always wore a hat, a fedora-type hat—a real, *real* man's hat!) I remember meeting Bob Hutton at my agent's office, and I was scared to death! I knew, number one, that the picture was going to be non-union; number two, I had been told about all of these casting couches in Hollywood. (In television, it wasn't necessarily the truth, but I didn't know anything about movies.) I knew that Bob was handsome and experienced in the business, but I really didn't know what to expect. So that's

why I requested that he come down to *my* agent's office — and I suppose he was very pleased to do so, because who knows if he even *had* an office of his own to work out of? But Bob was super. I think I only had one meeting with him, and he made his decision fast — he wanted me for the role and I guess my price (which was very cheap in those days) was right. I believe I was supposed to be paid nine hundred dollars a week — or was it three hundred dollars a week for three weeks? It was a paltry sum, but it was more than I had seen for three or four weeks' work.

I went to the May Company with Robert Hutton, and we picked out an outfit for me to wear — I had to pay for it, thirty-four dollars, but I was reimbursed. I remember the outfit very well because I wore it for so many days. Bob Hutton was several years older than I was, so I tried to make myself look older. I wore my hair up and carried a huge black purse. Why on earth they had me carry that big purse through every single scene, including encounters with the Slime People, I have no idea! Where was I going — shopping *[laughs]*?? I also wore four-inch high heels while running over hill and dale to escape these weird creatures. Wearing those heels killed me — my feet were never the same again after the movie. (Looking back on this, I question if perhaps this very experience may have prepared me for the sure-footedness that ice skating presents me with today?) But, hey, it was great fun and the cast and crew were wonderful people.

Any memories of the Slime People themselves?

One monster was a charming young kid by the name of Jock Putnam. His stepfather was a very famous neurologist — in fact, in some circles, he's known as the father of neurology. His name was Dr. Tracy Putnam. He was instrumental in discovering a medication called Dilantin, which epileptics would be very familiar with. Jock was doing the sound on the picture and he was also playing a slime monster. And he talked his stepfather into playing the role of a famous scientist. I also remember Jock running around with a big tank full of dry ice or whatever, to create the fog that's everywhere in the picture. Everybody did that — well, not the girls, but anybody that was strong enough.

Where were some of these exteriors shot?

About forty miles outside of L.A., in a canyon around Agoura or Thousand Oaks. We would arrive at dawn. On two separate occasions, we couldn't shoot because someone forgot to bring the film. Organization was not a priority here.

What did you think of the Slime People costumes?

You know, even in person, the things weren't scary. Looking back on it, they were pathetic — well, at least *funny*! And I believe that they spent a great deal of money on those costumes — they were probably a big bite out of the

Hart shrieks at the clammy touch of one of *The Slime People* (Bob Herron).

budget. Jock used to get so hot in there, and when he'd take it off, he did not look well at all—ill, almost. Another fellow who also played one of the monsters smoked, and it was the wildest thing to see—he'd smoke through that costume! Long plumes of smoke would pour from the ears and "shoulders." Once they got him all locked in, he didn't want to take it off—it took maybe a half hour to get him into it. So he'd walk around the set, smoking through the nose hole *[laughs]*!

What about some of the other people in the picture?

Judee Morton, the girl who played my little sister, was my roommate in Hollywood for about two years; she was later nominated for an Emmy for a *Dr. Kildare* segment. We would go home after a day on *Slime People* and I would say, "Judee, gosh, do you think that they could give me some lines instead of just screaming?" And she would say, "What? *I'm* the one that's doing all the screaming." And we used to argue! I'd say, "No, no. *I'm* doing all the screaming. You have more lines than I do." But now looking back at it, she was absolutely right—Judee *did* do all the screaming in that film! We still talk from time to time. Bill Boyce, the marine in the film, was a good friend of Judee's from her home town, Shawnee, Oklahoma. I don't know what ever happened to him. And Les Tremayne also was a real gentleman.

Was Robert Hutton a good director?
    To *me,* he was a good director; *any*body would have been a good director. I had never done a film before. He was not only directing, but he was also starring. So I suppose he was as good as anybody is able to be, who is doing both of those jobs. And he helped me as much as I, in those days, was capable of being helped. It was a very nice experience; I remember it being fun, I remember feeling like I didn't know what I was doing most of the time (or what I was *supposed* to do, or what it was all about). But the people that were there were all using it as a stepping stone. I didn't feel the way I might have if my career depended on this particular vehicle. I just knew that I was working and gaining experience, and, believe me, with the competition for any type of picture in those days, we all felt very fortunate to be working, Bob Hutton included.

Were you paid for The Slime People? *Hutton wasn't.*
    I *did* get paid the first week, and we even had a makeup person the first week. All of a sudden, in the second week, we started doing our own makeup. And people started disappearing, like lighting men and carpenters. All of a sudden, the crew was down to maybe seven—not counting the monster! I don't know how much money they had for it, but I'll bet you that it wasn't more than about thirty thousand dollars. When it was all over, I believe I was owed fourteen hundred dollars.
    In or around nineteen seventy, my husband Jim Nicholson and I were having some friends in for dinner. One of the couples happened to be Judee Morton and her husband Ian Fraser, who was and is a fine musical conductor/ arranger. During the course of the conversation, Ian looked over at me and said *[in a thick British accent],* "Susan! I caught your film on the telly last night." I assumed he was referring to one of my AIP films. I said, "Oh, really? Gosh, I didn't know that they went to television that fast." I looked at Jim: "Am I in any pictures that you've already sold to television?" Ian said, "Oh, no, the one you did with Judee." I looked over at Judee and I kicked her a

little bit under the table, signalling *her* to kick *Ian* under the table! *The Slime People* was something that I did not put on my resume, something that I didn't want Jim to know about. We'd been married for four or five years and I hadn't bothered to mention it. I didn't *lie,* but he didn't ask and I wasn't about to tell him *[laughs]*! But it was too late, Ian came out and said, *"The Slime People! The Slime People!"* — he repeated it three or four times! At first I feigned not knowing, but he kept at it: "Oh, God, it was *awful,* Susan! I just can't believe you *did* that, Susan!"

All the time this conversation is going on, Jim isn't missing a bite of his dinner. I turned to him and I said, "Well, gosh, Jim, I guess the cat's out of the bag now. I have to tell you." He said, "Tell me what?" I said, "Judee and I did a film a *l-o-n-g* time ago, and it wasn't exactly a great film. . ." He looked at me and he said, "I'm familiar with the film." Judee and I said in unison: "You *are*??" And Jim said, "Yes. We've been distributing it to television for the last five years."

What happens when you get your hand caught in the cookie jar? You either get mad or you go and sulk. I chose to get mad. I stood up from the table and I said, "Well, in that case, Jim Nicholson, you owe me fourteen hundred dollars!" *[Laughs.]*

The Slime People has a real Golden Turkey type of reputation today.

I don't want to say I was embarrassed over such a silly episode in my life, but I probably was. But time has a way of distorting any negative thoughts — at least, it does with me. Some people remember the negative, I try to remember the positive.

The Slime People was supposed to be opening in Los Angeles and I ran up to Seattle to get out of the city — as though anybody would even know or care who I was *[laughs]*! I went to Seattle to visit my brother, and my agent informed me that it was going to be sneak-previewing in Seattle! Of course my brother was all excited, and so we went to see it. There were maybe all of twenty-five people in the theater. And my brother reminds me — constantly — that he has never seen anybody sit so far down in their seat, for the full seventy-odd minutes or however long the thing was! But he got a big kick out of it, and so did the audience — it was kind of a hoot. But I remember seeing it that first time and badgering my brother, over and over: "Oh, please, Don, can we leave now?" I was embarrassed, not so much because of the film, but because I did a lot of things that were stupid.

Acting choices, you mean?

No, *lack* of acting choices *[laughs]*! Also, seeing yourself on the big screen can be a real shock — it magnifies everything that you see in the mirror that you wish was not there. In those days, so much emphasis was placed on the physical, and you had to be pretty vanilla-looking to be thought of as attractive. To me, I wasn't vanilla enough.

You took a year or so off from acting not long afterwards.

I was in the hospital for three months. I was very, very ill with pneumonia and I had streptococcus set in—I became poisoned. I lost about twenty pounds and they didn't know if I was going to live or not, and I lost all my hair. So for the next two years, I wore wigs, until finally my hair did come back. That's why I lost about a year in my career, mainly because I felt very self-conscious about my hair. It's different for men—people say, "Oh, he looks better." But a twenty-two-year-old girl bald is not exactly like a sixty-two-year-old guy with at least maybe some graying hair left over!

In nineteen sixty-three, I started getting back into it again—that's when I did *Dobie Gillis, The Beverly Hillbillies, Alfred Hitchcock*. I also had a small part in *For Those Who Think Young* and a small role in *A Global Affair* with Bob Hope. During those years, Paul Henning was producing *The Beverly Hillbillies*, and he was going to do a series on *Archie* and as I recall I was going to be Veronica. There was even some talk about perhaps marrying me off to Jethro in *The Beverly Hillbillies*! Mike Frankovich saw something that I was in, and that was how I got the role as a Hawaiian girl in *Ride the Wild Surf* [1964]. I went so far as to dye my hair black—blue-black—to get the role.

And not long after that, you met Jim Nicholson.

Jim Nicholson, who was then heading up American International Pictures, watched the rushes on *Ride the Wild Surf* because Columbia was perhaps going to be a competitor with the AIP *Beach* movies. Up until that time, I believe American International was the only company that was doing those types of films, and they did very well financially. Other studios were entertaining the thought of perhaps going them one better—spending more money, going three thousand miles further. Anyway, what Jim Nicholson happened to view were dailies of me. And—this is what I've heard from friends—he fell in love with me when he watched those dailies *[laughs]*! When I got back from Hawaii after making *Ride the Wild Surf*, I had an interview at American International; it was with [*Beach* series director] Bill Asher and Jim Nicholson. It was at that point that I was offered a very nice contract, and my agent Fred Briskin thought I should take it. So I signed with them.

Did you have your pick of roles at AIP?

Oh, gosh, no. *No*, no! You have to understand something: I was very torn about signing with AIP, because I had been under option for a time to Columbia, and I was told that they were going to be picking up my contract. When I went into my meeting with Jim Nicholson and Bill Asher, Jim offered me on the spot a very lucrative contract. Of course, I was feeling good because at that point I was technically with Columbia and I knew that I would probably be signing on Columbia's dotted line; plus, I had received quite good reviews from *Ride the Wild Surf*. Mike Frankovich, who had cast me in it, had at least *pretended* to have plans for me. So I was in a very good frame of mind at that particular time.

It was at this same meeting that Jim Nicholson asked me if I liked boats, and I said, "Well, yes, I *love* boats." Had he asked me if I liked boa constrictors, I would have said, "Oh, they're very nice!" He was handsome, charming and the kindest man I'd ever met. That was when he invited me onto his boat: Two or three weeks later, he had [director] Don Weis and his wife on his boat for brunch, and also myself and my agent, Fred Briskin. Our relationship started that soon, maybe a couple weeks after I met him.

Your first AIP film was Pajama Party.

There was something that left a very bad taste in my mouth about that picture. When they went back to do second unit stuff, nobody was around, so I think they shot somebody else's legs and inserted it in the final cut as though they were mine. That very well could have been something that happened as a result of the fact that I was Jim's girlfriend: Somebody working on the film might have been angry with me, and made that happen. It wasn't a very pleasant experience *[laughs]*!

People resented you for dating, and later marrying, Nicholson?

[Laughs.] Maybe. I was so naive in those days. I thought everybody loved me like I loved everybody, but it wasn't true at all, they *didn't*! I was greatly *feared*—why I don't know, but I *was*!

What was the atmosphere on the sets of these free-wheeling AIP Beach and Party movies?

That's exactly what it was, free-wheeling and fun. There was a great deal of camaraderie, and it was a wonderful feeling knowing that you were not saying goodbye at the end of a shoot, that you would be seeing these same people *[laughs]*—probably for the rest of your life! That's what you think when you're twenty; you think that the people you know, you will always know, and that the way life is, is the way that it will continue. It was a very closely knit group.

Did you enjoy going to England to make War-Gods of the Deep?

Of course. My mother went with me, and she stayed with me at the hotel there in England, the Carlton Tower. I had never been abroad before, so that was great fun for me and it was exciting for my mother. I was just happy that I was able to share those kinds of experiences with her. *War-Gods of the Deep* was wonderful; Tab Hunter and I had worked on *Ride the Wild Surf*, so it was fun working with him again, and David Tomlinson was just a kick.

What about Vincent Price?

You know, we didn't really have that many scenes in anything together, so the only occasion that I would have to know anything about him was just before we'd get ready to shoot, or perhaps on a social level with Jim. On a professional, working level, I think we had maybe two or three scenes at the most together, and not much dialogue. What I do know is that he was just a true professional through and through.

And socially?

Socially he was a lot of fun. I didn't go out with him as often as I would have preferred, but when I was married to Jim, we were in Europe half the time, because the company had many co-productions going in England, in Germany, in Spain. Most of our social life revolved around having people in for movies nearly every night of the week. And sometimes two movies a night. We'd see up to five hundred pictures a year! His life really centered around motion pictures—watching them, making them, talking about them and showing them. The times that we would go out to dinner with friends would be few and far between; most of our time was spent at our own house, having people in to share the films, dinner, coffee and conversation.

What kind of director was Jacques Tourneur on War-Gods?

I enjoyed working with him, he was absolutely lovely. We spent Thanksgiving [1964] together, as a matter of fact. The picture was shot in November-December, as I recall, because I remember having a Christmas tree in the hotel room. We'd shipped over everything; we even had Jim's cook accompany us on the trip so she could cook Thanksgiving dinner at the Carlton. We had an American Thanksgiving with all the trimmings. Anyway, Jacques was just lovely, and happy to be working.

AIP gave one-last-chance to direct to a number of older moviemakers.

Also to a lot of actors that weren't exactly being sought after, either. Jim always enjoyed doing that. Well, Vincent Price for instance. I don't suppose that Vincent mentions it, but AIP did pick up a lot of people, probably him included, whose popularity might have waned slightly had it not been for American International. Annette Funicello gained from it, Frankie Avalon— a lot of folks used AIP as a teething ring. Robert De Niro had a role in *Bloody Mama* [1970], Jack Nicholson wrote some scripts—he partially honed his craft there. And there's nothing wrong with that. But I think that sometimes people don't give as much credit to AIP as perhaps they should. Jim took chances on writers, actors, directors; brought people out of the woodwork; and I think he was responsible for a lot of actors' renewed popularity.

The producer on War-Gods *was Dan Haller—*

—who has also gone on to do really good things. He was an art director in the early days, and Jim thought Danny was very, very talented. Danny and George Willoughby co-produced *War-Gods of the Deep.*

Louis Heyward told me the two of them feuded.

Yes, but I don't know what the feud was about. I do remember George Willoughby being rather sour during the whole filming of that picture.

You had decorative, "fluffy" roles in a number of your pictures. Did you enjoy the change-of-pace straight role you had in War-Gods?

I enjoyed it, but somehow I always felt too young for that role and I don't know why. Like you say, it was a straight role and there wasn't a whole lot for me to sink my teeth into because she was just a simple girl. I did not really have a scene that was "mine" in that picture. I guess I *was* in there just for decoration, and I played nice, regular-type decoration. But not too much emoting was required.

What do you think of the film itself?

That it looks like a picture that was written as it went along. And I think that is the truth. Edgar Allan Poe was there, Vincent Price was there, the sets were there, the talent was there. The *story* wasn't *[laughs]*! Charles Bennett wrote the original script and it was good. But others added their two cents. It did receive very nice reviews.

War-Gods *may have been a bit muddled;* Dr. Goldfoot and the Bikini Machine *was just silly.*

Well, a lot of those pictures were rather silly. Silly albeit pure and entertaining. And they sure reeked of the vernacular of the day, the fashion of the day, and perhaps a lot of the attitudes in the early sixties.

Any special memories of Goldfoot *at all?*

Dr. Goldfoot was really a fun picture to make. I always felt as though I did a more-than-adequate job in that picture, and I think I have the reviews to back me up. I played a robot, a girl who was programmed to marry rich men and accumulate all the world's wealth. I was also programmed for different nationalities, and so consequently I took on the aura of whatever personality I was playing and I used a lot of different dialects in the picture. It was great fun and I felt very good about what I did in that picture. Now, I don't know about the picture *itself*; I think it made a little bit of money.

There was a sequel, so it must have made some *money.*

The sequel *[Dr. Goldfoot and the Girl Bombs]* was really rotten, as I understand it. The reviews were extremely negative and I doubt that it did well at the box office.

Did you enjoy working with the director, Norman Taurog?

He was probably one of the sweetest men I've ever met in my entire life.

Dull-witted spy Frankie Avalon begins to suspect that Susan Hart *might* be a robot in AIP's *Dr. Goldfoot and the Bikini Machine.*

He was so caring. I think of all the directors I've worked with, he was the most helpful; there was, again, a sweetness about him that I never really saw in any of my other directors. I didn't have very many of them, but none of them were as kind or as courteous as Norman Taurog. I think *Dr. Goldfoot* was an attempt by AIP to get out of the beach movie genre and into a new trend. One of the best scenes I've seen on film was with Vincent Price singing about the bikini machine — it was excellent. And I was told that it was taken out because Sam Arkoff thought that Vincent Price looked too fey. But his character *was* fey! By taking that particular scene out, I believe they took the explanation and the meat out of that picture. I would only love to see that footage again, but it probably disappeared long, long ago. It was a really unique explanatory scene and Vincent Price was beautiful in it, right on the money.

Wasn't someone killed during the making of Dr. Goldfoot?
    It was very, very hot up in the catwalks in the studio, and I guess one of the gaffers was overcome by the heat. He fell and landed about five or six feet from me — I remember hearing this *thud.* And I didn't know what happened until the next day, because they ushered me out very, very quickly and nobody told me until the next day. Maybe they thought I would be upset or

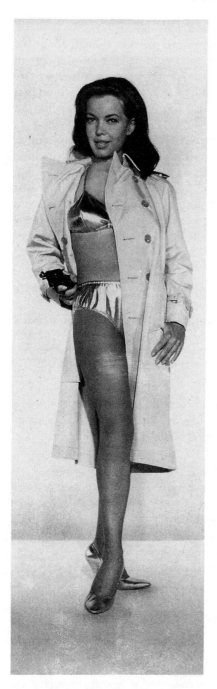

Doing Dr. Goldfoot's dirty work.

something. And I remember three or four people saying, under their breath, "Oh-oh. That's bad luck for the picture."

Bad luck for the gaffer, too.

[Laughs.] Oh, *extremely* bad luck for *that* poor chap! In those days, when someone died or was killed on a set, it was supposed to be very bad luck for the picture.

What can you remember about the Dr. Goldfoot *special that was made for ABC-TV?*

I believe that it was Ruth Pologe, who was head of AIP publicity in the New York office, who arranged for ABC to do a special relating to the picture. It was a half-hour show called *The Wild Weird World of Dr. Goldfoot,* and it had the highest ratings that night—everybody was thrilled about that. It was kind of a capsule presentation of the picture itself, with members of the cast doing maybe four or five songs. Tommy Kirk, who was *not* in the picture, *was* in this musical presentation of it, and I don't know why.

Where did you go on your world tour to promote Dr. Goldfoot?

Where *didn't* we go? London, Hong Kong, Italy, Spain—we went around the world! I remember landing in Frankfurt and running into Orson Welles. Both of our planes had been delayed about four hours, so we sat there and talked and had about six cups of coffee, and he was so nice! It was just the most delightful four hours, wonderful, wonderful fun.

What were your impressions of Sam Arkoff early on?

He had a good sense of humor and seemed to know enough about law to take advantage of people. He had no interest in making movies, only in making deals. Sam continues to take full credit for films he made with my late husband, which distorts true history. But he has to live with himself on that issue. Sam even tried recently to dismiss Jim's creativity by falsely claiming Jim was an alcoholic.

Only a few months ago, he was making derogatory remarks concerning Jim, like, "Jim would go home at night and sit there, and he'd have a drink or two, or maybe *more* than a drink or two, and he'd come in the next morning and say, 'What do you think of this title?'" And then Sam decided to twist the knife further and added, "Later Jim stopped drinking and after that, his titles weren't as good as they had been." I can't begin to tell you how many phone calls I received on those gems. I was shocked and hurt, and many of Jim's friends were simply appalled.

You were in London on your Goldfoot *tour when you announced you were marrying Jim Nicholson.*

Yes. Things were happening so fast in those days that I don't clearly remember it at all!

What became of two Susan Hart AIP films that were announced, Joan of Arkansas *and* Genghis Khan*?*

Joan of Arkansas I suggested to my husband, and he thought it was a fabulous title, a Jim Nicholson kind of title. We kidded around a lot about it, but it never got off the ground. *Genghis Khan* I wasn't aware of.

You were also going to co-star in Planet of the Vampires.

I was in Italy for two weeks the summer [1965] we were going to shoot that at Cinecitta Studios—I felt that it was going to be a very low budget, very yucky picture. And I remember Barry Sullivan got into a giant, violent argument with somebody, maybe Mario Bava. Why I didn't end up doing it, I can't remember, but I *do* remember being in Rome for a couple of weeks; meeting Mario Bava (a charming, colorful man); that the plot was explained to me in some fashion; and flying back to London *[laughs]*! That's all I recall and I'm shocked that it ever got made, because to the best of my recollection Barry Sullivan had some sort of a major problem either with the director or the producer.

What recollections of The Ghost in the Invisible Bikini?

The picture had been shot—without me—and it was such a mixed-up picture, it was not showable. You could make no sense of it! There was talk that one of the key production people was drunk through most of it; I don't know if that's true or not.

So after the picture was finished, they decided to put you in it?
   After the picture was supposedly completed, it was unreleasable. I was not in the film at all initially; a month or a month and a half after they saw they couldn't do anything with it, the idea of shooting additional scenes with a ghost was thought up. I don't know who wrote my sequences; it was Ronnie Sinclair, the editor, who ultimately directed them. For my scenes as the ghost, they put a blond wig and a black velvet bathing suit on me and they shot me against a black velvet backdrop. I was told where the people were in the scene into which I would be superimposed, what kind of instruments people had in their hands, so on and so forth—this went on for about two weeks. And then they had Boris Karloff come in and we shot our scenes in maybe a week.

I don't think I'd have had the nerve to ask an eighty-ish actor like Karloff to climb into a coffin.
   [*Aghast.*] You know, I wouldn't have *dared* ask! I saw *Ghost* again not long ago and I felt the same way, exactly—not when I was doing it, but now that I look back at it. *I* couldn't do it no matter *what* age I was!

Was Karloff fun to work with?
   That was just a great experience. He was just so easy to work with! It was very natural working with him, and he was such a gentleman. Jim, too, liked Boris Karloff very much, got along well with him; in fact, I think Jim and he spent a great deal of time together, the same way Jim and Buster Keaton were good buddies.

Why did Jim Nicholson leave AIP?
   He left AIP because his hands were tied in many respects. He had become an executive more than a filmmaker. He was very creative, he was always a hands-on type of guy as far as production was concerned. He knew what to make, how to make it, how to sell it, and had original ideas for what came next. He was wonderful with people; he liked the people that he had hired to work for him, and the people that he had hired liked Jim as much as he liked *them*. He was a very reciprocal type of person. He had loyalty like nobody I've ever met. People were extremely loyal to Jim Nicholson and he was extremely loyal to them. He required autonomy in his own specialized fields. He loved calling shots and he loved being responsible for his own bailiwick, which was all those things that I mentioned previously. What I think ultimately happened was that ... *other parties* got involved in his bailiwick. When that happened, I believe he lost his enthusiasm for working with those people who attempted to take away his expertise.

Scenes of Hart and Boris Karloff were added during post-production to help take the curse of incoherence off AIP's *The Ghost in the Invisible Bikini.*

Mr. Arkoff began hiring many people at American International at very large salaries, to do the very things that Jim Nicholson could do with his eyes closed. He was able to do this because, when Jim Nicholson got his divorce from [his first wife] Sylvia Nicholson to marry Susan Hart, he also gave up a lot of his stock, which put Sam Arkoff in the driver's seat in so far as the amount of stock held was concerned. So he allowed Sam Arkoff to do the driving, and I don't know how long AIP lasted after he left. I suspect that, after that point, producers simply came to AIP to make pictures; I would be surprised if American International itself made movies much after that. And the projects that *were* made after my husband left were many that he had chosen anyway. AIP was sold to Filmways in the seventies.

Jumping back a minute, why did you stop making movies for AIP after Ghost in the Invisible Bikini?

One of the reasons was because Mr. Arkoff informed me after I did four films that there was going to be no nepotism at AIP. And at that point, to go pound the pavement as Mrs. James H. Nicholson searching for roles at other studios probably wasn't worth it to me. I was at one time scheduled to do a picture for Jimmy Carreras, but that did fall through, and to this day I don't know what the film was. But that was the only thing that I rather pursued, a Hammer film [*The Lost Continent,* 1968] with Jimmy Carreras. (I personally found it difficult to be an actress, a mother *and* the wife of the president of AIP at the same time. Something was going to suffer.)

Also, I did not want to cause waves, and I think that may have caused waves. But I must say that I was in a state of shock when I was told that I was no longer going to be in pictures for that company because nepotism was not part of the bylaws of American International Pictures. I guess nepotism is in the eye of the beholder.

Everybody — including Arkoff — talks about the value of Nicholson's contributions to AIP. What would have been the point of subordinating him?
Ask Sam Arkoff.

Jim Nicholson later wound up with a deal at Twentieth Century-Fox.
He made a five-picture deal with Twentieth; I think he was one of the first producers that they allowed complete autonomy. He preferred never working on a studio lot; he preferred remaining his own person. Like using his own letterhead, his own stationery, and not the studio's. To hire his own publicity people. To make his own news releases. To totally produce. Well, they allowed him all of the things that he wanted, which included his own offices off the lot — he had beautiful offices at Nine-two-zero-zero Sunset Boulevard.

What were the five pictures?
The Legend of Hell House; Blackfather; Street People; The "B" People; and *Dirty Mary, Crazy Larry.* (The original title of that last one was *Pursuit* to begin with, and Jim changed the title. He thought *Dirty Mary, Crazy Larry* was kitschier, and he was right — as usual.) Anyway, they decided to go with *Legend of Hell House* first because that was the script that was ready, and that picture was shot in England. I made two or three trips to England with him.

And it was during Hell House *that he first became ill.*
Legend of Hell House was about three-quarters of the way through when Jim suffered his first seizure. It was later diagnosed that he had a malignant brain tumor. That would have been discovered in maybe October or November of nineteen seventy-two; *Hell House* was in its editing phase. And he died in December. *The Legend of Hell House* was put together ... released ... and did well. And then Fox decided to go with the next picture, which was *Dirty Mary, Crazy Larry* [1974]. Norman Herman and Mickey Zide were the two men left in charge of Jim's new company; they had been with Jim for about three months before his death.

I proceeded to get into quite a long lawsuit with them, which worked itself out after about three years. I think we all left the whole ordeal with bad tastes in our mouths. Since that time, I have spoken with Norman Herman and we are at the very least on speaking terms. He knows his craft very well and ultimately acted as producer on *Dirty Mary, Crazy Larry*, and I was always extremely upset because I was promised by Gordon Stulberg, the then-president of Twentieth Century–Fox, that Jim would without fail get screen credit since it was his original project. It was really his baby and everybody got credit except Jim Nicholson for it. I just about died when I saw the film and saw that Jim's name was left off of it.

And Dirty Mary, Crazy Larry *was a big moneymaker, wasn't it?*
      It was Fox's biggest grosser in nineteen seventy-four and it helped finance *Star Wars. Dirty Mary* was the first picture, by the way, where they tested spending as much money on advertising as on the film itself. Which was the thing that AIP *always* used to do—spend a tremendous amount of money on their advertising and *[laughs]* not as much money on their picture as they should, really! But it was the first major motion picture ever done like that.

Would you have any interest at all in getting back into acting?
      I would imagine that I'd be misleading you if I said I had no interest at all, because I will always have an interest in acting no matter who's doing it, somebody else or myself. Once you have experienced the fun of acting, it's something you never forget. In fact, I want to tell you something: Every actress that you will ever talk to in your lifetime that you ask that question, if they say *no,* they're probably fibbing!

SUSAN HART FILMOGRAPHY

The Slime People (Hansen Enterprises, 1963)
A Global Affair (MGM, 1964)
For Those Who Think Young (United Artists, 1964)
Ride the Wild Surf (Columbia, 1964)
Pajama Party (AIP, 1964)
War-Gods of the Deep (The City Under the Sea) (AIP, 1965)
Dr. Goldfoot and the Bikini Machine (AIP, 1965)
The Ghost in the Invisible Bikini (AIP, 1966)

Clips of Hart in *The Slime People* are seen in *It Came from Hollywood* (Paramount, 1982). Footage of Hart in *Dr. Goldfoot and the Bikini Machine* is seen in *Dr. Goldfoot and the Girl Bombs* (AIP, 1966).

Your imagination is far more *than what Hollywood special effects people can do.* Carnival of Souls *played upon fears that everyone can relate to.*

Candace Hilligoss

IF SOME ACTRESSES CAN WORK A LIFETIME and never achieve fame, does it seem possible that some can build a cult reputation on the basis of only a single film? It does when the film in question is *Carnival of Souls,* the micro-budgeted spookfest which has gone from lowly drive-in screenings in 1962 to playing at art houses and international film festivals in more recent years. Much imitated, never to be forgotten, the legendary Herk Harvey film continues to stand as a benchmark achievement in the annals of filmic horror, due in no small part to the haunting performance of its primary player, New York–based stage and TV actress Candace Hilligoss.

A product of Huron, South Dakota, Hilligoss was involved in acting from the early days of elementary school plays. After three years at the University of Iowa, she came to New York to study acting at the American Theatre Wing, and made her professional debut doing summer stock in Pennsylvania. She acted at the Cape Cod Playhouse, toured with Nina Foch in *Idiot's Delight,* turned up in New York TV shows and, as one of the world-famous Copa Girls, danced at the Copacabana night spot. In 1961 she was hired and spirited off to Lawrence, Kansas, to star in *Carnival of Souls,* and she later reinforced her horror rep playing the ingenue in Del Tenney's Connecticut-made shocker *The Curse of the Living Corpse.* Taking a break from her new avocation (novelist), she reminisces about her filmmaking experiences as well as her plans to reunite some of *Carnival's* principals in an all-new follow-up film.

How did you hook up with the people who made Carnival of Souls?

Sidney Berger was a graduate student at the University of Kansas at Lawrence who was helping Herk Harvey cast some of the smaller parts in *Carnival of Souls,* and Herk sent Sidney to New York to look for an actress to play the lead. Sidney called upon his friend Monty Silver, who was my agent, and said, "Would you have some actresses come in and read?" So I just auditioned in Monty's office, which was on the West Side in Manhattan. Sidney thought I was right for it. Now, *Herk* in his mind had originally envisioned a young Janice Rule; she was sort of the classic ingenue, with long dark hair. But when Sidney started casting, *he* saw *blond [laughs]*! I was not what Herk thought Sidney would be bringing back to Lawrence, and I think I was kind of a shock to him! Now, at the same time, I was being offered another picture, *Psychomania,* which originally was called *Black Autumn* (I think); Del Tenney was getting ready to shoot that in Connecticut. They were very interested in my doing a part in it, but I saw that the character had to be naked. *Carnival,* there was no nudity. So I chose *Carnival [laughs],* and an actress named Lorraine Rogers got the part in *Psychomania.*

If Carnival *hadn't come along, would you have done* Psychomania?

No, I probably wouldn't have. I would have found something else.

Previous page: Actress/authoress Candace Hilligoss.

Where did you stay while making Carnival of Souls?

In a hotel — the one hotel in Lawrence, which was on Main Street [*laughs*]!

Did you think Carnival *would be a good opportunity for you?*

[*Flatly.*] No. Because there were no known quantities attached to it. It was also very low-budget — under thirty thousand dollars — and movies of that sort usually don't take off, particularly if they don't have a major distributor. I felt it was going to be a take-the-money-and-run type of situation.

The people involved on Carnival of Souls — *did they seem to have confidence in themselves as feature filmmakers?*

Yes — why wouldn't they? They were very considerate, very sweet, like "innocents." There was a Mickey [Rooney] and Judy [Garland] attitude of "Let's put on a show!"

Did you have confidence in them?

I had no idea, because it all looked so strange on paper. I couldn't see what *they* were seeing in their minds, and I didn't know what they intended for it visually. And they wouldn't let me see the rushes, because they were afraid that somehow if I did see them, I'd become self-conscious. I had no idea what it looked like, because they wouldn't even let me *peek* at 'em!

How did you like working with Herk Harvey?

Herk was very together, very well-organized. Everything was on schedule, he got done what he wanted to do and so on. I'm sorry that he never went on to other movies, because he was very good with people. He did have some problems with me, I'm afraid: I was coming from a different training, which in those days was not familiar to people in universities. It was what he put down as "The Method." But I don't think he understood that the best acting comes from this way of working from the inside out. Many people in universities then were very used to a strong form of indication, which is working from the outside; more of what *I* felt was a superficial type of work. I think he didn't quite understand my terminology or my way of thinking. I had studied with Sanford Meisner and Lee Strasberg, and nowadays people are in tune with that style. But in the old days, to have someone come out and talk about "improvising" or "doing emotional memory" was so new, they didn't quite understand and it threw them a little bit. That made 'em very nervous.

And Harvey pushed you for a more conventional performance?

Yes, but I struggled hard to keep it very honest. He said, "I don't want people to really *care* too much about your character, because she's gonna come to a bad end." And I said, "But if they *don't* identify with her in some way, they won't sit with her for the whole movie. If they don't care, you'll lose your audience."

You shot mostly in Lawrence?
    Lawrence, and Salt Lake City, Utah. I think we were in Salt Lake a week or ten days, and we stayed in motels there. It was very strange: There was a crew of five, and me, all traveling together, and when we signed registries, we all had different names and different addresses *[laughs]*! The whole picture took three or four weeks; we'd work seven days a week, sometimes around the clock. But they planned it that way. And because they were shooting in sequence, they said it would be all right if I looked more and more beat toward the end, because I would be dying anyway. And it would look good for me to be beat-up, and a little green around the gills. They thought that would add to the character *[laughs]*!

Besides Herk Harvey, who was the most creative person that worked on Carnival of Souls?
    Herk credits Maurice Prather as the cameraman who set the tone and look of the film, but Reza Badiyi, who was the assistant director and the *other* cameraman, did a lot of the very complicated, tricky, almost "stunt" shooting: Hanging from rafters, dangling off the roofs of buildings upside down, lying on the ground and letting me almost drive over him. Really dangerous things. Herk had a good little crew overall. As he said, "Anyone can make a movie with two hundred people. Try making a movie with a crew of five!" *[Laughs.]*

What about the scene where you're almost run down by the van?
    As a matter of fact, that van did come pretty close. That was in Salt Lake City: Herk stopped a man—a stranger—and asked him if, for twenty-five dollars, he would drive down the alley and almost hit me. The guy said sure. The first take we took, I was a little nervous; it's no fun to be hit by a moving car! And Herk said, "You know, Candace, you didn't let him get close enough. Do it again. And this time . . . kind of let him hit you." I said okay. So the second time, he *almost* clipped me. Herk said, "Oh, that was wonderful!" You know *[laughs]*, stunt people get *paid* to do this! And the stranger was thrilled; he got his twenty-five dollars and went on his way!

Real seat-of-the-pants filmmaking.
    You bet. It was almost like the way Truffaut started making his movies. We'd be walking down the street, Herk and his crew of four or five, and he'd say, "We need a department store, and this looks like a very good one. Let's go in." *Today,* you would have to call the Chamber of Commerce, get a permit, this and that. *We* walked in, looked around, went upstairs on an escalator and found a saleswoman. Herk said, "Listen, for twenty-five dollars, would you

keep people out of the dressing room area? We'd like to shoot some footage of this woman changing her clothes." The saleswoman said, "Of course! No problem!" Five men and myself crawled into a dressing room cubicle, and we shot the scene. Then we came out, and Herk went up to a woman customer and said, "Look, for ten dollars, would you look the other way when this girl tries to speak to you?" "Sure." No questions! We went up to a cab driver: "For ten dollars, drive away when this woman runs up to you."

The only place we had a problem was at the train station, where Herk said to a conductor, "This girl is going to run for the train. Would you slam the door in her face, like you don't see her?" For twenty-five dollars, the man said, "That sounds good!" But the word got up to someone in the office that people with a camera were down in the station. Some very official-looking man came down and said, "Wait a minute! *Waaaiiit* a minute!" — it was the first time we ran into anyone who questioned what we were doing. Herk, who has a very calm way about him, sat down with the man in the boarding area and talked to him awhile, the official got to feeling better and better, and by the time Herk was through, we had our permission again *[laughs]*!

This was all in Salt Lake City, right?
Yes. In Lawrence, everybody knew who we were and what was going on. The rooming house was a real house in Lawrence; it was empty at the time. A young couple now lives in it with a little boy. They said when they bought the house, the realtor pitched it to them by saying, "This is the famous house from *Carnival of Souls*!" It's become Lawrence's answer to the *Psycho* house *[laughs]*! When the couple moved in, it took the little boy a week to get up the courage to go upstairs. He probably never saw the movie, but he knew enough to be nervous!

The finale, at the big pavilion, was also shot in Salt Lake City.
That was the only time Herk had to call up the Chamber of Commerce and get permission. The Saltair pavilion was the largest open-air ballroom in the world, unused for years, and the Chamber of Commerce people said, "It's *so* ruined, so filled with torn decorations — would you like us to send a crew out to clean it up?" Herk said, "No, no, no — leave it! We love it just the way it is." They said *[hesitantly]*, "If we charge you fifty dollars . . . would you be insulted?" An incredible bargain! Herk said, "W-e-l-l, if you have to, you have to." So we rented the entire amusement park, for a week, for fifty dollars!

Did you shoot both of your water scenes on the same day?
No. The first time was when I came stumbling out of the water, near the beginning of the picture. That was in warm weather, and I spent eight hours coming up onto that little beach there. First I'd go down, under the mud, and then I'd crawl up. That was still kind of Indian summer. When we came back

to shoot the end of the picture, the scene where I'm shown dead in the car, it was cold weather and the men were in down jackets and ear muffs, and their breath was showing. I had on a cotton dress. I stepped into the water and it was like thirty-five degrees. I said, "I can't do it." Herk said, "You *got* to do it, or we've got no end for the movie." I said, "I just *can't* get in there!" So they *dragged* me into the water, and I was screaming all the way! A highway cop came along and he said, "What's going on? What's going on here?" They told him we were making a movie. The cop said, "You're going to put that woman out in that car, in the middle of the river?" Well, the cop got very nervous and upset, and decided that he'd better stick around! Anyway, they got me out into the car, and Reza was in a little rowboat with the camera, going around it. Reza said, "You know, she's supposed to be dead, but she's got goosebumps, and her bottom lip is trembling!" *[Laughs.]*

Did Herk Harvey and the others have future movie plans?
    They hoped that *Carnival of Souls* would make money, and that they could start doing bigger and better-budgeted films. They were looking to launch a whole film complex there. But the film ended up with Herts-Lion, a crooked distributor, and unfortunately that took care of that.

Where did you see the picture for the first time?
    In New York. Herk came to New York to find a distributor, and I came to one showing with my agent, Monty Silver. After the movie, Monty said, "You know, you're just too weird. You're *so* weird, I can't represent you anymore." I said, "Don't you understand, that's the character? I was *told* to act that way." But he was so upset—he said he had a reputation to protect. And he got up and walked out, and never spoke to me again *[laughs]*!
    Eventually *Carnival of Souls* went to TV; in New York it became the *Million Dollar Movie* of the week, and it ran for a whole week, in prime time. Then, later, another local channel ran it, and someone from that channel told my new agent that *Carnival of Souls* and *Invasion of the Body Snatchers* with Kevin McCarthy were their two biggest moneymakers. They showed them every year, like clockwork, and they were always getting mail from people saying, "Please write and tell us when it's going to show again." People were crazy about it! From then on, wherever I went, people were staring at me and stopping me. One night I was on Broadway and Fiftieth Street at midnight, in the ninth month of my pregnancy, with my husband, and someone who looked like a Hell's Angel on a motorcycle hit his brakes and said, "Are you Candace Hilligoss??" I said, "No, no!" and my husband was saying, "Yes, yes!" He said, "I am so crazy about your movie! I am fighting with the Bleecker Street Cinema to get it in!" And then he took off *[laughs]*! All sorts of things like that happened!

Top: Hilligoss is about to be crowned by the mystery killer (director Del Tenney doubling for Roy Scheider). *Bottom:* As Dino Narizzano and Scheider battle it out, she ponders the problem of drowning with*out* getting her $50 wig wet. (Scenes from *The Curse of the Living Corpse.*)

Did the film's original release have a positive effect on your career?

[*Shrugs.*] It didn't have *any* effect. There was no publicity, no p.r., no agency pushing it; it was just out there on its own little legs. It should have done something for Herk Harvey, but it just went into this strange oblivion thanks to Herts-Lion, the distributor, who buried it, who played it at little drive-ins and so forth.

Were you paid for starring in it?

Yes, I was one of the few that was paid. I think I got two thousand dollars. Reza, for shooting it, got seventy-five dollars. Everyone else worked for a percentage. Next to the crooked distributor, I probably made more money than *any*body!

How did you get involved on The Curse of the Living Corpse?

I knew Del Tenney, who was a stage actor that had seen me work. He was already into making low-budget films; that was the era when they thought those kind of [horror] movies were easy to make. Del called up all his friends, "Let's get together and make a movie." He was going to be making it in Connecticut, so we didn't have to stay out of town, and so we said, "Well, okay, okay," and we did it. Like Herk Harvey, Del knew that those movies were easy sales, and could give you a good return on your investment. It was the end of an era.

What was Tenney like as a filmmaker, compared to Herk Harvey?

Del wasn't as experienced in the craft. He was okay, but he wasn't into it quite the way that Herk was; he wasn't looking for the values that Herk was looking for. He did *Psychomania* first, and he had wanted me for that; and then almost back-to-back he did *Curse of the Living Corpse* and *The Horror of Party Beach,* which had the sea monsters that looked like artichokes [*laughs*]. We shot *Curse of the Living Corpse* in Stamford, Connecticut, at a home that was originally the home of Gutzon Borglum, the sculptor of Mount Rushmore. His studio was an annex of the home, with a big high ceiling. Del Tenney's wife was [actress] Margot Hartman, and her father had bought the estate. We used what had been the studio for Mount Rushmore to film the interiors; they had built all the sets in there. The outside — the yard and grounds — were the exteriors.

And you just commuted out there every day?

Right. We drove out from New York each day; Stamford is very close. I was pregnant at the time, and they were worried that my waist would be expanding. So they said, "What if we just keep building her chest out? Then her waist will look smaller." I said, "But then my head'll look small!" I was the ingenue, five and one-half months pregnant.

Did Del Tenney play the killer in all the early scenes? He told me that he did.

If he said he did, he did; he probably didn't want to bother Roy Scheider to put on all that gear. In my one scene with the killer, it was Roy. He had to throw me in the quicksand, and I was told to drown without getting my wig wet. They had no replacement for my fifty dollar wig, they said they'd need it again, and told me, "Whatever you do, don't get your wig wet." It is hard to drown without getting your hair wet.

Any memories of working with Scheider?

I got Roy his part in that. Roy and I had done a couple of shows together at Arena Stage, a national repertory theater in Washington, D.C. He was *so* broke — he and his wife had just had a baby. I remember him saying to me, "Oh, I don't know what to do. I've got seventy dollars to my name. What'll I do?" I said, "Well, a friend of mine is putting together a movie. You look evil enough. I'll suggest you for the villain." He thought that would be really great. I put him in touch with Del, and Del said, "Yeah, he looks like a young George C. Scott." So I got Roy in it. At the same time, I sublet my apartment in Hell's Kitchen to Roy and his wife, and I finally let them live there a month free. So I was very instrumental in getting Roy Scheider's career off the ground. And he *still* owes me seventy-five dollars *[laughs]*!

The whole cast of *Living Corpse* were at that time very well-working actors. Robert Milli was playing Horatio to Richard Burton's Hamlet; Hugh Franklin was in *Luther* with Albert Finney; Dino Narizzano was on a soap opera — *all* of us were involved in other projects. None of them ever thought that *Curse of the Living Corpse* would see the light of day. The Paramount Theater in midtown Manhattan had been showing *Love in the Afternoon* [1957] with Audrey Hepburn and Gary Cooper, and it was such a bomb that they pulled it. *Horror of Party Beach* and *Curse of the Living Corpse* had just opened in Texas and broke all box office records, and so this double-bill now moved into the Paramount. *Curse of the Living Corpse* was suddenly playing within just a few blocks of where all these actors were working! There was a life-sized poster of me, running in a negligee, with Roy Scheider in a black cape swinging a saber at me! Right out in front of the theater! And all these actors, on their way to do all their artistic *Hamlet*s and whatever, were so terrified that their fellow cast members would walk down and see them in *Living Corpse*! Richard Burton was so excited to learn that his Horatio, Robert Milli, was down the street in *Curse of the Living Corpse* that he and Elizabeth Taylor wanted to run down and see this movie! And Horatio, of course, pleaded with him not to go!

Also, we all felt that movies like this didn't get reviewed; then, of course, not only did *The New York Times* go to town on it, but also *Time* magazine felt it needed attention *[laughs]*! Even Les Crane, who had a midnight talk show, went on about it. The lesson was that you *cannot* do these movies and feel that they're not going to be seen, because someone somewhere—and not just kids—go to see these movies!

And what do you think of Living Corpse?
[Laughs.] No comment!

Why have you made only two movies?
Now, I didn't retire after *Curse of the Living Corpse*; I did go on to do some theater. Then later, it became too difficult. I was married at that time to an actor who was still struggling, and it became necessary for me to make a choice between a career and staying at home. I elected to try to hold the family together and to raise my daughters, Candace and Dinneen, so that *he* would be free to go on. I began to concentrate on my writing.

And what keeps you busy these days?
I've just finished seven years of working on a novel, *Dakota Ashes,* based upon a screenplay which I *also* did. (I was urged by producer Hal Wallis, before he died, to do the screenplay as a book, and become the next Edna Ferber!) It took me seven years of writing night and day, and I'm now trying to find some way, as an unknown, to get my novel published. It was based upon family stories and memories as told to me as a small child, about South Dakota when it was the Dust Bowl in the Great Depression. It's really *The Grapes of Wrath* in reverse: My story's about the people who stayed behind, and their fight to save the land, told through a love story.

Also, Reza Badiyi (the original cameraman and a.d. on *Carnival of Souls*) and I are now trying to find a way to raise the money to do the sequel to *Carnival,* based on a story which I wrote. It's a new story, but with some of the same characters in another wonderful ghost story. This would be the first time in cinema history that so many members of the original cast of a film came back to reunite this late in history, to do a sequel. We would also love, we would *adore* to be able to go back and use some of the original Lawrence, Kansas, locations. Herk would like to be involved, both on- and off-camera, but now he would like someone else to take over all the headaches that go with directing and raising the money. So Reza, who is a very prestigious Hollywood director of many television series and movies-of-the-week, would come on board as the director this time around. If you know anyone who has two-and-a-half million dollars burning a hole in their hip pocket, and who wants to make a very low-budget film with a built-in audience, tell 'em to call me as soon as possible *[laughs]*!

The recent reissue of Carnival was a big hit, wasn't it?
Not only was it a hit, it was reviewed by Siskel and Ebert on their TV show as though it were an establishment movie, and it was featured on *Entertainment*

A characteristic shot of Hilligoss as the aloof young beauty plagued by phantoms in the eerie cult favorite *Carnival of Souls*.

Tonight with Leonard Maltin. And became of the success of the reissue, it ended up at the Munich Film Festival. Herk Harvey flew over for it, and on a night when he didn't think anyone would show up (there was a European soccer match), *Carnival of Souls* was sold out and people were sitting in the aisles. They kept him on stage till about three in the morning, after the performance, asking him questions! It's now on British television; it's gone through Canada, Sweden, Australia, New Zealand, and it's on laser disc. It's also played on three of the major pay–TV stations.

What do you think of the picture today? Can you see the qualities which make it such a favorite?
    Oddly enough, I almost see them more today than I did when we made

it. In their wonderful "innocence," uncorrupted by the Steven Spielberg syndrome, they allowed the audience to ask the question, "Who am I and what would I be if I were dead? Would I have an identity?" That terror of being alone, the possibility that, when you're dead, you may go into a no-man's land — that fear is universal. Everyone's imagination goes to work. And their own personal terror comes through. Your imagination is far *more* than what Hollywood special effects can do. *Carnival of Souls* plays upon fears that everyone can relate to.

CANDACE HILLIGOSS FILMOGRAPHY

Carnival of Souls (Herts-Lion, 1962)
The Curse of the Living Corpse (20th Century–Fox, 1964)

I was a sort of Jane Fonda in my day, but without her dough or her clout. So, I got blacklisted.

Rose Hobart

BORN IN NEW YORK CITY IN 1906, Rose Hobart responded to the lure of the theater at a young age, went on stage at 15, then drifted to Hollywood to embark on a frequently less-than-satisfying movie career. Rebounding between the theater and films, she enjoyed critical acclaim while waiting for the star-making breakthrough which somehow managed to elude her.

Hobart film-debuted in the 1930 Fox version of *Liliom* and went on to appear in over 40 additional films, both in the A and B category. But by the late 1940s, her progressive social leanings (and participation in the Actors' Laboratory Theatre) had marked her for condemnation by the political witch-hunters of the day. After a period of being blacklisted, she returned to acting in the 1960s on TV's *Peyton Place*, and today she resides at the Motion Picture and Television Country House, not far from Hollywood. Not accustomed to pulling punches, the actress disarms interviewers with her candor, outspokenness and good humor.

How did you first become interested in acting?

I used to spend my summers in Woodstock, New York, where my father, a well-known musician, had a quartet. One year they decided to have a festival, and the guy who ran it invited Edna St. Vincent Millay. At that point in my life, I had never seen a play. I spent the entire two weeks they were rehearsing talking to her. After seeing the performance, I made up my mind in the middle of a daisy field that that's what I wanted to be — an actress. I think I was seven then.

The scene dissolves to when I'm opening in Atlantic City in *Liliom*, playing the child, with Eva Le Gallienne. There was a knock on the door and it was Edna St. Vincent Millay saying, "You made it!" She was absolutely wonderful. So that's how I got on.

Backtrack a bit to when you got your first job.

It was under peculiar circumstances. My mother was Swiss and had gone to England for a time to work as a governess as a way of earning a living. In those days, women didn't *do* that! One winter, we were having a terrible time financially. We spent a week on Long Island with some of her actor-friends whom she met in England — a man named Percival Vivian and his wife. They played colleges, universities, etc., as Shakespeare originally was done in England. That meant there was no stage, just everyone performing outdoors. They all had to be clowns and tumblers, too, because that's what they did in Elizabethan theater.

At the time, he was directing for chautauqua, which was in tents. They were set for a tour of one-night stands which was to start in Abbeville, Louisiana, and end in Billings, Montana, eighteen weeks after. Two days before they were to leave, his ingenue quit! He came home frantic. But his wife said,

Previous page: "My mother was Swiss and my father was Belgian, so I say I'm French by a geographical average!" — funny, feisty Rose Hobart.

"Do you want to listen to her [Hobart]?" — I had been busily learning the parts and rehearsing with her. So in sheer desperation, I got my first job.

I learned an awful lot and was very fortunate because one of the character players was a fine Shakespearean actor. He took me out to the Redwood Forest when we got to California and coached me on projection. By the time I got through with those eighteen weeks, I could be heard in a tent that seated a thousand people.

Where did you go from there?

When I got back, Mother said the only people she knew in show business were the Shuberts. She was a singer, and the Shuberts were putting out operettas and that kind of thing. So she took me to the office where I saw these beautiful women in black satin. A little man came out and said, "Can you act?" I told him about my eighteen weeks on the circuit. I went up to one girl and asked, "Who was that little man?" and, looking at me with utter contempt, she said, "J.J." It was Mr. Shubert himself!

I was sent with a note to the Shubert Theater across the street. I opened the door to it and there was a bare stage. And remember, I had never been in a theater because I had only played in tents! There was Eva Le Gallienne, to whom I handed the note. She yelled out into this totally black auditorium, "Hey, Pepe! The Shuberts are finally showing some sense!" Apparently, they had been sending over those beautiful girls in their black satin dresses — chorines looking for dance jobs — to play the child in the last act of *Liliom*. So I went on tour for that whole year with Eva Le Gallienne and Joe Schildkraut. Then I did a play called *Lullaby* [her New York stage debut, 1923], which was my first long run in New York.

Did you come to Hollywood after that?

No, I didn't come out here until 1929 when I was already an established actress in New York and was playing Grazia in *Death Takes a Holiday* with Philip Merivale [as Sirki]. (He was great, by the way; he really looked like a death's-head when they shifted the lights. It was incredible.) It was a metaphysical play; I was very moved by it. I wouldn't read my mail after each performance because almost every night I would get a letter from someone stating they had seen the play and had gone home to commit suicide!

Fox and Universal both wanted to test me. I signed with Universal because they offered to wait until I finished my run with *Death Takes a Holiday* that June. About a week later, Fox called to say that they had already assigned me to [the film version of] *Liliom* with Charles Farrell. I said to myself, "Oh, shit! How can I *not* do that?" That was *my play*, I knew every line in it. So I came out here ahead of my contract, did *Liliom*, and went back to my contract with Universal. Of course, they were furious at me for doing that. Unfortunately, the movie was not a success because Charles Farrell was just a boy with a ukulele who hadn't the foggiest notion what *Liliom* was all about. And his voice was about an octave higher than mine.

Any other memories of Liliom?

Yes, that I was photographed *appallingly*—I really looked quite awful through the whole picture. And I always wondered about it until I found out quite recently, by accident, that Janet Gaynor was supposed to do it, and had refused to play it. But the cameraman was her cameraman. And he was so upset at her not playing it—oh! What he did to me was really awful! I looked so terrible, that may be one of the reasons why it was a flop.

Did you enjoy your stay at Universal?

They put me in *East of Borneo* [1931], which really floored me. I thought I would never do pictures again! The shooting schedule for *Borneo* was just incredible. We did two solid weeks of shooting from six at night until six in the morning. I lost about fifteen pounds, so they had to put gauze in my evening dress so my bones wouldn't stick out! Everyone was fenced off, but I was with all of those wild animals. They all kidded me and said, "Don't be afraid!" They built a chute and shoved one of the big cats down it. But the cat got to the bottom, said to himself, "No way!" and backed right *up* the chute! You should have seen how fast those people came over to *my* side of the fence!

In one scene, there's a damn snake over my head. They had a boa constrictor there, and they wanted about ten feet of him hanging over my head. The snake man came up to me when they got it all set up, and said, "I wish you'd tell 'em not to take this. Boa constrictors only are awake when they're hungry; and if ten feet of him is loose, ten men on his tail aren't going to be enough." So I said to the director, "Have you talked to your snake man about this?" I had to convince him that I wasn't going to do it.

It really is a fun movie. Have you seen it recently?

I'm not sure I could stand it! The whole premise was idiotic, but I know it's *still* playing in Australia and Germany because I keep getting letters about it. Before we filmed, the studio sent a whole troupe over to Borneo to shoot the exteriors. But instead of jungle-looking, it was like the flats of New Jersey. There wasn't a tree in sight, not an animal, not anything. They filmed forty miles of absolutely nothing before they found any vegetation. The crew knew if they came home with that, they'd be fired. So they made up their own jungle with monkeys and things. There *are* no monkeys in Borneo! They brought back a wonderful scene with monkeys, and at the end of the scene, one of the monkeys took a cigarette out of his pocket and lit it *[laughs]*. They had hired some guys and put 'em in monkey suits! Everything in the picture was totally wrong.

I hated my stay at Universal. I fought with Junior [Carl Laemmle, Jr.] the whole time. The trouble with Junior was that he had no real talent and was a lousy administrator. His father was pretty good and had some idea what he wanted. But Junior didn't know his ass from a shotgun! After *East of Borneo,* they asked me if I wanted to leave. I said, "I sure as hell do! I want to get back to New York and the theater. This stuff with animals is ridiculous!" So I went to Junior's office to sign what I thought was a release. Fortunately, I had one of the top theatrical lawyers in New York, who was sharp as hell. He said, "Rose, read the small print, *please!*" And down at the bottom of this "release," in very small letters, it said that during the suspension of this contract, which could be continued by either party giving notice to the other in writing, I was not permitted to work for myself or in any other business whatsoever. So I said to Junior, "Screw you!" I stomped out of the office and slammed the door behind me. I found myself in another office, so I stomped through that and slammed *that* door. Then I found myself in a *third* office! It wasn't until I got home that I got the giggles.

Junior was really a good name for him. He was just a kid.

He was only around nineteen. I never saw him except for when he was bawling me out for not showing up or for losing weight and they had to spend so much money filling in the costumes. Junior really wasn't interested. He was a good Jewish boy, and when Father hands you the business, you run the business. He couldn't have cared less about it. Universal made a fortune off of me because they were always loaning me out to other studios. Finally, they let my contract lapse. The next day I was on a train heading back to New York.

How did you like working at Paramount when Universal loaned you out to do their Dr. Jekyll and Mr. Hyde?

I was just on the set and ready to work! That's what happened when you were loaned out. The whole business was very odd then, it was really paternalistic. If you were part of the family, all of the red carpets came out. If you weren't, you were damned lucky to get in the door!

How did you enjoy working with Rouben Mamoulian?

He really was a fine, fine director. There was only one thing that really bothered me about the way he directed. I figured he always must have dotted his *i*'s and crossed his *t*'s because when he finished a scene, he would always have to have something symbolic to finish it up with. That was really overdoing it! He died here at the Motion Picture Hospital a few years ago. I went to see him, but he didn't recognize me. I was warned by the nurse that he wouldn't, but it still broke my heart.

So what was he like personally?

He was very intense and had no sense of humor, unfortunately. That was true of many of the European directors. Otto Preminger was an absolute bastard because he had no sense of humor about anything, least of all about himself. The Europeans really think of filmmaking as an art, while most directors here think of it as just another job.

Miriam Hopkins was known for being difficult to work with. Did you get that impression of her?

Difficult is an understatement! I had no scenes with her, but I used to go on the set and hear about her endlessly from Freddie March. She was always upstaging everyone, all of the time. I don't even think she thought about it anymore because she was so used to doing it. She'd maneuver around until Freddie would have his back to the camera, practically. So in this one take in the music hall, Mamoulian set up a camera for a two-shot. But he also hid a camera behind her, behind a curtain. They took the whole scene, she upstaged him, and then she heard "Cut!", coming from behind *her.* She *wheeled,* and said, "Is *that* where the camera was?!" And Mamoulian said *[smugly]*, "Yes, *that's* where the camera was. *Print!*" *[Laughs.]* And she didn't do it quite as often after that! She was an excellent actress, though.

Have you ever worked with her?

No. You don't get to know the whole cast of a picture — but people think that you do, because you're all in the same picture. (I've been in movies with practically all the stars in the business — but I've never met half of 'em *[laughs]* — because I'd work with the "underlings"!) I only ran into Miriam Hopkins when I was handling the seating for an Equity ball, the fiftieth anniversary. I had a table for people who were working with me on the seating and the rest of it, and one of the people was a Negro, a friend of mine. Miriam Hopkins said, "I will *not* sit here," and I said, "Well, *don't,* then, girl. Go somewhere else." She *did* sit there, but when he asked her to dance, she *froze [laughs]*!

Fredric March had the reputation of being "all hands" where his female co-stars were concerned.

He had the worst reputation, but probably was the most faithful of all the husbands in Hollywood. He put on such an act! Oh, he'd kiss people behind the set, but that's as far as it went. Because he and Florence [March's actress-wife Florence Eldridge] had this incredible relationship. She knew what was happening, but her attitude was, "Oh, go ahead, have your fun."

Did you think the makeup on Mr. Hyde was effective?

We all saw the [1920] Barrymore version, which was the pinhead look. So they wanted to get away from that. I think it was the makeup man who suggested they go for the Cro-Magnon type regression rather than just inventing something.

Hobart is about to meet her fiancé's fearsome alter ego (Fredric March) for the first time, in the Rouben Mamoulian–directed *Dr. Jekyll and Mr. Hyde.*

Jekyll and Hyde *was a "lost" film for years, then only became available in a heavily edited version.*

The uncut version, which is now once again available, is great because the ending of the shorter version didn't make sense. What they cut out was what made the whole picture meaningful. The cut version isn't really good at all. You need those explanations.

Despite Fredric March's womanizing reputation, Hobart says he was "probably the most faithful of all the husbands in Hollywood." (A scene from *Dr. Jekyll and Mr. Hyde;* pictured: March, Hobart, Halliwell Hobbes.)

Your father in the film was played by veteran character actor Halliwell Hobbes.

He was just a charming English gentleman. I knew most of the English colony, including Ronnie Colman, Leslie Howard and Roland Young. They were incredibly beautiful actors. I loved all of them.

I was really fascinated with the guys who doubled for Freddie March and Halliwell Hobbes when they had the big fight in *Dr. Jekyll*. They were on the set for quite a long time and I got to know them. For instance, they got into a big argument one day over a hypothetical situation. Question: If you were doing fifty miles an hour on Mulholland Drive and you went off the bank, would you get hurt worse if you stayed in the car or if you jumped out? So one day, they did it! One of them stayed in the car and the other jumped out. The one who jumped ended up in the hospital for six months because the car landed on top of him and broke almost every bone in his body! But they really were great guys. I learned a lot from them. Stunt men are a breed apart.

Do you remember the cameraman, Karl Struss?
Again, he was a typical European. He concentrated only on what he was doing; he was always absolutely absorbed. Karl invented all kinds of things on that picture because the transformation of Dr. Jekyll into Mr. Hyde was really tough to do. Of course, the worst thing that happened to Freddie on that picture was when the makeup man (who should have known better) tried to make the masks. All of them were just *too* mask-like and Freddie couldn't move. So they just put liquid rubber on his face — *that* was the makeup. And when they took it off, his face came with it! He was in the hospital for two or three weeks, he was lucky he wasn't ruined for life. That's the kind of thing they used to do in those days, and that's why I hated pictures! They didn't give a shit about people.

Were you on the set when they shot the transformation scenes?
I was for some of them. I had gotten friendly with the crew, and when they did something special like that, I wanted to see what they were doing. Most of it was done with color slides over the camera lens which were gradually pulled out. Each layer of makeup was a different color, so you blocked out one layer by putting on another slide. They had to get Freddie exactly in the same spot every time. They finally drew the outline of his head on the wall.

Did you have any hint that he was giving an Oscar-worthy performance?
No, actually; nobody on the set anticipated that. First of all, he was very unhappy with it because that makeup was so rough for him to work in. He could only stay in that makeup about twenty minutes or so, and then he'd have to go relax — it *hurt,* finally. It was ruining his face, wearing that makeup.

Did you get to know Boris Karloff during those early years at Universal?
He was a lovely, true gentleman — the gentlest man I've ever known. Why he and Vinnie Price ended up as monsters, I'll never know. It's just incredible. Well, maybe that's why they're so good, because even when they played monsters, you *did* kind of like them, you felt sorry for them. I knew

Hobart acted opposite horror icons Boris Karloff and Basil Rathbone in Universal's lurid *Tower of London*.

Karloff when I was at Universal, and I used to watch some of the things he was shooting. I must have been on the set of *Frankenstein* because it feels familiar whenever I see it. I thought he was really a fine actor being wasted on all of that stuff.

A few years ago, they were selling the property of Elsa Lanchester out here. Of course, she played the Bride of Frankenstein. Well, she had this awful little replica of herself in that makeup [the Aurora model kit] which they were trying to sell. And I kept thinking, why would she want to be remembered as the Bride of Frankenstein with all of the other things she'd done in her life?

Were any of your scenes cut from Tower of London? *Your part somehow seems incomplete and your character simply drops out of sight.*

They must have been, because I worked on that for almost six weeks. When I see it now, I think, "They could have shot that in three days!" Universal was always a cheap studio and went on being that way even after the Laemmles left. They really didn't care about the pictures, they just cared about making the money. You can't do a decent picture like that.

Do you remember Basil Rathbone?

I worked with him even before *Tower of London*. We were both doing summer stock up in Newport, Rhode Island. I remember he and his wife Ouida used to give the goddamnedest parties out here when he was doing all of those Sherlock Holmes pictures. I think the thing that made his parties so special was that he was the first one (that I can remember) that used tents outside, so that you could go outside and do things out there—you weren't stuck in a room.

All of those English actors were terrible womanizers and they were always telling stories about their conquests. I remember Rathbone telling me one story about Marlene which really made me kind of sick—you don't do that, even if it's true. We always stopped for tea and I was the only one of the women invited to join the guys. And their conversation was getting dirtier every day. It was really getting *obscene!* One day when they had just finished one really bad one and they were laughing and having a ball, I decided that I couldn't put up with this. They were talking about gals that I knew, and *[laughs]* I also wasn't sure that they really did all the things that they said they were doing with 'em! I said, "How do I stop this?" to myself. Finally I asked, "What are the three most insulting two-letter words that a woman could say to a man?" And the answer was, "*Is it in?*" The reaction was fantastic because I knew exactly who had been asked this question and who had not. And they were so shocked that all conversation on the subject ceased for the rest of the time I was invited back. They were trying to outdo each other, of course. The boys were showing off. Actually, they were lying through their teeth!

Was Karloff one of the storytellers?

No, no, Karloff was never in that. He was a good family man and a British gentleman.

You played an emissary of the Devil in a very minor Columbia horror film, The Soul of a Monster *with George Macready.*

I remember spending all of one night shooting a scene on the back lot. I was walking down a street while black cats were supposed to hiss and all the street lights were supposed to buzz. We did that all night long—and it was colder than hell! They never warned me when all of this was going to happen, so I jumped each time. I wasn't meant to, as I was supposed to be *causing* it, so we had to do an awful lot of retakes. I enjoyed working with George Macready. We had previously done a play in South Carolina, an Elizabethan type of thing. Then, later on, I worked with him on *Peyton Place*. He was a great villain because he always underplayed. That makes the portrayal much more villainous, actually. Of course, he had that great scar which he won as a young man at the University of Heidelberg. They used to duel in those days, and that was his mark of distinction.

They shot three endings of that. I'm awfully sorry they didn't use the original one. In it, I fall out of a window, get run over, and the cat just gets up and walks away. That was the one I loved. They sent it out with three different endings to see which really appealed to an audience. But they ended up with a compromise.

Did you like playing a villainess?

I loved it. It was much more fun than playing those nice girls. I would have given anything to play the Miriam Hopkins part in *Dr. Jekyll and Mr. Hyde*. That's why Ingrid Bergman chose it in the MGM remake. Lana Turner loused up my part.

For that MGM version, Katharine Hepburn somehow wanted to play both parts.

I'm not very fond of Katie Hepburn. She was the original gal in the play *Death Takes a Holiday*. She was playing it in New Haven just before it came to New York, but they canned her and got me. I had two days to learn the part, and I had never even seen the play. No one had ever given me the script. I went out to New Haven, had a rehearsal one morning, saw Hepburn play it that night, and had to go on the Saturday matinee the next day. I was standing backstage waiting for my first entrance when I suddenly realized I couldn't hear what was going on on stage—next to where I was standing was a Victrola playing music. I ran up to the stage manager and said, "I can't hear my cue." And he said, "You're on!" I tore on stage and started talking all out of breath. I suddenly realized that that was the perfect voice for the part. And that's how I played it from then on.

Why was Hepburn fired from Death Takes a Holiday?

She was working with a very famous New York lady voice coach who told her that since she was playing this spiritual part, she must not let anyone touch her on the upper arm. Supposedly, the upper arm was the physical part, while the lower arm was the spiritual part. So that is what she was doing to the actors—while they were rehearsing, she wouldn't let anyone come near her. Needless to say, the producer was not happy! Then she wouldn't let me into the dressing room that Friday night to see if the costumes would fit me. I had to wait until she left the theater. I've never seen her since.

Did you ever see the movie version of Death Takes a Holiday, *with Fredric March?*

Not until many, many years after it was made, because I was so mad I wasn't playing my old part *[laughs]*.

Any recollection of The Brighton Strangler *with John Loder?*

Oh, sure—that was one of my favorites, actually, because it had an all–English cast. I loved that English group. I had a ball with 'em. Max Nosseck, who was the director, had a *thick* Austrian accent. For the very last scene, where I had to say, "Applaud, applaud!", he told me, "I want you to say, 'Applowed, applowed!'" I couldn't get that out of my head *[laughs]*, and I kept pronouncing it *applowed* when I tried it! They had to have about six takes because of me. And if he hadn't said anything, I'd have been all right!

John Loder was always a good actor, I thought.

He was excellent in that. It's interesting, the way certain people are very good actors but they never get to be really good stars. Because their personality isn't *alive* enough in some way. John Loder was very gentle and very sweet, but he never got to be the really important guy he should have been. He was just kind of dull, as a human being.

The bottom line, in a lot of cases, is sex appeal.

Well, look at Bogie, for God's sakes, who was the last person in the world who would have had sex appeal. And yet, *something* came across, and he was absolutely great. You just have it or you don't. And some gals, too. There are some girls that guys just slobber over, and women look at them and think, "She isn't that good...!"

I did a picture called *Conflict* [1945] with Bogie, and he was playing three games of chess, by *mail*, while that picture was being shot. He was a chess player, and apparently a very good one; the minute he wasn't acting in front of the camera, he was working out a chess play. Sydney Greenstreet was also in *Conflict*, and he had trouble remembering his lines in those days. And they kept changing the script, and that drove him crazy. So they never changed his stuff, they *couldn't*, because he just couldn't retain it. He had to learn his part before he ever came on the set, and that was *it*, kiddies—if you changed a *word*, he was dead!

He did a lot of his films with Peter Lorre, who ad-libbed all over the place, and that screwed him up like crazy!

Well, of course it did! I hate actors that ad lib, because it's really dirty pool. They always throw the other actors off.

You were originally cast as the entombed woman in Val Lewton's Isle of the Dead, *but had to be replaced by Katherine Emery after production shut down for a time. How much shooting did you actually do?*

We shot for about two weeks before Boris Karloff got sick and they had to stop shooting. And by the time they put it back into production again, I was on another picture, so I couldn't come back. They had shot all of my long shots first, and they used them at the end of the film, so I'm still in there. They were able to replace me without redoing everything they had done.

Did you have any acting scenes opposite Karloff in Isle *before it was closed down?*

Not that I remember, no.

Of all the directors you've worked with, do you have a favorite?

There were very few directors I worked for that I thought were really fine. Frank Borzage, who was the director of *Liliom,* was the one who taught me about working in pictures. He's the one who told me that the camera only picks up what you're thinking; emotion doesn't mean a goddamned thing. (*I* thought, "Oh, he's just used to picture actors who don't know how to act.") When we came to Liliom's [Charles Farrell] death scene, my big scene in the picture, Frank said, "Do you want to shoot or do you want to rehearse?" I said, "I think I know what I want to do with it. Can we just shoot it?" He said sure. So we shot it, and I gave a real theater performance—cried real tears and so on. And the crew was standing behind the lights with tears in *their* eyes— that's when I said to myself, "I did it!" But Frank said, "I'm sorry, we have to do it again"—there was some technical difficulty, he said. (I thought to myself, "Oh, shit!") We shot that closeup *thirty-six* times, one right after the other. Finally, Frank said to print takes eighteen and thirty-six. I said, "Frank, will you do me a favor? Will you print the first take?" He said he would.

We went into the projection room the next morning and saw the scene— it was an enormous head shot, a closeup of me. After about five seconds of watching the first take, I realized it was ludicrous. *Awful.* Absolutely nothing happened on my face—it was so frozen, it looked like a goddamned Benda mask. You could hardly hear what I was saying because I was really crying and the tears were muffling my voice. (Plus, sound wasn't very good in those days.) In the eighteenth take, when I was talking to myself with the camphor tears rolling neatly down my cheeks, it was perfect. I said to Frank, "Thank you so much for doing this. I never would have believed it if I hadn't seen it." And he said, "The one thing you've got to remember is that you must emote for that one first take before you can give the one that is great for the film." That's how I learned to be a movie actress.

Do you have a least *favorite director?*
Sylvan Simon. God, he was a bastard *[laughs]*! But I never worked with the *really* bad ones, like Otto Preminger and those guys. They were *real* stinkers.

How about a favorite actor to work opposite?
I guess Bogie, because I knew him best. I had played his wife twice in the theater, in New York. The interesting thing about him was that he was a *bastard* when he was a failure; before he became successful, he was an absolute stinker. That's why he had three wives before Bacall. But when he fell in love with Bacall, and was a successful guy, he turned out to be great. He's the only guy I know that improved with success *[laughs]*!

Do you have any recollections of the 1946 film The Cat Creeps?
I don't think it was very good. All I remember of that one was that my character couldn't stand cats. I love cats and even had a black one once.

How did you come to be blacklisted?
I was very political and was pretty horrified by the conditions out here. I belonged to Equity in New York before we had a Screen Actors Guild. At that time, actors were working twelve hours a day, and I thought, "We have to get a union. This is ridiculous!" I was a sort of Jane Fonda in my day, but without her dough or her clout. So, I got blacklisted.
Some kids from the high school around here came over to talk to the actors, and one or two of them knew about me being blacklisted. One of them said, "President Reagan said that there wasn't any blacklist." And I said, "Bullshit!" They were shocked, but I also think they were delighted. Reagan was president of the S.A.G. at the time of the blacklist. That's why I know everything that comes out of his face is bullshit! The man doesn't know anything!
At one point during the time I was blacklisted, I wanted to make sure that I would be able to get a passport if I wanted to go to Europe. So in order to get myself cleared, I privately went before the committee with my husband's Republican lawyer. They were bringing up such stuff that you wouldn't believe; papers that said things like, "Workers of the world revolt!" with my signature on the bottom. Of course, it wasn't my signature, it was printed. I thought, why don't they just *ask* me if that's my signature? My lawyer tried to get them to listen, but they threw him out of the room! He almost became a Democrat, he was so horrified.

They said I had been to a meeting of the Communist Party in Mexico City on such-and-such a date. And I said, "If you are interested, I was in a hospital in Culver City on that date, having my son!" When I finally got a transcript of my testimony, whatever I said to defend myself was cut out. It was just "...", and then it went on to something else.

How did you occupy yourself during the blacklist?

I'm just like a cat—I always land on my feet. I'd been told all my life that I couldn't have children because I had too much acidity in my system, etc. Then I suddenly found myself pregnant. I was forty-two, so I was really fascinated about being a mother. That was my next role for about six years until my son started going to school. Then I tried to get back into pictures, and that's when I *really* found out I was blacklisted.

Do you still feel repercussions from the blacklist years?

Sixty Minutes did a segment here about the Motion Picture Home, and the fact that I was blacklisted came up. Later, a guy came up to me here and he said, "I want you to know that I'm your friend." And I thought, *this* is a charming friend! There are people who were very happy to be warned about me because I'm a "subversive" character. I went around for days trying to figure out who was speaking to me and who wasn't. I finally said, "Come on, Hobart, you went through this before. Stop being silly and get back to normal!" So I went back to saying "Hi!" to everyone. Besides, half the people here can't see who you are anyway!

How many other actors are here at the Home?

Just me. Most of the other people here are [behind-the-scenes] people, or the wives or husbands of people that were in the business. That really startled me; I thought when I came here, "I'll be with my pals." No way.

Is this a nice place for you? Are you happy here?

Yes, actually. If you have to be somewhere like this, which I do, this is *it,* the *crème de la crème.* They really do everything they can to make us feel comfortable and they try to keep us happy. They have things every day that we can do, like painting; they take us out to concerts and certain other things. But the real problem is that there still isn't enough to do. All my life I wanted to be constructive, to help people, to do things for people. That's one of the reasons I wanted to be an actress. Most people sit here in their cottages, watch TV, go down to breakfast, come back, watch TV, go down to lunch, come back, watch TV, go down to dinner, come back, watch TV, go to bed. Well, that's not a life to me *[laughs].* So it's very difficult.

How do you spend your time these days?

Rose Hobart at the Motion Picture Home in 1992.

I do a lot of writing. I wrote my autobiography, and a piece which I sent to *The New Yorker*. I have my first rejection slip, so I guess now you could say I'm an official writer!

ROSE HOBART FILMOGRAPHY

Liliom (Fox, 1930)
A Lady Surrenders (Universal, 1930)
Chances (Warners, 1931)
East of Borneo (Universal, 1931)
Compromised (Warners, 1931)
Dr. Jekyll and Mr. Hyde (Paramount, 1931)
Scandal for Sale (Universal, 1932)
The Shadow Laughs (Invincible, 1933)
Convention Girl (Falcon Pictures/First Division, 1934)
Tower of London (Universal, 1939)
Wolf of New York (Republic, 1940)
Susan and God (MGM, 1940)
A Night at Earl Carroll's (Paramount, 1940)
Ziegfeld Girl (MGM, 1941)
Singapore Woman (Warners, 1941)
Lady Be Good (MGM, 1941)
Nothing but the Truth (Paramount, 1941)
I'll Sell My Life (Select, 1941)
No Hands on the Clock (Paramount, 1941)
Mr. and Mrs. North (MGM, 1941)
A Gentleman at Heart (20th Century–Fox, 1942)
Who Is Hope Schuyler? (20th Century–Fox, 1942)
Gallant Lady (Prison Girl) (PRC, 1942)
Dr. Gillespie's New Assistant (MGM, 1942)
Salute to the Marines (MGM, 1943)
The Adventures of Smilin' Jack (Universal serial, 1943)
Swing Shift Maisie (MGM, 1943)
Air Raid Wardens (MGM, 1943)
The Mad Ghoul (Universal, 1943)
The Crime Doctor's Strangest Case (Columbia, 1943)
Song of the Open Road (United Artists, 1944)
The Soul of a Monster (Columbia, 1944)
Conflict (Warners, 1945)
The Brighton Strangler (RKO, 1945)
The Cat Creeps (Universal, 1946)
Canyon Passage (Universal, 1946)
Claudia and David (20th Century–Fox, 1946)
The Farmer's Daughter (RKO, 1947)
The Trouble with Women (Paramount, 1947)
Cass Timberlane (MGM, 1947)
Mickey (Eagle-Lion, 1948)
Bride of Vengeance (Paramount, 1949)

Rose Hobart (a.k.a. *Tristes Tropiques*) (Joseph Cornell short, 1939) is a cut-down version of *East of Borneo*. According to Hobart, she appears in long shots (as the mad Mrs. St. Aubyn) at the end of *Isle of the Dead* (RKO, 1945).

*I liked Roger Corman. He's a monster, but he's a man
with a great drive, a tremendous energy and tremendous
charm. I wanted to* kill *him a lot of times, but I liked* him.

—— *Betsy Jones-Moreland* ——

HOW OFTEN DOES IT HAPPEN THAT THE STAR of sci-fi and horror movies faces greater dangers when the cameras *aren't* running than they do in the pictures themselves? As part of Roger Corman's circle of actors in the late 1950s, Betsy Jones-Moreland coped with a sea serpent (in *The Saga of the Viking Women*), the Cookie Monster-ish *Creature from the Haunted Sea* and even with a disaster that brought about the end of the world (in *Last Woman on Earth*), but the cameras ought to have been facing the *other* way and recording her encounters with runaway horses and riptides, real-life mounted bandits, deadly manta rays (and good old Roger himself).

I was born in Brooklyn, New York—by accident. My mother's from the South, from Virginia, and I was supposed to be born in Virginia, but she got caught short in Brooklyn and that's where I got born. My real name is Mary Elizabeth Jones and I was born April 1, 1930. So I have been stuck all my life with being Mary Jones, born April Fool's Day, Brooklyn, New York. And if I didn't know how much my mother loved me, I would have thought that she had it in for me from the beginning *[laughs]*! I've never lived all that down! When I was in school—I lived in Madison, New Jersey—everybody had adenoid problems, and they would call me *[in a nasal voice]*, *"Mare-reee!"* And I hate the name *Mare-reee,* so in fifth grade I changed it to Betsy.

When did you decide that you were going to be an actress?

I never did, when you come right down to it. I weighed about one-sixty—which is not bad, because I'm five feet ten inches tall. I was zoftig, but I wasn't fat. But I also wasn't *thin.* I was working in New York, office work, public relations, publicity—I worked for *Howdy Doody* and *Gabby Hayes,* TV shows like that, for an organization called Martin Stone, which was the company that owned those shows. I wanted at that point to be in public relations and publicity for the rest of my life. Then I left there and went with Philip Morris, and I was distributing free cigarettes—they did that at all the fashion shows and all the shows of any magnitude in New York. You would put these little tiny packs of cigarettes around and you would talk to people and try to get everybody to change to Marlboro cigarettes.

Well, while that was going on, I was going to a beauty/exercise/"make-over" salon and losing twenty pounds, and that twenty pounds made all the difference in the world. A friend of mine, who was a costumer, made me an absolutely staggering costume and we went to a ball and won first prize for the most beautiful costume. That night, photographers and reporters came *pouring* out of the hotel where the ball was held—they kind of *trapped* me and pushed me up a flight of stairs, the flashbulbs popping and all that. They

Previous page: **Poor Betsy Jones-Moreland looks like she may be reacting to Roger Corman's newest directorial demand. (Photo from** *Creature from the Haunted Sea.***)**

said, "Are you a showgirl or a model?" I said, "I'm not either, I'm a stenographer." And while *they* fainted, I thought, "They *really* think I could possibly *be* a showgirl or a model. . . ?" Those words changed my life—that was the end of being a stenographer.

I was very, very shy. I was tall; I was awkward; in my teens, all my boyfriends came up to my boobs. It was *very* uncomfortable. I was so terribly shy, I couldn't talk to anybody. So I decided I'd better take an acting class—I'd better do *some*thing! I took an acting class at Carnegie Hall in New York. I had *no* intention of being an actress, I just wanted to be able to stand up in front of people and get over being tongue-tied and shy. One day I saw an ad for showgirls at what *had* been Billy Rose's Diamond Horseshoe (it was then called the French Casino). I thought, "Well, this ought to scare me to death!" So I went and auditioned for that, and I *got* the job, which I didn't *want*. I had no idea what being a showgirl involved or anything else, I was just trying to come out of my cocoon. Now here I was, *out* of it, and didn't exactly know how to handle that! I went home to Mother and said, "What'll I do?" and she said, "No *way* am I going to tell you what to do. You make up your own mind. We'll sit down and make a list, pros and cons. If you do it, most of the people that you now know will *never* speak to you again. On the other hand, if you *don't* do it, you will always say, 'What *if*. . . ?' There is no way that I am going to make that choice *for* you." Which I think is one of the greatest things any mother ever did for any kid.

So I decided to become a showgirl and I did *that*; I was a showgirl at the Latin Quarter. One friend of mine had been in *The Solid Gold Cadillac* on Broadway, she got married and she was going to leave the show, and she called around to other showgirls and said, "Why don't you come on in and audition?" I went in and auditioned, and *again* I got the job; *again* I didn't want it, I still had it in my mind that I was going to do public relations and publicity, and that this showgirl bit was a passing thing. I took the job, I played on Broadway, I went on the road, and came to California. (By the way, Majel Barrett was my understudy in *Solid Gold Cadillac* on Broadway *and* on tour; we were roommates together all across the country.) Out here there was a lady agent who was a wonderful friend of my mother's, and she became my agent in California. And I became a movie actress! That's how that happened: I never decided to become an actress, it sort of happened to me, one step after another. And at each step, I was saying, "No, I don't want to do this." Each step was a *lark,* for the *moment,* for *today,* but I didn't want to act, I had this whole other life cut out for myself. But here I was, out in California, doing movies!

Where did -Moreland come in?

My mother's mother's name was Moreland, and my family in Virginia were all Moreland. When I went to join the [acting] unions, there *already* was a Betty Jones, and they won't let you have two names that similar to each other. So I put the -Moreland, which I've always loved, on the end of the Jones.

Most of your early movies were at Columbia. Were you under contract there?
I wished I had been, but I wasn't. They were putting me in front of the camera and grooming me — that is what I was *told*. They were trying to expose me without exposing me, and get me some experience. But then the whole business started to fall apart — that was nineteen fifty-five, when I first came out here. My first movie was *The Eddy Duchin Story* [1956], and I learned an awful lot in the few days I was on that picture. I always thought of Columbia as my home studio — that's where I started out, and I still feel very partial to Gower Gulch. None of it exists as I knew it anymore.

Roger Corman?
Roger Corman, as I have said many times — many, many, *many* times! — could charm snakes off bird eggs *[laughs]*! He could charm any*body* into doing any*thing* on the planet. I thought he had the most engaging smile of anyone I have ever known in my life, and he has a gift for making you feel like you're part of something important. Albeit it's *not* important and you're *not* part of it *[laughs]*, he makes you feel as though it *is* and you *are*. I think that's how he's gone as far as he has gone. He just has this incredible ability to charm people.

The first picture you did with him was Viking Women and the Sea Serpent.
At that point, Roger was going along making a movie every *month* — two weeks pre-production, two weeks shooting, two weeks pre-production, two weeks shooting. And, oh God, every picture that I did with Roger was *such* an adventure! When I would come home at night and try and tell people about it, I think they had a hard time believing me! Or when a picture was *over* and I had *survived* it — 'cause there was always a question of survival with Roger. You really had to check yourself every day to make sure you were still alive, because you're *always* in danger. There's always some goddamn thing about to kill you or eat you, or you were going to fall in a pit and never get up — there was always *something*.
There was a scene in *Creature from the Haunted Sea* with a manta ray. I had it put in my contract that I was *not* going to get into a tank, or any *other* place, with a manta ray, but there we were in the water together! Knowing Roger, he would have you *eaten* by the manta ray and still have the camera running, and say, "The bloody part, we'll fix it in the lab." That was his answer to everything, "We'll fix it in the lab." *Whatever* it was. If there were people running around in the background in a world that's supposed to be totally dead — "Don't worry about it, we'll fix it in the lab." If Roger exposed film —

it didn't matter what was on it, just so long as it was exposed—he was happy, he was just overjoyed. That was all he needed to do, expose the film. And anything that was *on* it, was a blessing. And I guess he always *did* "fix it in the lab"; somehow or other, it always got to the screen.

Anyway, on *Viking Women,* there was a girl who was supposed to star in it, Kipp Hamilton. The morning of the first day, we got into vehicles that were to take us out to the ocean—which at *that* point was somehow a lot farther away than it is now. There was nothing out there, no condos, no restaurants, no place to get coffee, no telephone, no *any*thing. It was a long time ago and nobody had really "discovered" the Pacific Ocean yet. We were at Cabrillo Beach, which is sort of "up" from Santa Monica, and at that point it was desolate—*nobody* went to Cabrillo Beach. There was a big undertow and it was very rocky and craggy, and quite *dangerous,* I guess.

Roger took us out into this wilderness—got us out of our vehicles—and Kipp Hamilton was not there. (By the way, neither was the key to the wardrobe truck!) So he waited, he stormed, he pounded. He had a baseball cap, and whenever things started to fly totally apart (which was at least once an hour), he would grab that cap and *slll-lam* it down on the ground! Well, no Kipp Hamilton. So finally he sent somebody to the phone, some phone a thousand miles away—it took a *l-o-n-g* time. And it turned out that Kipp Hamilton had had a call to do some other job, in New York, or *some*where. Anyway, not *there,* not on the coast with us. And she simply didn't come. Abby Dalton was supposed to play Kipp's sister, so when Kipp didn't show up, Abby got Kipp's part and Abby's [real-life] sister got Abby's old part. Abby and her sister were personal friends of Roger's and Abby's sister was home in bed asleep when Kipp did not show up and "the fit hit the shan." So Roger had her get out of bed and race to the location and become her sister's sister in the film. They also had to send back to Hollywood for the key to the wardrobe truck, which was like sending back to Mars, we were so far out. So Roger was in high dudgeon right off the bat.

Talk about the ship-launching scene.

The rudder on our Viking ship fell off; the girl who was supposed to be holding onto the rudder had long fingernails, and of course they all snapped when the rudder broke. Well, this ship wasn't seaworthy, and we floated out into the ocean in it. And *sat* there. No way to get back. *No way.* We thought we were going to end up in Hawaii! Roger was going crazy, up and down the beach, storming and screaming. We could see him waving his arms, we could see him ripping the cap off, throwing it into the sand. We knew that what was coming out of his mouth were things we were glad we weren't there to hear *[laughs].* (And *we* were out there cussing in our own way!) I had gotten bloody beforehand running up and down the beach, over rocks and so on, and I was not *about* to put my feet in the water 'cause there were sharks out there.

Also, we had on leather costumes that were left over from some John Derek movie. They were *leather*. We are now in *salt water,* so the leather *shrank.* We were in the hot sun; we were in these already-abbreviated costumes; and they abbreviated even *more*. There *were* no doubles [duplicate costumes]; forget doubles! On a Roger Corman picture, you're lucky if you have anything *single,* let alone double. We didn't have anything else to put on, so for the rest of the picture we were sort of shrunk. We also lost our shoes so they *stayed* lost — that was the end of the shoes *[laughs]*!

Also, I should tell you that I am not very good in the sun, I never *have* been — I get sunstroke and heat prostration. When it got hot that day, I collapsed, I passed out. So they shot around me — it was one of those Roger Corman things! I started again, tried to launch the boat . . . and, again, the sun got me. Finally, [actor] Jay Sayer took a reflector that they had been using and he brought it over to me, and set it up so that it shaded me. If he *hadn't,* I don't know what would have happened to me. Nobody else was paying the slightest bit of attention to me. Not that I *need* attention on a movie set, but I didn't want to *die*!

You launched a second ship at the end of the movie, but that was shot the same day?

Right. The second ship was a longboat, a hollowed-out log — a *very* heavy thing. We were all supposed to push it out into the surf and then jump into it. It was the end of the day and the surf was coming in really big. The stuntmen had nothing but absolute contempt for actresses — they wouldn't save your life no matter what, they're not the least bit interested in being friendly or in being concerned about your well-being. But my agent also represented a man who *was* a stuntman on that show, and this stuntman came over to me and said, "No matter *what* happens, do not let go of that boat. Hold onto that boat no matter what it does, because if you let go of it and it hits you in the head, there is a riptide here. They'll never even find your body. *Do not let go."* That was the second launching we had to go through.

It was that way every day, every day was an adventure. Also, we were always running one step ahead of the unions. Roger would keep one long gallop ahead of the unions, they were always trying to come and shut him down because he was always working with not-enough-crew and the crew doing the wrong things and everybody was doubling and doing this, that and the other thing that they weren't supposed to be doing. The unions frowned upon that sort of thing. Of course, I didn't know diddly-squat, and I certainly didn't know anything about the crew and who's supposed to do what. Each day we were shooting at a totally different place, and I didn't realize until later that we were shooting at each location for only one day for a very good reason!

After the beach, you shot at Iverson's Ranch.

Between life-threatening experiences on *Viking Women*, Jones-Moreland giggles as she comes to Brad Jackson's rescue. Susan Cabot (right) is not amused.

Roger thinks horses have brakes. He does not understand that horses *don't* have brakes. We [the Viking women] had these eight-foot steel spears and Roger would gallop us into a pile of rocks — a *big*, dead-end pile of rocks — at Iverson's Ranch. And we were supposed to put on the brakes. Well, the horses don't know that! And we've got eight-foot steel spears comin' up our rear ends! There were a whole bunch of stuntmen on horses behind us, chasing us, and we would practically *splatter* ourselves all over these rock faces. We were all tired; we were riding bareback; our legs were *raw* from riding. (We'd already had riding scenes on the beach the day before.) We were not *any* of us used to that, and our legs were *way* beyond the point of shaking. It was very dangerous, because we were riding rough territory.

And at least one person did *get injured, right?*
A *couple* of people got injured; Richard Devon shattered his knee, I think he still has problems with that. And Abby Dalton's sister fell off her horse. Now, this is a girl who was riding her own horse — she and Abby had sent home and got their own horses. Abby's sister pitched over the head of her horse during one of these "brake jobs" and plowed her head right into a

rock. The first-aid man came flying over—he really liked the Dalton girls very, very much and he was beside himself. He went *flying* down into the scene to try to shield her, because there were many more horses coming and he didn't want her to start to come to and put her head in the path of all these horses. Everybody went galloping on by and he had his body over the top of her, trying to keep her down. She was unconscious; she had to be taken away. And when Roger went to the hospital to see her—she was not even conscious yet—he tried to get her to sign a release, that he was not responsible or liable for any of this. (I was not there so I can't swear to this, but this is what I was told.) That was Roger to the core *[laughs]*! [June Kenney came in at this point and took over the part.]

Any memories of Susan Cabot?
    I *loved* Susan Cabot, I got along with her just fine. We had lots of fun together. We were sitting on the beach that first day and we were having lunch under a tree after that boat adventure, and we were still in these damp costumes. Very short costumes, getting shorter by the second. And a lizard ran right up an embarrassing part of her anatomy. She didn't bat an eye, she sat there and toughed it out. The rest of us were screaming hysterically, having fits laughing, falling down—she just sat there, and waited for it to leave. I *loved* her for that, and I have never forgotten it.

Richard Devon was very outspoken when he talked to me, and he said that Corman was a monster on the set when things weren't going his way.
    Roger was *real* put-out if things didn't go his way. But he was *never* abusive. I've worked with directors who *are* abusive, and he was never that. He would scream at everybody *equally [laughs]*, he didn't find *one* person to whip. I worked with another director later on that liked to find *a* woman, and then beat the crap out of her—humiliate her, and beat her down. The stronger the woman, the more they gotta do it.

Did you see Viking Women *when it came out?*
    Yes, I did. What did I think of it? I thought I was wonderful; I thought I was terrible. I thought it was the most wonderful thing in the world; I thought it was a piece of trash. *All* those things go through your head. There's a scene where the girls are incarcerated, and somebody says to me, "We've got to get out of here." I was supposed to say, "But how?" But because I had come from New Jersey not too long before that, I said, "But *hhhooowww?*" All in the nose—nasal New *Joisey*. Everybody in the theater laughed, and I thought I was going to *die*! God Almighty, I thought I would never live it down!

You didn't work for Corman for several years after Viking Women.
    When we were on *Viking Women*, I kept track of my hours. I had been

Jones-Moreland and Haze weather a rear-projected sea squall in the campy *Viking Women*.

a secretary and a stenographer and an office person, and I was accustomed to doing that. I kept track of my hours and I felt that I should be *paid* for those hours—we went way the hell beyond the hours we were supposed to work. Well, when I said I wanted to get paid for these hours, and I *didn't* get paid for 'em, I went to the Screen Actors Guild. Everybody said, "You'll *never* work for Roger again!" I said, "The man's a crazy man. Who the hell would *want* to work for him again!" Not working for him again wouldn't have bothered me at all. But I *did* like him, I liked Roger. He's a monster, but he's a man with a great drive, a tremendous energy and tremendous charm. I wanted to *kill* him a lot of times, but I *liked* him. I never felt hostile toward Roger, but I wasn't going to be "had" by him, either—I worked for that money, I earned it and I wanted to get it.

Did you get that extra money?

Oh, absolutely. Then time passed, and I did *A Streetcar Named Desire* on stage in Hollywood—I played Stella and Virginia Arness [wife of James] played Blanche. We were extremely successful and I got some *staggeringly* good reviews, which just blew my mind. The day after some of the reviews came out, Roger called me and he said, "I have been testing a title for a movie for two years. People are ready to beat down the doors of the theaters to get to see this movie. This is the most excitement there's ever been for any title that I've ever done." I said, "What's the title?" He said, "*Last Woman on Earth.* I want *you* to star in it." He told me that we were going to San Juan, Puerto Rico, we were going to stay at the Caribe Hilton, we were gonig to do *this* and we were going to do *that*. "It's going to be in CinemaScope and Technicolor; I have *never* had this much money to spend before; this is my first big picture and I want you to star in it." I said, "All right. Send me a script," so on and so forth. I read the part in the script about going in the water with manta rays and I said, "None of that for *me,* thank you!" Other than that, I signed and I went.

    I got to Puerto Rico . . . I got off the plane . . . I was supposed to be met at the airport, and there was no one there to meet me. I had this enormous amount of wardrobe (I had seventeen wardrobe changes) and I literally dragged it through the airport, *crying,* I was so goddamn mad. It was hot . . . it was wet . . . it rained every twenty minutes (that is *not* an exaggeration) . . . and it was *humid.* I was furious. Anyway, they finally took me out of the airport and they took me to the location where they were shooting that day, out in the jungle. Here I see for the first time in my life real thatched roofs, houses up on stilts, chickens, three and four generations living in a one-room house — it looked like a movie set, except it wasn't a movie set, it was real. No fences; cows wandering from property to property, from house to house; they used palm fronds and coconut husks to cook outside. People had said to me, "Don't put your foot down on the ground in the jungle. There will be ten million bugs on you before you can get your foot back up off the ground." I said, "For God's sake, I've got to *shoot* in the jungle. How am I gonna *not* put my foot on the ground?!" You just cannot believe the bugs — I *lived* with a can of bug spray in one hand the whole time.

And, of course, you ended up not *staying at the Hilton.*

    [Laughs.] No, we stayed in a house, all . . . of . . . us . . . in . . . a . . . *house,* one house, with *one* bathroom. The entire company had to come back from work and everybody had to go to the bathroom, 'cause there weren't any bathrooms in the jungle, believe me. And if there *had* been, you wouldn't have used 'em, because a barracuda would have gotten your parts *[laughs]*! So everybody would come back and use the bathroom and the toilet *immediately* plugged up — that would always happen. We were always out of hot water because there were twenty or twenty-five of us trying to take a shower! Well, [director of photography] Jack Marquette and two or three of the others *promptly* moved out. *I* didn't have the clout to move out; Roger said, "Stay in this house," I stayed in that house. *Finally* I got the hell out of there, but I stayed for as long as I could. I was doing my own makeup, my own hair, my own wardrobe, my own everything. Looking at the movie today, I can't believe how good my hair looks in that movie *[laughs]*, considering that I had

Not unexpectedly, Jones-Moreland's status as the *Last Woman on Earth* is the source of some discussion between Robert Towne (enjoying the upper hand) and Tony Carbone.

absolutely everything working against me. I had no mirror, no nothing. I had to dress and undress on the beach in the middle of everything and everybody — there was no trailer or anything like that.

The second day in Puerto Rico, my ankles swelled up to be the size of my thighs. I had a terrible reaction to the water. Well, I ran all over the place, running to doctors, trying to get pills, anything. And the *first shot of the movie* was between my ankles, with me putting sun tan oil on my legs! My ankles looked like elephant ankles, they were so swollen. Then there were those goddamn air tanks that we had to carry on our backs. Roger was too cheap to have 'em pumped out so that they would be light; he didn't want 'em pumped out 'cause then he would have had to pump 'em back *up* again! They were very heavy, sixty or seventy-five pounds, and at one point the three of us [Jones-Moreland, Tony Carbone and Robert Towne] had to jump in the water with these tanks on. Supposedly we were jumping off a boat, but actually we were jumping off a dock. The Puerto Rican crew was standing up on the dock. Well, I can't swim, not worth a nickel, and this thing started to pull me over backwards. I'm gulping water, gulping water. And we're practically in a sewer — we were in a place where people lived on their houseboats. This was *not* the best water to have going in your eyes and your mouth! I'm swallowing water and choking, and I cried out, "Throw me a rope! Throw me a rope!"

And they threw me a rope—both ends. *Both ends*! And I was so goddamned *mad*! Tony and Robert Towne finally helped me, they kept me up—they could swim and I couldn't. (Bob Towne could swim like a fish.) I finally got the damn tank off and got up there, and I stood toe-to-toe with Roger and I cussed a streak. A *streak*! 'Cause I damn near drowned in that sewer, and I was *not* happy about it! That was *one* of my days with Roger.

Did the fact that your leading man [Towne] was also the film's writer cause any problems?

No. It was 1959 and I guess the drug culture was starting, and he was kind of involved with a lot of people who were doing . . . things like that. I don't mean that *he* was on drugs on the picture, I don't mean that at all, but he was sort of "spaced," I had the feeling that he was always off on a cloud somewhere. If anybody had said to me that this man was going to go on to win Academy Awards, I would have said they were stark raving mad *[laughs]*! However, he had things to say—you *had* to know that. There was something about Bob that you *knew* that he had things that had to be said. There are some lines from *Last Woman on Earth* that *to this day* I remember, and quote to myself. It was his first sale of a script, as far as I know, he was just beginning, and that sort of pleased me, the fact that we were all puppies in a basket together, all doing this "wonderful" movie. ('Cause Roger made us think it *was* a wonderful movie!)

And Tony Carbone?

He was a wonderful actor. I met him for the first time way before *Last Woman on Earth*: [Producers] Clarence Greene and Russell Rouse were going to do a TV series, Clarence asked me to come in and read with a bunch of actors, and Tony was one of 'em. I was very impressed with him and I liked him very much. I thought he was a very exciting, dynamic, *interesting* actor and that the others were sort of white bread—totally blah. I didn't know Tony at all but I thought he was a great choice for the series. Clarence Greene tried to explain to me that an actor coming into the home every week [on TV] needed to be a blah one—then you could bring in the more dynamic people to play *off* the blah one. That was the thinking at the time, you wanted white bread coming in every week, you didn't want anything that was going to rock the boat. Tony was much more a rocker-of-the-boat. I just thought that was awful, because he was such a good actor.

Was Corman less of a "traffic cop" and more of a director on Last Woman?

He made a couple of noises in that direction. I think that was around the time when he was going to [acting teacher] Sanford Meisner, and I thought, "Well, boy, now I'm gonna get directed, this is gonna be great, it's gonna be Elia Kazan time!" I thought we were going to get Direction with a capital D.

Well, *no*, that didn't happen. Roger does not direct — maybe he did later, but he didn't then. He moved the camera, he got it from Place One to Place Two, and if you happened to be in the shot, that was fine, but he didn't tell you what to *do* in that shot. On *Last Woman on Earth,* it was business as usual and "We'll fix it in the lab!"

Let me tell you about the bandits. We were shooting in the jungle, and all of a sudden, all the Puerto Rican guys started to disappear — they would just vanish into the weeds! We didn't know what the hell was going on. Then these small horses with people on them came *flying* by! And they were *bandidos* — they were *really* bandits! I thought it was a joke the first time, but it was no joke. The Puerto Rican guys took off and I stood there like an idiot — what did I know? They went by ten feet from me, fifteen feet max. Two or three days later, the same thing happened again; by that time, of course, I knew what was coming when I heard the horses' hooves, and I was fascinated. I didn't run and hide behind a tree, I was just fascinated! I couldn't believe my eyes — the romance of it all was more than I could stand *[laughs]*!

Any other near-fatal memories of Last Woman on Earth*?*

[Laughs.] There was a scene where Bob Towne comes up to my hotel room to give me legal briefs or something. I've been drinking, I'm loaded, and I'm walking on a bannister on the balcony. First of all, you have to remember that we're all sleeping in this house, we're all up half the night trying to get into the shower and go to the toilet, the toilet's not working. I then had to get up at the crack of dawn to get ready to go out and shoot — do my hair, do my makeup, do all this stuff. I was getting very little sleep. We get to this scene, which we shot at the Caribe Hilton as I recall, and we were on the top floor. And I was walking on the bannister, like an *idiot,* doing the tipsy, gonna-fall-off routine. Jack Marquette was shooting it from the floor *up,* not from the top *down* where you could see how high up I was. And I realized later that I could have been standing on a *chair* — or *any*thing! I didn't need to be walking on a goddamn bannister, thirty floors above the ground or however the hell high that hotel is! This is why I say, you have to pinch yourself and be sure you're alive every day when you're working for Roger — this kind of thing goes on all the time! I don't know what in the world possessed me to do it!

The other thing I remember is Jack Marquette saying, "Betsy, you've got deep circles under your eyes. You're going to have to put on some Erase." Erase was a makeup that you'd use to hide the dark circles under your eyes — it goes on underneath other makeup. And I said, "Jack, I have got half a tube under each eye. There is no more that I can put on!" And he said, "Well, Betsy, there's nothing I can do for you." And this is one of my big scenes *[laughs]*! What a *hell* of a way to go into your big scene, thinking that you're supposed to be as beautiful as you can possibly be, and you're told by the cinematographer, "There's nothing I can do for you." Lord Almighty!

Did you have any live sound in that film?

[Laughs.] Oh, God, you just had to ask that. A *year* or so after we made that picture, Roger calls—this is ten thousand miles and at *least* twelve months later. He says, "We have no sound. 'Beach' Dickerson didn't get any sound. You gotta come in and wild-track it." *Not* loop it—wild-track it. We didn't have [a guide track], we didn't have *anything* to go by. We just had to throw in some words and just *hope* that it matched the mouth somehow or other! I stood there with tears running down my cheeks and the microphone in front of my face, trying to figure out *some* way to put *some*thing to make *some* kind of sane marriage between my voice and what was on the film! And it broke my heart, because if I *had* done any good work [in *Last Woman on Earth*], that took care of it! If *any* of it had been any good, that blew it right out of the water.

Years passed. *Years!* Then all of a sudden Roger called again and he said we were going to do some added scenes—the film had to be longer for TV. By this time, I was heavier, and my hair was darker. (By the way, Roger had originally wanted me to go blonde for the movie, and I don't look good as a blonde. I wish that I did, but I don't. So I had my hair streaked and it looked great, *I* thought.) Anyway, when we shot these additional scenes on a beach in Malibu (or wherever), I was a totally different person. I *tried* to be the same person but I was much more mature—that girl [in the movie] was a dip, and I couldn't *be* a dip anymore somehow! This was the scene where I'm sitting on a rock and Tony Carbone finds the dead girl on the beach, and then comes back all a-twitter. That whole sequence was added on much, *much* later. Roger got all three of us back together, me and Tony and Bob. We just had to add minutes, so there's a lot of scenes of us just walking up the beach. We also shot another added scene in some little bar on Santa Monica Boulevard.

Also, all the stills that I've seen from *Last Woman on Earth* were taken while we were shooting the extra scenes, they were *not* taken in Puerto Rico. I'm heavier in those pictures, my hair was darker, and it was not nearly the way it was style-wise in the movie.

Was there ever a movie where you had a better role than the one in Last Woman on Earth?

No. Uhn-uh. My favorite scene in the movie is the scene where I run after the baby chicks. That, and where I'm cutting the fish. I think I looked best in those two scenes.

Were you enjoying the experience of working in Puerto Rico?

I fell in love with the Puerto Ricans. Because of the humidity and the climate, I can understand their totally different tempo. I adjusted to *theirs* better than Puerto Ricans adjust to New York. *Their* tempo is a hell of a lot *nicer* than ours in New York. I ended up having a lot of friends in Puerto Rico in a very short period of time. You *cannot* run around tap-dancing to New York tempo in Puerto Rico, 'cause you will simply drop dead. It is too damn wet, it's just *unspeakably* humid, and the bugs are everywhere. There are groups of dogs, fifteen or twenty of 'em, that lie in the middle of the roads when you get a little bit out into the country. They lie there and they don't move — you can be going any-number-of-miles per hour that you want and they don't move, you have to drive around them. It's unbelievable!

There was one young Puerto Rican boy who had a crush on me, and he would go down to the water — the beautiful Caribbean sea — and throw a line in the water and pull in fish. One day he said he wanted me to have one of the fish for lunch. He cooked it out of doors at his house and brought it to me on a beautiful leaf, and told me how good the fish would be and he wanted me to eat it. Well, I'm not a big fish eater, but I thought, "I'm *not* going to create an international incident, I am going to eat this fish, and if it's the last fish I eat, if I choke to death on the bones, that's just gonna have to be the way it is!" *[Laughs.]* I started to eat the fish, and all the Puerto Ricans were standing around saying, "The head is the best, and the eyes the sweetest." And I thought, "Oh, my God, what have I gotten myself into here?!" Well, of course, I ate the whole fish, I ate the head, I ate the eyes and they were absolutely fine — it was a *great* delicacy, *marvelous*. And they were just cheering me as I went on, and it made for very good feelings amongst us — because there was so much anti–American sentiment at that point. There were riots in 1959, there had been riots before that — we were not the most welcome people on the planet Earth. So any little thing I could do, like eat the eyes of the fish, was for the good *[laughs]*!

How did Creature from the Haunted Sea *come about?*

Creature from the Haunted Sea was shot because, after *Last Woman on Earth* was done, Roger had some film left over; that's all *that* was about. Roger called back to Hollywood and he told a writer [Charles Griffith] to rewrite a picture that Corman had already shot twice, once in Hawaii [*Naked Paradise*, 1957] and once in the snow somewhere [*Beast from Haunted Cave*, 1959]. He told the writer, "Rewrite it for Puerto Rico and we'll shoot this picture again." He told us he had the film left over and he said, "Let's spend five more days here and we'll shoot this other picture," which we did. Roger was supposed to be in it, he was going to play my brother and he was going to play it like an idiot. Then at the last minute, this kid named Robert Bean came down from Canada (as I recall) and he played the part. Robert Bean was fine, but I wish that Roger had done it — I think it would have been a lot of fun.

The only problem with that movie is that it started out to be a takeoff on everything Roger had ever done before. It was to be a comedy, a laugh a minute. Then all of a sudden, somewhere in the middle of it, that got lost and it got to be serious! You never knew whether it was a fish or a fowl, and it turned out to be — foul, I guess *[laughs]*!

Did your paycheck double when you agreed to do a second picture?
No, no. We did *Creature* in only five days. *Last Woman on Earth* took two weeks, I think.

So what about the experience with the manta ray?
I literally had to go into the ocean where we saw the sharks and the manta ray. We had been shooting in the jungle and Roger had some of the guys construct a platform out in the ocean; they wanted me to go out onto this platform (which was supposed to be part of the boat) and then fall off of it. All the Puerto Ricans came running out of the water screaming, "Manta! Manta! Manta!" We looked out and right under the surface of the water we could see this big black shadow. I said, "Oh, God, Roger, I can't go out there—" He said, "Just *do* it! Just get in the goddamn water! I don't want to hear any more about these fucking fish!" And I was so mad at him that I thought, "If a goddamn shark comes along and takes off my leg, I am going to beat Roger to death with the bloody stump!" I was just fit to be tied! And yet I have always *liked* Roger—you can't help but *like* Roger! He never did harm to me. He tried to *screw* me in that I wasn't going to get my money and that kind of thing, but who doesn't do that?

Most of the people I've interviewed have that sort of attitude toward him. The one who came away with a real healthy dislike was Richard Devon.
Well, Richard got really badly hurt on *Viking Women*; the last time I talked to him, he was still suffering from Roger making him do something that was not necessary to begin with, and not *sane* secondly. I've never disliked Roger at all. I remember I was utterly *stunned* when he started importing ["artsy"] pictures from Sweden. I said, "Roger *who* is distributing these pictures?!" I couldn't believe it!

Were you doing much improvising and ad-libbing in Creature?
Yes, I think we were. Every day was a new adventure, and we didn't quite know from minute to minute what we were doing.

Did you find playing comedy appealing?
Yes, I did. I'd like to know a lot more about it than I do, I've never felt secure. I also sang in that picture; that was my singing debut *and* my singing end.

The fact that the film was a spoof—did that make it more fun to work on?
Yes, it did—especially since it was a spoof of *Roger*.

What do you remember about the Creature itself?
Not very much. It was all made of chicken wire and Brillo pads; the footprints were made with a toilet plunger. I don't remember who played it.

According to Jones-Moreland (seen here with Tony Carbone), *Creature from the Haunted Sea* wasn't a fish, so it must have been "foul."

What does a picture like Creature from the Haunted Sea *do for—or to—an actor's career?*

Probably bottoms it out. I just assumed that nobody would ever see it. In the beginning, because it *was* going to be a "sophisticated" spoof and it *was* going to be an inside joke, I was not ashamed of it. Later, when it *didn't* turn out to be that way, when it got off the track and got dumb, then I wished that I'd never heard of it. You're there, the camera's running, you just do whatever you gotta do and you just go on.

Jacques Marquette told me that, once the pictures were done, getting out *of Puerto Rico was the toughest part for you guys.*

We finally got to the point where Jack, who was the cinematographer, hid the last reels of the films. He *hid* them, because we didn't have tickets to get home, we didn't have money to get home, the crew wasn't getting paid. We were truly stranded. Roger was going on to other things—and we *weren't*! Roger talked to his brother on the phone a lot, and the brother, I understand, is even tougher. Good cop, bad cop—*he's* the bad cop. Roger and his brother were going to go on and do something else, and his method of operation was to leave everybody [connected with the finished pictures] and go on. I don't think that was really Roger's m.o. Jack hid the film—he stashed it in a freezer or something—and he wouldn't let Roger have it until we not only got our checks, but we got our checks cashed and we had the money in our hot little hands, to do with as we pleased!

One other story: I found out that *Last Woman on Earth* was going to premiere in San Diego. I went camping with friends of mine, we went down and spent the night in the mountains, and came down to the theater in our fatigues and so on. I'm sure the poor manager of the theater could have killed me, could have shot me dead. He probably thought that this glamorous person was going to appear, and in I walk in army fatigues, wild hair, sunburned (and having a wonderful time). The double feature was *Last Woman on Earth* and *Little Shop of Horrors.* So I will always feel a close kinship to Jack Nicholson, because of that moment when our two pictures came out together!

Did Corman ever offer you a part that you turned down?

No, but a funny thing happened later. I had done a soap opera called *Morning Star* on NBC and I had money in the bank, and that's when Roger called my agent and wanted me to do a part in *The St. Valentine's Day Massacre* [1967]. Jason Robards was the star and he was very insecure as a *movie* actor, and Roger wanted to make him feel *very* secure. Roger wanted me to play one of the reporters in Robards' first scene—Robards' first scene was going to be shot at some big mansion that Roger rented. Roger offered me some amount of money, I forget how much, but I had money in the bank and I was being very snotty at the moment and I said to my agent, "There's not enough money!", meaning that there wasn't enough money in the *world* to tempt me to get onto another Roger Corman picture and get killed, which is what was in my head. (Also, it was a small part and I had starred in this soap opera for a year and I didn't want to bring myself down to a small part.) Well, *he* thought I said, "*It's* not enough money"—there is a world of difference. So Roger doubled the price and then I thought, "Well, *okay,* I can't turn *that* down!" So here I was, the very experienced "old hand," gonna help Jason Robards *[laughs]*!

By the way, I hope that nowhere along the line have I made it seem that I don't like Roger. You cannot help liking Roger, he has such great charm, and you can't beat the fact that he started out with a nickel and a half and built what he built. He discovered people, he employed people, he *used* people. Yeah, he *used* people—he found talented people that needed to work and were not working and he *used* them, but *he gave them work.* I want to make all that clear, because it'd be easy to mistake a lot of what I'm saying for Roger-bashing. By no means do I intend to do that. You can't *not* like Roger. You have to be *lured* by that wonderful, wonderful smile and that ability to make you feel important. *Anybody, anywhere* has got to respond to that—I don't care who you are, you have to respond to that feeling that he's taking you in and you're part of the family and your input is important. He just *generates* that, and I don't even think he *works* at it, I think it just *happens.*

What do you recollect about working on The Outer Limits [*"*The Mutant*"*]*?*
   That was shot about a block and a half away from my old house on Tuxedo Terrace in Hollywood, up in Bronson Canyon—the cave where we shot *Viking Women.* The first night that we were there, my voice went hoarse, I lost my voice from screaming in that cave. I had one hell of a time—it was very cold and very damp. It was very difficult from then on to sound like anything but a frog *[laughs]*!

You were also in the famous Route 66 *episode with Boris Karloff, Lon Chaney and Peter Lorre.*
   We went to Chicago to shoot that, just after Labor Day as I recall. Peter Lorre and other actors of that sort, Humphrey Bogart and so on, were always loved by "the darker side," if you know what I mean. The Mafia. The hoods of this country. Those actors were always treated with great respect and love and devotion. We went one night, Peter Lorre and I and I forget who else, a whole bunch of us—we were taken by "gentlemen" from that world to a nightclub, to dinner, and we were treated like royalty. Absolutely like royalty! Peter Lorre wasn't allowed to pay for anything, there was no way that anybody like Lorre could ever pay for anything when the *other* kind of people were around. And everything was done first class. It was very interesting. You sort of had a feeling there was an undercurrent *all-l-l-l* the time, that other things were going on that you didn't know about and didn't *want* to know about, but you'd read about them in the paper tomorrow. There'd be little exchanges at the other end of the table, somebody would step out from the shadows and whisper in somebody else's ear, and you thought, "Oh, God, somebody was just macheted somewhere!" *[Laughs.]*

Did you get the feeling that Lorre knew more than you did about what was going on?
   I don't think so, I don't think he was part of it. I think he was like a mascot. He was a pet, but *not* a pet who knew anything! Peter Lorre was wonderful fun. I have not too many other recollections about that *Route 66* except that George Maharis got *very* sick. Very, very, *very* sick—he had hepatitis. I *think* that in the episode before that, they had him in the water at night in the cold. He got real sick, and they would *not* take care of him. They would not double him or do any of the things they needed to do to protect their star. And so in the middle of our shooting, he took off! Nobody could find him. We were there, as I recall, an extra two weeks, on salary, *all* of us. Finally he was found, or allowed himself to be found, or came back; he had tried to recover. They were not good to him.

Talk about Betsy Jones-Moreland today.

I did seven *Perry Mason* [TV movies], which I was *very* grateful for. We shot them in Denver and I played the judge. And I have a kennel in El Monte and I do rescue work; I have dogs and cats and a few chickens and ducks, and I try to find homes for animals that people can't keep anymore. I've formed a not-for-profit organization—*believe* me, it's not for profit *[laughs]*—and everything I make goes into it and much more besides. I get food donated to my organization and I try to spread that out amongst other people who are doing rescue work. That's the biggest thing that I do: I can't personally rescue hundreds of animals, but I have been feeding hundreds of animals for a long time and I feel *real* good about that. It started out when I lost a cat in nineteen sixty-six, and in trying to find that cat, I went around to the pounds and saw what was happening to so many animals. You can either say, "I was never here . . . I will walk away . . . I will forget that this happened," and put it out of your head, or you can say, "I have to do something about this." I chose the latter and it changed my life, and of course it totally ate up my career. (Ate up everything *else,* too.) But it's very satisfying, makes me feel good. It's something that I'm very proud of and that I work very hard at.

BETSY JONES-MORELAND FILMOGRAPHY

The Eddy Duchin Story (Columbia, 1956)
The Best Things in Life Are Free (20th Century–Fox, 1956)
The Garment Jungle (Columbia, 1957)
Operation Mad Ball (Columbia, 1957)
The Saga of the Viking Women and Their Voyage to the Waters of the Great Sea Serpent (AIP, 1957)
Screaming Mimi (Columbia, 1958)
Thunder in the Sun (Paramount, 1959)
Day of the Outlaw (United Artists, 1959)
Strangers When We Meet (Columbia, 1960)
Last Woman on Earth (Filmgroup, 1960)
Creature from the Haunted Sea (Filmgroup, 1962)
The St. Valentine's Day Massacre (20th Century–Fox, 1967)
The Hindenburg (Universal, 1975)
Network (United Artists, 1976)
The Last Tycoon (Paramount, 1976)
Joni (World Wide Pictures, 1980)

I think from time to time that a sequel to
The Brain from Planet Arous *would be*
worth doing. Know any investors?

Jacques Marquette

IN A SHORT BUT ACTIVE PRODUCING CAREER, Jacques Marquette was responsible for three of the most conspicuous low-budget sci-fi/horror films of the frantic
1950s: *Teenage Monster,* a "werewolf" Western (also directed by Marquette);
The Brain from Planet Arous, featuring John Agar and a giant floating brain; and
the all-time cult classic *Attack of the 50 Foot Woman.*

   Born in Brooklyn in 1915, Marquette moved to Hollywood in 1919 and attended
Hollywood High School. Breaking into the business as a "gofer" for his older
brother Joe, a newsreel cameraman, Marquette's first job was assisting his brother
on coverage of the 1933 Long Beach earthquake. Later, after a World War II stint
as a cameraman for the Air Force's Film Division, Marquette accepted a $69-a-
week job at Technicolor Labs as a technician. By 1957 he had moved up to camera
operator on various studio pictures and was still facing the difficulty of climbing
to the next notch of director of photography. It was at this time, according to
the filmmaker, that his "interest in sci-fi and producing all merged into a new
project known as Marquette Productions."

What were your first jobs in Hollywood after the War?

   First as a technician at Technicolor Labs. Soon I was in Technicolor's
camera department, which in those days meant *on the set* — the old three-strip
color required Technicolor people, not studio employees, on the camera. I was
a camera assistant on many color films like *Anchors Aweigh* [1945], *Niagara*
[1953], etc. Finally, film crews on color films went back to studio personnel
and I went to work at Twentieth Century–Fox as an assistant cameraman.
There I met actor Jeffrey Hunter, and he coaxed me into serving as camera
operator, director of photography and co-producer on *Living Swamp* [1955],
a Disney-style documentary film on Georgia's Okeefenokee Swamp. After
that, I returned to Hollywood now advanced to camera operator, first on
Warners' *The Helen Morgan Story* [1957]. I "operated" on many films thereafter but wanted to advance to director of photography — which was not easy
to do at the time.

What made you decide to get into the business of making movies?

   I'd been working in the business for quite a while, and I was seeing some
of the ineffectual things they were doing with a pretty good amount of money.
For instance, an actor's agent could talk a producer into almost any amount
of money they wanted — particularly if the producer was "stuck" on that one
actor. They would pay probably ten times the amount they would have to pay
at *scale* — that's the minimum amount of money any actor gets if he belongs
to the Screen Actors Guild. This went through the whole business. Cameramen, actors, producers — their agents would up 'em, up 'em, up 'em. I knew
a hell of a lot of people in the business that were not working (and would

Previous page: Cinematographer Jacques (now Jack) Marquette, long active in movies
and (especially) television, once combined his love of science fiction and a desire to
make movies into a short-lived producing career.

like to keep working), that would be *more* than pleased to work for scale. Consequently, I got together with a writer-friend of mine, Ray Buffum, and we wrote *Teenage Thunder* [1957], a drag race movie. Sweet old guy, Ray; I paid him out of my pocket for it.

And you also raised the money to make the film.

I had been raising the money all along. I finally got it all together, hired a director named Paul Helmick and cast it. We shot about two days when all of a sudden I got a phone call from an outfit in New Orleans called Howco International. Somehow they'd gotten a copy of the script — I don't know how! — and they wanted to talk to me about getting together. They wanted to contribute to make it, and they would distribute it. I had a board of directors, about five guys, and we talked this over — it was like money from heaven, because we knew damn well that we were thin on what we were doing. And, naive as we were in business, we went for it. Howco made up the contract and it seemed okay. We made the picture, made the prints, Howco released it and it did pretty good.

"Did good" for them or for you?

[Laughs.] For *them*! Howco was a dishonest outfit, one of too many distributors who take your product and "creatively account" their costs, leaving you, the independent producer, without a dime. After *Teenage Thunder* — but *before* we knew what thieves they were — Howco wanted to make some more pictures with us. I told 'em, "Well, you'll have to put up *all* the money. We don't have the money to do it" — 'cause we hadn't received any money from Howco on *Teenage Thunder* yet. So I had Ray Buffum write another story, *The Brain from Planet Arous*. I wrote about twenty pages of a treatment, because I wanted to give Ray an idea of what I was trying to do. He got the idea, and he did real well. Eight days, we shot it in; we paid everybody scale.

Where did your idea for Brain *come from?*

It was a story which I had sort of halfway stolen from *Amazing Stories*. I used to read that, *Astounding Science Fiction,* all of those — I loved science fiction. One of them ran a story about a guy on the beach in the summer, and this thing came out of the ocean, went up into his foot and took him over. So I used that idea. John Agar and Robert Fuller are scientists working out of a house in the desert, and their equipment tells them that radiation is emanating from one of the mountains in the desert nearby. When they get there, they're attacked by the Brain from Planet Arous, which kills Fuller and takes over Agar's body. We shot those scenes in the cave at Bronson Canyon.

According to The Hollywood Reporter, *your shooting title was* Superbrain.

We never called it that. What *The Hollywood Reporter* and *Variety* would do is this: They'd call me up and ask, "What pictures have you got start-ing?" I'd say, "Well, we're about to do..."—whatever it was. They'd say, "What other ones are coming up?" "At the moment, we don't have any other ones." And then they'd say, "Well, just make up some titles and tell 'em to me!" *[Laughs.]* Honest to God!

What was your budget on Arous?
The budget, as I recall, was about fifty-eight thousand dollars. I did all the optical effects in the camera; otherwise, it would have cost probably five hundred dollars for *one* effect.

Where did you shoot your interiors?
My neighbor Walter Studt was an optometrist, and he had a much bigger house than we had. We used his house, and also part of the backyard, I think. We were there about three or four days. (Part of the film we shot in my house, too.) This neighbor also came up with the silver contact lenses for John Agar to wear when the alien brain was in control of his mind. John Agar didn't like 'em, but he wore 'em—he had no choice! It was very uncomfortable for Agar, the lenses could not be worn for more than fifteen minutes at a time.

What do you remember about your brain prop?
We told the people who were going to make it what we wanted, and that we wanted lights inside. It was made of plastic and held up with wires. Later on, after we finished the picture, my kids got a-hold of it and put on a show. They'd get other kids together, charge 'em five cents and put on a show with the brain in there *[laughs]*!

Where'd it eventually go? In the garbage?
That's right. That's where everything eventually goes *[laughs]*!

Dale Tate, the associate producer, was also the voice of the brains.
That's right. Dale Tate was a guy that worked for Consolidated Film Labs, which did all the processing of our films. He was dying to be an actor, but never quite made it. He did the voices for the brains and also played a scientist. Later on, he played the TV announcer in *Attack of the 50 Foot Woman*.

What made you think of Nathan Juran as director?
I think we had worked together on something in the past. We got together and talked a little bit, and I hired him. He worked for scale, too.

Next you did Teenage Monster, *a Western with a werewolf-ish monster.*
That one we originally called *Monster on the Hill*. We hired a director, looked at all the locations, did all the casting; I was going to photograph it,

According to Marquette (and everybody else!), the problem-plagued horror Western *Teenage Monster* was the least of his 1950s films.

and we were going to start on a Monday. The director came up to me on Sunday and he said, "Jack, I can't do the picture. I've got a fourteen-week deal at Universal, and I have to take it." Well, what could I do? I called another board of directors meeting, and they said, "It's too late to stop it, and we can't call in another director on one day's notice. *You* direct it, Jack." It was one of those things—when you've got the ball, you've got to run. So I became a member of the Screen Directors Guild, five thousand dollars worth, and I went ahead. It was my first and only directing job.

Who dreamed up the plot for Teenage Monster?

I think that just came from a talk I had with Ray Buffum. We talked a little about it, and he took it from there. To play the Teenage Monster, we hired Gil Perkins, with whom I'd worked in the past. He was basically a stuntman from Australia, a real nice guy. He was about six feet five inches tall and I knew I needed a tall guy for the monster. We had special boots on him that raised him up about four more inches, and so (in relation to other people) he was pretty tall. We couldn't give him any dialogue, other than the grunts and groans and stuff like that.

Watching the film, it looks as though Perkins is delivering dialogue, even though grunts and groans is all we hear.

No, the grunts and groans were intended from the beginning. There *was* some dubbing. The women in the film [Anne Gwynne and Gloria Castillo] were supposed to intuitively understand—almost like a pet dog—what the creature meant and wanted. English was not spoken by the creature on the set, he grunted and emoted, but this is what was intended, poor dubbing and looping aside.

Where was Teenage Monster *shot?*

We were shooting out at a place called Melody Ranch, which was a big old Western street way out in the Valley. I'd hired another cameraman—I didn't want to have *that* chore, too!—and the first day of shooting was all what we call "day-for-night" scenes. The editor got the rushes the next morning, and he came driving out to where we were shooting and he said, "We can't print any of this stuff, we can't do *any*thing with it." Shooting day-for-night is an *art,* and this cameraman evidently didn't know how to do it. He had under-exposed the film so much it couldn't be printed, there was no image on it! Howco found out about it and they said, "Fire the cameraman." I said, "No, I'm not going to do that. He's just given me another job to do"—which was to watch *him*! Anyway, what had been an eight-day picture was now a seven-day picture, because a whole day had been lost. But I went ahead and completed it, and it was *bad,* naturally. For instance, when situations called for a closeup or a tight two-shot instead of a master shot, we couldn't do it, we had to stay with the master. We couldn't "punch up" situations that *should* have been "punched up" in a closer shot, I knew I had no time to do it. *Teenage Monster* was produced on a budget of fifty-seven thousand dollars with a full I.A. [the International Alliance of Theatrical State Employees] union crew.

How was the special effect of the falling meteor achieved?

With sparklers. Held by my hands with a black felt covering, then superimposed over the landscape shots.

After these three films, you figured out that the people at Howco were only looking out for themselves.

[*Laughs.*] It was the typical thing. The exhibitors cheat the distributors, and the distributors cheat the producers. For instance, just recently when Art Buchwald sued Paramount over *Coming to America* [1988]; even the *judge* said how ridiculous the accounting was. It's always been that way. For each picture, Howco would send me producer's reports which showed the amounts of money received in the different areas where the pictures had played. And it was almost impossible to figure out if the pictures were profitable or not. Maybe there'd be thirty or forty different areas where the pictures were released, and (for instance) some of the drive-ins reported rain, which means no income from there on those days. The majority of the problem, in *my* case, was that I had no real business experience. We tried to force the issue in a suit against Howco, and one of their claims was that the pictures was "cross-collateralized." (There was never anything in the contract that said that, but that's what they claimed.) That means that if one picture makes a profit and the other makes a loss, Howco "evens it out." There are so many areas where they can cheat you; you can't tell how many theaters the thing played in, or how many nights or days it played, unless you had somebody there taggin' along. We just got our salaries, on all three pictures. On paper, *Teenage Thunder, The Brain from Planet Arous* and *Teenage Monster* all lost money and returned nothing to the thirty investors in Marquette Productions.

Why did you photograph these films, when you already had all the producing responsibilities?

The dual roles of director of photography and producer grew out of my previous role as a camera operator. My career in the film union hierarchy was stagnated. To jump the next step up to director of photography required (by union rules) that a producer hire me as d.p. and (by union contracts) producers can only do that when nearly all available d.p.'s are working. So, as producer, I hired *myself,* at an opportune time.

Did you derive more creative satisfaction directing, producing or photographing your pictures?

Photographing was always the most satisfactory task. Producing— secondarily. Directing was not my favorite job—dealing with agents, actors and egos was not enjoyable. In photographing, I feel more directly involved with the medium and process of filmmaking, rather than the personalities and bureaucracy that seem, so often, to get in the way.

Who came up with Attack of the 50 Foot Woman?

If I remember right, Bernie Woolner had the idea for that, and we had this friend of mine, Mark Hanna, write it. (Nice sweet guy. He still owes me two thousand dollars!) Bernie was one of the producers on *50 Foot Woman,* he was the one that actually put all the money situation together. He was a theater owner in New Orleans—I think he had two drive-in theaters, which then were very lucrative. (Drive-in owners could take a picture, play it, and then tell the distributor, "We got fogged in, we couldn't play it." Then they'd keep all the money! As I said before, that was typical of exhibitors.) Anyway, Bernie was a real sharp guy, and he'd made at least one or two pictures years before.

Talk about your special effects on 50 Foot Woman.

Making Allison Hayes fifty feet tall was another optical effect. We had to shoot the background that she was going to be walking in front of, then we had to shoot her separately, on a stage covered with black velvet. We had to light her so that she was totally lit all over, because anyplace where there was

A big hand for the little lady: Allison Hayes has a close encounter in Marquette's *Attack of the 50 Foot Woman*.

dark or shadow, the background image would bleed through. The lab would put the two together. We built a giant hand for her; the miniature electrical tower; and also a miniature house. We either built these things ourselves, or we paid to have 'em built. We also built the interiors of the outer space giant's spaceship; that was built out of pegboard. The giant was played by a guy named Mike Ross, who also had another part in the film, as the owner of the bar. The last time I heard of him, he was a used car salesman in the San Fernando Valley.

Where was the film shot?
    Partly in an old house near Beverly Hills, a house that was sort of built like a castle. We did quite a bit of it in there. It was very expensive to rent the place, like five hundred dollars a day. The exteriors were mostly shot in a canyon near my residence in Tarzana.

Nathan Juran directed again.
    "Jerry" Juran was another one of these directors (they're basically all the same) who don't give a goddamn about your budget. That's *your* problem. They want to shoot on and on and *on*. So he and I went through arguments like you can't believe. I said, "Keep it up and you're gone." And I meant it, too—I had no choice.

He must have been better on Brain from Planet Arous, *or you wouldn't have rehired him for* 50 Foot Woman.

There was a *beginning* of that argument with him on *Arous.* Juran was good in the respect that he knew what he was doing and he completed each day's work in the proper sequence and in the proper time — *until* he got to certain things, and then he'd get a little stiff about 'em. That's when I'd lower the boom.

He did both pictures under the name Nathan Hertz.

He's like so many people, they have a real ego. He felt that his name was well-known (or *some*thing!), and he would be put down if people saw that these were his pictures. He didn't want people to know that he would make that cheap a picture.

Any memories of star Allison Hayes?

She seemed like a very nice gal, very willing. Not like a lot of the actors and actresses today; today, they think they know more than the producers or the directors and they don't give a damn about the budget. After the picture was done, she became involved with this director, a guy I didn't think could even direct traffic. She got hooked on this guy, who was about five feet three inches tall; *he* never got a divorce from his previous wife and he was boozing pretty good. At the rate he boozed, he has to be dead by now.

The 50 Foot Woman *script ended with Hayes crushing William Hudson in her giant hand while Hudson shoots up her face with bullets.*

I chose, together with Juran, to omit this ending in favor of a slightly less violent one. It seemed at the time too violent, and not really necessary to serve the purposes of the plot.

Most of the humorous business in the film is not *in the script. What made you decide to "spoof it up"?*

No "spoofing" was ever intended. It was an exploitation film, simply that. Think of it as an honest period piece.

And the fact that people derive so much fun from it — does it hurt your feelings that people laugh at the film you made seriously?

No. I made it seriously, and I made it in the contingency of what I had to make it with. I know that *initially* people didn't laugh at it; *I* didn't laugh at it. But you have much more "intellectual" people that look at it and laugh. They have no idea of what it was like at that particular time. You can look at comedies from forty years ago today, and *some* of that comedy stands up. *Most* of it doesn't.

Allison Hayes' growing techniques are revealed in this behind-the-scenes glimpse at the special effects of Marquette's *Attack of the 50 Foot Woman*.

You released 50 Foot Woman *through Allied Artists.*

Right. We had a budget from Allied Artists of ninety-nine thousand five hundred dollars to complete it. When we completed it, it came in at eighty-nine thousand dollars. There *were* a few optical effects I would have liked to improve, but unless you do it right at the time that you're shooting it, you have to go *back* to do it over again and, my God, the expense is terrific. Allied

Artists told us we should go back and improve some of the effects. Well, it would have probably cost twenty thousand dollars. I said, "My friends, *that's* the picture. Period." So they had to buy it, what could they do?

Was Allied Artists a more honest place to work for than Howco?
Oh, yes, far more. Allied Artists reported over four hundred thousand dollars at the box office on *50 Foot Woman.* I think I owned twenty percent of that picture, and my share finally ended up about eighty thousand dollars net.

You photographed several films for Roger Corman. How did you hook up with him?
Roger Corman's "legend" is well-earned: He's too stingy to believe. I had worked on one of his pictures where what he had done was this: There was an independent picture [*Diary of a High School Bride,* 1959] that Roger either had something to do with, or maybe he just found out about, and Roger had his eye on the sets. He had one of his writers knock out a screenplay that would make use of *this* picture's sets! So as soon as the first picture quit, *he* went in there and used every set they had and he made his own picture, which was *A Bucket of Blood.* I think that was my first time working with him. Later on, he decided he was going to make two pictures in Puerto Rico [*Battle of Blood Island* and *Last Woman on Earth,* both 1960] and I was going to be the director of photography. He drew up all the contracts and I was to get two percent of each picture's gross; he didn't want to pay me, he wanted me to defer. You can't do that; [by union rules] I had to be paid at least scale. I got off the plane at Puerto Rico, and Roger was right there. Whenever you arrive in Puerto Rico by plane, Puerto Ricans give you a free drink at the airport—"Welcome to Puerto Rico!" Well, *Roger* was there for the free drinks [*laughs*]!

He said to me, "Do you realize that the cost in Puerto Rico is twenty-five percent *more* than it is in the United States?" I said, "What are you trying to tell me, Roger?" He said, "I've rented a house, a big mansion, and we're all going to stay in this mansion" [rather than at a hotel]. I said, "Oh? I don't think *I'll* stay there." We went to look at it: The place had about four or five bedrooms, and in each bedroom they had four or five army cots. It was like a dormitory. I also remember that there were two big deep-freezers in the "mansion," filled with all kinds of frozen food. I said, "Wait a minute. Where are we going to put all the film?"—we had to keep the film frozen as much as possible before the high humidity got to it. So we threw all the goddamn frozen stuff out of the freezers and put the film cans in there. Then they went and got some more freezers and put the meat back *in,* which means it's refrozen meat!

I told him, "Roger, I'm not staying here." This was still five days before we were supposed to start shooting, so he had plenty of time to get somebody else to come. So Roger and I got into his Volkswagen and he showed me another place I could stay if I wanted, a cabana on a major hotel. A cabana off the swimming pool. No bathroom, no place to eat, and there would have been drunks and people using the pool until two, three in the morning. No way! Finally, after all day looking at all these different horseshit places, he took me to the Caribe Hilton. I said okay, I'd stay there. *Now* what happened is that, all the people that were staying at the "mansion" came into town on the weekend. They'd come to my hotel and eat dinner with me, and I'd sign the check for all of 'em *[laughs]*!

Corman ended up making three *pictures there.*

It was so cheap to make pictures in Puerto Rico that Roger did decide to make a third picture *[Creature from the Haunted Sea]*. By this time, I was ready to go home; I told him, "If this third picture takes over eight days, I'm gone. I can't stay. I've got commitments and so forth." He said, "Okay, we'll do it in eight days." Meanwhile, his secretary never paid the bill at the Caribe, the bill for me and the other people I'd signed for. I told Roger, "Your girl hasn't paid the bill. They won't let me out until the bill's paid." He said he'd talk to her. *Another* couple of days go by, and still the bill is unpaid. I said, "Roger, if this bill isn't paid, you're not going to be able to release *any* of these three pictures you've made because part of 'em *is going to be missing*." 'Cause I had the negatives *[laughs]*! *That's* when Roger finally paid the bill and I went home!

Did he at least give you creative freedom in how you shot these films?

Roger did give me complete photographic freedom — he was too busy with logistic problems to solve. As long as my suggestions did not cost any extra money, it was fine.

How did you get involved on Flight of the Lost Balloon?

Barney Woolner and I had done *Attack of the 50 Foot Woman* together and that was very successful, so when he got *Flight of the Lost Balloon* going and realized that he couldn't do it all by himself, I had to put in money. I put in (I forget how much) cash, and then also I put my house up as collateral with the film lab. Then we went ahead and started to make the picture in Puerto Rico. One incident that stands out in my mind about *Flight of the Lost Balloon* was the day we shot a scene where the two stars, Marshall Thompson and Mala Powers, were supposed to run over to the hot air balloon, climb in and take off. (Of course, we didn't *have* a hot air balloon, just the basket and some straps going up from it.) We rounded up all the blacks we could get and we had them playing cannibals, and they were supposed to be chasing Marshall and Mala and trying to catch the balloon. Instead, they're standing and just running in place *[laughs]*! Nathan Juran was directing, and I said to him, "We can't get by with this!" And he looked at me and said *[sneeringly]*, "Let 'em write letters." He had *that* kind of an attitude.

Marquette's main memory of *The Strangler* involves star Victor Buono's avoidance of the shower.

Just the opposite of the problem he gave you on Attack of the 50 Foot Woman.

Well, by that time he was probably getting very annoyed with me because we were running into problems in Puerto Rico; a lot of the people that we'd hired there were striking.

Any memories of photographing a thriller called The Strangler *[1964]?*

That was for a director named Burt Topper, with whom I've worked a few times. One thing I remember about *The Strangler* is that we were working on a stage at Paramount, and it was a scene where Victor Buono (who *was* the Strangler) was supposed to go into a shower that this woman [Diane Sayer] was in. The woman was supposed to be nude. And Buono said, "No way I'll go in there with her nude." He wouldn't go in there *[laughs]*! So that loused Burt up!

How about shooting Burnt Offerings *with Oliver Reed?*

That was a thing we did in Oakland, in a big old house up there. The director was Dan Curtis, and this supposedly was his "biggie." He would have us set up in a corner for a shot of a whole room. We'd get the room lit properly, which might take a half hour or more. Then he'd come back and say, "No, now I want to do it from *that* corner over *this* way." *[Laughs.]* One day we were having lunch, and Curtis' assistant came over and said that Curtis' daughter had jumped off a building in Pasadena—committed suicide. Drugs. He said, "We're shutting down the production." So everybody went home. Some time later, they were ready to start back up, and my agent felt that I should be paid for all the time that production was shut down—which, by union rules, I *was* entitled to. I said, no, this shutdown was *not* the type that called for that, and they didn't have to pay me anything for the time we didn't work. The next thing I know, I find out that they don't want to use me for the balance of the picture. It wasn't until later that I found out that, sure enough, my agent had sent these earlier letters [demanding full payment]. So I got rid of *him.*

Of all your pictures, 50 Foot Woman *is the one with the big following. Is it your favorite of the bunch?*

No, I liked *The Brain from Planet Arous* best, maybe because I wrote the initial treatment. I like science fiction so much, and I thought that was more "authentic" to science fiction than the others. It was exciting to see it realized. I think from time to time that a sequel would be worth doing. Know any investors?

I don't like gore pictures, I won't see them.
I make 'em, but I don't have to look at 'em!

Cameron Mitchell

NO ONE EVER SAID THAT LIFE WAS FAIR (especially not in the film business!), but it's still a cruel irony that Cameron Mitchell, the intense, dark-haired leading man of many a celebrated Broadway play and Hollywood hit, should wind up the human emblem for the low-rent horror and slasher flicks of the recent past. Over the past dozen years, he has appeared in such dross as *The Toolbox Murders, Frankenstein Island, Space Mutiny* and *Screamers,* a far cry from the caliber of films and the type of celebrities with whom he was associated during the 1940s and 1950s when he was a rising star at MGM and Fox. The only one who *isn't* complaining, it seems, is Mitchell himself: Now in his 70s, he's only too happy to still be working steadily, and in some ways, he says, he is pleased about having enjoyed some of the unique acting opportunities which an actor gets only by working the wrong side of the Hollywood tracks.

Scotch/German/Irish Cameron McDowell Mitzel was born in Dallastown, Pennsylvania, one of seven children of a country minister. At 18 he told his parents he wanted to become an actor, and was promptly disowned by his father who intended for Cam to become a minister like himself ("He forgave me when I did the voice of Jesus Christ in *The Robe!*"). Arriving in New York with a thick Pennsylvania Dutch accent (he had never used a telephone or an elevator, or been in a movie house or a restaurant), Mitzel held the usual variety of odd jobs (42nd Street movie house usher, mail clerk, dishwasher) while at the same time beginning a letter-writing campaign to all the big-name Broadway producers and actors. The legendary husband-and-wife acting team of Alfred Lunt and Lynn Fontanne took an interest in Mitzel (Fontanne got him to change his name), and he stage-debuted in the Lunt/Fontanne play *The Taming of the Shrew* in 1939. After doing his part in World War II (as an Air Force bombardier), Mitchell got an MGM screen test through the auspices of actor/director Richard Whorf, an old friend from his stage acting days, and was signed to a Metro contract the following day. Mitchell appeared in a number of MGM films and then reached what he considers the apex of his career when he appeared as Happy Loman in the Pulitzer Prize–winning stage production of *Death of a Salesman* (1949) under the direction of Elia Kazan.

After several more years in Hollywood, Mitchell broke into TV (he starred in NBC's long-running *The High Chaparral*) and began globetrotting, turning up in dozens of mini-budgeted horror and action items in every corner of the world (including 30 films made behind the Iron Curtain!). Now filling the void left by John Carradine as the patron saint of rock-bottom horror movies, Cameron Mitchell looks back over a long career in horror, sci-fi and exploitation.

Your first science fiction film was Flight to Mars, *made in 1951.*

Flight to Mars I made for Monogram, and they had high hopes for it. We had to shoot it in like five days, and I remember I said to them, "How the hell can you shoot this in five *days?*", but they did! The technical stuff—the miniatures and special effects—were done by another unit. It was fun to work at Monogram, and they knew it was gonna make a ton of money, which it did. And, by the way, it was that picture that put the Mirisch brothers on the map.

Previous page: **From Hollywood classics** *(Death of a Salesman, Les Miserables, Love Me or Leave Me)* **to rock-bottom exploitation fodder: The Cameron Mitchell story.**

Men meet Martians on the Red Planet in Monogram's Cinecolor *Flight to Mars*. Left to right, Morris Ankrum (in spacesuit), John Litel, Virginia Huston, Cameron Mitchell, Richard Gaines.

Flight to Mars opened the door for Walter Mirisch, who zoomed to the top as a producer not long after doing this one little film.

Did you enjoy working with costars Marguerite Chapman and Arthur Franz?
    Marguerite Chapman was a doll, an absolute doll; Arthur Franz, I haven't seen or heard from him in years. I remember that I really enjoyed doing that film; I don't know why, but I did! It was interesting because it was primitive and it was second-class, but a lot of the things that they did in the real space program *we* did in that film *[laughs]*! I'm embarrassed to look at it today because my performance was awful.

How did working at Monogram compare to working at the larger studios?
    They weren't calling it Monogram then, they had a fancy name for it, Allied Artists—years later, a picture I did with Mario Bava, *Blood and Black Lace,* was a big hit for them. Needless to say, the larger studios were better— Lesley Selander [director of *Flight to Mars*] was strictly a B picture director, of course, and you had to go very fast. I do remember that John Litel, who was a good actor, was in it, and he had a lot of scientific razzmatazz to say.

Well, he was having trouble, and starting to perspire *[laughs]*—it happens to an actor! Finally I went to Selander and I said, "For God's sake, write it on a board for him—put it on a card!" That's what they finally did, and he got it.

The producers promised a sequel, Voyage to Venus.
    Voyage to Venus was never made. But I remember that they did talk to me about it.

Did you enjoy working in these older sci-fi and horror films?
    Many years ago, I liked every picture—and today, I don't like *any* *[laughs]*! As a kid, to see a movie was a joy for me, and there *were* no bad films—to my mind, every film was great. I used to see triple features when I was in New York, going to drama school; you saw three pictures for a dime. I made six dollars and seventy cents a week, and had to live on that, but for a dime I could see three movies! So I used to sit through 'em twice, no matter what they were. Today I don't like any movies. I don't like Stallone, I don't like (what's his name?) Clyde Westwood, I don't like Bronson, none of 'em. They made 'em better in the old days. I watch American Movie Classics to see guys like Gary Cooper, who was a very underrated actor, Clark Gable (I did three films with Gable), Spencer Tracy, the true greats.

In general, do you enjoy science fiction in films or literature?
    Some of it is very good, like Ray Bradbury's stuff; George Orwell's *1984* was good. Yeah, I do enjoy it. I saw a flying saucer years ago, and I do believe in those things.

Where did you see a flying saucer?
    In the Saskatchewan, about forty years ago. I've also been operated on by a doctor, a very religious man, by the name of Alex Orbito in Manila. I had heard about him, and when I got a chance to do a film in Manila, I really went not to make the film as much as to see Orbito, because I knew I had to have a big operation. He performed it, and it worked. He operated on me with his hands—he did three big operations, cut me with his fingers. He's now a close friend of Shirley MacLaine—in fact, she wrote a whole chapter about him in her book.

At Twentieth Century–Fox you appeared in the classic musical fantasy Carousel.
    That was from the play *Liliom* by Ferenc Molnár. Originally Frank Sinatra was supposed to play the lead part in that, and we were all on location in Boothbay Harbor, Maine—beautiful place. Frank and I had left California on a Thursday, and on Sunday Frank *quit*. But we had prerecorded all of his songs, including a duet with me! It was a comedy number and we had a long sustained note, and I was very nervous about it because I'm no singer, and I

Exhibitor Edwin Zabel and Mitchell, joined by actresses Barbara Ruick and Joanne Woodward, at a showing of Mitchell's musical/fantasy *Carousel*.

had heard that Frank only did things one time. But it came off. We had a one hundred fifty-piece symphony orchestra conducted by Alfred Newman and I was scared to death, but luckily we did it.

Why did Sinatra walk off the picture?

Several reasons. One, I think, was that he wanted Judy Garland to play the girl, but Shirley Jones got the part — she had done *Oklahoma!* [1955] and she was a very nice girl. The second thing was, we were going to do the picture in fifty-five mm, but the camera made so much noise that we had to do it twice, once in fifty-five and once in thirty-five. And Frank's basic reason for walking off the film was that he felt he should be paid twice if he had to do it twice. They sued him, and he settled the lawsuit by agreeing to do *Can-Can* [1960]. I heard his recordings, by the way, all of them, and when I saw him recently in Palm Springs I said, "Frank, I wish to God you had done *Carousel* because I never heard you in such great voice." And he said, "Cameron, that was the greatest my voice ever has been in my life." Gordon MacRae sang it on the nose, Gordon had a great set of pipes, but he didn't have what Frank had. I still think that Frank's sorry he didn't do it.

Well, when Frank walked off the picture we were stuck in Boothbay

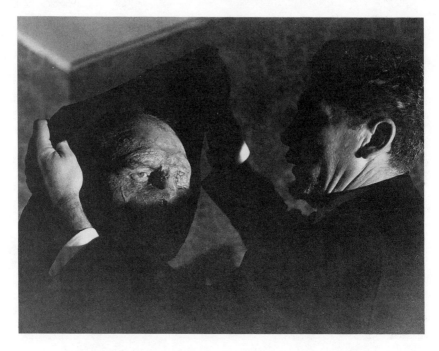

Mitchell unveils James Whitmore's hideous *Face of Fire*.

Harbor without a leading man. And at one point the director and all the executives wanted *me* to play that part, and I thought I was gonna get it, but I was sold out by my agent at MCA and they finally gave it to Gordon MacRae. And that was the last film Gordon made.

Carousel *was a very expensive picture, wasn't it?*
      Carousel was the most expensive film made until *Cleopatra* [1963] — the film cost a fortune. Because they redid some of the musical numbers six times, and that's money! And when they ran it for the first time for Darryl Zanuck and Buddy Adler and all the other Fox executives, they all said, "Jesus, what a mistake we made. If we had put Mitchell in there, we'd have had a new star." That's true. I've missed out on a lot of things like that.

One of the better horror films you did was the Swedish-made Face of Fire.
      The original story was written by Stephen Crane, author of *The Red Badge of Courage,* and was called *The Monster.* In the story, "the monster" was a black man from the South, which gave it an added dimension, but for the film they made him white and James Whitmore played him. [Director] Albert Band, going over to Sweden on the plane, met Clare Boothe Luce, and she told him *The Monster* was one of the three best stories she had ever read.

How did you enjoy working in Sweden?

I loved working in Sweden because we worked at Svensk Filmindustri and I met Ingmar Bergman — they pronounced the *g* like a *y*, Ingmar *Ber-ry-mon*. He reminded me so much of Kazan. We had a deal, we were going to do *Siddhartha* by Hermann Hesse in India, and I was very excited about it. But at the last moment, he pulled out — Hesse was still alive, and Bergman said, "I'm so insecure. I can only do my own things." Finally somebody did a terrible, synthetic, sugary version of *Siddhartha,* but, boy, it could have been a great film.

Why was Face of Fire *done in Sweden?*

Because I think they had most of the money there. It was shot in a town outside of Stockholm, a little town that looked like early America, and we did the interiors at Svensk Filmindustri in Stockholm, where Bergman did all his films. It was tough shooting, because we had a lot of rain — I think we had three good days in four months, and they were Sundays so we weren't working *[laughs]*! But I enjoyed my trip to Sweden, I love Sweden and I love the people there. I went back there later, after *The High Chaparral,* and they treated me like a king. There's a certain crayfish there for three weeks of the year, which you eat with fresh dill, and I once made a trip from Rome to Stockholm just to eat three dishes of that!

Were you happy with your performance in Face of Fire?

Yes, I liked it, I like that kind of low-key stuff. I also liked James Whitmore; the girl who played my wife, Bettye Ackerman, was the wife of Sam Jaffe. Robert Simon, Royal Dano, Richard Erdman — it was a fairly good cast. I felt *Face of Fire* was a pretty good film, although it probably could have been better. I don't think that I've ever been happy with anything I've done, I always see things I could have done better. I can't recall ever seeing a film I've made that I felt was absolutely right from my point of view, and I've never been truly happy with a performance. The closest I think I came was when I played Barney Ross in *Monkey on My Back* [1957], which was one of the first films on drug addiction.

You made a number of films for Mario Bava in the nineteen sixties, most notably Blood and Black Lace.

I did about six films with Mario Bava, I loved him, I thought in many ways he might have been the best director — certainly the best one I've worked with in Europe, and maybe the best of them all.

Better than Kazan?

I thought Mario was one of the greatest directors in the world. I've worked with Kazan, Orson Welles (I did his last film, *The Other Side of the Wind*

[1976]), John Ford, I've worked with the best. Bava's right up there. And when I think of the limited money he had and the corners he had to cut, it's unbelievable! He never had a really good script, but he could make a film out of anything. I remember the vampire film with Barbara Steele, *Black Sunday*— Bava was the first to use slow motion with the black horses and the coach and all that, and in actuality that was shot on a soundstage and they had about twenty feet to run and that was all! Only Bava with his mastery, his know-how, could have done that—he was a miracle man in the film world. He would use a little boy's wagon as a dolly, he did incredible things with nothing. I did one picture for him called *Knives of the Avenger* [1967] which was really a hodgepodge, but he made it so good—even with the dubbing, it was good. He was so clever! He made the first face mask—he could make a mask of your face and put it on anybody else. I always felt we would get together to make one of the great pictures of all time, but unfortunately we never did and he passed away. His son is now directing.

Bava certainly was a good cameraman.

He was a *very* good cameraman. In *Knives of the Avenger* I wear a mask, an armored mask, you can't see my face, and I rape a young girl; I later meet her, and she doesn't know that it's me. Anyway, on the day we shot the rape scene, she had a couple of pimples on her face and I said to Mario, "Maybe we oughta shoot this in a few days. . ." He said, "*Che? Che?* Son of a bitch!" That's all he knew in English, "son of a bitch!" I said, "Mario—her *face!*" He said, "*Va bene!*", he put two or three lights in, and, by God, she looked gorgeous. I felt that the way he shot *Blood and Black Lace* was unbelievable, and it came out so good.

How close were you two personally?

We were very close personally, very friendly. I really think that I was his favorite actor, because he would always call me. He was really a wonderful man and I loved him personally. There's a Mario Bava cult all over the world.

Blood and Black Lace *was fairly successful at the time.*

Blood and Black Lace was a big release, made a lot of money. Eva Bartok was the female star, and I liked her very much—there was a big scandal about her years before, when she had had a baby by a leading member of the British royalty. We shot *Blood and Black Lace* in Rome.

How does working in Europe compare to making films in Hollywood?

I loved Italy; you make better films in Hollywood, but I loved the Italian people, they were wonderful and friendly. I did a lot of co-productions with them in the Iron Curtain countries.

Nutty nobleman Cameron Mitchell demonstrates his carnivorous plants to anxious onlookers in *Island of the Doomed* (a.k.a. *Maneater of Hydra*).

Many of the Italian horror films make up for what they lack script-wise and acting-wise with rich color, lighting effects and striking decor.

Then it all comes down to who directs it. I felt that Bava was always in good taste.

Any general comments about the amount of globetrotting you've done?

Well, it's one way to see the world! I feel like Willy Loman, because I'm always packing my suitcases *[laughs]* — I don't think anybody's traveled more than I have. And I don't think anybody's made as many films as I have; I must have made close to three hundred.

You're adding in TV.

I'm talking strictly about *features*. I've never counted them, but I think I've done a thousand TV shows! Maybe this is awful to say, because I should have been more selective.

In what countries have you had the best filmmaking experiences?

I would say Italy; parts of Africa; Mexico I enjoyed. I had some pretty bad experiences in Yugoslavia; some terrible ones in the Philippines, because it's so hot over there you almost can't work.

Do you speak the languages in all these countries?

Yes, I did—I *had* to, in some of these films. I didn't know the tenses or grammar, but I could make myself understood. Many directors I worked with, including Bava, didn't know English at all. And so for other American actors, I could translate for them, too. I speak pretty good Italian, German and Spanish. You pick up that stuff—you *have* to.

Horror-wise, you next turned up in Island of the Doomed.

Island of the Doomed has made a lot of money for that producer, Jorje Ferrer. We shot it in a big estate near Barcelona; it was a dreadful film, but it's made a lot of bucks. Every time the producer needs money, he leases it to a cable company, and it's kept him going! I enjoyed playing the villainous Baron, although I didn't think the dubbing was very good.

What else can you recall about where the film was shot?

It was a very expensive house; the producers paid the people who owned the place five thousand dollars, which then was a lot of pesetas—and, believe me, the owners were sorry, because the crew did a great deal of damage. The crew laid dolly tracks and stuff like that; they cleaned the house before they left, but they didn't fix what they broke.

Did you enjoy working on the film?

Yes and no. It was a German/Italian/Spanish coproduction, and I enjoyed being in Spain. I saw a bit of Ava Gardner while there.

Around that same time you made Autopsia de un Fantasma *in Mexico.*

Right, with Basil Rathbone and John Carradine. Basil Rathbone in his mind was Don Quixote, and if you think about it—he was about seventy then—he *was* a perfect Don Quixote. That face, that aquiline nose! It's a damn shame that nobody ever did the real *Don Quixote* with Basil Rathbone, he was a brilliant actor. He was very neat, very well educated, read many books—and he was a great fencer, really one of the world's best. In *The Mark of Zorro* [1940], they had one of the greatest fencers in the world doubling Tyrone Power, but Rathbone did his swordwork himself, he was that good. The fencing scenes in *The Mark of Zorro,* because of Basil, were the best I've ever seen. And he was really one of the nicest men I ever met.

Did Rathbone seem unhappy to be in Autopsia de un Fantasma?

Not at all. We enjoyed it, and we had a good time in Mexico City—this was before the smog came, when it was still lovely. I don't think either Rathbone or Carradine spoke Spanish, or, if they did, just *poco [laughs]*—a *little.* And the director was an interesting man, Ismael Rodriquez—a bit crazy, a real wacky sense of humor. *Autopsia de un Fantasma* was a comedy which really did not come off, but it had its moments.

Mitchell says that his suggested script changes helped to turn the trick in the shock schlocker *Nightmare in Wax.*

You've worked in a few films that featured John Carradine. What were your impressions of him?

I liked John, he was a good old ham. I like ham if it's good, like Charles Laughton, one of the finest, a marvelous actor. Carradine was a fun person to work with, but he had a terrible arthritic condition in his knuckles and his feet—his toes curled up under the soles of his feet! He was playing the Devil in *Autopsia de un Fantasma,* and he tried to be light and limber. And of course it came across very funny—he was a very old, limping Devil *[laughs]*! Which really added to the humor, which Carradine was not even aware of!

Do you recall how you got involved on Nightmare in Wax?

I'm sure somebody just called me and asked me. [Director] Bud Townsend and I had worked together on a TV series called *The Beachcomber*—he directed about twenty-eight of 'em. They were having trouble with the script on *Nightmare in Wax,* and I told Bud, "Don't worry, we can fix anything"— we had fixed many terrible scripts on *The Beachcomber.* So on the first day of shooting I went to the Movieland Wax Museum in Buena Park, which is where the film was going to be made, I read the script for the first time and Bud said, "Well, Cam, you missed this time. There's no way we can save this." In the original script, my character skins the people—but if you skin people, there's a lot of blood, right? Well, it was impossible — you wouldn't have seen anything but blood, and I don't think anybody would allow us to do a film where we skinned like twenty people! It was way overboard in bad taste.

Then I said, "Well, gimme a few minutes. Let me think about it." So it was my idea to make a dream sequence out of it: The film opens with a phone call and ends with a phone call, and it was all a dream. That saved the picture, because it could not have been made the way it was written. I also created the scenes with the red-headed girl [Victoria Carroll] in the wax museum, where we're talking; the scene in the car, after I've killed her and I'm talking to her corpse. Those scenes I thought were interesting. We had all these ideas and we could have done more with the picture, but we just didn't have time. When you consider that we did that from scratch, it was a hell of a film.

Any problems entailed in shooting at a real wax museum?

No, it was really quite a thrill, especially because they had the Rolls-Royce there from *Sunset Boulevard* [1950], a picture I love, one of the greatest films ever made. What I thought was clever in *Nightmare in Wax* was when I was putting the finishing touches on these wax dummies, we were actually using the real people — they had to stay perfectly still. And they came out beautiful, especially some of the girls — they looked like works of art. Berry Kroeger was in it, he was a good actor; Anne Helm was a good actress, and she was very big then; Scott Brady played a detective; we had a pretty good cast. And, as I said, I also liked working with Bud Townsend. That was the first film that he did, and he was a very intelligent and fast director and he should have been one of the great ones in the business. He was damn good, and I loved Bud.

In nineteen seventy-seven, you did a very muddled suspense film called Haunts, *with May Britt.*

That was a strange film — I didn't understand a lot of it, and I don't know what [director] Herb Freed was trying to do. But they cut the end of it. At the end of the film now, the uncle, the part that I play, goes to the sink and turns the faucet and blood comes out. Then he hears the shower running, he walks over to it and parts the curtains, and there May Britt is, nude, and they embrace. The embrace was cut — taken out of the film — and I don't know why. It should have been left in — that would have shown that he was as crazy as she was, that madness ran in the family. It was an interesting film.

What can you tell me about May Britt?

She was wonderful, and lovely to look at. For the nude scene she covered her nipples — she looked naked, but there was tape on the nipples. We shot *Haunts* in some very lovely country above San Francisco, where no one is allowed to make any improvements — you have cattle grazing on farms by the sea up there. It was a great location.

Do you remember appearing in The Swarm *for Irwin Allen?*

Irwin Allen you can have *[laughs]*! I did a lot of work for Irwin, but I thought *The Swarm* was dreadful. It cost a lot of money, but the bees—it looked like there were two hundred and that's all! They had this all-star cast and a geriatric love story between Olivia de Havilland and Fred MacMurray, which didn't make much sense. And I remember Irwin Allen wanted me to cut my hair, to get a military haircut, and I said, "Okay, Irwin, for sixty thousand dollars, I'll cut it." So naturally I didn't cut my hair *[laughs]*!

Many horror fans probably remember you best for The Toolbox Murders.

Boy, did *that* make money! The producer, Tony Didio, he's now a big Hollywood producer. I have been in so many horrible little films that have "made" people! He now smokes ten dollar Cuban cigars, he goes to the Cannes Festival every year, and he made his fortune off that picture!

Did you actually play the killer in the murder scenes?

Yes, I did. In the scene where I chase the nude girl, we used a gal who was a porno star [Kelly Nichols]. I shot her in the head with a nail gun.

Does the type of gore seen in pictures like this influence young viewers?

I'm sure it does. I don't like gore pictures, I won't see them. I *make* 'em, but I don't have to *look* at 'em!

Was it a challenge playing this type of murderer?

I think I did enjoy the challenge. The scene where I sing to the girl I'm holding prisoner was my idea; I thought that actress was quite good, Pamelyn Ferdin. The lollipop I carry around, anything weird like that was my idea! A lot of the odd touches that were any good were mine *[laughs]*! The human touches—'cause even a killer is human, you know.

What about the sequel that we've been threatened with for years?

It's supposed to be done—I read that in the papers all the time.

What do you think of horror film fans?

Horror fans are interesting people. They love these kinds of things! I don't know how I got hooked up with this horror thing, 'cause I never thought of myself as a horror actor, but I am. I mean, once Vincent Price is dead, nobody's done more than I have!

You played a comic book–style mad scientist in the campy Supersonic Man.

I liked the director and the producer of that film, and I had a wonderful time doing it in Madrid. The dubbing was dreadful, and it was badly sold—it was a takeoff on *Superman* [1978], and it didn't quite come off. But the people involved on that were nice people.

What about The Silent Scream*?*

The Silent Scream made a lot of money; they tell me it's done over sixty million dollars. It had to have something going for it to do that kind of business; I thought Denny Harris, the director, was a creative guy. I remember them shooting the opening scene in slow motion, and thinking it wasn't much of an idea until I saw it. They did a hell of a job there and really set a mood for the picture.

Without Warning*?*

I don't remember much about that, except that I did have to wear some gross makeup. One film that I did around that same time was *The Demon,* and that I thought was a pretty good film; we shot that in Africa. *The Demon* had a kind of an E.S.P. angle to it, and I played an army colonel who's called in on a case. It was an interesting film, not all bad.

Raw Force, *about kung fu zombies?*

We shot that in Manila. It's so humid there because you're almost on the equator. You can go out to some of the outer islands and get a breeze, but most of the things I did were in Manila, and you couldn't really act. The only place where you were *halfway* comfortable was in your air-conditioned hotel room, because even in cars, even though they had air conditioning, you just perspired. I don't want to have to go back *there* again!

Cataclysm*?*

I went up to Salt Lake City, Utah, to work in that; Phil Yordan wrote and directed. Many years earlier he wrote the screenplay for a picture I was in called *No Down Payment* [1957]; if *No Down Payment* had been sold properly, I might have been close to getting an Oscar nomination. *Cataclysm* had to be done and redone four or five times, I don't know why, and I haven't seen it. Marc Lawrence was in that, too, playing two parts—I have no idea why they did that, but I thought he was very good. I think *Cataclysm* might have had some interesting things in it.

Do you still try to pitch in creatively on any of these horror things?

Oh, always. Some of the scenes are terrible! Years ago I helped out on a very good film called *Ride in the Whirlwind* [1965] with Jack Nicholson and Millie Perkins; I got top billing in that, and some people said it was the best Western ever made. They made it for like seventy thousand dollars and they shot it in Utah, and they lived on nothing. I got quite a bit of money out of 'em for the money they had, 'cause I didn't know how much of a skin-and-bones operation it was. It was written and produced by Jack and he was very good as an actor, and he was getting ready to *quit*! I really saved his skin: I said, "Jack, you *can't* quit, you're too good." I told him, "Beg, borrow or steal the money, but take this to a festival in Europe." He did, and it ran for thirteen months in the Champs Elysées in Paris! That's how he wound up in *Easy Rider* [1969]; instead of getting out of the business, he became one of the biggest stars. He owes a lot of that to me, I really helped him.

Are directors open to suggestions on these newer, schlockier pictures?
Some of them are, some of them aren't. The intelligent ones are.

Screamers*?* Frankenstein Island*?*
Don't remember 'em.

Blood Link, *with Michael Moriarty?*
I remember doing that in Berlin, and I'd never been there; I'd been to Germany, but never Berlin. And I loved Berlin, it was wonderful. I enjoyed doing the picture but I don't know what happened to it and I never saw it. The director, Alberto De Martino, was pleasant and the producer, Italo Zingarelli, was the Commissioner of Wines and Spirits for Italy. And he is as big as Orson Welles *[laughs]*!

One of your best supporting parts in recent years was as the gang boss in My Favorite Year *[1982].*
I'll tell you how that happened: I was having lunch one day with an Egyptian director in the MGM commissary, and Mel Brooks came by. "My God!" he said. "The star of my favorite picture!" I asked, "Mel, what's your favorite picture?" and he said, "*Gorilla at Large*!" At first I laughed, and then I understood because Anne Bancroft [Mrs. Brooks] was in that, and she is very good and very sexy in the film. Then he said, "Listen, how would you like to play Jimmy Hoffa in a movie?" and I said, "I would love to." [Director] Richard Benjamin did a helluva job on *My Favorite Year*, and as I did my scene I was not aware of the grunts and animal noises I was making — it was just the way it happened. I thought it was a great picture and that Peter O'Toole deserved the Award that year.

You've worked with Fred Olen Ray a time or two, most prominently in The Tomb. *Is he a good director?*
Well, he's a nice guy *[laughs]*! And for the amount of money he puts into these pictures, I guess he does all right.

You had another sadistic role in an anthology horror film called The Offspring.
I enjoyed making that because the Civil War is one of my favorite topics. We couldn't do the story of Sherman's March but we did the next best thing, a sergeant as wicked as Sherman, and I played that part in the film. Do you

A carnival background and a rampaging ape (George Barrows) added to the flavor of Fox's 3-D *Gorilla at Large* (1954) with Mitchell and Anne Bancroft.

remember the house that the maimed children lived in? In actuality, Sherman spent several nights in that house. We shot it there in Georgia, and I thought my segment of the story was good. And the kids, I thought, were wonderful.

Is it fun to work with today's aggressive, hurry-up young directors, or just hard work?

It depends. Sometimes it's fun and sometimes you die gettin' up at 4:30.

Deadly Prey? Teenage Exorcist?
[Laughs.] Don't remember either of 'em!

Have you ever turned down a role?
I turn down a lot of things. In the last week alone, I must have turned down six offers — not that any of them were great things *[laughs]*! But I've just signed with a new agency, Contemporary Artists, I have a good agent and I'm very happy with him.

Do you think you'll ever retire from the business?
I can't really answer that . . . I don't think I could ever retire. If the right vehicle came along, I think the vinegar would work and the fire would still burn. But it doesn't burn for mediocre films anymore — I would like to do something good. And I think I will always like to do something good. But it's very difficult today to find a good script, to find a good director, and to find the kind of production we had years ago.

One of your newest flicks is Space Mutiny *with John Phillip Law.*
I had to wear a beard longer than Moses and it was awful. I couldn't eat, I couldn't smoke, I couldn't do anything *[laughs]*! I haven't seen the film.

What hopes do you have for your acting future?
I did a play at the Burt Reynolds Theater in Florida several years ago, *Family Planning,* written by Bill C. Davis, who I think is the finest young playwright in America. The play was about an old caretaker in a very poor old folks' home — it's a great part for me — and the play is about the fact that we don't know what to do about senior citizens. But it isn't all sad, it also has a lot of laughs and it's just the way life is. It's the only play I've ever done where, every performance, we got a standing ovation. Because it is a terrible thing, the way we treat seniors, and I feel that this play that Bill wrote could make a statement about that. This could be Academy Award time for me if we were to do this as a feature, and that is what we are trying to do. It's really very touching and funny.

Even though you're now in this low-budget rut, you've got a lot to be proud of overall.
It was my honor to be the first actor to read aloud the words of supposedly the greatest play in the history of the American theater, *Death of a Salesman.* I read it for Elia Kazan and Arthur Miller at the Taft Hotel, which was next to the Shubert Theater, in nineteen forty-eight. Kazan was directing a Kurt Weill musical, and between the matinee and evening performance we met in his room, we ordered dinner, they threw the script in front of me and Kazan said, "Read." I said, "The whole script?" and he said, "Yep." So I read the whole

play, beginning to end, including all the characters. And they sat there with smiles on their faces, and not one word was changed. It was my privilege and honor, and luck I guess, to have been the first actor to read those wonderful words aloud. And I'm unique in another way: I did *The Taming of the Shrew* with Alfred Lunt and Lynn Fontanne, and that's considered the greatest comedy ever made. Sydney Greenstreet was in it, Celeste Holm, Richard Whorf, Thomas Gomez — a bunch of good people. So it was unique that I did the best tragedy and the best comedy.

Do you feel you've lived up to your early promise as an actor?

Sometimes yes. I came to Hollywood when Brando came out, and Montgomery Clift, and I was considered the third good Broadway actor from *Death of a Salesman,* and I feel that if I had been more selective my career might have fared better. I had a great, low-key part in a Kazan picture called *Man on a Tightrope* [1953], and the picture he did after that was *On the Waterfront* [1954]. And I was supposedly the number one choice for the lead and Brando was number two. But Kazan had a fight with Darryl Zanuck — I was under contract to Zanuck — and they didn't talk for like five years, so I lost *On the Waterfront.* So I've come close to some big things. But on the other hand, the way things have turned out, I did get a chance to experiment, and as an actor, a pure actor, I could do and try many things which you couldn't do in a major film. I have been lucky in many ways.

CAMERON MITCHELL FILMOGRAPHY

The Last Installment (MGM short, 1945)
The Hidden Eye (MGM, 1945)
A Letter for Evie (MGM, 1945)
They Were Expendable (MGM, 1945)
What Next, Corporal Hargrove? (MGM, 1945)
The Mighty McGurk (MGM, 1946)
High Barbaree (MGM, 1947)
Cass Timberlane (MGM, 1947)
Tenth Avenue Angel (MGM, 1948)
Homecoming (MGM, 1948)
Command Decision (MGM, 1948)
Leather Gloves (Loser Takes All) (Columbia, 1948)
Adventures of Gallant Bess (Eagle-Lion, 1948)
The Sellout (MGM, 1951)
Smuggler's Gold (Columbia, 1951)
Death of a Salesman (Columbia, 1951)
Man in the Saddle (Columbia, 1951)
Flight to Mars (Monogram, 1951)
Japanese War Bride (20th Century–Fox, 1952)
The Outcasts of Poker Flat (20th Century–Fox, 1952)

Okinawa (Columbia, 1952)
Les Miserables (20th Century–Fox, 1952)
Pony Soldier (20th Century–Fox, 1952)
The Robe (voice only; 20th Century–Fox, 1953)
Powder River (20th Century–Fox, 1953)
Man on a Tightrope (20th Century–Fox, 1953)
How to Marry a Millionaire (20th Century–Fox, 1953)
Hell and High Water (20th Century–Fox, 1954)
Gorilla at Large (20th Century–Fox, 1954)
Garden of Evil (20th Century–Fox, 1954)
Desiree (20th Century–Fox, 1954)
Strange Lady in Town (Warners, 1955)
Love Me or Leave Me (MGM, 1955)
House of Bamboo (20th Century–Fox, 1955)
The Tall Men (20th Century–Fox, 1955)
The View from Pompey's Head (20th Century–Fox, 1955)
Carousel (20th Century–Fox, 1956)
Tension at Table Rock (RKO, 1956)
Monkey on My Back (United Artists, 1957)
All Mine to Give (RKO/Universal, 1957)
Escapade in Japan (Universal, 1957)
No Down Payment (20th Century–Fox, 1957)
Face of Fire (Allied Artists, 1959)
Inside the Mafia (United Artists, 1959)
Pier 5 — Havana (United Artists, 1959)
Three Came to Kill (United Artists, 1960)
As the Sea Rages (Raubfischer in Hellas) (Columbia, 1960)
The Unstoppable Man (Sutton Pictures, 1961)
Last of the Vikings (L'Ultimo dei Vichingi) (Medallion Pictures, 1961)
Dulcinea (Nivi Films, 1962)
The Black Duke (Il Duca Nero) (Production Releasing Corp./Eldorado Pictures, 1963)
Caesar the Conqueror (Giulio Cesare il Conquistatore delle Gallie) (Medallion Pictures, 1963)
Erik the Conqueror (Fury of the Vikings) (AIP, 1963)
Dog Eat Dog (Ajay Film Co., 1964)
The Last Gun (Jim Il Primo) (British Lion/Spanish, 1964)
Blood and Black Lace (Sei Donne per l'Assassino) (Allied Artists, 1965)
Ride in the Whirlwind (Favorite Films, 1965)
Minnesota Clay (Harlequin, 1966)
Hombre (20th Century–Fox, 1967)
The Treasure of Makuba (Producers Releasing Organization, 1967)
Autopsia de un Fantasma (Rodriquez/Peliculas Nacionales, 1967)
Knives of the Avenger (I Coltelli del Vendicatore) (World Entertainment Corp., 1967)
Island of the Doomed (Maneater of Hydra) (Allied Artists, 1967)
Nightmare in Wax (Crown International, 1969)
Rebel Rousers (Four Star Excelsior, 1970)
Buck and the Preacher (Columbia, 1972)
The Big Game (Comet, 1972)
Slaughter (AIP, 1972)
The Midnight Man (Universal, 1974)
The Klansman (Paramount, 1974)

Political Asylum (Panamericana Films/IF, 1975)
Haunts (The Veil) (Intercontinental, 1977)
Viva Knievel! (Seconds to Live) (Warners, 1977)
Slavers (Lord Films/ITM, 1977)
The Swarm (Warners, 1978)
The Toolbox Murders (Cal-Am, 1978)
Texas Detour (Cinema Shares International, 1978)
Supersonic Man (Topar, 1979)
The Silent Scream (American Cinema Releasing, 1980)
Without Warning (The Warning) (Filmways, 1980)
Cataclysm (1980)
Captive (1980)
The Demon (Gold Key–Holland, 1981)
Texas Lightning (Film Ventures International, 1981)
Screamers (New World, 1981)
Raw Force (Shogun Island) (American Panorama, 1982)
My Favorite Year (MGM/United Artists, 1982)
Frankenstein Island (Chriswar, 1982)
Kill Squad (Summa Vista, 1982)
Blood Link (Zadar Films, 1982)
The Guns and the Fury (A&Z/Bordeaux, 1983)
Killpoint (Crown International, 1984)
Prince Jack (LMF Productions, 1985)
The Tomb (Trans World Entertainment, 1985)
Low Blow (Crown International, 1986)
The Offspring (From a Whisper to a Scream) (Conquest Entertainment, 1987)
The Messenger (Snizzlefritz, 1987)
No Justice (Richfield's Releasing, 1989)

Night Train to Terror (Visto International, 1985), a horror anthology, features Mitchell in a much-abridged version of *Cataclysm*. Mitchell also appears frequently in made-for-home video movies like *Swift Justice, Ninja Nightmare, Memorial Valley Massacre* (1989) and *Easy Kill* (1990) as well as made-for-TV movies. This list represents only a starting point for future compilers of his extremely convoluted (and confusing) filmography.

*I was always looking to sustain myself [in the business]
for a long period of time rather than ever being
a "star," so to speak, or going for "The Big Time."
That was never very important to me ... I have six children
and eleven grandchildren, a very happy marriage—it's been
that way for forty years. And that kind of solidification
was more important to me than being an unhappy star.*

Ed Nelson

A REALISTIC ACTOR JOINING THE ROGER CORMAN stock company during the maverick director's 1950s heyday came on the scene knowing that short pay and long hours were two of the few certainties attached to the job. In store for Ed Nelson was one of the widest assortments of roles enjoyed by any of the Corman regulars, from scientist to caveman, from gang leader to attorney, and from cops and robbers (sometimes in the same picture) to the giant fiberglass crustacean in *Attack of the Crab Monsters*. Behind-the-scenes, too, Hollywood newcomer Nelson tried his hand at many trades, working without credit (and sometimes without pay!) as a screenwriter, stuntman, location manager, wardrobe and prop man, alligator wrestler, cameraman and even producer (on Corman's *The Brain Eaters*).

Happily, it all paid off for Nelson, who went on to become one of television's most recognizable faces (1500 + performances, including five years on TV's hottest nighttime soap opera, *Peyton Place*). Backstage at the Catskill Actors Theatre in Highland Lake, New York, where he's appearing with Beverly Garland in a stage production of *The Gin Game*, Nelson is more than happy to talk about the days before his TV successes, when he paid his dues in movies like *A Bucket of Blood*, *Devil's Partner* and *Night of the Blood Beast*.

When was your first encounter with Roger Corman?

I met him when he came to Louisiana to do *Swamp Women* [1956]. At that point, I didn't know he was just starting out in the business; all *I* knew was, when everybody wanted to go to town 'cause it was Saturday, I would volunteer to stay in the jungle and watch the equipment. Roger was very grateful, and he helped me out a great deal in those early days. He's every bit as cheap as everybody says he is—that's what he calls "frugal." They tell a story about Roger, who I love dearly, that he made two or three pictures before he found out you could go "Take Two" *[laughs]*! I did a lot of work for him, for free, so that I could get parts in his pictures. Just like Jack Haze and Dick Miller and all the rest of 'em. He used us and we used him. But it was no more than that—it hardly ever got personal.

A lot of people have that attitude about Corman; people like Richard Devon just couldn't stand him after a while.

Well, Richard was brighter than a lot of us *[laughs]*, and I could understand that from him—Richard is theater and he's a noble person. I don't have time, really, to dislike Roger, I have no reason to. He was very kind to me. Yeah, he used me, but so what? I mean, I used him, too, if you want to use the term *used*. But I didn't know of a single person that worked with Roger and really was personal with him. I didn't know who went home with him and sat up and played cards—you know what I'm saying? Nobody, as far as I knew.

Previous page: **Before his days of TV prime-time success on** *Peyton Place,* **actor Ed Nelson had a baptism of fire in Roger Corman's notorious exploitation movies.**

So what exactly did you do for Corman on Swamp Women*?*

I did everything on that picture: I was the location manager, I wrestled the alligator, I held it up in the water so that Touch Connors—Mike—could wrestle it. The guy that brought that alligator out ran an alligator farm/snake farm on Highway 90, outside of New Orleans; now he is one of the wealthiest men in America, and lives in a compound with high walls outside of Atlanta. Very paranoid—he has guards with guns and carries guns and knives on him. A very short guy with a lot of muscles—and he invented Nautilus.

Two of your first films—Swamp Women *and* New Orleans Uncensored—*starred Beverly Garland.*

Beverly Garland was one of the first "stars," so to speak, that I ever worked with, and she has been consistent from that day to this. An underrated actress; even though people know who she is, people don't really know the work she can do. We've been very good friends over a period of time and I think the world of her.

Your very first film was The Steel Trap *[1952], wasn't it?*

That's right, I was an extra in that. *The Steel Trap* had a great director-and-producer husband-and-wife team, Andrew and Virginia Stone, and that was the first picture I was ever in. They were shooting at the old New Orleans airport and were using extras like crazy. Joseph Cotten and Teresa Wright were going to run up to the ticket counter, past a line of people, because they had to get on that plane—he had robbed his own bank and now she has convinced him to return the money, and he has to get the money back in. And it's turning out to be harder to get the money back in than it was stealing it in the first place *[laughs]*! I was the last one in the ticket line, and just before the first rehearsal the director Andrew Stone looked down the line and said, "You!" Everybody turned their heads looking back, back, back—I didn't know I was last, *I* looked back, too! I pointed to myself and said, "Me??" He said, "Yeah, come up here." So I came up, in front of my fellow New Orleans actors. Stone said, "You get in the front here." And here I am at the front of the line, at the ticket counter, and Joseph Cotten is gonna come up and stand next to *me*! And Teresa Wright! My God!!

So they rehearsed once—"Cue Joe and Teresa. Come on!" They come running in and the camera pans with them up to the counter and Joe goes into his dialogue. "Okay, good rehearsal," Stone says. Then he looks at me and he says, "You. What are you doing?" I say, "I beg your pardon?" He says, "What are you doing?" I say, "Well, I'm doing the same thing I thought I was doing at the back of the line." He says, "You're in the front of the line now!" When you see that picture, you'll be amazed, because I do the biggest non-acting job—I close my eyes real slow and open 'em real slow, almost do a half-yawn and I don't pay any attention to these people who come runnin' up screaming! It's absolutely embarrassing. Stone said to me, "Listen, I'm gonna give you some advice. Don't act." That was my first picture.

After you did Swamp Women, *how did you hook up again with Corman in Hollywood?*
    I went to see him right away, because he and the crew were very good to me. I mean, I did a lot of work for 'em down there in New Orleans for very little, and I guess they thought I could make it. So I came out and I knocked on his door. He knew I had had training in production, so I gathered his wardrobe, I got his props together, I'd help rewrite the scripts—

So you worked on a lot of Corman pictures that you didn't act in.
    Well, sure!

Where did you learn production?
    In nineteen fifty-two, I went to New York to study direction and production. There was a school there called S.R.T. — School of Radio Technique — and it was live medium. You worked camera, direction, you worked switching, you worked the boom, everything. And I learned all about the production side of television there. It was a very good school. At the end of the six months, they put on a one-hour program and they invited all the network people in to watch it.

In nineteen fifty-three you were back in New Orleans working as an assistant director at WDSU-TV.
    WDSU was the only station in New Orleans at the time, it was the NBC flagship of the South and I was the floor manager there. One of the guys working out there, doing a fifteen-minute sustained show, was Dick Van Dyke.

Then between nineteen fifty-four and nineteen fifty-six you narrated a show called N.O.P.D.
    N.O.P.D. was a series that a buddy of Jack Webb's, Stacy Harris, starred in. It was shot in New Orleans and it was shot with a group that used to do the trailers for motion pictures — Motion Picture Advertising was the name of the production company. I wrote some of those because the guy that wrote 'em was drunk half the time and he couldn't come up with 'em, so he hired me for one hundred dollars a script. Because I narrated that series, I knew I couldn't act in it also, so I wrote one where the heavy didn't have any lines — but you saw him throughout the episode. So I played in that one. (And I had acted in a couple of other ones before they decided I was going to narrate it.)

You arrived in Hollywood with one hundred five dollars in your pocket.
    Well, it was in my *wife's* pocket *[laughs]*. We had three kids at the time,

Stardom at last: Somewhere underneath all that heavy fiberglass, Ed Nelson is playing the title role in *Attack of the Crab Monsters.*

and I got a job — I never felt that I couldn't get a job, earn enough to support my family.

What did playing the crab in Attack of the Crab Monsters *entail?*

Weight, mostly. The crab was made by Dice, Inc., and it was a heavy piece. What they did was, they had piano wires on the end of every elbow of the crab, and on a long stick way up in the air they had these wires connected. And people out of the frame would be holding these sticks. They would alternate picking them up and lowering them, so the legs would move. That worked fine. Inside the crab was a hole no bigger than maybe four feet, and I would get in there. They would put pads on my shoulders and I would bend over and pick up the body of the crab and walk along, in a squat. In my hands I held two wires which worked the eyelids, and I could pull on those and the eyes would open and close. So I had that double job. Roger would set the camera up so that there would be rocks in front of the lens, down low, so that you wouldn't see my feet. And it worked pretty good.

Most of the time.

Yeah, there *is* one place where you see my feet, and I'll tell you where it is. The girl scientist, Pamela Duncan (the first plastics I ever saw in my life, incidentally, Pamela Duncan wore) — she is in a scientific lab, and she shows one of the professors stills of the Crab Monster that she has taken and she notices that the crab is pregnant. You cut to one insert of the photographs of the crab, and in that insert you can see my feet hangin' out the bottom. I saw it on the big screen in downtown L.A., and I said *[loudly]*, "There're my feet!"—people were lookin' at me *[laughs]*—!

What was the crab made of?
    It was fiberglass, and I would say it weighed like a hundred forty pounds, something like that.

You also played the ensign who brings the scientific team to the island.
    And that's one example I always give of one of the most impossible lines I ever had to say in my life. We were shooting a scene on the beach at Malibu where one of my men was killed falling out of a motorboat. And Roger had me yell to the other guys in the boat, over the surf, with emotion (because the dead guy was supposedly a friend of mine), "Bury him!" I mean, the boat was sixty feet away and the surf was pounding, and Roger wanted me to holler, "Bury him!" with emotion! How the hell *[laughs]*...! Chuck Griffith played the guy who fell out of the boat; he also wrote the picture.
    Another one where I played two parts was *She Gods of Shark Reef* [1958]. I swam across San Pedro Harbor and climbed up a dock or something, doubling for one of the stars. Then I played a guard and got into a fight with the guy I just doubled for!

Would you go out and see these movies after they were made?
    I've seen some of them; I think I might have seen all of them. I wouldn't go see 'em today, I don't think *[laughs]*.

You had minor roles in several non–SF Corman pictures, like Rock All Night *[1957].*
    Did you know that in that movie Russell Johnson really shot me with a wad—a blank? We'd already done it two or three takes, I ran by Russell and he turned, *pow,* and shot me, without aiming off to the side which is what you're supposed to do. The wadding went through my sports coat, through my shirt, and into my back. I may still have the scar, on the left side of my back. I went to the hospital and they took the wadding out. And, you know what?, they didn't use the take where I really got shot, they used the one where I pretended.
    There's another scene in there where Roger had Mel Welles beating breadsticks on the counter to the music—which he didn't have. Later on, Roger put the music in and the breadsticks don't go to the music! Talk about lookin' like an ass *[laughs]*!

Teenage Doll *[1957]?*

I put rubber hoses up into my nostrils to play that blind man, so people wouldn't recognize me, 'cause I play a cop in that, too.

How about Carnival Rock *[1957]?*

They brought a New York actor in for that, an older man [David J. Stewart]. He looked at me on the set one day, on the side, sitting in his chair with his name on it, and he said, "My God, what I couldn't do with a face like that..." I had some plans for it myself! He thought I was gonna waste it, you know what I mean? — that was the connotation *I* got out of it! I felt like saying, "Well, what're you doin' with yours?"

Dick Miller hated him.

This guy was easy to dislike. Dick's still around and working — I like ol' Dick, he was very nice to me the last time we were together. He's married to a swell gal.

I, Mobster *[1958]?*

I, Mobster I remember because Stosh was in that from *Stalag 17* [1953] — Robert Strauss. I had done the play in earlier years, and so I was anxious to meet him and all. And in that picture I invented — or I thought I did — a bit where, in taking my hat off, I hold it for just a moment in front of his face and I sucker-punch him, *boom.* And it worked out really great. It's nice to invent little bits of business like that.

You were back to science fiction with Teenage Caveman.

We had a tough time in that. I was like Number Two Bad Caveman. The Number One Bad Caveman was a great heavy, had a pockmarked face — Frank deKova. When we were running, Roger had us bunched up so tight together that we had to carry our spears straight up and down. Well, Frank wouldn't do it. He kept carrying his spear [horizontally]. I was the second guy and, Jesus, he was almost gouging me with the thing *[laughs]*! So Roger says, "Frank, will you carry the spear straight up and down?" Frank grumbles and curses under his breath, we try it again and he carries it down again. Roger's yelling, "Nelson! Keep in close! Keep in close!" I holler back, "I can't keep in close, the guy's gonna *get* me!" All I had on was a sheepskin! So I go to Frank, "What the hell's the matter with you?" And Frank grumbled, "Well, no Number One Bad Caveman carries his spear up in the air like that..." I told him, "He'd carry it up in the air if the director *told* him to carry it up in the air!" Jesus!

Was that just the way deKova was?

No, it's just that he was upset, or because Roger had him runnin' through the bushes with Mexican sandals on, made out of rubber tires—he was just angry at that moment, that's all.

Did Robert Vaughn seem to be enjoying himself?

No, not really. He's not the type of actor that enjoys himself anyway. Bobby's not a happy person; he always plays the erudite, sophisticated prick, and he was a little bit like that in real life!

Later on in *Teenage Caveman,* there's the scene with the dogs—it was incredible. A guy comes out in a truck with a bunch of dogs in the back— Roger got this guy, who was a "dog wrangler" *of sorts*. I think the guy went down to the pound *[laughs]*, 'cause he had mastiffs, he had Doberman pinschers, Russian wolf hounds—! So this guy is out there throwing meat to the dogs out of a leather bag, and he says, "Who's fightin' the dogs?" Somebody says, "The fellow over there, Nelson." The wrangler says *[growling]*, "Tiger, get over here! Fang, come here! Killer, let's go!" I thought to myself, "Jesus Christ—Tiger, Fang and Killer!" Besides three other ones! So he says to me, "Look, watch out for Missy here, 'cause she's the one, she'll go right for the throat." I said, "Well, uh, hey, I don't have any padding on—"

He interrupts me, "You're not carrying that spear, are you? I wouldn't let 'em see ya with the spear. The dogs see ya with the spear, they're gonna become very aggressive." I said, "Well, it doesn't stand to reason, here come the dogs and I throw the spear away!" The wrangler goes, "Yeah, well, I'm just tellin' ya fer yer own protection, you figger out the rest." *[Laughs.]*

This is a true story, as God is my witness! I said, "Roger, look, before I hear the dogs I get tired or somethin' and I lay the spear down. Or something like that. I can't throw the spear away!" I mean, it's tough enough I had to fight these dogs! Roger said okay, okay. And, you know Roger, we gotta get it on the first take—we were losin' the light, or he only had the dogs for ten minutes, or some damn thing. So I put the spear down, I hear the dogs coming, I brace myself and I go, AAAARRRRGGGGHHHH!, like that. The dogs stop—stare at me—and they *take off*! They take off in the opposite direction, and they run away from the guy! He never caught all of 'em, he caught like four or five of 'em.

And then you had to do it over again.

Yeah! And the wrangler's complaining, "He scared my dogs!" I said, "Scare your *dogs*??" What the hell, *I* was scared, too! Roger called over Jonathan Haze and Dick Miller and all those guys, and he said, "Grab a dog! Everybody grab a dog!" They grabbed the dogs and Roger got a waist-shot of me and they threw the dogs into the frame, onto me. The dogs now are so frightened they're pushing against my body to get away from me, and I'm havin' to hold onto them and force one of 'em's mouth open and stick my arm in it! Now, if you watch that movie, you'll see that those dogs are afraid I'm gonna choke 'em to death with my arm. It's one of the funniest things that ever happened to me, and that was *Teenage Caveman*.

Susan Cabot's gripe with Corman was that he had no regard for actors' safety.
     You had to watch out for yourself, but you generally have to do that anyway — not as much today as in those days. He didn't want to hurt anybody, but if anyone got hurt, they could recover — he wasn't gonna *kill* anybody. He didn't have a great deal of knowledge in those days about safety; I'm sure he's much more aware of it today than he was then. I mean, he didn't have much knowledge of *any*thing in those days — what he had was a great deal of courage [to become a moviemaker]. And he had connections who would release his stuff.

Did you have any contact during those years with Jim Nicholson and Sam Arkoff?
     No, not much, other than I worked for them on several other pictures over the years. Nicholson was a very thin man, and Arkoff of course quite the opposite! Sam I saw quite often later on because he liked to go to Mardi Gras, and being from New Orleans I was there most of the time, too. We used to have some chats about the old days.

Any memories at all of Invasion of the Saucer Men?
     [Laughs.] Just that Frank Gorshin and I got along great, and struck up a friendship that lasted many years.

Your acting career wasn't enough to support a family for a while.
     Oh, no, I did the other things. But we lived way out of the city, and I think that was very smart, too — inadvertently! We lived out in Pomona because it really was less expensive, and that was a long way out in those days. Consequently, the kids weren't into the "Hollywood thing" — they just went off to school like everybody else, and it worked very good. And I could get jobs out there. I met a wonderful guy who had a cab company there, he knew I was an actor and I could take the cab whenever I wanted and if I had to take off to make a movie, fine. That worked out great. Then every year at the Fair Grounds we had the largest county fair in the world, and I'd sell beer and ice cream in the grandstands at the races. And jobs like that. But mostly drove the cab in Pomona, to make ends meet.

You also worked with Jack Nicholson during this early period, in a picture called The Cry Baby Killer *[1958].*
     In it, Jack played a guy who held a pretty girl hostage in the back of a restaurant, in a storage room, and I was a TV news reporter who came on the scene, *[in an announcer's voice]* "live, to bring you the drama of this hostage

situation." But Jack was so strange, in those days even — the crew hated him. Poor Jack was defeated, I think, after that picture for two or three years — he went off to the Northwest or someplace to "find himself." About ten years ago, we were on a flight together coming back to Los Angeles from Vancouver and he was very nice to me. We recalled those old days and the rough stuff we had together. He was very good to me and he's always been one of my favorites, and certainly one of my favorite actors.

What was it about working with Roger Corman that made many of his co-workers feel that they should be out making movies on their own?

I don't know, I suppose they thought that if Roger could do it, *any*body could. Obviously, that's not true. I never felt that way; I never wanted to do it. I mean, I produced *The Brain Eaters* only because I needed the money. I knew I could do it — I could always produce a picture. But I just don't like it, it's not my bag.

So how exactly did The Brain Eaters *come about?*

Roger Corman called me into the office and he said to me that he and Bruno VeSota (who was going to direct this picture) needed a producer. But we had to do it non-union, we had to do it with N.A.B.E.T. crew rather than I.A. And since Roger knew that I had been in production for many years, he felt that I could produce the picture. I'm vague about the figures, but the budget was astronomically small — it was something like thirty thousand dollars to make the picture. And I would come up with all of the who's, where's and why's.

I was living in Pomona, and I knew a lot of the folks there — the mayor, chief of police, people like that. So I asked them to help us, and they did — they volunteered a lot of equipment that normally you'd pay for. Like the hospital facilities — we made a contribution to the nurses' fund, and shot some interiors at the hospital. All the policemen, all the guns, all of that stuff was donated because we contributed to whatever charity they had. I had a carpenter/neighbor/buddy of mine make the half-shell [the alien craft] — it was only half because we only photographed it from one side. When we went to the other side, we just turned it around! It was close to thirty feet tall, and he made it for like two hundred fifty dollars. We used sheet metal — aluminum sheets — around a wood structure, then we rented the scaffolding that we used alongside it.

You and VeSota cast the picture, right?

Yep. A lot of my friends, and friends of Bruno's, did the picture — played ghouls and things like that. And of course Leonard Nimoy, who was a buddy of mine, played the old man that protected the Brain Eaters. We shot all the interiors of the vehicle that came from "inner Earth" in my garage, with the

Nelson gave producing a shot in 1958, putting together—and starring in—the non-union *The Brain Eaters* with Joanna Lee.

lights off—just in darkness, with one light on Leonard. And, you know *[laughs]*, I never paid Leonard for that day. I owe him about forty-five dollars, or whatever it was I promised him.

The Brain Eaters was originally not called *The Brain Eaters*—Roger loved our original title so much he took our title off of it and Bruno and I had to make up *The Brain Eaters*. The original title of *The Brain Eaters* was *Attack of the Blood Leeches*—that was the title Roger loved! So he took the title to make another picture [*Attack of the Giant Leeches*]—he got somebody to hack out a script for him.

Tell us how you made the Brain Eaters themselves.

We made the creatures out of a little toy wind-up beetle that was around in toy stores at the time and quite plentiful. They had antennae and, if they bumped into a piece of furniture, they would turn and go the other way. We put crepe hair on 'em, and pipe cleaners for their antennae.

Were you happy with the way they looked on film?

No, not really. But we were not trying to make a flawless picture, we knew we had limitations and we just tried to make it the best we could with the money we had available. Most of the time you never saw the creature, it was always on the back of somebody's neck, under their clothes. Also, I knew what they really were, so it's hard to judge *[laughs]*!

So just about the whole thing was done in Pomona.

Right. We shot in a very famous park in Pomona called Ganesha Park — we got permission from the local park people. Remember the scene where we finally get rid of the machine — "electrocute" it? We did that in my backyard, using telephone lines as the high tension wires. We lit 'em and threw a line over the telephone wires going to my little tract house.

How much did you get paid on Brain Eaters?

I got (I think it was) one thousand dollars a week for the part, and to be the producer also. Because of the non-union crew and all, we could work long, long hours, so we did that, but I always made sure that we fed the crew well — having been on crews so much, I knew that was important. So we always went to a restaurant and let 'em order whatever they wanted. And we always had a lot of good food on the set, a lot of beer and stuff like that, so they wouldn't mind being there. And they did a good job, they worked very hard on it. One day the camera operator didn't show up, and we had to shoot. So *I* shot that day. I didn't have a light meter or anything, so I went down to the store and bought a thirty-five mm light meter that had settings for CLOUDY, HAZY, CLEAR, BRIGHT SUN *[laughs]*...! That's what I used, and it came out perfect!

Did you supervise the picture in post-production?

No, Bruno did — I have very little knowledge of that. Bruno and Roger together, probably. I understood that Roger sold the film to AIP for something like two hundred thousand dollars — and then later on he got an offer of three hundred thousand dollars. He was quite upset that he didn't wait!

Do you have any inkling how well it did for AIP?

No, but *[laughs]* I don't have any trouble believing that it made money!

An SF writer named Robert Heinlein claimed the film plagiarized a story of his.

Never even knew about it.

So you enjoyed working with Bruno VeSota on Brain Eaters.

Dear Bruno, he was a wonderful guy — had nine children. He was only married like three or four years but he had a set of twins, and triplets —! He had a great face, but *[squeaking]* had this terrible, terrible voice! A sweetheart of a guy — he died way ahead of his time, he was so overweight.

I later did another picture with Bruno, a thing called *Valley of the Red-woods* [1960] that we shot in Eureka, California. We were staying at a hotel way out in the middle of nowhere, and a bunch of gals that worked at a lumber mill, in the office, invited us to a cafe in Eureka—"on Saturday night it really moves." I wasn't interested, Bruno wasn't interested, but a couple of the younger guys were. And I had to get us the car. Gene Corman said, "No way"—he didn't have the insurance and all of that, and he was afraid that we'd all get drunk and wouldn't be at work the next day. Or that we'd get into trouble. I said, "Look, Bruno's gonna be with me. How much trouble could I get into with Bruno?" I mean, the guy weighed like four hundred pounds, he was like five feet tall—! Gene hemmed and hawed and I said *[calmly]*, "Gene, I'm takin' the car. I can hotwire it—steal the thing—or you can give me the key and nobody'll know the difference." "Okay, okay, it's over there on the dresser. . ." It was a little Studebaker wagon. The two young guys sat in the back, Bruno in the front and I was driving.

We got to this place, the Blue Moon Cafe, and it was a long shotgun bar—it just ran forever. From the bar to the wall was five feet—I mean, it was just the bar, the stools, and enough room to walk by and hang your coat up. We were there for quite a while, and a guy came over and was talking to Bruno. (Looked like he was gay.) The other two guys were talking to these gals, and I was in there telling "Hollywood stories." Now, Bruno and the guy took off, and I thought to myself, in my own sick mind, "Bruno, poor guy, what the hell can he do, he's four hundred pounds." I mean, he's not going to go with some secretary, eighteen years old, from the lumber yard *[laughs]*! Bruno said *[in a squeaky voice]*, "I'm gonna get some cigars, Eddie." "Right, Bruno, right!"

Half an hour goes by. There's a mirror that runs the whole length of the bar, I look up at it and in comes two cops. These two cops come in and they're talking to everybody (there's not that many people in the bar) as they're work-ing their way down: "Is your name Wilson or Nilsson?" they're asking. "My name is Nelson," I tell 'em. "Are you from Hollywood?" "I'm with a film crew that's shooting outside of town." "You got a buddy, a big fat guy?" "Yeah—he's a sweetheart of a guy," I said. The cop said, "Well, we got him in a pad-ded cell." Oh, my God, I said to myself, poor Bruno.

I told the two cops, "Okay, no problem, I'll come right down and we'll straighten this thing out," and I got my coat. We get out front—we could see the police station from where we were—but the street's one-way. So we gotta drive a-l-l the way around the park. I get in the police car and I hear over the radio, "This guy's giving us a lot of trouble down here." I told the cops, "I don't understand! Bruno's one of the sweetest pacifists—he's a non-violent person!" We get to the police station and we go in, and I can hear him scream-ing in the back of the place! I get in the back and he's got one cop on each arm and he's flailing 'em around the room! I grabbed him and I yelled, "Bruno! Bruno!"

And he busted out laughing. And the *cops* started laughing. These were

No girl was safe
as long as this
HEAD HUNTING THING
roamed the land!

NIGHT
OF THE
BLOOD
BEAST

Unforgettable poster art for a movie Nelson doesn't remember at all, AIP's *The Thing* inspired *Night of the Blood Beast*.

two cops that were buddies of Bruno's, that he'd met at a roadblock three days before when he went to get some cigars! He went into the police station and said, "Listen, why don't we rig this up for Nelson?" I'm telling you, I was out of it, it worked so well. I'd already started to sweat, I could already hear Gene Corman bawlin' me out—! Then on the way back to the location in the car, Bruno, big as he was, leaned back against the seat *[Nelson arches his back]* to straighten his pants—his crotch—and broke the back of the seat in this little Studebaker. Broke the seat! Oh, my God, Corman is gonna kill me, I told myself. We got back, claimed total innocence, finished the picture. But that was the joy of Bruno and that picture.

What do you remember about Night of the Blood Beast?
    Not much *[laughs]*.

It was one of the first films of Bernard Kowalski, who was twenty-eight at the time.
    I've worked with Bernie a lot—he's a wonderful guy. Even back then, so early on, he was a very confident young man, very knowledgeable.

Blood Beast *was for Gene Corman. How was he different from Roger?*
    They were very similar, as far as I was concerned, and I think they had

Nelson is braced for action in AIP's *Night of the Blood Beast*.

just about the same amount of knowledge. They always treated the work "light-heartedly," as far as I was concerned—I never had any problems with Roger or Gene. And having just come out from Louisiana, I can remember some very kind things that Roger did for me. Gene was very much like that, too.

Beverly Garland resents the fact that, when Corman moved up to slightly better pictures, he left some of his old stock players behind. Was it that way with you?

I guess—I don't know. I know I never worked for him again *[laughs]*, but who knows why? But also, money is a question—my money went up, and I'm sure Beverly's did, too.

So he was looking for more affordable people.

Oh, absolutely. He never took headliners, people who wanted big money. The ones that he did get, people like Vincent Price, he probably worked 'em for one week, and then the rest of the picture was with the other people.

What's the story on Devil's Partner?

Devil's Partner was made by a guy named Hooker—he made a famous little picture that made millions of dollars, *The Littlest Hobo* [1958]. *Devil's Partner* was his second picture, and it was directed by Charlie Rondeau—big guy, pretty much of a bullshitter *[laughs]*. But we got along fine.

Richard Crane and Jean Allison are on hand as *Devil's Partner* Ed Nelson takes his last breath. The 1958 film, co-written by Bowery Boy Stanley Clements, collected dust for three years before its 1961 Filmgroup release.

You played a dual role in that, as an old man and a young man.

Yeah, it was a Faust story. And I lived with goats *[laughs]*! I remember them shooting the transformation effects [from old to young] — I had to hold my head still while they took some makeup off, shot a few frames, took some more makeup off. À *la* Dr. Jekyll and Mr. Hyde — lap dissolves. The makeup didn't take that long to put on — an hour, maybe two.

Do you remember where that was shot?

No, but it was out in the San Fernando Valley somewhere, out in the sticks. I don't think I ever saw the picture.

You had a good heavy role in Soldier in the Rain *[1963], one of your better pictures.*

There were some great things in *Soldier in the Rain* — I loved the fight scene that I did at the end, that was one of the great fight scenes of film, they say. They had me rigged up on a wire so Jackie Gleason could pick me up over his head. And then the fight scene between Steve McQueen and me, at the bar — a wonderful stunt coordinator figured that out for us. That's where I met my stuntman (he's dead now), Howard Curtis — he was killed in a parachute leap. He was my stuntman from then until the time he died.

Did you hurt your back in that fight scene? It looks as though you did.

I don't remember—I may have. Those were the days when you wore bruises and such like a medal; today, the guy takes off three weeks. But in those days you got a little extra joy out of doing those things. I came up through the Westerns, too, and in those days we fell off the horses—not at full gallops, but we reared and did things like that. We were physical people, and they cast us a lot of times because of that.

Do you remember working with Boris Karloff on Thriller*?*

[Emphatically.] Sure. I did a lot of those—I had been at Universal under contract for awhile, and the producer of that show, Bill Frye, used me quite a bit in other things later on. I was glad to get on *Thriller,* 'cause I wanted to work with Mr. Karloff so badly. He only came in and worked the show Tuesday, Wednesday, Thursday—Thursday night he would fly to London, stay in London two days, then fly back on Monday. He was very, very nice to the cast, but I just—*pestered* him, almost, sitting with him and talking about the old days and talking about his friend Bela. He would tell me how sad it was, that Bela had been almost the number one actor in Europe, and when he came to the United States, because of his language problem, he became this *creature* here! How sad that was, Mr. Karloff thought. So I just loved working with him—he was a very gentle man. He had window flowers in his flat in London, and he loved to talk about flowers!

How about Twilight Zone*?*

Twilight Zone I did only one, and it was a classic—they reran the hell out of it. It was called *Valley of the Shadow* and it was ninety percent "my" show, so to speak. A wonderful script. I was pleased to do that, because it was a hot show at the time.

You were also on The Outer Limits, *in an episode called* Nightmare.

Yeah, I remember that, too—that was one of Marty Sheen's first jobs. We shot it over on Melrose Avenue, at one of the independent studios, and one day when we went to lunch we talked John Anderson into going in his creature outfit *[laughs]*! And we almost caused a traffic accident on Santa Monica!

Going into Peyton Place—*would you call that your Big Break?*

No, I think my big break's in front of me. *Peyton Place* was the biggest break I had at the time, although we didn't know it at first—don't forget, the reviews on *Peyton Place* were hideous. *Terrible!* As a matter of fact, as a joke one time, after the show became number one, Ryan O'Neal and I cut one of the *TV Guide* reviews out and sent it back to the reviewer on bread, with mayonnaise *[laughs]*!

Once you started working real regular in TV, you hardly ever made movies again. Was that by choice?

That's just more or less the way things worked out. They say if you're in television, people are not going to use you in motion pictures. Generally that's true. And usually directors and producers who are in television, when they make the jump to motion pictures, they don't bring their people along — they have a whole new entourage. Like what Beverly [Garland] said about Corman. That's just the way it goes. And so there's no way to measure [your worth as an actor]: You can't measure it by the final result, you can't say, "Well, if I was any good, I'd be way up there." Because a lot of guys that are "up there" aren't any good at all!

And vice versa.

Yeah. Of course a guy can look good in a twenty-five million dollar picture — they shoot every scene about eight times, six different ways, and they take eight months to do it! Now, to find out if he's any good or not, I'd like to see him in a *Highway Patrol.* Done in two and a half days. With a bad script. And a new director.

I've done some films you don't know about because they've never been released — one with Brooke Shields called *Brenda Starr,* and then I just finished one in Asheville, North Carolina, *The Boneyard* with Phyllis Diller. That one, I think, is not going to be around in the United States *[laughs].* It was made, really, for Japan — that's where the money came from — and it was a monster picture. I'm sorry you won't see it, 'cause they had a wonderful ten-foot Phyllis Diller monster *[laughs]* — it looked just like her, only ten foot high! And a guy inside, up on stilts. Incredible! But who knows what it looks like on film. These were "monster people" — they make creatures in Asheville. They have their factory there, and they make some wonderful ghouls and creatures. [*Brenda Starr* was finally released in 1992. *The Boneyard* went directly to video.]

So what's ahead for you?

I don't know what's ahead; I put so many restrictions on my agent this last year that I hardly get called for *anything!* But I'm going to take 'em off, and see if I can work a little more. They're calling me always about soap operas, asking me if I'm interested in doing another one. I'm not. It isn't hard work, it's just the quality of 'em is so poor — five, six, eight people writing the same character, it doesn't make sense. I watch them, and they're terrible for the most part. I hate to do something I wouldn't watch.

No regrets, then, that you never fully made "The Big Time"?

I was always looking to sustain myself for a long period of time rather than ever being a "star," so to speak, or going for "The Big Time." That was never very important to me. Also, because I had a lot of children, I had to work a lot. I couldn't sit out and turn down a lot of things, and wait for the big plum. Which didn't bother me a great deal. Once in a while it bothers me, when I see other contemporaries that have gone on and done very well by doing that — by *not* taking everything. But, hell, I have a lot more to show for it, in the long run. I have my eleven grandchildren and my six children, a very happy marriage — it's been that way for forty years. And that kind of solidification was more important to me than being an unhappy star.

ED NELSON FILMOGRAPHY

The Steel Trap (20th Century–Fox, 1952)
New Orleans Uncensored (Columbia, 1955)
Swamp Women (Woolner Bros., 1956)
Bayou (Poor White Trash) (United Artists, 1957)
Hell on Devil's Island (20th Century–Fox, 1957)
Invasion of the Saucer Men (AIP, 1957)
Teenage Doll (Allied Artists, 1957)
Carnival Rock (Howco, 1957)
Attack of the Crab Monsters (Allied Artists, 1957)
Rock All Night (AIP, 1957)
She Gods of Shark Reef (AIP, 1958)
Night of the Blood Beast (AIP, 1958)
The Cry Baby Killer (Allied Artists, 1958)
The Brain Eaters (AIP, 1958) Also producer
Street of Darkness (Republic, 1958)
I, Mobster (20th Century–Fox, 1958)
Teenage Caveman (AIP, 1958)
T-Bird Gang (Filmgroup, 1959)
The Young Captives (Paramount, 1959)
A Bucket of Blood (AIP, 1959)
Valley of the Redwoods (20th Century–Fox, 1960)
Elmer Gantry (United Artists, 1960)
Judgment at Nuremberg (United Artists, 1961)
Devil's Partner (Filmgroup, 1961)
Killers' Cage (Code of Silence) (Sterling World Distributors, 1961)
Soldier in the Rain (Allied Artists, 1963)
The Man from Galveston (Warners, 1963)
Time to Run (World Wide, 1973)
Airport 1975 (Universal, 1974)
That's the Way of the World (Shining Star) (United Artists, 1975)
Midway (Universal, 1976)
For the Love of Benji (Mulberry Square, 1977)
Acapulco Gold (R. C. Riddell, 1978)
Brenda Starr (Triumph Releasing, 1992)

*People ask me how we were able to
keep a straight face making* Cat Women
of the Moon. Well, we didn't*!*

William Phipps

IN THE EARLY DAYS OF 1950S SCIENCE FICTION, before the floodgates opened wide, one of the first people to become identified with the genre was actor William Phipps. Aside from furnishing the voice of Prince Charming in Disney's cartoon classic *Cinderella* (1950), Phipps also hid his boyish face beneath a beard as the star of Arch Oboler's end-of-the-world melodrama *Five*; made a token appearance in Oboler's *The Twonky*; encountered Martians in both *Invaders from Mars* and *The War of the Worlds*; and took on the Abominable Snowman as one of the leads in *The Snow Creature*. Probably most notoriously, he even grappled with Moon maidens set on world conquest in the almost indescribable *Cat Women of the Moon*.

Hailing from St. Francisville, Illinois, Phipps knew from boyhood that he was destined to be an actor, and appeared in several plays in grade school and at Eastern Illinois University. Hitchhiking to Hollywood in 1941, he worked on the stage and later in films, beginning with RKO's *Crossfire* in 1947. In the nearly half-century since, he has amassed a list of credits that is nearly staggering, not only in films but also in television, commercials and in voiceover work (he provided the narration for the special 190-minute TV version of David Lynch's *Dune*). Aggressively feisty, William Phipps has some surprising things to say about some of the biggest names in science fiction.

How did you get interested in becoming an actor in the first place?

That's kind of the wrong question. People in my profession will understand this, but I don't know if you will or not: I never thought of *becoming* an actor, or of being interested in acting. I always *was* an actor. Either you are or you aren't. I always just felt, "I *am* an actor." The first thing I did was in the second grade, when I played Bluebeard—the man that killed all of his wives *[laughs]*! Then I did a couple of plays in high school; went on to college (Eastern Illinois University in Charleston, Illinois), and did some plays there. At college, I was president of the freshman class—every office that I ran for, I was elected. The one office that I was *not* elected to was the president of the drama society, because the advisor to that, Dr. Robert Shively, said, "Oh, we can't elect Bill. He's going to go to Hollywood this summer"—I had told everybody that I was going to Hollywood to become an actor, and everybody took me seriously *[laughs]*! And so I *had* to go, to save face!

Did you get work there right off the bat?

I did a play out here called *Families Are Like That*—that was in forty-one—so I've been in Hollywood fifty years. Right after that, World War II broke out, so I was interrupted by three years in the Navy. (Across the Pacific sixteen times, on six different ships.) Then I came back and I started in at the Actors' Lab, which was a very famous school. It was *the* school, the only one that was considered any good at that time. (And I don't think there's been a better place since.) They had body work, fencing, speech, pantomime, the whole bit. I went there on the G.I. Bill. I did a play there, and Charles Laughton and Mrs. Bertold Brecht came to see it 'cause they were getting ready to do the play *Galileo*. *Galileo* had over fifty speaking parts, and so it was hard to cast. So Charles Laughton saw me and came backstage and asked me to do the play with him because he thought I was a terrific actor. And Mrs. Brecht, too — "Ah, yah, so, you *vunderful!*" So I did the play — I played Andrea, who was Galileo's [Laughton] number one pupil. It premiered at John Houseman's Coronet Theater on La Cienega Boulevard in Hollywood.

Your first fantasy film work was as the voice of Prince Charming in Disney's Cinderella.

I auditioned for it. They recorded me at a sound studio at Disney, and Walt Disney heard the tapes before he met the people. I later met him, and I did the film.

After the picture was done, Disney had a nationwide contest where the winner would get to come to Hollywood for free and have a date with the man whose voice brought Prince Charming to life — in other words, me! I don't know how they selected the winner; I suppose the people that entered it competed in some way. (*How* I don't remember — didn't care then — don't care now *[laughs]*!) I met the winner for the first time on the stage at the Pantages Theater in front of a full house, thousands of people, on coast-to-coast radio — *Art Linkletter's House Party*. I was in white tie and tails, and top hat. While I was backstage in the wings, waiting to go on, I noticed that there were a lot of mannequins — for what reason they were there, I don't know, they were for some other production, I assumed. There were several of them, female mannequins, and they were naked. And I was pretending to make love to them while on my hands and knees, in white tie and tails and top hat! Art Linkletter's announcer Rod O'Connor was so broken up, laughing so hard, so distracted, that he had trouble announcing the show. Rod and I thought that was hysterical — but I don't know what the *other* people around us thought *[laughs]*!

Anyway, she and I went out on our date. They gave me (I think) one hundred dollars pocket money and gave me a limousine and a driver, so we could go anywhere we wanted. We went to Ciro's and the Mocambo, which were the two most famous places on the Sunset Strip at the time, and we went to the Trocadero, too. At the end of the night, around midnight, the limousine driver and I took her back to the Roosevelt Hotel, where she was staying. And then the chauffeur took *me* back home — a rooming house we called the House of the Seven Garbos, a home for fledgling *actresses,* where I lived in a room in the basement for seven dollars a week! The next day I went to the tuxedo rental place and turned in my stuff. I was a pauper again!

Several articles that came out about Five *called you a radio actor. Were you?*

You know, I'm so amazed that there are so many "authorities" in this business that seem to know every-fuckin'-thing about it. I was *never* a radio actor—I wasn't then, I never became one and I'm not one now. I hadn't done *any* radio at all at the time of *Five*. When Arch Oboler was casting *Five*, he had Leo Penn—Sean's father—signed to do the lead. Then Oboler went to Charles Laughton looking for advice on casting the mountain climber. Laughton had an acting group by this point, a group that I was very active in. Oboler asked him, "Who's your best person?" and Laughton said, "Bill Phipps." We were doing a play at that time, Chekhov's *Cherry Orchard*, and I was playing Petya, the perpetual student, so I had a scraggly beard. Oboler came to see the play, and then he had me come up to his place in the mountains above Malibu—a ranch, the buildings all designed and built by Frank Lloyd Wright. I was all prepared to test for the part of the mountain climber, and when I got there, Arch said, "I want you to test for the lead." I said, "You've already got somebody for that part, I thought." He said, "Well, nothing's set in *concrete*." So I tested for the part of Michael. Arch Oboler liked my test and he paid off Leo Penn.

Oboler said he turned down name stars when he did Five. *He wanted unknowns.*

You'll have to make up your own mind about that. I would take it with a grain of salt. For one thing, he couldn't have *paid* a big name star *[laughs]*! He had a very limited budget, so he *had* to go with unknowns. He paid all of us S.A.G. minimum, and the only reason I did it was because I was getting top billing and a percentage. Then, too, *Five* was a non-union film, so I don't think that many big stars would go out on a limb with that. When we were making the picture up at Oboler's ranch, union people from all the different guilds came to see him, and there were big objections. What Oboler finally did was sell the picture to Columbia and pay off the unions.

Did that leave him any profits from Five?

Yeah, but I don't think very much. I had a percentage of the picture—a percentage of *his* profits—and I *did* get some money, I don't remember how much. But I think that he came close to breaking even, that he didn't make very much money.

Were all of your scenes shot on the ranch?

There, and also some down on the beach, which was just down the hill. The empty city that Susan Douglas and James Anderson go into was Glendale. My car was one of the abandoned cars sitting on the street. It was a real shoe-string production.

How much of a shoestring? How hurried were you?

We weren't hurried, but he didn't have any expenses, though, because we were all staying there at the house. And he had five students from U.S.C., kids who had been students of the very famous montage director Vorkapich, for the crew. (I'm sure Oboler, in his cheap way, went to U.S.C. and said, "I'm making an experimental film, non-union," and he got the best students.) They all doubled in brass—in other words, they all did *everything*. They gripped and they lit and they assisted the cameraman, everything the crew normally does. And there was a very ugly incident on *Five*: College students will be college students, they're not people of long professional standing in the business. One of the crew, a very nice fellow name of Art [presumably assistant director Arthur L. Swerdloff], said something that Oboler didn't like and Oboler *hit* him. With his fist. Cut him real bad—nasty gash, blood, the whole bit. I wasn't there to see the blow struck, but I was there shortly afterwards and saw the guy—Oboler had broken his glasses and cut him all up. And there was a big lawsuit over it. That was a terrible thing; no matter *what* the guy said or did, there's no excuse for that. But that's Oboler for you.

You've *[laughs]*—you've got me started on Oboler now. I never thought much of the man. I thought he was silly, about as silly as *The Twonky* is.

But initially, going into Five, *were you looking forward to working with the Great Arch Oboler?*

I didn't know a thing about him. Never heard of him. Years after *Five*, I appeared on an album that he did called *Drop Dead*, and a lot of it was scripts from his old *Lights Out* radio show. I just didn't think they were any good! And I appear on *The Chicken Heart*, which is the *famous* one! I played this *Chicken Heart* segment for a writer-friend of mine, John Paxton, who wrote *Crossfire* [1947], *The Wild One* [1954], *On the Beach* [1959] and so on. I played it for him and he said, "It all sounds phony, it's terrible! And as much as I think of your acting, Bill, *you* even sound false on there. I don't believe you." I agreed with him, and if you play it, I think it'll bear me out.

When it comes to Oboler and this genius bit, I don't see it. Never did. I don't think he was a genius at all. Not by any stretch of the imagination *[laughs]*! When Oboler directed, he didn't so much watch as he *listened*—he was a radio man. He always had the earphones on. Sometimes a scene would end, you'd look over at him and see that he wasn't even watching.

Did you and he get along all right?

Oboler had a "hands-off" thing with me. He didn't want to clash with me; he had clashes and run-ins with everybody else. Why *not* me? I have my own theories about that, but I couldn't really tell you why. I was his leading man—

So it wouldn't pay to clash with you.

Well, but he *could*. He clashed with Susan Douglas—very, very badly. She was one of the biggest pain-in-the-asses I ever worked with!

With her, then, he might have been in the right?

Except I think he had the hots for her! The nearest thing I had to a run-in with Oboler was a very interesting one. We were shooting on the beach and I had a microphone under my shirt. I was doing my dialogue and Arch came up to me and said, "Bill, I want you to do that again, but use your lower register"—meaning, bring the voice down, and use my normal voice, the way I'm talking to you now. I said, "I am." He said, "No, you're not." This went on for a few hours, doing it over and over; he kept saying, "I want you to get it down." It got to be where I was saying, "But I am," and he was saying, "No, you're not." It was a standoff, an impasse. I never came unstuck, though, I kept very calmly saying, "I *am* speaking in my normal voice, Arch." Then, the next day, he played it all back and it was just perfect, natural and normal. He came up to me and apologized. But, coming from him, it wasn't really an apology. In fact, he *didn't* apologize, he admitted he was wrong. No— that's *still* not right, 'cause Oboler Could Do No Wrong. What happened was that he told me that what I did *was* the lower register. Boy, that was delicious to me *[laughs]*!

And, by the way, I never, ever, *ever* called him Mr. O. or Mr. Oboler. He was Arch. Most of the others called him Mr. O., because they were scared, I suppose. *I* wasn't scared of him.

In what way was Susan Douglas a pain in the ass?

Oh, she wanted this and she wanted that, she wanted her own way and nothing was right. She bellyached and bellyached. She was just a thoroughly unlikable person. Thoroughly!

James Anderson, who played the bad guy?

James Anderson was at the Actors' Lab when I was, and he was in Laughton's acting group. Jimmy Anderson was a very nice, very talented person, but a person out of control. He'd let his emotions carry him away, he would get almost irrational at times. He was a very heavy drinker and he died very early—it was brought on by dissipation.

And what's your opinion of the film?

Oh, I never did like it. I didn't like the script, didn't like the picture, still don't. I quarrel a lot with the writing. Oboler did a lot of sermonizing, and there's a lot of sermonizing in the picture. But it always rang shallow with me.

Did you feel it would be a successful picture?

No, no, I did not. I had no hopes for it at all.

In the late sixties, a theater in North Hollywood decided to run *Five* and *The Twonky* as a double-bill. They invited Oboler, and Oboler invited me. I didn't really want to go, but I did because he made a special thing of wanting me to be there. Hans Conried, who was the star of *The Twonky,* he was there, too. When something like that happens, people come from out of the wood-work, buffs of these things; there was a full house. During an intermission, Oboler spoke, and do you know what he did? After asking me to be there, he introduced Hans Conried to the audience but not me *[laughs]*! I suppose he thought that would hurt me, but, you know what? It didn't. I didn't care. Oboler was a . . . he was. . . Oh, hell, he was a *creep [laughs]*!

Did appearing in Five *help you move up the Hollywood ladder?*

Who knows? You never know. But the premiere of *Five* was the first premiere that was ever televised — television was in its infancy then. I was still living at that same rooming house that I mentioned before, which was called the House of the Seven Garbos. I wore a tux and went to the premiere with the seven girls who lived there, all of them dressed in rented furs. The girls were Suzan Ball; Ann McCrea, who was a regular on *The Donna Reed Show* for years; Valerie Cote, who is now the wife of John Guedel (Guedel produced Groucho's *You Bet Your Life*); and four others. So I got fantastic publicity out of *Five*, all over the United States, probably the world. So that can't *hurt* *[laughs]*!

Speaking of the House of the Seven Garbos, I wasn't the only male there, there was also Hugh O'Brian and Leonard Nimoy. O'Brian was ostracized, because he was like an octopus, and because he was so *cheap*! Every girl that lived there, when nobody else was around he would paw them. So after a while he was just "frozen out"! And Leonard Nimoy used to drive me up the wall! I was already in movies, and he used to follow me around and pester me to death. I used to *hide* from him, honest to God *[laughs]*!

You have an unbilled bit part at the end of Oboler's The Twonky.

He called me one day and said he wanted me to appear in a scene, the last scene in the movie, where a bunch of guys barge in in their white coats and take Hans Conried away to the nuthouse. Oboler wanted to know if I would play one of the guys, as a "good luck" thing — we had done *Five* together, and I guess he was happy with *Five* and what I did in it. So, would I do it as a gesture? I figured, so what? Sure, I'd do it. And that's all I did in the picture.

And did you see the film?

I saw it when it came out, but I don't remember too much about it outside of the fact that I thought it was a silly film and I got very bored with that animated TV set running around the house. It just didn't make sense.

You had another small part, as one of the soldiers, in Invaders from Mars.

That was produced by Eddie Alperson, one of several movies I did with him—he was a big fan of mine. I don't remember too much about *Invaders* except that on a soundstage at Republic they built a whole floor that was like the surface of the earth—they brought in dirt and everything. But it was done way up off the floor of the stage, so that underneath it there was a whole world of tunnels, like a rabbit's warren or a prairie dog town, and there were all kinds of entrances and exits. It was hard work: I wore a helmet and a uniform and I carried a lot of equipment, and it was hot and sweaty and miserable. And I was on that picture for quite a while.

Any memory of the director, William Cameron Menzies?

I never got to know him, but my memory of him is that he was always lost in thought, like he was far away someplace.

How do you feel about science fiction in general?

Just this morning I was talking at breakfast with a director friend of mine, Jack Hively; he was just the executive producer of a new film called *The Giant from Thunder Mountain* with Richard Kiel and Jack Elam. I was telling him, "Thinking back, I have been involved with a *lot* of science fiction. I didn't try it, I didn't plan it that way, and I remember that at the time it was happening, I would remark on it with wonder. How is it that I kept getting in?"—*Five, The Snow Creature, Invaders from Mars, The War of the Worlds*, etc. It just happened, and I *still* don't have an answer *[laughs]*! But I'm happy about it because I like doing science fiction, and I like watching it—I like the visual possibilities. It's exciting to do.

Was Cat Women of the Moon *exciting to do?*

[Laughs.] People ask me how we were able to keep a straight face making that movie. Well, we *didn't*! Marie Windsor did, and so did Victor Jory, because they took themselves so seriously, but Sonny Tufts, Douglas Fowley and I had a ball. We were laughing and making fun of things all the time, trying to make the day as pleasant as possible. We shot it in five days, and I remember on the last day, we quit before the picture was really finished. That was it—they pulled the plug—because it was quittin' time and they didn't have any more money and couldn't go another day. Or another *hour* *[laughs]*!

The conclusion of the movie takes place off-camera. Victor Jory chases some Cat Women out of camera range, you hear gunshots, and then you hear him yell, "The Cat Women are dead."

Susan Morrow (left) and her fellow Moon maidens roll out the red carpet for Earthman Phipps in the 3-D camp classic *Cat Women of the Moon*.

Wasn't that wonderful? That's the thing that really stays with me about *Cat Women,* because I thought then, as I think now, "Boy, what a shitty way to end a movie!" *[Laughs.]* It just stopped! The director, Arthur Hilton, was a very, very nice man, though; he was a short man, and he walked with a pronounced limp. He was an editor before he became a director. And one of the producers was a fellow by the name of Jack Rabin, who had an optical special effects lab and he did work for lots of other studios. He had those facilities already, in his own business, so there was ninety-eight percent of the budget right there. That's how the picture came about.

Do you remember your first impressions of the spaceship set, and some of the props?

[Laughs.] When I saw that spaceship set, I thought I was workin' for Soupy Sales! And that giant spider! They held it up with big ropes above us on the cave set and dropped it down on our heads. At the time, we thought it was the most outrageous, absurd thing in the world—how did spiders get on the Moon?! It was all just incredible—I thought, "How can anybody put this in a movie? It's gonna ruin it!"

What can you recall about the attitudes of some of the other actors involved, like Marie Windsor and Victor Jory?

Well, Marie Windsor has never been one of my favorite people, I'll tell you that right now. A couple of years ago, I did a play called *Daddy's Dyin' ... Who's Got the Will?*, and I played the title role. *The L.A. Weekly* picked it as the outstanding drama of the year, and gave us its top award. There was a big dinner and presentation, and the mistress of ceremonies was Estelle Getty. Del Shores, the guy who wrote the play, and I sat together at a table; and before things got started, Marie came by and said hello to me. Estelle Getty was calling up the different presenters, and Marie was one of them. So when Estelle called her to present us with our award, Estelle mentioned *Cat Women of the Moon* and how it was a cult film nowadays, blah, blah, blah. And Marie even commented upon it. Now, she could so easily have said, "And one of my co-stars is sitting right over there, Bill Phipps." She did not—she did not say a word about it—and yet *I'm* getting one of the awards *[laughs]*! You know what that is? It's a person who relates everything to themselves.

It's surprising she acknowledged it at all. She can be a little touchy about Cat Women.

Well, that's Marie Windsor for you. If she had any class at all, she'd be tickled to death about *Cat Women of the Moon*. Look at Elsa Lanchester; what if she took that attitude about *Bride of Frankenstein*, where she walked around with her hair standing on end? She didn't; in fact, she had the [Aurora] model kit sitting on her mantelpiece! Me, I'm glad that *Cat Women* does have this kind of Worst Film reputation today, that it's funny and cultish and people can laugh at it. What do I care? Why should *any*body care? And if it embarrasses Marie Windsor, I feel sorry for her.

And Victor Jory?

Oh, what a pompous ass. Terrible! The day before we started shooting, he and I happened to walk into a little coffee shop which was on the Goldwyn lot. I was very young at the time, and Victor Jory said, "Sonny Tufts is gonna do this picture, eh? Well, he'd better not take a drink while he's working, 'cause I'll knock him on his fuckin' ass!" I remember thinking at the time, and I still do, what a thing to say! And what a thing to say about a fellow actor, before he's *done* anything! Sonny Tufts was a known carouser and heavy drinker, but so were a lot of other people. But they *worked*! In other words, Victor Jory was trying to establish himself as top dog, but that didn't mean shit to me.

Did you like Sonny Tufts?

He was a marvelous fellow, and he had the greatest sense of humor of anybody I've ever known. He should have been in vaudeville! They always made him like the amiable leading man or second leading man–type, but that wasn't really his nature at all. He was a funny, funny guy, and wonderful to be with. I loved him. Also in the cast was Susan Morrow, who played one of the Cat Women, the one I have a little romance with. Do you know who her sister is? Judith Exner, the lady that was having an affair with John F. Kennedy and the Chicago mob boss [Sam Giancana] at the same time, and wrote a book about it!

And, on the opposite end of the SF spectrum from Cat Women, *what can you tell me about* The War of the Worlds?

I have wonderful memories of that, because Byron Haskin and I became very good friends. Before I met Byron, I met his wife Terry at Preston Sturges' nightclub, a fabulous place called the Players. She had seen *Five* and was very impressed with me, and so she introduced me to her husband. I ended up doing a number of things with Haskin, like *The First Texan, The Boss* [1956], even some TV, but *The War of the Worlds* was the first one. Paul Birch, Jack Kruschen and I were three townspeople that were in a lot of the early scenes, and we're also the first three people killed by the Martians. Jack later got an Academy Award nomination for *The Apartment* [1960], and Paul Birch was a wonderful actor and a really nice man. One of my lines is the nearest thing to a laugh in the whole picture—"Welcome to California!"—and I immediately get zapped! We shot those scenes indoors, on a stage at Paramount.

Did you meet George Pal at all?

George Pal was very much the European, mannerly gentleman, very cordial, always smiling, very accommodating—"How good to see you," "How nice of you"—and you never knew who he was or what he was or what he was thinking *[laughs]!* You know the type! There was something very indeterminate about him. I remember that Byron Haskin used to give himself all the credit for making these pictures good or making them a success, always intimating that George Pal just got in the way. But Pal was a great promoter and he was the one that got them off the ground, got the backing and the financing and etc.

Haskin's notorious for taking the credit for other people's contributions to movies.

I'll tell you something about Haskin. You can always spot a liar when they say certain things. Haskin was always saying, "And I can show you proof," or, "You can ask so-and-so," things like that. You don't talk like that when you're telling the truth. He would lie about things for no reason. He was a cameraman and he was great in special effects; he was a good mechanic. But as a director I don't think he could handle anything poetic or sensitive or warm or touching. Things like that would have been completely out of his realm.

Did you have any inkling, as you were making War of the Worlds, *that it would be a classic?*

You never do. And a lot of times, when people *do* think they're making a classic, that's usually the kiss of death *[laughs]*!

Next you were one of the two leads in the first Abominable Snowman film, The Snow Creature.

The director on that was W. Lee Wilder; I first worked with Willie on a TV series called *Gangbusters,* and he said to me then, "I'm gonna do a movie" — meaning *The Snow Creature.* He told me a little about it and he said he wanted me to play the detective, and of course I thought to myself, "Oh, sure" — you hear this kind of stuff every day. But then he contacted me when he was about to do the movie, and we did it. I liked him, by the way, very much — he was very open and direct, very warm and friendly. (The opposite of Oboler.)

Do you recall the end of the movie, when I shoot the Abominable Snowman, down in the sewers? You don't actually see me shoot the gun, there's a big closeup of the gun going off. Well, the problem was that the gun wouldn't fire. Little things like that will make an impression on you, because *[laughs]* I remember thinking to myself, "How in the fuck can they get all the way down here, under the city, in these sewers, and not know that they have a gun that won't work and ammunition that won't fire??" It was idiotic, it *upset* me, because I've never had it happen before or since, and I've fired guns thousands of times. But I remember Willie saying to me, "Don't worry about it, I can fix it." And he did, he put in the closeup.

Were you still associated with Charles Laughton when he directed The Night of the Hunter?

Oh, yes. After Laughton and [producer] Paul Gregory bought the book *The Night of the Hunter* by Davis Grubb, Charles asked me to come over to the house, and he handed me the book. He shut me in the library and he said, "Don't come out 'til you've read it!" *[Laughs.]* So I read it, and I told him, "My God, this'll make a great movie. . . !" He was all hot to approach Gary Cooper to play the preacher; Laughton had done a movie with Cooper and Tallulah Bankhead called *Devil and the Deep* [1932] years before. He wanted Cooper, but I kept saying, "No, I think Robert Mitchum would be great." But he didn't know Mitchum.

So you kept after him?

I kept working on him and working on him, that Mitchum had to play this part. And he wouldn't hear of it. Finally he said, "Well, have you got his phone number?" I did. So I called Mitchum, and I put Mitchum and Charles on the phone together. Laughton told him, "This character's a shit — a real meanie. So, if you play it, you've got to play it in a way that you don't give the little kids nightmares!"

After they got off the phone, Laughton handed me the book and said, "Here, take this out to him." I said, "Nope. I won't take it to him." He said, "What do you mean?" and I told him, "I won't take this book to Mitchum unless you go with me." "No, no, no, no!" he cried out. This went on for an hour or two, but I was adamant: "I will not take the book to Mitchum unless you go with me."

So he drove out with me; I had a Mercedes roadster at the time. Laughton lived in Hollywood, up the hill from Hollywood Boulevard, and Mitchum lived way out west in Mandeville Canyon. We parked in the interior of the grounds where Mitchum lived, and I went up to the door with the book. Mitchum answered the door and I said, "Here's *The Night of the Hunter.*" He said, "Come in. Say, who's that in your car?" "Oh, a friend of mine came along." Mitchum looked and looked and then he finally walked out to the car, and he of course saw who it was and invited Laughton in for a drink.

Mitchum had some relatives over at the time, and several days after that he said to me, "When those relatives told me they wanted to come over, I said, 'What do you want to come over for? It's dull here on Sunday, nothing ever happens.' Then all of a sudden Charles Laughton walked into the room!" It made a liar out of him, made him feel like a fool *[laughs]*! Because for Charles Laughton to walk into a room, believe me, it was like leading an elephant into a living room. Wherever he went, he would stop traffic — people would just stop and stare. He had that kind of presence, as you can very well imagine.

How come Laughton directed only one movie in his career?

About that time, he directed some big successes on the stage — *The Caine Mutiny Court-Martial*, Shaw's *Don Juan in Hell* — and I remember he was saying he didn't care about acting anymore, he wanted to spend the rest of his time directing. (He was not an old man when he died, you know — he died at the age of sixty-three.) So he was looking forward to directing a lot more movies — whatever came up, whatever he got hold of. Once I got him and Mitchum together, but before he started doing *Night of the Hunter*, at a projection room at Nosseck's Studio he ran every classic picture he could get his hands on, just to "bone up" on directors' techniques. All that stuff, I saw with him — silents and everything. I went with him every day.

Did he like the way The Night of the Hunter *came out?*

Oh, yeah. I was on the set several times, and here's another anecdote about the film that you may not know. He would never say *cut*, unless the camera ran out of film. "Everybody be quiet; get settled; if you're standing up and you're uncomfortable, sit down; if you're sitting down and you're uncomfortable, stand up *[laughs]*; if you've got a cough or a cold, leave; but I want it quiet until this camera runs out of film." Then he would start a scene. I remember being there one day for a scene with Mitchum and Shelley Winters.

They started it, but Charles interrupted, "No, no, that's not right. Do it again and *this* time..." blah, blah, blah. Most people would have said *cut*. But in order to start up again, they have to call "Quiet!" again, they have to slate it again, lots of things. That all takes up a lot of time, and it also breaks the mood, breaks the rhythm. Laughton did all that preparatory stuff *once,* and then never stopped until the camera was out of film. That way, he got a lot better work out of people. Still today, very few people do it that way.

In the late nineteen sixties, you dropped out of the business for several years.
   My problem at that point was, I wasn't a juvenile anymore; I didn't look old enough to be a father; I was sort of in no-man's-land. I dropped out for five years and moved to Hawaii. I arrived in Maui in nineteen sixty-nine and came back here in March of seventy-five. While I was over there, at one point they were shooting *Hawaii Five-O* and they were trying to find me, and I got the message two weeks later. The people said, "Why don't you try to get work in this series?" and I said, "Either you're in this business or you're out of it. I am *out.*" I wanted to see if I could get out, cut the umbilical cord, forget about agents and managers and casting people and the Screen Actors Guild, etc., etc. — I wanted to get out of the *reel* world and into the *real* world and see what would happen! I had a couple of commercial fishing boats when I was over there; I also had a radio program, and a cable TV program for a while. I had a wonderful time.

You made your comeback as Teddy Roosevelt in TV's Eleanor and Franklin *[1976], and later appeared as a regular on the short-lived* Time Express *[1979].*
   That was very exciting. It was created by Ben Roberts and Ivan Goff, who did *Mannix* and *Charlie's Angels,* and who wrote one of the best Cagney pictures of all time, *White Heat* [1949]. *Time Express* was a mini-series, we did four of them, and they had a lot of back-up scripts. It starred Vincent Price and his wife Coral Browne, and it had a great format: People would get lured to the train station downtown on some pretext, and they'd come up to the ticket office, where there'd be fog swirling around. The ticket master in each episode was Woodrow Parfrey, and he would greet them by name and have their tickets ready. Now they would get on the train and suddenly they'd be talking to Vincent Price, and he'd take 'em to his car. His car was the most elaborate, swankiest car that you ever saw — from the eighteen hundreds, with the bright red cushions and upholstery, beautiful woodwork and all that stuff. Price would get around to saying, "Remember when such-and-such a thing happened in your life..." Now, the format of it was that they could go back in time to any turning point in their lives in hopes of changing their futures.

And you ran the train.
   Right, I was the engineer of this diesel streamliner. My name was

Phipps (center) co-starred with Vincent Price, Coral Browne (Mrs. Price) (seated), Woodrow Parfrey and James Reynolds in the short-lived teleseries *Time Express*.

Callahan and I did it with an Irish brogue, and I was dressed in the engineering uniform of the eighteen eighties—the striped cap, red bandana, the works. I had been on an old steam locomotive that went off of a trestle into a river 'way back in eighteen ninety, and I perished with it. But now here I was, back on the Time Express!

Well, I thought, "Vincent Price, Ben Roberts, Ivan Goff—it *can't* miss!" And we weren't doing a pilot, we did four! I remember saying to Vincent Price, "God, I'd like to be in a really big, hit TV series before I die," and he whispered, "So would *I*!" [*Laughs.*]

Phipps (now billing himself as William Edward Phipps) in a recent pose.

You were also in another SF pilot that didn't take off, Space Force *[1978].*

It was first called *Fort Leo,* then they changed it to *Space Force.* That was a good experience. The two leads were Fred Willard and I and we were on a space station; I was the commander and Fred was under me. It was written and produced by Norman Stiles and John Boni, two writers from *Sesame Street.* I would have been the star of the series, and we thought we were all in like Flynn. But unbeknownst to Norman and John, the same studio and the same network were also making another science fiction pilot with Richard Benjamin and Buzz Henry, called *Quark.* Norman and John were intimidated when they found out about that; they didn't know we had competition, they thought theirs was the only one being made. I imagine because of the Richard Benjamin name, and Buzz Henry's, that they got priority; *Quark* got picked up and several episodes were made, and *Space Force* wasn't. And I think we would have had some wonderful stuff happening on there.

Your overall career: If you had it to do all over again, what would you do differently?

You know *[laughs]*, I was asked that once before, and I answered by saying, "Well, you do what you have to do." Which, when you think about it, is *not* a flip answer; it really boils down to that. I always knew that I was an actor, and you have to have that inner knowledge to go ahead and "do what you have to do." I never did what a lot of actors have done (right or wrong, smart or dumb, I don't know): I just went with it. Whatever came along, whether it was *Cat Women of the Moon* or *War of the Worlds* or *Five*, I'd stick my toe in the water and if it felt okay, I'd do it. I never thought about what any of these would do for my career, never thought ahead to whether it would be a success or what it would do for me. I never had any kind of plan or blueprint, never tried to capitalize on anything. But I kept busy throughout a forty-year career, and I'm still busy today. I know that I've always been a good actor, I know that I am now, and I know I still get work. And I have the respect of my peers. Hey, what more could you ask for?

WILLIAM PHIPPS FILMOGRAPHY

Crossfire (RKO, 1947)
The Arizona Ranger (RKO, 1948)
Train to Alcatraz (Republic, 1948)
Desperadoes of Dodge City (Republic, 1948)
Belle Starr's Daughter (20th Century–Fox, 1948)
Station West (RKO, 1948)
They Live by Night (The Twisted Road) (RKO, 1948)
The Man on the Eiffel Tower (RKO, 1949)
Scene of the Crime (MGM, 1949)
Cinderella (voice only; RKO, 1950)
Key to the City (MGM, 1950)
The Outriders (MGM, 1950)
Rider from Tucson (RKO, 1950)
The Vanishing Westerner (Republic, 1950)
The Red Badge of Courage (MGM, 1951)
No Questions Asked (MGM, 1951)
Five (Columbia, 1951)
Fort Osage (Monogram, 1952)
Rose of Cimarron (20th Century–Fox, 1952)
Loan Shark (Lippert, 1952)
Flat Top (Monogram, 1952)
Invaders from Mars (20th Century–Fox, 1953)
Julius Caesar (MGM, 1953)
The Twonky (United Artists, 1953)
Fort Algiers (United Artists, 1953)
Northern Patrol (Allied Artists, 1953)
The War of the Worlds (Paramount, 1953)

Savage Frontier (Republic, 1953)
Cat Women of the Moon (Rocket to the Moon) (Astor, 1953)
The Blue Gardenia (voice only; Warners, 1953)
Red River Shore (Republic, 1953)
Francis Joins the Wacs (Universal, 1954)
Riot in Cell Block 11 (Allied Artists, 1954)
Executive Suite (MGM, 1954)
Jesse James vs. the Daltons (Columbia, 1954)
Two Guns and a Badge (Allied Artists, 1954)
The Snow Creature (United Artists, 1954)
The Indian Fighter (United Artists, 1955)
Rage at Dawn (RKO, 1955)
The Violent Men (Columbia, 1955)
Smoke Signal (Universal, 1955)
The Far Horizons (Paramount, 1955)
The Eternal Sea (Republic, 1955)
Lord of the Jungle (Allied Artists, 1955)
The Man in the Gray Flannel Suit (20th Century–Fox, 1956)
The First Texan (Allied Artists, 1956)
Great Day in the Morning (RKO, 1956)
Lust for Life (MGM, 1956)
The Wild Party (United Artists, 1956)
The Boss (United Artists, 1956)
Kiss Them for Me (20th Century–Fox, 1957)
Badlands of Montana (20th Century–Fox, 1957)
The Brothers Rico (Columbia, 1957)
Escape from Red Rock (20th Century–Fox, 1958)
The FBI Story (Warners, 1959)
Black Gold (Warners, 1963)
Showdown (Universal, 1963)
Cavalry Command (Parade, 1963)
The Kidnappers (Manson, 1964)
Harlow (Paramount, 1965)
Dead Heat on a Merry-Go-Round (Columbia, 1966)
Incident at Phantom Hill (Universal, 1966)
Gunfight in Abilene (Universal, 1967)
Valley of Mystery (Universal, 1967)
Homeward Bound: The Incredible Journey (Buena Vista, 1993)

Phipps also appeared in additional footage shot for the American television version of Hammer's *The Evil of Frankenstein* (Universal, 1964).

*I know of so many people who are miserable
in this business — really miserable — and I never could
understand it, because they're so bloody lucky to be
in and to stay in it. I really think it's a wonderful business.*

Vincent Price

HE REQUIRES NO INTRODUCTION IN A BOOK OF THIS SORT: Vincent Price was a living legend to fright film fans for most of the 50-plus years since he took the horror plunge with Universal's *Tower of London* in 1939. In the years since, he played a variety of roles in approximately 100 films, made all over the world, but it was as a screen villain—sometimes haunted, often heinous, occasionally humorous—that Price made his most popular and acclaimed pictures. And in recognition of his preeminence in the horror field, Vincent Price was the very special guest of honor at the May 1990 *Fangoria Weekend of Horrors* in Los Angeles where, following an introduction by the one and only Roger Corman, the screen's foremost aristocrat of evil received ovation after ovation during an on-stage interview with director Joe Dante.

Per Price's request for a "different" type of interview, the questions (devised by Dante and yours truly, and supplemented with questions from the audience) were an eclectic and wide-ranging bunch, touching on his horror movies, the 1982 Disney short *Vincent* (shown at the tribute), his dramatic and comedy roles, the work he'd done on stage and the music scene, and more. (Price died after a long illness in October 1993 "closing the book" on the screen's great horror stars.)

How did you come to be involved with the Disney short Vincent?

Somebody sent me from Disney a storyboard for *Vincent* and I thought it was such a wonderful idea—I loved the story. So I went over to meet [director] Tim Burton, and Tim is kind of a mad fellow, a wonderful, mad little fellow. He had this marvelous idea and he showed me a little mockup of Vincent, the character, and then read me the script. And I said, "I will do it." Because I think this is something that you must do when something like it comes along. So I went in and did the narration for him. It won a lot of prizes for Tim in little festivals, all over the world. One of the reasons he did *Vincent* was that he was fascinated with (as he called it) "the Vincent Price persona"—how I was able to hide behind the evil. I think it's a wonderful film.

I'm going to do another film for Tim very soon, called *Edward Scissorhands,* and I'm playing the professor who creates Edward Scissorhands. He's a marvelous fellow, really brilliant talent, this boy. Wonderful designer—he's sent me other things that he's designed, and we've sort of kept in touch. [*Edward Scissorhands* was released in 1990.]

You are also the voice of the haunted house in the new Euro Disneyland.

They asked me if I'd do it and I asked, "In what language?" and they said, "French." I said, "*Mais oui!*"—that's about as much French as I speak *[laughs]*! They sent the script to me and they spelled it all out phonetically, and I learned it—I got French friends to come in and help me, and I had a terrible time because it's all sort of in pseudo-verse. I really had a big three weeks of work

Previous page: Vincent Price reigned as King of Horror Films in the 1950s and 1960s, beginning with the starring role in Warners' 3-D blockbuster *House of Wax* (pictured).

Out of the musty mufti of AIP's creepy Poe series, Price played a fanatical peacemonger in the company's science-fictional *Master of the World*.

to get it right, I got over to the studio—and they had changed almost every word of it *[laughs]*! But I got through it and I think it's going to be very nice, and it's kind of fun to be part of Disneyland.

When you made the Three-D House of Wax, *was that the point at which you had to decide whether you wanted to be a stage star or a movie star?*

Yes. I was offered a wonderful play in New York called *We're No Angels,* and it was a big, big hit, and every time I'd go by that theater in New York [after turning down the role], I'd say, "Did I do the right thing?" But it was playing and it was about to go off after a year, and *House of Wax* is *still* playing after forty years *[applause]*! I don't know, really; you always wonder whether you've done the right thing or not. But I think I did, because I loved

House of Wax, it was great fun to make. And it was fun to be part of the grow-ing technology of the motion picture industry.

The famous story about House of Wax *is that the director, Andre de Toth, only had one eye —*
  —and he couldn't see any of the Three-D effects! He'd go in and look at the film, and he'd ask, "What are all those people screaming about?" He never saw a thing!

One of your co-stars in that film was Charles Bronson.
  Yes—Charles *Buchinski.* He was wonderful in it; he had no dialogue, but he was awfully good *[laughs]*!

Did you think he would go on to bigger things?
  Yes, I did—he really has a wonderful face. We did another picture together, *Master of the World,* and I think Charlie was practically a deaf mute again *[laughs]*! And I saw one of his first pictures as a great star and he was almost a deaf mute in *that [laughs]*! He didn't talk very much, he talks more now.

In preparing to do House of Wax, *which was a remake of* Mystery of the Wax Museum, *did you look at Lionel Atwill's performance?*
  No, I think that's a big, big mistake. No, I've never seen *Mystery of the Wax Museum* unless I saw it as a kid—it came out when I was a youngster. So [in preparing for *House of Wax*] I never did see it—on purpose—because I didn't want to copy Lionel Atwill. And *House of Wax* was a different story.
  While *House of Wax* played for about thirty weeks at the Paramount Theater in New York, I was doing a play and I used to sneak into the back of the movie theater. And I'd have more fun watching the people with these silly Three-D glasses on *[laughs]*. And they couldn't tell who I was, because *I* had glasses on, too! I'd always pick two teenage girls to sit behind, 'cause their reactions were marvelous. At the end of one of the showings, these two girls were riveted and they were moving forward in their seats. And when finally I'm thrown into the vat of wax and I'm burned up and the steam comes up and it says THE END, I leaned forward and I said, "Did you *like* it?" Right up into orbit, they went *[laughs and applause]*!

A lot of people might not remember that you were directed by Alfred Hitch-cock in an episode of his television series.
  I was really terribly excited about working with Hitchcock, he's one of the great movie makers of all time. There were only two of us in it [Price and James Gregory], just two characters, and I thought it was going to be wonderful. It was a very elaborate thing called *The Perfect Crime,* and I was really very thrilled to think of Hitchcock telling us what to do.

His entire direction was, he came on the set one day and he said, "Faster." *[Laughs.]* And so we did it a little faster and he said, "That's better. A little bit faster." Then he went over and slept *[laughs]*! I've read four books about Hitchcock recently and he slept all through everything—or gave the appearance of sleeping. He set things up so brilliantly that he didn't really have to watch very carefully.

Another director people might not remember your working with was Orson Welles, who directed you on stage when he was twenty-two.
     Yes, after I had done *Victoria Regina* and a couple of other plays, I joined the Mercury Theater with Orson. And I did two plays which were really wonderful: *The Shoemaker's Holiday,* which is a very bawdy Shakespearean farce, and *Heartbreak House* by George Bernard Shaw. Wonderful cast, we had, and he was a brilliant director, Orson—mad as a hatter, but brilliant *[laughs]*!

Angel Street *was one of your major successes on Broadway, and it was eventually made into the film* Gaslight *[1944]. But you didn't end up playing the lead in the movie, Charles Boyer did.*
     You never get a chance in the movies to play the same leading role that you've done on Broadway, or very seldom. But I did the play, and it ran for five years. It was an extraordinary story, a real theatrical story. The Shuberts [the theater owners] hated the play so much when they came to see a run-through that they refused to print the tickets for Monday. So the play opened on Friday, and Saturday the reviews were raves, one hundred percent. I've never read reviews like that in my life—"The best melodrama of all time" and so forth. And there were no tickets! The line outside the box office was there and the girls in the box office were writing the seat numbers down on slips of paper!
     Finally Sunday came around. My wife was out on the West Coast and I called her from New York and I said, "Isn't it wonderful?" There was a dead silence and then she said, "What do you mean wonderful? It's the greatest tragedy of all time." I said, "The play is a *hit*! It's the biggest hit in town! What's this tragedy bit?" She said, *"Pearl Harbor."* I had read the papers, but I'd only read my own notices, I hadn't read about Pearl Harbor *[laughs and applause]*. Isn't that a terrible story? Almost every show in New York closed sooner or later right after that, except *Angel Street,* which ran five years.

You also wrote a play yourself.
     My God, how did you know that?

Poet's Corner. *Were you happy with it?*
     I loved it, I had a wonderful time. I was up in a famous summer theater called Skowhegan in Maine and I showed it to the director at Skowhegan (I'd worked there before) and he said, "Well, it needs some work, but I like it and

I'll do it—if you'll play in it." I said, "My God, I can't play in it—I'd be so nervous and self-conscious." So he put me in a small part.

Well, I was a disaster, because every time somebody else would open their mouth and say one of my brilliant lines, I'd go *[Price gasps with awe].* Or if it was a funny line *[Price bellylaughs]*—and I wasn't meant to laugh! But it was fun to do. I never tried another one, but it wasn't too bad.

When you did Victoria Regina *with Helen Hayes, there were two other great screen villains-to-be in the cast, George Zucco and George Macready. How did you enjoy working with them?*

Oh, they were wonderful. *Victoria Regina* I had done in London first, in a little theater, and then [American producer] Gilbert Miller came to see it and decided to buy it for Helen Hayes. And it was of course the peak of her career—this was fifty-five years ago. (I was only ten years old, playing Prince Albert *[laughs]*!) It was a wonderful play. George Macready played my brother, and became one of my best friends. He was a wonderful villain. I remember when he did *Gilda* [1946], a critic said he was "an icicle dressed by Wetzel." (Wetzel was a great men's tailor.) And George Zucco was also a really great villain.

When people see Invisible Man *movies they often think, "How much work does this really involve?" Like, when you're not there, do you come in those days?*

You come in. It's endless! *[Laughs.]* There's a scene in *The Invisible Man Returns* where I take the clothes off a scarecrow, because I'm only invisible if I'm naked. (It's very cold!) I have to undress this scarecrow and put the clothes on myself, and it took nine hours. Today they have blue screens and chroma-key, but the way they did it in those days, the set was built and the camera anchored and they draped the whole set in black velvet. And then I was draped with black velvet. And whatever I put on myself, I put around the black velvet. But it took forever, because anytime you'd make the smallest mistake, you could be seen. So it was very laborious, and rather boring!

Is it true that the director of The Invisible Man Returns *didn't speak English?*

Joe May spoke very, very little English. Thank God I spoke a little German—we could curse at each other. He was a great director in his day in Germany, but he really did have a bad time here because he didn't speak very much English at all. I saw *The Invisible Man Returns* in a theater and there were two fellows in front of me, and at the end, when I returned to visibility, one of 'em said, "That'll teach you not to drink ten-cent whiskey!" *[Laughs.]*

There was a wonderful triple bill that I went to see about ten times: the original *Invisible Man* with Claude Rains, myself in the second one, and a cartoon called *The Invisible Mouse* [1947]. Which was heaven, because they used all the tricks: The cat even put flour on the floor so that the feet of the mouse would leave tracks *[laughs]*!

You worked with another great director, James Whale, on what is generally regarded as not his finest hour, Green Hell *[1940].*

Probably one of the ten worst pictures ever made. If you ever get a chance to see it, you must, because it is hysterical. I had a line where I am going up the Amazon with Douglas Fairbanks, Jr., who was playing a character named Brandy. For some unknown reason, going up the Amazon, I say, "Brandy, do you think it is possible for a man to be in love with two women at the same time, and in his heart be faithful to each, and yet want to be free of both of them?" *[Laughs.]* Opening night, the audience fell on the floor—it was hysterical! It was the funniest picture in the whole world!

Another one of the funniest pictures in the world is Champagne for Caesar *[1950], in which you played a mad soap tycoon* [applause]. *And in* His Kind of Woman *[1951], you gave another wonderful comic performance.*

I loved playing comedy, but I looked like a villain. And they were all villains, really, those comedic parts. But I love comedy, and I think it's much more difficult to play comedy than the straight roles. *His Kind of Woman* is really a funny film; I play a movie star who believes in himself, believes that everything he does is true. Mr. [Howard] Hughes didn't direct the picture but he fell in love with the character that I was playing, and six months after we finished the whole film, he called me back and built a set which cost at that time two hundred fifty thousand for that scene where all the Mexican policemen and I go down in the sinking boat. The policemen all go underwater, I'm standing on the prow and I turn around and say, "Stop mumbling and abandon ship!" And their heads pop up out of the water *[laughs]*! It cost him two hundred fifty thousand to add that scene and he loved it—*loved* it!

You were hilarious in Tales of Terror, *in the wine-tasting contest.*

That's a funny scene, I must say. They hired a fellow to come on the set and show us about wine-tasting, because people don't really taste wine, they *drink* it. And so he was showing us all these fancy things. So all Peter Lorre and I did was just exaggerate them a tiny bit, and they were hysterical. I loved doing that.

George Sanders is a person about whom much has been written—some of it by himself—describing what "a dreadful man" he was.

He wasn't. He was a dear man, a wonderful man. One of the first pictures I ever did *[The House of the Seven Gables]* was with George, and I knew him really intimately and was very, very fond of him. He pretended to be a dreadful man, but he was a brilliant raconteur, spoke Russian superbly (he was born in Russia), he was a wonderful pianist, had a beautiful singing voice. But he really didn't care. I remember one day he said to me, "I'm going to Egypt to do a film," and I said, "Is it an ancient film or a modern film?" He said, "I

The cast of *Tales of Terror* discussing a scene (or maybe just posing for a publicity shot!) behind the scenes: Debra Paget, David Frankham, Price and production assistant Jonathan Haze.

really don't know yet, old boy." I said, "Well, aren't you going to find out before you go?" He said, "Really doesn't matter. You smoke cigarettes *this* way *[Price holds up a hand]* if it's an old film and *this* way if it's modern." *[Laughs.]* I loved it!

Who instilled in you your appreciation of the arts?

    I went to college in the East, I went to Yale; it was during the Depression, and there really were no jobs. And I thought that being a teacher would be a wonderful job, and what I would love to teach is visual arts. So I majored in the arts, in the history of art, at Yale, and then when I got out I taught school for a couple of years—and found out how little I knew! So I went over to England, to the famous Courtauld Institute, which was just started at that time, and I stayed there for two years and started in the theater then, too. But it's really my hobby, I know a lot about art. I don't know much about anything else, but I know a lot about art!

Have you ever tried your hand at painting?
    I took it up about six months ago and I quit about five and a half months ago *[laughs]*! I have no talent whatsoever!

Do you ever seek out and watch your old pictures?
    Every once in a while, if it was one that I enjoyed making. The ones with Roger Corman I loved, because we had such a good time making 'em. We worked hard, really hard—oh, boy, he was a slavedriver! But it was wonderful fun, because he had it so carefully planned. He had Danny Haller doing the sets and Floyd Crosby on the camera, he got wonderful people around him and he just did a superb job. And, again, they were great fun.

When Ray Milland was asked how he liked working with Roger, he said, "I can't remember, because the pictures were made so quickly that I have hardly any memories of them."
    Roger did make pictures very quickly, but they were made thoroughly. They were brilliantly designed and brilliantly thought out. He was one of the best directors I ever worked with in my life. [Mr. Corman was present at the tribute.]

Which of the pictures you made for Roger was the most satisfying to you?
    Well, I kind of loved *The Masque of the Red Death*. We had one of the great cameramen in England [Nicolas Roeg] and we had a wonderful cast. And all the extras were from the Royal Ballet—but that you can do in London, you can't do it here. You'd have to bring 'em out from New York! But it was a very exciting film, and I found it fun to work on.

Another fan favorite is The Tomb of Ligeia, *which was written by Robert Towne.*
    I think *The Tomb of Ligeia* was closest to Poe—it was *very* close to Poe, as a matter of fact. Roger and I had often talked about the idea of doing a film in an actual location. We had this wonderful twelfth century abbey and most of it was done right in there.

Pit and the Pendulum?
    Pit and the Pendulum I think was one of Roger's triumphs, because that

Price, a script girl and Roger Corman on location in England for AIP's *The Tomb of Ligeia.*

is a really difficult thing to bring off. You know, one of the problems with doing Edgar Allan Poe is that those are short stories, and you've got to make them into long films! And Poe doesn't take the trouble to explain why people are where they are, so you have to explain that. It was a very difficult film to do, *Pit and the Pendulum,* but I enjoyed it.

Were there Poe stories that you would have liked to have done with Roger Corman, but didn't?

    Yes, I would love to have done *The Gold-Bug* with Roger. *The Gold-Bug* was the first detective story — Poe was an extraordinary writer, and it would have been fun to do that "version" of him. Because a lot of people don't recognize that something like sixty-five percent of Poe's work is satirical — it isn't heavy, it isn't horror, it's satirical work. I did a television show one time called *An Evening with Edgar Allan Poe,* and in it I narrated a Poe story called *The Sphinx.* It's about a man who thinks that he sees a monster, and it turns out to be a little moth.

Tell us a little about Dragonwyck *[1946].*

If only one Vincent Price movie still exists a thousand years from now, *he* **wants it to be** *Dragonwyck* **(1946).**

Dragonwyck I think was one of the best pictures I ever made *[applause]*. It was Joe Mankiewicz's first picture [as director] and it was the fourth picture that I'd done with Gene Tierney; I also did *Laura* [1944] with her, and I think that's really one of the best pictures ever made *[applause]*. It's not a pretentious picture, but it was perfect — the best thing that Otto Preminger ever did.

Did you enjoy working with Gene Tierney?

Yes. I did four pictures with her *[Hudson's Bay* (1940), *Laura* (1944), *Leave Her to Heaven* (1945), *Dragonwyck]*. She was divine. You know, when you see *Laura*, it isn't dated at all. Gene Tierney didn't date! Her hair was sort of contemporary, no matter what period. . . .! It's almost fifty years ago that we did *Laura*, and *Laura* holds up — it's just as modern today as it was then, largely due to Gene Tierney. She was wonderful to work with but she had a rough time [in life].

Your "typing" in the late nineteen-fifties as a horror star began with your association with William Castle. He brought a sense of fun to going to the movies, a kind of showmanship that is sadly missing today.

He was a *great* showman. There was a wonderful article in one of the airplane magazines not too long ago about "What Happened to Show Biz?", and it brought up Bill Castle and the things that he did. The crazy things, like *The Tingler [applause]*. But he was wonderful! I mean, who would ever do a black-and-white movie and have one scene in color, where the lady turns on the water in the bathtub and it's *bloo-oo-ood [laughs]*! Wonderful!

When Castle would come to you with a script, would he already have the Gimmick in mind?

Yes, I think so. Like *House on Haunted Hill,* with the emerging skeleton *[applause]*! When he was looking for a haunted house, he went out and found a great Frank Lloyd Wright house — one of the most modern pieces of architecture in the world — and he used this as the haunted house! And there's nothing like that first scene, where all the guests that I've invited arrive by hearse. . . ! He was a nutty fellow, but great fun and very inventive.

The opening night of *House on Haunted Hill*, I was in a little theater in Baltimore. In the movie, I reeled this skeleton in using a winch, and then there'd be a real skeleton in the theater that would shoot over the audience. Well, I was in this theater with a great many young people in it — and they panicked! And they knocked all the seats out of the theater *[laughs]*! They just took down the first five rows. I loved it!

You were on The $64,000 Question *a number of times, on art. Was that before or after the quiz show scandals?*

It was before the quiz show scandals. *The $64,000 Question* had a very good premise: The contestant would be a person who was, say, an actor or a shoemaker or whatever, who knew about some other subject. *One* other subject. Then, because it was so popular, there came shows where a guy knew about *everything*. Well, I never could believe that, I couldn't go along with that for a minute. Ours was very honest — at least, it was with me. I studied — I never put down books on art. I studied the whole time I was on it!

Could you tell us a little about Peter Lorre?

    [Holding his nose and imitating Lorre.] Peter? *[Laughs.]* The greatest imitation I ever heard of Peter Lorre in my life was by Peter Lorre. He held his nose and talked like that, and that sounded just *exactly* like Peter Lorre *[laughs]*! At his funeral, I read the obituary address for him, because all of his friends were dead—Humphrey Bogart and all of them were gone, and I guess I knew him as well as anyone at that time. He called himself a "face maker," and he always denigrated actors. He always played 'em down, said we're face makers, we're nothing else, we really don't have a brain in our heads. But he was a wonderful actor.

    He also loved to rewrite the script. One time, in one of Roger's films, there was a scene where all Peter and I were doing was getting from one place to another, and there was some exposition there. I always know my lines and I was saying them, and Peter was sort of vaguely saying something else, I don't know what it was. And I said, "Oh, for Christ's sake, Peter, *say the lines!!*" He said, "You mean that, old boy? You don't like *my* lines better?" I said *[sharply]*, "No!" So he said all the lines—he knew every line in the script! But he didn't like to say them *[laughs]*!

Boris Karloff found Lorre a little off-putting, because he would not stick to the script.

    Yes, it's very annoying, it really is. Because no actor is funnier than a good writer.

Basil Rathbone?

    Basil—I sound like Pollyanna, don't I?—he was one of the nicest men that ever lived *[laughs]*! I did a picture with him called *Tower of London [applause]*, years ago, he was Richard III and he was absolutely marvelous in it. And he did a wonderful thing, sort of to keep everybody's spirits up (it was a rather heavy play and too many stars in it). He got us all together, all the cast—being the star, he could do this—and he said, "Let's make an agreement amongst ourselves. Let's never tell a dirty joke that we didn't hear after we were fourteen." Well, we'd all go home at night and think of all the dirty jokes that we'd heard before we were fourteen. And they're *very funny [laughs]*! They're not particularly dirty but they're very funny, and we'd come on the set the next day and tell these stories...! Basil was a sweet man—a great prankster and joker, but a wonderful actor.

What were some of your most difficult films to make?

    I did a couple of pictures in Italy, which shall be nameless—

Queen of the Nile [1964] with Jeanne Crain?

    God Almighty! And another one with Ricardo Montalban called *Gordon, il Pirata Nero* [1962]—"Gordon the Black Pirate." I said, "Why *Gordon?*"

[Laughs.] Gordon, what kind of terrible name is that? Well, Gordon, I finally found out, was because of Byron, who was Lord Gordon—he had lived in Italy. On *Gordon* they lost the soundtrack, so we dubbed it. But we had so many different nationalities in it that we had to hire lip-readers in everything but Watusi *[laughs]*—it was impossible! I don't think anybody ever saw it.

What was it like doing The Last Man on Earth *in Rome?*

The problem doing *The Last Man on Earth* was that it was supposed to be set in Los Angeles, and if there's a city in the world that doesn't look like Los Angeles, it's Rome *[laughs]*. We would get up and drive out at five o'clock in the morning, to beat the police, and try to find something that didn't look like Rome. Rome has flat trees, ancient buildings—we had a terrible time! And I never was so cold in my life as I was in that picture. I had a driver and I used to tip him a big sum to keep the car running, so I could change my clothes in the back seat.

How about The Abominable Dr. Phibes?

Dr. Phibes, and *Dr. Phibes Rises Again,* were really funny pictures, I think two of the funniest pictures ever made. Scary, but funny—each one of the murders had a little fillip to it that made it funny. But the guy who directed it [Robert Fuest] was a madman—and wonderful. He would say, "Do this" and you did it, because there was nothing else to do! It was so mad and so crazy but they were great fun to do. I loved doing those two *[applause]*.

How did you and Charlton Heston get along when you worked together?

Charlton Heston? Who's he *[laughs]*? Oh, *that* one! Charlton and I got along all right. We did a couple of television shows—the first *Playhouse 90* and a few other ones—and I did *The Ten Commandments* [1956] with him. I always loved him because he was practically brand new to the screen and he was telling DeMille how to direct *[laughs]*!

How about Errol Flynn?

I did two films with Errol, one with Bette Davis called *The Private Lives of Elizabeth and Essex* [1939], which was one of the biggest films made in its time. It was exciting because it was the very beginning of my movie career and I was thrilled to be working with Bette. And with Errol, who was a little difficult, but an extraordinary, charming man. Charmed the pants off every girl that he ever met *[laughs]*—and the dress, too!

How did you get involved with Alice Cooper and his Welcome to My Nightmare *album?*

I did a show for a long time called *The Hollywood Squares,* and on

Price's horror bow, as the foppish Duke of Clarence in Universal's *Tower of London*.

Hollywood Squares you met *every*body *[laughs]* — everybody in the *world*! It was great fun because the comics were all on it, and I love comics. Alice and I became friends, and he asked me if I would do this thing. Just like Michael Jackson asked me to do *Thriller* — which is still the biggest-selling album in the history of the medium *[applause]*. I notice that I am now sort of the grandfather of the raps, or the *great*-grandfather *[laughs]*! *Thriller* was a wonderful rap, really marvelous.

Can you tell us about working with Diana Rigg in Theater of Blood*?*

Diana Rigg — she's a killer, that girl, one of the most sexy and attractive ladies I've ever met in my life. She took over my spot in *Mystery!* as the host; I'd done it for eight years and I thought that was enough of that, and so she's come in and is doing it now. She's awfully good, a wonderful actress.

You've worked a number of times with your fellow Geminis Peter Cushing and Christopher Lee, and you're very close to both of them.

Christopher, when you first meet him — if you don't get along right away, he's a rather pompous man *[laughs]*. He's very sort of British and terribly sort of proper. For some reason or other, we got along wonderfully, and we're like two girls — we get on the telephone together and we crack jokes. We save up jokes and gossip and all kinds of things! I don't think he does that with anybody else — we just have the best time together and I'm devoted to him. Peter Cushing is a very proper man, a very sad man — he lost his wife years ago and he's never gotten over it. But we're all born within a day of each other — not in the same year, as they hasten to point out *[laughs]*!

What was it like to work on the set of the old Batman *series?*

Egghead *[laughs and applause]*? I've run into a large amount of criticism over the years, people would say, "Why did you *do* such a crappy thing as *Batman?*" Well, *Batman* wasn't crappy, it was one of the funniest shows ever on the air, really hysterical *[applause]*. They were broad, they were farcical, but they were wonderful. I must get a hundred pictures of Egghead a week to sign — *Batman* is all over the world now, they replay it in England, in Germany, everywhere. I'm so sick of that picture of me holding the egg....! *[Laughs.]*

What did you think of the new version of The Fly*?*

When the new *Fly* opened, I thought they were going to call it *The Zipper [laughs]*. Anyway, when it came out, I got a lovely letter from Jeff Goldblum saying, "I loved your *Fly,* hope you like mine." *[Laughs.]* I thought that was very sweet, it was an adorable letter. And he loved the original *Fly.* So I went to see his, and I thought parts of it were marvelous, up until the end. Then he didn't turn into a fly, he turned into a glob. And there was nothing left of him. I really thought they went too far. And it lost credibility.

I have a feeling that horror films must be logical. You must be able to believe some part of them — not all of it, but you must be able to believe that this could happen. Otherwise, it's not frightening.

Being that you're the true master of classic horror, what is the attraction for you for horror and terror?

You. People who enjoy it. And when they're made with the imagination that Roger Corman put into 'em, and that the other people I've worked with put into 'em, people love 'em. They're like fairy tales—they have a quality of the unreal and yet they're real. They scare you and you scream and then you laugh at yourself. I think they're great fun.

There are no derogatory stories about you.
There are very few, because I like people. And I think that if *you* like people, you get along with people and they don't dislike *you*. I know of so many people who are miserable in this business—really miserable—and I never could understand it, because they're so bloody lucky to be in and to stay in it. I really think it's a wonderful business and people should be very grateful for being part of it.

A thousand years from now, there's only one Vincent Price picture surviving. Which one do you think it should be?
I think *Dragonwyck [applause]*. *Dragonwyck* was a very difficult part to play, because he's a crazy man, a monomaniac, and yet didn't know it. So it was a challenge to play it. I think *Dragonwyck*'s a very good film.

Conqueror Worm *reportedly was a very troubled film to make; your conflict with the director stemmed from the fact that he had originally wanted someone else for the part—*
—and *told* me so *[laughs]*! When I went on location to meet him [Michael Reeves] for the first time, he said, "I didn't want you and I *still* don't want you, but I'm stuck with you!" *That's* the way to gain confidence! He had no idea how to talk to actors. He came up to me one day after a take and he said, "Don't shake your head!" I said, "What do you mean? I'm not shaking my head." He said, "You're shaking your head!! Just don't shake your head." Well, that made me so self-conscious that I was poker-faced—and, as it turned out, he was right! He wanted it *that* concentrated, so it would be that much more menacing. He could have been a wonderful director . . . such a sad, sad death. . .
When I made that picture in England, it was called *Witchfinder General*, from the title of a novel. And when I came back here, I wanted very much to see it and I kept looking in the paper to see if it was going to be released. And when it was released here, they called it *Conqueror Worm*. So I started to look around, to see where the hell they got this title. And I found it. I read it one day in a book of poetry and I thought you might like to hear it because you're going to *[laughs]*!

> Lo! 'tis a gala night
>   Within the lonesome latter years!
> An angel throng, bewinged, bedight,
>   In veils, and drowned in tears,

Sit in a theatre, to see
  A play of hopes and fears,
While the orchestra breathes fitfully
  The music of the spheres.

Mimes, in the form of God on high,
  Mutter and mumble low,
And hither and thither fly—
  Mere puppets they, who come and go
At bidding of vast formless things
  That shift the scenery to and fro,
Flapping from out their Condor wings
  Invisible Woe!

That motley drama—oh, be sure
  It shall not be forgot!
With its Phantom chased for evermore,
  By a crowd that seize it not,
Through a circle that ever returneth in
  To the self-same spot,
And much of Madness, and more of Sin,
  And Horror the soul of the plot.

But see, amid the mimic rout
  A crawling shape intrude!
A blood-red thing that writhes from out
  The scenic solitude!
It writhes!—it writhes!—with mortal pangs
  The mimes become its food,
And seraphs sob at vermin fangs
  In human gore imbued.

Out—out are the lights—out all!
  And, over each quivering form,
The curtain, a funeral pall,
  Comes down with the rush of a storm,
While the angels, all pallid and wan,
  Uprising, unveiling, affirm
That the play is the tragedy "Man,"
  And its hero the Conqueror Worm.

               —*Edgar Allan Poe*

[Applause and standing ovation.]

VINCENT PRICE FILMOGRAPHY

Service DeLuxe (Universal, 1938)
The Private Lives of Elizabeth and Essex (Elizabeth the Queen) (Warners, 1939)
Tower of London (Universal, 1939)

Continued clashes with the film's director may account for Price's dour demeanor in this shot from AIP's *Conqueror Worm*.

Green Hell (Universal, 1940)

The House of the Seven Gables (Universal, 1940)

The Invisible Man Returns (Universal, 1940)

Brigham Young—Frontiersman (20th Century–Fox, 1940)

Hudson's Bay (20th Century–Fox, 1940)

The Song of Bernadette (20th Century–Fox, 1943)

The Eve of St. Mark (20th Century–Fox, 1944)

Wilson (20th Century–Fox, 1944)

Laura (20th Century–Fox, 1944)

The Keys of the Kingdom (20th Century–Fox, 1944)

Leave Her to Heaven (20th Century–Fox, 1945)

A Royal Scandal (20th Century–Fox, 1945)

Dragonwyck (20th Century–Fox, 1946)

Shock (20th Century–Fox, 1946)

The Long Night (RKO, 1947)

Moss Rose (20th Century–Fox, 1947)

The Web (Universal, 1947)

Up in Central Park (Universal, 1948)

Abbott and Costello Meet Frankenstein (voice only; Universal, 1948)

The Three Musketeers (MGM, 1948)

Rogue's Regiment (Universal, 1948)

The Bribe (MGM, 1949)

Bagdad (Universal, 1949)

The Baron of Arizona (Lippert, 1950)

Champagne for Caesar (United Artists, 1950)

Curtain Call at Cactus Creek (Universal, 1950)

His Kind of Woman (RKO, 1951)

Adventures of Captain Fabian (Republic, 1951)

The Las Vegas Story (RKO, 1952)

House of Wax (Warners, 1953)
Casanova's Big Night (unbilled guest appearance; Paramount, 1954)
Dangerous Mission (RKO, 1954)
The Mad Magician (Columbia, 1954)
Son of Sinbad (RKO, 1955)
Serenade (Warners, 1956)
While the City Sleeps (RKO, 1956)
The Vagabond King (voice only; Paramount, 1956)
The Ten Commandments (Paramount, 1956)
The Story of Mankind (Warners, 1957)
The Fly (20th Century–Fox, 1958)
House on Haunted Hill (Allied Artists, 1958)
Return of the Fly (20th Century–Fox, 1959)
The Bat (Allied Artists, 1959)
The Big Circus (Allied Artists, 1959)
The Tingler (Columbia, 1959)
House of Usher (The Fall of the House of Usher) (AIP, 1960)
Master of the World (AIP, 1961)
Pit and the Pendulum (AIP, 1961)
Naked Terror (voice only; Joseph Brenner, 1961)
Tales of Terror (AIP, 1962)
Convicts 4 (Reprieve) (Allied Artists, 1962)
Confessions of an Opium Eater (Souls for Sale) (Allied Artists, 1962)
Tower of London (United Artists, 1962)
Rage of the Buccaneers (The Black Buccaneer; Gordon il Pirata Nero) (Colorama
   Features, 1963)
The Raven (AIP, 1963)
The Haunted Palace (AIP, 1963)
Twice-Told Tales (United Artists, 1963)
Diary of a Madman (United Artists, 1963)
Beach Party (unbilled guest appearance; AIP, 1963)
Queen of the Nile (Nefertite, Regina del Nilo) (Colorama Features, 1964)
The Comedy of Terrors (AIP, 1964)
The Masque of the Red Death (AIP, 1964)
The Last Man on Earth (AIP, 1964)
The Tomb of Ligeia (AIP, 1964)
War-Gods of the Deep (The City Under the Sea) (AIP, 1965)
Taboos of the World (voice only; AIP, 1965)
Dr. Goldfoot and the Bikini Machine (AIP, 1965)
Dr. Goldfoot and the Girl Bombs (AIP, 1966)
House of a Thousand Dolls (AIP, 1967)
The Jackals (20th Century–Fox, 1967)
Conqueror Worm (Witchfinder General) (AIP, 1968)
Spirits of the Dead (voice only; AIP, 1969)
The Oblong Box (AIP, 1969)
The Trouble with Girls (MGM, 1969)
More Dead Than Alive (United Artists, 1969)
Cry of the Banshee (AIP, 1970)
Scream and Scream Again (AIP, 1970)
The Abominable Dr. Phibes (AIP, 1971)
Dr. Phibes Rises Again (AIP, 1972)

Theater of Blood (United Artists, 1973)
Madhouse (AIP, 1974)
The Devil's Triangle (voice only; Maron, 1974)
Journey into Fear (Stirling Gold, 1976)
It's Not the Size That Counts (Percy's Progress) (Joseph Brenner, 1978)
Scavenger Hunt (20th Century–Fox, 1979)
Days of Fury (host and narrator; Picturemedia Ltd., 1980)
The Monster Club (ITC, 1981)
House of the Long Shadows (Cannon, 1983)
Bloodbath at the House of Death (Wildwood, 1984)
The Great Mouse Detective (The Adventures of the Great Mouse Detective) (voice only; Buena Vista, 1986)
The Offspring (From a Whisper to a Scream) (Conquest Entertainment, 1987)
The Whales of August (Alive Films, 1987)
Dead Heat (New World, 1988)
Edward Scissorhands (20th Century–Fox, 1990)

Clips with Price from *The Bribe* are used in *Dead Men Don't Wear Plaid* (Universal, 1982). *It Came from Hollywood* (Paramount, 1982) includes an abridged version of the Price-narrated *House on Haunted Hill* trailer. Price's scenes in *Forever Amber* (20th Century–Fox, 1947) were reshot with George Sanders. His cameo appearance was cut out of *Bustin' Loose* (Universal, 1981). His 1989 feature *Backtrack* was released theatrically in Europe (as *Catchfire*) but went directly to cable and video in the United States in 1991. He also narrated numerous shorts and documentaries, many on art.

[The War of the Worlds] *was a big responsibility and I
was* very *inexperienced, so they took a big chance on me.*

Ann Robinson

YOU DON'T HAVE TO STAR IN A *lot* of movies to become a famous actress, sometimes you just have to be in the right *one*. Ann Robinson's fling at film stardom in the mid–1950s put her at the head of the casts of such *un*remembered titles as *Gun Duel in Durango*, *The Glass Wall* and *Gun Brothers*, but her starring stint in George Pal's knockout science fiction adventure *The War of the Worlds* has, all by itself, made her one of the top female science fiction stars.

Growing up in the proverbial shadow of the studios, the California native acted in grade school plays and later fibbed her way into the movie business as a stunt woman. She was part of Paramount's "Golden Circle" of new stars in the early 1950s but had only one leading role at the studio, in Pal's *War of the Worlds*. In 1977, after falling away from acting to attend to marriage and motherhood, she masterminded the movie's 25th anniversary celebration at the Holly Theater in Hollywood, and in 1989 she took up arms again, backing up Richard Chaves and the rest of the cast in TV's *War of the Worlds* in *their* battle against the newest wave of Martian marauders.

Your publicity says you thought about a career in medicine while you were in school. True?

That's not true; you can't believe any of that publicity stuff. When I was a little girl, I think I wanted to be a policewoman *[laughs]*! I guess acting was always interesting to me, but I didn't realize that I would ever have a chance to *be* in a movie. I liked plays and at school I always entered into plays 'cause I liked the attention, I liked showing off. The first play that I can remember being in was *Snow White*, which we did in the eighth grade at Flintridge. I was one of the ladies-in-waiting who tells the story. But I don't really know if I had any particular ambition or not in *what* I would be when I grew older.

How did you break into show biz?

As a stunt girl and an extra. One of the first films I ever did was called *Black Midnight* [1949] with Roddy McDowall. I was on a horse, doing the stuntwork for some young actress. (That's what I did the best, horseback riding.) I also doubled for Shelley Winters, when a stagecoach or a buckboard turned over in a movie called *Frenchie* [1950]—little things like that. Another one was *The Story of Molly X* [1949] where I doubled for June Havoc—in fact, that might have been my very first job as a stunt girl. I had to escape from Tehachapi State Prison, over a fifteen-foot barbed wire fence. I didn't know *any*thing about stuntwork—I had lied like crazy to get the job, telling everybody how experienced I was! I looked and I thought to myself, "What have I got myself into?", but when you're that young and stupid, nothing fazes you *[laughs]*! I took a big brown wool army blanket and threw it over my shoulder, I climbed the fence and I threw the blanket over the barbed

Previous page: Ann Robinson and Gene Barry in their signature screen roles — the leads in George Pal's *The War of the Worlds.*

wire. (I got "prickled" quite a bit, I got stuck here and there.) So now here I am up on top of the fence, and I'm saying, "Now how the hell do I get down?" I could hear the assistant director yelling, "Jump, damn it, the film is running!" And so this stupid girl jumped. Fortunately, all the sod was plowed very deeply so that, if anyone *did* escape, they could follow the footprints. So, when I jumped, I didn't hurt myself. By the way, before we did the scene, all the prisoners from that side of the compound were made to go someplace else, so they couldn't see me climb the fence. They didn't want 'em to see how easy it was for an inexperienced stunt girl to climb over *[laughs]*!

And how about your first movie acting job?

I did my first bit in *A Place in the Sun* [1951]: I was an extra and director George Stevens walked by and said, "Who has an S.A.G. card?" I said, "I do!" And he said, "Fine. Stand there, and when Elizabeth Taylor walks through the door, say, 'Hello, Angela.'" That was my first bit. After that, I don't know if I went back to being an extra or not; I probably did, but I don't recall. Then, down the line, I read in the newspaper or somewhere that they were casting at the Circle Theater. I went down and auditioned; I'd never been in a play like *that* before, this was semi-professional now. I got the part, and we were there about ten weeks. The play was called *The Wind Without Rain*, with Marty Milner, written by Ivan Tors.

All the talent scouts in those days went to plays (they still do, that's still the best place to get "discovered"). Milt Lewis from Paramount came, and he said, "When you're finished with the run of the play, come over and read for us." I *did* read, several times, but I didn't seem to be material for them at the time. But Milt liked me a lot, he thought I had potential — he was a sweetheart. One day Robert Walker was doing some retakes [for *My Son John*, 1952] at Paramount; director Leo McCarey was there and they had a complete crew. But Robert Walker became ill. Milt Lewis called me up and said, "How fast can you get down here? We've got a whole crew standing by, doing nothing, and we can make a screen test!" This was all Milt Lewis' plan. I hurried down, they ran me through wardrobe, I wore some beautiful gown that belonged to Joan Fontaine, they fixed my hair, ran me through makeup and sent me to the set. Milt said, "Do you have anything memorized?" I said, "Well, yeah, but it's got three parts in it." He said, "Make it a monologue." So, *on the spot*, I was able to incorporate all three parts — I was talking and saying all three characters' dialogue, just changing the tenses and all. We managed to get through it, and a few days or a week later, Paramount said they were interested in signing me.

You were part of a group of actors called the Golden Circle.

The Golden Circle started back in the twenties or thirties; it was Paramount's group of "stars of the future." Then in the forties and fifties they had new groups, with Susan Hayward and Robert Preston and William Holden — a whole lot of them. *Everyone* in the first and second group became a star; the only one who really became a star in the third group — *my* group — was Barbara Rush. By the way, Ann Robinson is my real name, but when I first went into the business, I found out that I couldn't use it — there was another Ann Robinson in the Screen Actors Guild, a stunt woman. I dropped the -son and went as Ann Robin for awhile. I went under contract to Paramount as Ann Robin. Then, when they did *War of the Worlds*, they said they didn't like that name and they were going to change it to Susan Roberts. I said, "Oh, my God, haven't you had enough Susans around here? Why can't I just use my own name?" They said, "What is it?" and I told them, "Ann Robinson." And they said, "Okay — works for us!" That's how *that* took place.

What did a Golden Circle player do when he — or she — was not in a movie?
      They had a room called the Fishbowl — it's still there at Paramount, but now it's all filled with electrical equipment, they use it for a storage room. Back then, it had all props — pianos and couches and things that you might need to do scenes. We used to memorize scenes and do them every week, and the heads of the studio would come in and sit and look at us. They'd sit behind a glass wall, in this darkened theater, and watch us.

Did you have to test for your part in The War of the Worlds?
      Yes. I don't think George Pal was particularly impressed with me at first — my hair was very, very short, bright red, and I just didn't look like what George had envisioned a library science teacher to look like. So I had to read for the part — here we are, back in the Fishbowl again! I did a radio play on tape called *Alter Ego*, where I had to do two voices. I played two girls; one was a sweet, innocent, adorable creature who had an inner self, an inner voice — she was possessed. And this awful, *horrible* creature came out of her and told her to murder her boyfriend [Vince Edwards]. So she stabbed him with scissors (and ended up being hanged!). I still have a copy of it and it isn't half-bad, considering the fact that I was inexperienced and just doing it from instinct. The drama coach, Charlotte Clary, told George Pal, "I want you to listen to this recording that Ann did." So he listened and he was *very* impressed. Gene Barry thought it was a trick, he said, "Oh, she's recorded it twice, it's a trick." And so Charlotte told me to go in the Fishbowl and do it again, for George Pal. I've never been really nervous, but twice in my career, my legs gave out from underneath me. Once was when Gene Kelly wanted me to walk down the stairs as a showgirl in *An American in Paris* [1951] and I couldn't walk down the stairs in a bathing suit and high heels because Gene Kelly was staring at me. The second time was when I had to go into the Fishbowl and read for George Pal. (Gene Barry and the director, Byron Haskin, were there, too.) I had to sit down, my knees gave way, I got so nervous.

But I repeated what I had done on the tape and he realized it wasn't a trick, I was able to do it all by myself. That impressed him, and he said, "Well, we'll *make* her look the way we want her to look." He was afraid my short, bright red hair—my "poodle cut"—would date the picture. So they put these ghastly hair pieces on me, these terrible bangs and this awful hair hanging down my back, and if *that* hasn't dated the picture, nothing will *[laughs]*!

Anyway, after they decided they liked me, *then* we did have to do a screen test, Gene Barry *and* I together, from the movie. We did the farmhouse scene—sitting down, having the eggs. That was our screen test, I guess to see how we looked together, or to see how we looked in Technicolor.

Do you happen to know what other actresses might have been up for the role?

Oh, everybody that was in the Golden Circle. They read a lot of people. But they wanted unknowns. George Pal didn't want a well-known person. I asked him once how I got the part and he said, "Because I wanted *you* . . . and because my *wife* approved!" By the way, I met his wife Zsoka, too, and she was a lovely, gracious woman.

Was it shot mostly on the lot?

Yes, everything was done on Stage eighteen except a couple of things on the back lot. Gene Barry went downtown, to Sixth and Hill or Eighth and Hill on a Sunday morning and did some shots down there, running through L.A. They did that around six o'clock on a Sunday morning when there was no traffic. Then we did some things in the Hollywood Hills, up on location. And we went to Arizona to use the Arizona National Guard, who were on maneuvers. All that stuff you see with us running around tanks and things was done in Arizona—that's what we did first. I always figured they had us do *that* first so that if we got flattened by one of those tanks, they could recast pretty easily *[laughs]*!

What about the "exteriors" at the crater at the beginning?

That was all Stage eighteen. Even the miniatures were done on eighteen—*and* the farmhouse. With the exceptions I mentioned, there wasn't anything that wasn't done on Stage eighteen. (Sounds like Hangar eighteen where the government supposedly has all the U.F.O.s hidden!)

What kind of guy was Pal?

The most wonderful man in the world. I'd never met such a kind, sweet gentleman. Brilliant, soft-spoken—he was *everything,* everything anybody could imagine, just the nicest person in the world. Not a mean bone in his body.

His "rep" these days is that, if he'd been a little less sweet and a little more tough, he could have gone a lot farther than he did.

I think everyone took advantage of him, no question about it. MGM took advantage of him, and so did Warner Brothers. And I'm not sure he was treated very well at *Paramount* at the beginning — he wanted to do *War of the Worlds* and Paramount threw it in the trash! Cecil B. DeMille pulled it out of the trash and said, "You're crazy if you don't do this," and I believe that DeMille was responsible for convincing them that George should do it.

Was he on the set much?

Every day, absolutely. And so was Byron Haskin. You never saw any discord or harsh words. And Byron was adorable, *so* nice. This picture was a big responsibility and I was *very* inexperienced, so they took a big chance on me. I've heard that an awful lot of people don't like [my performance] — fans and people like that — but then a lot of people think I was *great*!

So Haskin was a good director for you?

He was very, very nice and very helpful. And he taught me lots of little camera tricks, like how to use my eyes in a suspenseful manner, and *not* to over-mug. He taught me how to move my eyes first, and *then* my head — things that would add a little suspense to the scene, but things that an inexperienced young girl wouldn't think to do.

Was Pal giving Haskin directorial suggestions?

Oh, I would imagine so, they had *lots* of conferences. They worked extremely well together. The associate producer was Y. Frank Freeman, Jr., and he also was a very nice man — very quiet, but a good friend and a nice person. His father was one of the heads of the studio.

Are Pal and Freeman really in the movie, playing bums?

Yes, they are — they're listening to a radio out in front of some store. But I *think* that that was actually shot for *When Worlds Collide*.

Was War of the Worlds *perceived as a "big" picture for Paramount while it was in production?*

Oh, yes, because it was a George Pal picture. It was a big, *big* picture and everybody treated *us* very big — "star treatment." I was terribly excited, this was big stuff. Lots of publicity and attention — it was wonderful. They took great pains with this, every step of the way.

How long were you on the picture?

We started in pouring-down rain the first or second day of February nineteen fifty-two. They had to bring Gene Barry out of Laurel Canyon in a weapons carrier because everything was flooded — we were having torrential rains. It was quite an opening day! How long did we work on it? Two or three months maybe,

I *really* don't know—we didn't work on it physically as long as it took for the special effects. It came out on the twenty-fifth of November, nineteen fifty-three.

Have you ever read the H.G. Wells book?
No.

How was acting opposite Gene Barry?
Oh, he was great. I just felt so good with him—he was strong and protective and helpful. He'd come from Broadway and he was a song-and-dance man, and he was *awfully* kind and *awfully* nice to me, and helped me out a lot. My son and his daughter took ballet lessons together twenty years ago, and so one day he came to pick her up. I ran over to his little Mercedes and he couldn't believe who was running across the lawn—he was just *so* tickled to see me. Then, when he was doing *La Cage aux Folles* down at the Pantages in Los Angeles, I went to a matinee one day. I went to the stage door and wrote down my name, and in case he didn't remember my name, I put *War of the Worlds* underneath it! I wasn't taking any chances *[laughs]*! And he came *racing* to the door, grabbed me by my hand and dragged me through—he hugged me and kissed me and said, "Look at you! Look at you!" He was just so kind, so sweet! He dragged me around to meet all the cast members—he said, "Did you see *War of the Worlds*? This is my leading lady!" He's such a neat guy! He's in Palm Springs now and friends of mine see him quite often. I, being a mountain person, not a desert person, will *not* go to Palm Springs. It's ninety or one hundred degrees at twelve o'clock at night!

According to Byron Haskin, Barry was "terrible" in War of the Worlds.
I thought he was great. And he never looked more handsome. I don't think they could have cast anyone else who was as good as he was, or suited the part better.

Was Lee Marvin really considered for that part?
Yes. But he didn't know it! Years later, my son was working on *The Mike Douglas Show* and he told me Lee Marvin was going to be on. I said, "Ask him about being up for that part in *War of the Worlds*." And it was all news to Lee Marvin, he hadn't had the slightest idea.

What about Les Tremayne?
I "grew up" listening to Les Tremayne on radio, the same way I grew up with George Pal and his Puppetoons. And suddenly here I was with my "heroes" that I knew when I was a little girl! Les and I used to sit and he'd reminisce about *Orphan Annie* and *Jack Armstrong,* and he would tell me all the characters he played. And we would play games about who the sponsors were—Ovaltine for *Orphan Annie,* on and on. I loved him! And he and I still

do see each other off and on and he looks just the same, he looks *wonderful*—mustache, full head of hair, distinguished and, of course, that *voice*.

If you had been picking your own parts in those days, what kind of parts would they have been?

Gee, I don't know. I was so inexperienced, I don't know *who* I identified with—I was so swept up in the whole thing, things like that didn't occur to me. I couldn't sing and dance, as much as I would have loved to, and I never pictured myself as being a comedienne. (Everybody compared me to Ann Sheridan in looks; in fact, Warner Brothers wanted to hire me to do the Ann Sheridan part in the *Kings Row* TV show, but I had signed with Edward Small to do *Fury* with Peter Graves.) So I imagine that it would have been normal, regular dramatic parts.

Did you have an "approach" to your War of the Worlds *role?*

Oh, I just did what I was told to do. I never even heard of the expression "approach," it was really just flying by the seat of your pants. I was so young, what was there to call upon? I was really playing *myself* as if I were a young girl at that time, living in a small town. It was a nice, *quiet* era anyway, the fifties—everybody was just *nice!*

Were you still living at home at that point?

I was. My father didn't believe that unmarried women should live by themselves. I don't think he did me any favor, though, because I should have learned how to manage my affairs, my money and rent, that sort of thing. Things were too easy for me. The first time I moved away was when I married and went to Mexico. And *that* was quite a departure—living in a foreign country and *barely* speaking the language.

How much money were you making at Paramount?

Hah! One hundred twenty-five dollars a week, that was my contract. But I was making twenty-five dollars *more* than the other contract players, and I don't know why. And they didn't put me on hiatus, they paid me right straight through, fifty-two weeks, and again I have no idea why—maybe I just had a good agent! And when I was loaned out to do *The Glass Wall* [1953], Vittorio Gassman's first [American] movie, they charged the other studio one thousand dollars a week for my services. But *I* still got one hundred twenty-five dollars!

Apart from War of the Worlds, *did you make any other movies at Paramount?*

No. When I was loaned out to do *The Glass Wall*, I thought, "Gee, my career's on its way. Another studio, another group of people want me!" I got a little full of myself, I thought it was so great.

The Martian (Charles Gemora) in *The War of the Worlds* indulges in an *E.T.*-ish impulse to reach out and touch someone—unsuspecting Ann Robinson.

What was your best scene in War of the Worlds?

Everybody likes the sitting-at-the-breakfast-table, cooking-the-eggs scene. That's probably the *nicest,* the most *normal.* I wasn't over-acting, I was just being a normal girl, none of this screaming and running around. It was a nice, quiet scene and a *thoughtful* scene. It was such a departure from all the hysteria and noise and racket—finally you have these two people talking to each other. By the way, my character, Sylvia, and Gene's, Clayton Forrester, we were thrust together, we were *not* lovers. He was stuck with me through the whole movie! Everybody keeps saying there was a romantic interest. Sylvia might have had a crush on him when she was doing her thesis, and she was tickled to death to meet him in the opening scene, but they were never, *ever* sweethearts, or fell in love with one another. It was a nice scene when he held her in his arms and she was sleeping; I liked *those* types of scenes.

Your best-remembered scene is the one with the Martian.

Charles Gemora was the Filipino chap who played the monster. He must have made that costume to fit his own body, because he was a slight individual. He put that latex suit over his head and body—it came down to his hips. His fingers reached as far as the elbows, where there were three little rings attached to wires—that would make the suckered Martian fingers open and close. He knelt on a wooden dolly and very gently they rolled him into the scene. He couldn't see very well—in fact, maybe he couldn't see out of that tri-colored eye at *all*. Then that big arm of his was placed upon my shoulder—someone had to do it *for* him, place his arm on my shoulder, and then get out of the shot. I could hardly feel it, it was so gentle. We had to do that several times to get accustomed to it. Gene Barry pulled me away from him, Gemora got yanked out of the shot on the dolly and Gene threw a hatchet. Then in the next shot, you see the Martian's shadow run by and you see the hatchet sticking out of his chest. And I always thought, "This guy might have been nice!" Maybe we ruined a chance for peace because Gene Barry got overzealous and threw that hatchet! This Martian was just coming up behind me to tap me on the shoulder—he wasn't aggressive, he wasn't mean. Of course, the Martians *had* blown my uncle apart, along with a bunch of other people, but maybe *this* guy was the nice one who wanted to negotiate. And Gene "thanked" him with a hatchet in the chest *[laughs]*!

My biggest surprise was when I came on the set one day and they had the "cobra" there—the ray-zapper. That's the only prop that was life-sized. I walked up to look at it and somebody turned the damn thing on—and it scared me to *death [laughs]*! The light came on and noise came out of it and, Lord!, I jumped. They had great sport with me *that* day!

Do you remember where you saw the picture for the first time?

Yes, at the sneak preview at the Fairfax Theater on Fairfax and Third Street in Los Angeles. Everybody [involved in the making of the movie] was probably there. Those were the days when they passed out cards for you to write your opinion on, and leave in a little box when you walked out. I remember standing there in the lobby, and not a person recognized me. It was a riot!

Why did you leave Paramount?

[Laughs.] Because they *asked* me to! When my contract was to be renewed in September-October 1953, it was not renewed. George Pal, Frank Freeman, Jr.,

people like that begged [Paramount] — they said, "The movie hasn't even come out yet, what are you *doing?*" It did no good. I don't know what I did, I don't know what happened, I don't know if I stepped on someone's toes, if somebody was jealous, if somebody was angry with me. In those days, you didn't do *any*thing wrong — in the Golden Circle, you couldn't even smoke or drink, even if you were twenty-one. But somebody got a bee in their bonnet, somebody didn't like me, and they were *adamant* about not renewing my contract. So to this day it's a mystery. Then later, in November when the picture was out, Paramount wanted me to tour! It was so strange, they had to hire me back because they needed me to publicize the movie. So they paid me two hundred dollars a week to tour!

Who else toured with the movie?

Just me. I went to New York for the opening at the Mayfair Theater. I remember there was a Saturday or a Sunday when all the publicity people left me alone in New York City — they just headed for the hills on the weekend. I'd never been there before — I got lost on the subway, took a hansom cab ride, all that sort of stuff. I was walking in Times Square and saw myself two or three stories high on this big billboard for *War of the Worlds* — it was just incredible. I took pictures of it and there was a soldier there, and I asked him if he would be kind enough to take a picture of me with this theater in the background. Afterwards he said, "What did you do that for?" I said, "Well, you see that great big character over there? That's me." He said *[sarcastically]*, "Sure it is." I said, "Well, we'll go across the street to the theater, there are some pictures of me out in front."

After that, I said, "You want to see the picture?" and he said, "Sure." But the line to get in was around the block for two miles, three or four people deep! So I went up to the ticket-taker and I explained to him that I was Ann Robinson and I was in the movie and Paramount said I could come and see it if I wanted to. I'm sure he thought I was a dingdong. So he called the manager and I said the same thing to *him*. He said, "Who's the soldier?" and I blurted out, "Oh, he's my *cousin!*" Because all of a sudden I realized I had "picked up" a stranger — I was so embarrassed, so humiliated, that they might think I had picked up some soldier off the street! (He looked a lot like Jimmy Lydon, oddly enough — that's how I remember the kid.) The manager scratched his head and he said, "Do you have any i.d.?" So I showed him my California driver's license and he said, "Well, you don't *look* like her but I guess you can go in." *[Laughs.]*

What other cities did you visit?

The entire eastern seaboard, all the way down to Norfolk, Virginia. I remember arriving there late at night, and Paramount forgot to pick me up. I had spoken to a young man on the plane and he said, "You're going to Norfolk

When her interplanetary telecommunicator is on the fritz, Queen Juliandra makes do any way she can. Ann Robinson behind the scenes on *Rocky Jones, Space Ranger.*

and you've never been there before? Let me tell you something: This is a navy town, you've got to be careful." So now here I am waiting—Paramount forgot about me. About a half-hour, forty-five minutes later, back comes this young man with his wife—his wife had picked him up and they had left, but this guy somehow *knew* that something would go wrong. He and his wife took me to my hotel, and he said, "I'll tell you what to do. You move your bed in front of that door, and don't come out till morning." And all night long, my phone was ringing and notes were being slipped under my door! It was just a *sea* of sailors in white suits, and I was scared to death *[laughs]*!

On TV's Rocky Jones, Space Ranger, *you were a regular as Juliandra, an alien queen. How did you get that part?*
I probably went out on an interview; I don't exactly remember. Maybe they said to themselves, "Gee, she's been in a great big science fiction Paramount movie. We'd be dumb not to hire her for *our* show." And so I got the part. Richard Crane [Rocky Jones] was a very charming man—very personable, very likable, and very much to himself. He wasn't outgoing or gregarious and he wasn't a flirt. Just a nice person.

Where were these shot?
Out at the Hal Roach Studios in Culver City. And these were quick—you'd learn fifteen, twenty pages of dialogue for a half-hour show, and they shot one half-hour show every three days or so. It was almost like working on a soap, *very*, very fast. It was a case of memorizing your lines, hitting your mark and staying out of the other guy's key light—*that* is the secret to television!

Was it fun working that fast?
Yeah, I guess. See, we weren't doing Ibsen *[laughs]*, it was just fun. As long as you didn't hold up production by not knowing your lines, as long as you didn't stutter, everything was fine. [Producer] Roland Reed was a very nice man; he used to always tease me about going on his yacht, knowing perfectly well I wouldn't go. He was just a nice guy. I had a cat that scratched my face and gave me impetigo, which is terribly contagious. We had to shut down the whole production because I could have spread it through the cast. That sweet man paid for all my medical bills—he sent me to a doctor to have special X-ray treatments. (Later on in life they can possibly *kill* you, but who knew then *[laughs]*?) He didn't bat an eye—it had to cost him a lot of money to close down production and pay my bills and it wasn't even his fault, it was *my* cat. He was a lovely man.

Sounds like you've had a lot of luck meeting nice producers.
I really did. I think I had some sort of an attitude, or an upbringing, or an *aura* about me—people didn't bother me. Nobody molested me, nobody approached me. Either I was totally sexless *[laughs]*, or they thought to themselves, "No, she's not the type." No casting couches, nothing like that! I was either terribly innocent and people realized it, or I was totally unappealing.

What about the Rocky Jones *director, Hollingsworth Morse?*

He was really nice, too, a gentleman. I remember going to his house years ago with a boyfriend of mine, I had to pick up something, and he had a magnificent home in Beverly Hills with wonderful souvenirs of every place he'd ever been on locations. I was very impressed with the man.

You also played Juliandra's evil sister Noviandra. Did you enjoy that?
Oh, God, yes! I was Bette Davis, I was Agnes Moorehead, I was John Barrymore—I was all of them rolled up into one. I chewed up the *walls*, it was *wonderful!* I did everything but *snarl!* I was so awful, I was so corny! I *loved* doing something like that—but I didn't get paid any more for doing two parts *[laughs]*. To play opposite me when Juliandra and Noviandra were in the scene together, they got a girl about my height and build for over-the-shoulder shots. They didn't have that wonderful electronic stuff that they have now, where you can walk right in and put your arms around each other. But for the time, I thought it was done very well [with a split-screen]. Those episodes with the bad sister were, I guess, the ones that were the most fun.

Whose idea were your sexy costumes?
I got to tell 'em what I wanted. They said, "What kind of a skirt would you like to wear?" and I said, "I want something slit up the leg." I really had a neat figure and a nice, tiny waist—those were the years of the waist-cincher. And because I wore my hair parted in the middle, they fixed a skullcap for me.

Did anybody wonder if maybe you were too sexy for a kids' show?
Well, look at the comic books, look at how they draw those bosomy heroines. No one ever objected to *those* round hips and full bosoms. Look at the Phantom and his girlfriend, living in that cave with him—she was well put together! So they never objected to drawing women who looked like women. I didn't show any cleavage—it was just a nice, long leg and a narrow waist. I didn't have bosoms hanging out—I didn't *have* bosoms in those days *[laughs]*!
I had some great publicity pictures taken at Warner Brothers one time. I was trying to get out of the image of the straw hat and the cute little girl, I said, "Please put me in a black negligee." And so they had me in pillows, lying around with this laaaazy look on my face and my hand through my hair and my hand on my hip. And I was trying to pull the top down as low as I could, to get some cleavage. And when I saw the final pictures, they were all air-brushed out. I looked like a *boy!*

How busy were you acting-wise in the nineteen fifties?
I did a *lot* of work in the fifties, a lot of television shows—all of 'em. I can't think of any that I *didn't* do! But then I ran off to Mexico in nineteen fifty-seven and blew my career right out of the water—I married a very famous

Robinson in a sultry 1950s glamour pose.

Mexican matador, Jaime Bravo, and had two children. When I got back home, Hollywood had passed me by. I just ruined it, I blew it. I should have stayed around and paid more attention. Now I realize why they call it "the business" — because it *is* a business. I thought it was all fun and games and glamour, and I didn't take care of it *as a business*. We had two sons, Jaime, who is a director with ABC Sports, and Estefan, who's a back-up singer with a singing group called Human Drama. Both of them are doing what they like to do and they're very good at *what* they do; Jaime's won three Emmys! Their father and I were

The *War* 25th anniversary re-premiere, attended by Forry Ackerman, Zsoka and George Pal, Les Tremayne and Robinson, was such a success that the actress hopes to arrange a 50th celebration, too.

married until nineteen sixty-seven, and now I'm married since nineteen eighty-seven to Joseph Valdez, who's a real estate broker.

So you did very little acting in the nineteen sixties?

After my second son was born in nineteen sixty-three, I think I did a *Gilligan's Island* and that was about it. Motherhood suddenly took over. Then in the seventies, I found out that *War of the Worlds* was going to be reissued. I went to Paramount and I said, "Why don't you do a 'premiere' for the twenty-fifth anniversary?" The Paramount publicity people said, "Gee, that sounds like a good idea—but *you* do it." I said, "Yeah, but *you* pay for it!" And they said okay—they gave us a budget of two thousand dollars. So we did it—my husband-to-be and I put that twenty-fifth anniversary on. And there was a lot involved—you have to hire off-duty policemen, you have to rent klieg lights, rent barriers, get insurance, champagne, flowers, a cake . . . a *lot* of work! Well, the thing snowballed; it got so big, so huge, that a lot of people started *asking* to come. It was shown that night [September 7, 1977] at the Holly Theater on Hollywood Boulevard in tandem with *When Worlds*

Collide, so we had some stars from *that*; George Pal flew in from Europe, Les Tremayne, people came from all over the country, all over the *world*. It became so huge that Paramount was absolutely flabbergasted that we put this thing on. They'd never seen anything like it in their lives—people were lined up all over the street. And the Holly was only a seven hundred–seat theater!

Had all the years of being kicked around by Hollywood changed Pal at all?
No, he was the same wonderful man. By that time, he'd decided to move his office to his home so he wouldn't get ripped off anymore. Everybody was coming in and stealing his storyboards. Like Forry Ackerman, he liked people and trusted everyone, and they walked off with everything! So in his later years he had his office in his home, so nobody could look over his shoulder and steal his ideas.

And that "re-premiere" also helped you to get back into "the business"?
Yes, it did. I got a job on *Police Woman* and I did a running part on *Days of Our Lives,* a soap opera. Somewhere down the line I found out that Paramount had something up their sleeve about *War of the Worlds*—we contacted them and they said *[gruffly],* "Send us a picture." They were so *cool.* So my husband took some great pictures of me, they were eight by tens the next day, and they were in Paramount's hands a day later! And the day after *that,* Paramount said, "Let's do lunch"—and they signed me on the spot. Working on the show was fun—it was *great.* Those people treated me like royalty—I can't imagine being treated any better, I got top-drawer star treatment. [Producer] Sam Strangis and his son [Greg] are just charming people, and Richard Chaves was so adorable. It was just a thrill. We shot up in Toronto.

You were also in a low-budget item called Midnight Movie Massacre.
Here's what happened on that. Robert Clarke and I went to Kansas City, Missouri, to star in a movie version of the old television show *Space Patrol* for [producer] Wade Williams. The director who Wade had selected, thinking that the guy knew what he was doing, made a wonderful, beautiful bunch of scenes. But when they were edited together, there was no continuity. Meanwhile, Wade's backers were saying, "We'd like to get our investment back," so Wade had to capitulate and make it something kids would like. So Wade made *Midnight Movie Massacre,* about a monster that eats up everybody in a movie theater, and *Space Patrol* became the movie-*within*-a movie in that. I saw Robert Clarke just the other day, and as much as we both love Wade Williams, Bob said, "I have a mental block about that movie!"

On this, the fortieth anniversary of War of the Worlds, *tell me what your opinion of the movie is today.*
I've gotten more mileage out of *War of the Worlds* than Vivien Leigh did with *Gone with the Wind.* And now—in a totally different genre, of course—

Ann Robinson (seen here in a current shot) still enjoys the occasional TV role, as well as looping dialogue into features (*The Dead Are Alive, To Begin Again,* many more).

here I am, up with the classics! So how can I *not* be proud of the movie? Even Gene Barry, as wonderful as he was in *La Cage,* is going to be remembered one hundred years from today for *War of the Worlds.* As long as there are still prints and laserdiscs and videocassettes, it'll still be playing. It was a wonderful movie and a wonderful experience. My husband and I had a great time doing that fortieth anniversary "premiere," and in ten more years, we're going to do the fiftieth!

ANN ROBINSON FILMOGRAPHY

As Ann Robin:

The Story of Molly X (Universal, 1949)
Black Midnight (Monogram, 1949)
Frenchie (Universal, 1950)
Peggy (Universal, 1950)
An American in Paris (MGM, 1951)
A Place in the Sun (Paramount, 1951)
Goodbye, My Fancy (Warners, 1951)
Callaway Went Thataway (MGM, 1951)
I Want You (RKO, 1951)
The Cimarron Kid (Universal, 1951)

As Ann Robinson:

The War of the Worlds (Paramount, 1953)
The Glass Wall (Columbia, 1953)
Bad for Each Other (Columbia, 1953)
Dragnet (Warners, 1954)
Gun Brothers (United Artists, 1956)
Julie (MGM, 1956)
Gun Duel in Durango (Duel in Durango) (United Artists, 1957)
Damn Citizen (Universal, 1958)
Imitation of Life (Universal, 1959)

Basil Rathbone had sunk low [by doing The Black Sleep*],
and I think he found it uncomfortable to accept the
lesser members of the hierarchy as being social equals.
Now, I'm accusing him of a kind of snobbery and I can't
be sure that that's an accurate evaluation ... but at
least that was my feeling at the time.*

Herbert Rudley

No OTHER HORROR MOVIE, not even Universal's campy "monster rallies" of the 1940s, had a cast to compare with the lineup of fright film luminaries that turned out for 1956's *The Black Sleep*. And consequently no leading man ever appeared with as many great ghouls in a single session than the hero of *Black Sleep*, stage and screen actor Herbert Rudley.

A former Philadelphian, Rudley left Temple University at the end of his second year, journeyed to New York and won a scholarship with Eva Le Gallienne's Civic Repertory Theatre. He made his first stage appearance in 1928 and went on to do many more, including the Judith Anderson / Maurice Evans *Macbeth* (with Rudley as Macduff). He repeated his stage role in *Abe Lincoln in Illinois* in the 1940 Hollywood version, appeared in over two dozen films since, and also worked regularly in TV (including a two-year stint as husband to Eve Arden on NBC's *The Mothers-in-Law*).

How did you get the leading man part in The Black Sleep?

The director, Reginald LeBorg, had apparently seen some of my other work, and when he was engaged by [producer] Howard Koch to do the film, he called me in for an interview and wanted to know if I'd be interested in working with him in that particular picture. I was a working actor at that time, and I said, "Certainly!" And it became a very happy association.

Wasn't that heroic role a change of pace for you, movie-wise?

That's kind of a hard question to answer. You see, I have never been a personality actor, I've always been basically a character actor. The range of my acting career has gone from A to Z rather than from A to B. From one point of view, that [being an "A to B" actor] was an asset; it can be helpful in some ways if you're known for playing a certain type of role, whether it's a heavy, a leading man, a comedian or whatever. When you're established along those lines, you're called for anything that might come up in those arenas. People didn't quite know who *I* was, because whatever role I was involved in was totally different from most of those other roles; it was not predicated upon a personality. Now, I'm not denigrating that approach; there've been some wonderful stars created out of that approach. But I was theater-trained, and as a person in the theater, each role was an adventure in itself. It was stepping out of your own personality into the character. I was basically a character actor, and therefore I never established a persona as an individual.

To answer your question — boy, did I take the long way around! — yes, it was different, but so was every *other* role that I played.

What did you enjoy about working on The Black Sleep?

Previous page: Stage and screen actor Herbert Rudley played an uncharacteristic "monster fighter" role in the all-star horror free-for-all *The Black Sleep,* with Patricia Blake.

Basil Rathbone, Patricia Blake and Herbert Rudley don't look like they wanted their picture taken. Publicity shot from *The Black Sleep*.

I think the interesting thing about *The Black Sleep*, as opposed to a great many of the other horror films, is that it was predicated upon a script which had an element of warped but actual reality. In other words, it was not so far beyond the ken of probability that you had to dismiss it, or accept it with a big jump of imaginative acceptance. It was based on a simple but basically realistic concept. Now, it *did* go far afield in the subsequent development of the story, but it was rooted in some sort of off-key reality as opposed to so many of the other horror films which were *per se* just horror films. So everything that was done in relation to the film had that basis in some sort of elemental truth—distorted though it might have become! I think that was true for Howard Koch, who was the functioning producer, and also for Reggie LeBorg. He strove to keep in touch with an essence of reality throughout that film. I think he was successful at that, and that that's one of the reasons why *The Black Sleep* has become kind of a celebrated film of its genre.

How quickly was the film shot?
    Oh, very quickly. It was a low-budget film, and we had it done in ten or eleven days.

The big draw for fans, of course, is the all-star horror cast.

One of the interesting things about the all-star cast of horror people was in relation to Bela Lugosi. He played the mute butler in that, and, amusingly enough, he had numerous discussions with Reggie, pleading for a chance to "break his silence" and speak, even if it was only a couple of words. He did not want to feel that he was playing a voiceless character. Reggie was very touched by that, I remember, and he tried to explain to him that that was the character — Reggie couldn't suddenly switch and have him talk, because it would destroy the basic concept of the character. I think Bela knew that from the beginning, but it was just a case of actor's ego — everybody else was talking, why the hell couldn't he *[laughs]*?

Could he have handled a speaking role at that point?
I think he could have, within certain limitations. Now, Akim Tamiroff, of course, had a ball, and he was marvelous in it. He had no problem with silence — his problem was *verbosity [laughs]*! But he was not responsible for it, it was written that way.

Did you have any chance to socialize with Lugosi?
No, I did not. As a matter of fact, I had very little socialization with anybody outside of Reggie and Howard Koch. That included even Basil Rathbone, with whom so many of my scenes were played. But I have never been an actor who could not disassociate himself from the function in a particular project. I've always been married — many times! *[laughs]* — and my life was not devoted to the social life of mingling with actors *per se*. There have been a few exceptions, like Gregory Peck, whom I had a long-standing relationship with — we went all the way back to a play of Irwin Shaw's called *Sons and Soldiers* in which Greg played my fantasy son.
When I came out to Hollywood, I had no concept of "the Hollywood scene." I had been theater-trained and theater-bred. And in the theater, there is no caste system. I came out here in forty-two to make *Rhapsody in Blue* (and that was only because I thought I was going into the Army, and I wanted to make a few bucks to leave for my wife and child). I had known, from New York, a number of people who had subsequently become out in Hollywood big-name writers, producers, directors and so on. I used to invite them to evenings at my home, along with actors who were making maybe five hundred, seven hundred fifty dollars a week. I remember [Philip and Julius] Epstein being present at one of these evenings — I must have had maybe thirty or thirty-five people there, all of varying groups, representatives of different phases of the theater from an economic point of view. Phil came over to me and said, "Herb, what the hell are you trying to do? Revolutionize Hollywood?" I said, "I don't know what you're talking about." He said, "Well, look at the group of people you have here tonight. You've got the three or four thousand dollars a week writers, you've got a producer who's making five

thousand dollars a week—and then you've also got people who are bit players!" I said, "But they're my *friends*!" And he said, "*You can't do that in Hollywood.* There's a caste system." I said, "Oh, fuck off—don't give me that shit!" I was really very put out by it.

It wasn't until many years later, in my relationship with Greg Peck, by the way, that this came home to me. He would on occasion be invited to my place and I would be invited to his, and one evening, he invited me to a big party at his place. I got there, and only the *crème de la crème* of the motion picture industry was present—*except for me.* And I suddenly realized how valid that comment about the caste system was. Because *I* suddenly became uncomfortable—this was the only time in my relationship with Greg that I did. *So* uncomfortable that, though Greg continued to attempt to maintain our relationship, I veered away from him. I just didn't feel that I could mix comfortably in that upper echelon. I was just a working actor. I was a *respected* actor, but I was not in the star category, I was not important in that sense. And we drifted apart as a result of that. Which was a lesson to me. I had been naive.

Basil Rathbone gave a lot of parties, too. Were you ever at any of those?

No, I was never invited to a party of Rathbone's. As a matter of fact, I don't think Basil socialized with *any*body in the cast of *The Black Sleep.* I have a sneaking suspicion that this was at the nadir of his career, and that he had sunk to a level which was uncomfortable for him. The reverse of what I was telling you about myself. Rathbone had sunk low, and I think he found it uncomfortable to accept the lesser members of the hierarchy as being social equals. Now, I'm accusing him of a kind of snobbery and I can't be *sure* that that's an accurate evaluation of his position, but at least that was my feeling at the time. He would leave the studio as quickly as possible. (But then *[laughs],* so did I!)

Did you enjoy your scenes with him?

Oh, yes, he was a professional and he was excellent. There was no friction, no attempt to take advantage of a fellow actor in a scene. He was a very generous and nice person to work with.

He may not have thought much of The Black Sleep, *but he gave a very good performance in it.*

He did—he gave an *excellent* performance in a role which could very easily have become a caricature. And that was a mark of his professionalism, his ability and natural talent. I thought he was marvelous in it. I never worked with him before or since.

You were both in The Court Jester *[1956].*

Well, yes, come to think of it, and there *were* a few scenes in which we were both involved. But we had no real contact.

Lon Chaney, Jr., can't be bothered to set aside his cigarette for this publicity photo with Rudley for *The Black Sleep*.

How about Lon Chaney?

Not much recollection. My whole approach as an actor was that I had a job to do, and I was concerned with doing it to the best of my then-ability. And that was the end of it. There were no lingering social aftermaths, at least on my part, in the main. John Carradine I admired; as a talent, I think he was quite extraordinary. And as an intellect, he was quite *brilliant*. His classical knowledge was outstanding. I think he deserved a much better fate than what he got.

Your leading lady, Patricia Blake, didn't seem to go too far in the business.

I was not impressed with Patricia. I don't know whatever happened to her. She was pretty, and she had a nice personality, but I didn't think she had any plusses from the point of view of abilities.

LeBorg told me his one problem on Black Sleep *was that the horror stars were trying to outdo one another.*

That's true. But I think, in the main, that he did an excellent job of keeping control. Reggie had a Prussian background, and *[laughs]* when his authority was challenged, he was quite capable of handling that. As a matter of fact, I think that that aspect of his personality may have had something to do with his lack of acknowledged success in the industry, as opposed to his ability. We talked so much, and he very often told me about his experiences, that I had the feeling that he got into a lot of trouble because of that. He was bucking the system. And he didn't have the acceptable requirements. For example, when Bette Davis bucked Warner Brothers, she was in a position to make her rebellion effective. Reggie, when he would rebel against the institution, was not in that position. And I think he suffered because of that. I think his ability was far above what his success was.

He left Universal because they kept giving him horror pictures to direct— then, right after he left, Universal dropped the horrors and started doing more prestigious films!

It was really kind of sad. He should have been more creatively productive in a higher level of film than he was relegated to. He was a very, very interesting man.

The Black Sleep *was a big moneymaker.*

Yes, it was, especially in relation to its investment—which was minuscule *[laughs]*! I saw it when it came out and I thought that overall, considering the minimum amount of time and the minimum amount of money that was expended *in* that time, it was a *very,* very good film. There were things about myself that, in retrospect, I was not too happy about, but *again,* it was a melodramatic situation (to say the least!). I think I may have gone overboard on a few occasions, although I attempted to stay within realistic bounds. And I don't think Reggie let me get *too* far out of hand! Reggie got as much out of that film as could have been expected, if not more.

Reggie LeBorg and I became very close friends. Out of that relationship, we developed a writing combination, and based on an idea that he had about Mary Magdalene and Matthew, we wrote a religious script. Initially, he had hired a writer who was very well-known in the industry to collaborate with him on it. Reggie knew that *I* wrote, and at the end of work one evening, he asked me to read it and tell him what I thought. I felt that the idea was fascinating, but that the development was very poor. I told him so, and he asked me, "What would *you* have done with it?" I began to improvise, and as a result of that, he said, "I think your ideas are marvelous. Would you like to collaborate with me?" I said, "You already *have* a collaborator." (Collaboration is a difficult thing, very close to marriage; if you have a third party in there, it's not a very advisable program!) "However," I said, "if you feel that strongly about it, and if you can relieve yourself of your other obligation, I'd be very interested in doing it with you." So he bought the other writer out and we collaborated on it. Reggie was a multi-talented man, and I was extremely fond of him and respectful of his ability.

What are you doing these days?

    I retired in eighty-four or eighty-five. I was given a television script to read with a certain part in mind, I took the script home to read it, and it included a list of the characters with a minuscule description of each. One was described as "a middle-aged man of thirty-five." I thought to myself, "Something is very screwy here. When does a man of thirty-five become middle-aged?" I realized that the handwriting was on the wall, and that I would very soon be faced with a choice: Either to be retired, or to be unemployed. I chose retirement.

    These days, I'm enjoying my release from having to prove myself. I play a good bit of golf, and I continue to do some writing. My wife and I have a very active social life. I am, for the first time, happily married—this is my fourth attempt, and the one that I think will last. (We've been married thirty-five years, and went together for four years prior to that.) And occasionally, when my wife gets a little out of hand, I tell her, "Look, honey, you're my next-to-last...!"

HERBERT RUDLEY FILMOGRAPHY

Abe Lincoln in Illinois (RKO, 1940)
Marriage Is a Private Affair (MGM, 1944)
The Seventh Cross (MGM, 1944)
The Master Race (RKO, 1944)
Rhapsody in Blue (Warners, 1945)
A Walk in the Sun (20th Century–Fox, 1945)
Brewster's Millions (United Artists, 1945)
Decoy (Monogram, 1946)
Hollow Triumph (The Scar) (Eagle-Lion, 1948)
Casbah (Universal, 1948)
Joan of Arc (RKO, 1948)
The Silver Chalice (Warners, 1954)
Artists and Models (Paramount, 1955)
The Black Sheep (United Artists, 1956)

The Court Jester (Paramount, 1956)
Raw Edge (Universal, 1956)
That Certain Feeling (Paramount, 1956)
Tonka (Buena Vista, 1958)
The Bravados (20th Century–Fox, 1958)
The Young Lions (20th Century–Fox, 1958)
The Big Fisherman (Buena Vista, 1959)
The Jayhawkers! (Paramount, 1959)
Beloved Infidel (20th Century–Fox, 1959)
The Great Impostor (Universal, 1960)
Hell Bent for Leather (Universal, 1960)
Follow That Dream (United Artists, 1962)
Falling in Love Again (International Picture Show, 1980)

*The thing I remember most about writing [horror and
science fiction] was how much fun it was. It's an
interesting kind of writing because you don't use much of
your own life and experience in it; it's out of your head,
it's fantasy, it's imagining. I was very fortunate that
so much of what I wrote got on the screen.*

Harry Spalding

THE NAME MIGHT NOT BE INSTANTLY RECOGNIZABLE, even to diehard fans of science fiction films, but throughout the late 1950s and early 1960s, writer Harry Spalding was right-hand man to Robert Lippert, the exhibitor-cum-mini-movie mogul who (under his Regal Films and Associated Producers banners) was responsible not only for the swarm of *Fly* films but also a flock of other B titles in that same period. Spalding started out as story editor to Lippert, then built up to screenwriter of *Curse of the Fly*, *The Day Mars Invaded Earth*, *The Earth Dies Screaming* and many more.

Born in Victoria, British Columbia, and brought to the States when he was six, Spalding credits his interest in writing to his mother, who read the classics aloud to him when he was still a child. His affinity for fantasy and horror subjects also dates back to his youth, when he was enamored of then-new films such as *The Lost World* and the Lon Chaney classics; the first "grown-up" magazine to which he subscribed was *Amazing Stories*. Early on, Spalding did some short story and newspaper writing, then went into the theater business as a film booker/buyer in San Francisco. Working in this capacity brought him in contact with Lippert, who asked Spalding to read and critique scripts that his company was preparing to shoot in Hollywood. In 1956, when Lippert got the go-ahead to make a steady flow of low-budget features for bottom-of-the-bill 20th Century–Fox release, Hollywood's doors opened wide for Spalding, who moved down from San Francisco to become part of the Lippert unit.

Bob Lippert loved movies from the beginning, all his life long. He got started when he was a kid in high school: He had a sixteen mm projector, so he was in charge of running films at school assemblies. He'd acquire a film on, say, a Thursday and, being a natural-born dealmaker, he'd show it Thursday night at the Elks, Friday afternoon at the school, Friday night at the American Legion, Saturday at the Presbyterian Church...! As one of his suppliers said, "If we were lucky, we'd get it back by Wednesday!" He always loved theaters — which he pronounced "the-*a*-ters" to his dying day. I first got to know him in the late forties.

How did he get started as an exhibitor?

He got hold of a small theater but had trouble getting films, so he sued his opposition, Fox West Coast, which was run by the Skouras brothers. He won his suit, and got enough money to get himself going. He started acquiring theaters and then, after awhile, he fell in love with the idea of going down to Hollywood and making movies. I always felt that that was the connection between he and Spyros Skouras. The Skouras brothers had taken over a theater circuit in trouble and built it into a dominant corporation. With these similar backgrounds, Spyros and Bob got along. The whole deal with Fox was between Lippert and Skouras, it did not involve the other people over at Fox

Previous page: Screenwriter Harry Spalding (a.k.a. "Henry Cross"), the brains behind such horror and science fiction favorites as *Witchcraft, House of the Damned* and *Curse of the Fly.*

During his story-editing days, Spalding was involved on "Terror-Topping, Supershock Thrill Sensations" like this Lippert/20th Century–Fox twin bill.

at all. If Bob had a problem, he called Skouras, and if Skouras wanted something done, he called Bob. It was very much a personal deal. The initial Regal deal called for one hundred twenty-five thousand dollar budgets, more under different circumstances. That went on for quite a while. Then, when that expired, Associated Producers came about—and they made even cheaper pictures than *Regal [laughs]*! That's when I got involved as a writer. Then at the *very* end, he co-produced a few things in England, which he put into the Fox deal.

He always seemed to have good luck with science fiction.

Rocketship X-M was one of the best science fiction things that he did; then he had a dinosaur picture called *Lost Continent* which he also had good luck with. Then he did *The Creeping Unknown* with Hammer—that was "before Hammer was Hammer." Bob and James Carreras hit it off. Carreras had a property called *The Quatermass Experiment,* and so Bob and Carreras together made that. In England, it was released as *The Quatermass Experiment* and here it went out as *The Creeping Unknown.* Of course, Hammer went on to bigger and better things in a hurry, but that was really the beginning of it.

Richard Landau, an American who'd worked for Lippert before, gets a writing credit on Creeping Unknown.

Landau had to have come in through Bob; he had been friendly with Lippert for years, and had worked for him at different times. The film starred Brian Donlevy and Margia Dean, whom Bob furnished—that was *his* end of it. Under England's Eady Plan, an American partner could only provide a very limited amount. What the financial arrangement was, I don't know.

Can you say why Lippert's name isn't in the credits?

Curiously enough, he didn't really care too much about credits. Also, if you were going to get the Eady Plan money, they were very persnickety about the percentage of non–English contributions to the film. Lippert had a good, healthy ego, but he really wasn't all that concerned about getting screen credit and that sort of thing, as many people are. His attitude towards Hollywood was always "pretty boys" and "pretty girls" and "don't take it too seriously."

He went without screen credit on The Fly *as well.*

Essentially he *did* do that first one, but it was kind of a strange thing. [Director] Kurt Neumann was a very talented man and a very cultured one— he played the piano, knew a lot about music, understood art. But he had the German background and he was fiercely independent. He was one of those people that just did not feel like fitting into "the Fox arrangement" or "the Metro arrangement" or what have you. He just loved to be out there, picking something with possibilities, and putting a deal together. And he had a lineup of people who worked with him when he found something. He also had a friend (whose name I forget, I'm sorry to say) who liked spotting properties and telling Neumann about 'em. Neumann probably paid him finder's fees and things like that, but the main point was that this gentleman just enjoyed being "part of the action." Anyhow, I came to work one Monday morning, and Kurt Neumann was there already. He handed me a copy of the newest *Playboy,* which contained a short story called *The Fly,* and said, "I've got an appointment with Bob at ten. He'd like you to read this." I read it, and loved it.

The phone rang and it was Bob, and he asked me, "How'd you like it, kid?" I said, "It's great, Bob, but I imagine everybody in town is already dickering for it." But that did not turn out to be true — *nobody* was dickering for it. So Lippert went right to work on the thing, and got an option, and set up the deal. But he didn't *complete* the deal, because he had to talk to Fox first. We were the small tail on the big dog and the production people at Fox hated to have Lippert find something that they overlooked! Fox got hold of it and read it, and wanted it. They simply made a deal with Bob: "*We'd* like to make this, but *you* buy the property" — it would be cheaper if Lippert bought it than if Fox did, naturally. So Bob and Fox worked out some financial arrangement, Kurt Neumann was included as director and producer, and it was made as a Fox picture, in color.

Who brought in James Clavell as screenwriter?
Kurt had James Clavell — always *James*, never *Jim* — whom none of us had heard of. As I remember, prior to this, Clavell had written one script (*with* somebody else) which was never produced, for RKO. Clavell's first draft [of *The Fly*] was, I think, the best first draft I ever saw, it needed very little work. Kurt practically shot it "as is," it was a really great job. Kurt produced and directed, with no further involvement by Lippert. The picture did very well.

Any other recollections of Clavell?
I remember him talking about an idea he had for a novel. He had been in a Japanese prison camp during the war, and the thing that had interested him was that the people who got along best in the prison camp, the ones who *survived* the best, were the same people who would probably land in jail in *normal* life! The very things that made them undesirable citizens made them great survivors in prison camps — and that became *King Rat,* his first novel, and subsequently a picture. Clavell was also very anxious to direct, and Lippert had an idea that he wanted to do — a war story in Asia, more or less modern-day. So Clavell wrote the script, and again the first draft was practically perfect — he's one of the few writers I ever ran across that had that facility. Lippert was having trouble getting a director, and I said, "Why don't you use Clavell?" He thought about that for a while, and the next thing I knew, Clavell came in the office and said, "Thanks very much!" And he did direct the picture, which was called *Five Gates to Hell* [1959]. During the main titles, there's even some fine print saying, "With thanks to Harry Spalding," which he just sort of sneaked in *[laughs]*! Then, of course, he went on from there. I was up at his house one time, a lovely house up in the hills, with a great view — and he said, "I always get a kick out of looking at this. It represents a hundred typewritten pages!" *[Laughs.]*

Lippert had no misgivings about using a first-time director?
The great advantage for Clavell was, we were used to this sort of thing.

Being a small Fox unit, we used to have thrust upon us the relatives of the Fox brass, who wanted to be producers, directors or whatever. We used to call 'em the Sons of the Pioneers. We had quite a number of them over the years, so we knew how to do it. We used to put the film editor up there with a new director, and we'd get certain cameramen who were good at working with new directors. All the director really had to do was work with the actors, because he would turn around and the cameraman would say, quietly, "I think you should get a reverse on that." And of course the director would say, "What's a reverse?" *[Laughs.]* But Clavell was quick to learn.

Arch Oboler went after Fox, claiming that The Fly *was very much like some story he'd written way back when.*

I didn't know that; never even heard of it.

Were you on the set of The Fly?

I don't know whether I was ever on the set at all. I *was* involved on the script but not to my usual extent, because Clavell did such a great job. In fact, probably most of the few changes that *were* made to that first draft were changes to fit in with production problems of one kind or another. I remember they brought the Fly mask over to the office, and I did put it on *[laughs]*! It was just a plain head mask, the simplest kind of a prop.

What was Lippert like? Edward Bernds told me that, if there was such a thing as reincarnation, then Lippert used to be a pirate.

I used to accuse *Clavell* of being that, a reborn pirate! Clavell was very ambitious, very talented—never forgot an enemy! He had a little plaque on his desk, TIME WOUNDS ALL HEELS. But, back to Lippert. He came from Alameda background, lived with his mother all his early life. He loved movies and theaters, and when he was nineteen he married his wife Ruth, who was an Irish girl, seventeen, if I remember correctly. Ruth's father protested vigorously, and it wound up in court when the father wanted the marriage annulled. The judge asked, "Why do you want the marriage annulled?" and the father said, "He's too young, he doesn't have a steady job. I want someone who can support my daughter." Lippert took two thousand dollars out of his pocket, held it up and said to the father, "Well, here's two thousand dollars. How much have *you* got?" And the judge was convinced! That's the kind of guy that Lippert was.

He was the quintessential entrepreneur, really; even in school, turning the sixteen mm into a going thing. And then, following that, he got into the giveaway dish business, selling dishes to the theaters to give away on Dish Nights. All his life he spent buying and selling theaters, buying and selling film, opening exchanges. He was an easy man to get along with, but he was totally concentrated. He and I had a pretty good relationship, 'cause we were

**Robert L. Lippert, production manager Harold Knox and Spalding during the
threesome's filmmaking heyday.**

both from San Francisco, we both knew the theater business, all that kind of
thing. As a matter of fact, Lippert's employees were kind of his family a good
deal of the time. He really took that attitude. But he had no interest in the
world at large; what he was interested in was what he was going to do tomorrow. This is not to disparage him; it's just that he concentrated on the bottom
line at all times. Like others of that kind, he was a little "innocent," in a way,
because he was so concentrated in the one area he was successful in. As a result,
some people didn't understand him. They'd come out of meetings with Lippert scratching their heads! He had certain people that he trusted, and *un*like
a lot of people, he didn't like "yes men" around. Unfortunately, he was *too*
fond of making deals. If he had made fewer deals and concentrated more on
the ones that he did make — in other words, made bigger pictures — he would
have probably been better off, and his reputation would have been better.

Did he seem to have a soft spot for science fiction?

Yeah, he liked that kind of picture — because he'd had some success with
it, for one thing. There were other angles about it that he liked, too. For example, if you're doing a rocket-to-the-moon film, basically you only have one set.
And that's very cheap, you see *[laughs]*!

Where were Lippert's headquarters?
Oh, we moved around—he also liked to buy real estate *[laughs]*! He
didn't believe in ever having offices in a building he didn't own. We were in
Culver City right across from MGM at one time, we had offices on Wilshire
Boulevard, we had offices in Beverly Hills. Actually, it was a very small staff
of half a dozen or so, including Jack Leewood, a producer and troubleshooter
for Lippert. Bill Magginetti was production manager and Jodie Copeland film
editor. And the story editor—me. (Also, I was running some theaters for Bob
in my spare time *[laughs]*!) We brought everything else in from the outside,
hiring as we needed.

Were you involved on Lippert's Kronos *and* She Devil?
Kronos, no. *She Devil* was going on while I was there, but I was really
not much involved on that, either.

The Unknown Terror? Back from the Dead?
Unknown Terror, not that I recall. I worked with Charles Marquis Warren on *Back from the Dead;* Warren did the directing and Robert Stabler did
the producing. It was based on a novel [*The Other One*] by Catherine Turney,
who also wrote the script. The only thing I remember about that involves Warren and his sardonic sense of humor. He was not a man who loved everybody,
and he particularly didn't like lady writers with convertibles and huge dogs
in the back seat—which is the way Catherine Turney arrived at Lucey's, a
restaurant across from Paramount, where we met to discuss the script. This
lady loved her dog and worried about it and brought it over with her. Halfway
through this meeting, there was a problem involving a dog in the script. I
made some suggestions, Stabler made some suggestions—and Warren settled
it: "Why don't we just *kill* the dog?" Catherine *blanched*—but killed the dog
anyway!

Any recollections of Space Master X-7?
That was produced by Bernard Glasser and directed by Ed Bernds. I
remember that we had to go over budget on the script, but actually the thing
I remember more about the overall situation there was that they did a very
good job. Ed Bernds was just great to get along with, a capable writer and
director, and Bernie Glasser had lots of production experience. In an outfit
like ours, where we were making a lot of pictures with a small staff, it was great
to have units that you could turn the picture over to, and not worry about
anything other than acts of God. When we decided to make *Return of the
Fly,* I suggested them, and Lippert went along with that idea. He liked both
of them, too. The big problem on *Return of the Fly* was figuring out where
to start. *The Fly* was a one-shot deal, an accident. It's not like a Frankenstein
Monster, someone you could revive.

Also, you killed the original Fly pretty thoroughly in the first movie.

Yeah, we crushed the hell out of him in a press! So we were really puz-
zled, how do we make a sequel to this thing?! We finally got (sort of) a
reasonable answer, setting it years after the first *Fly* and having the son recreate
his father's experiments. Ed Bernds wrote every word of the script, I'm not taking any credit along those lines, but we would kick things back and forth and
bring back memories of other films that might have something that would
possibly help us. And it worked out quite well. They shot it over at Fox and
it had a higher budget than the usual one hundred twenty-five thousand
dollars. It went smoothly, and the picture was very profitable.

Did you have a chance to meet Vincent Price while making Return of the Fly?

Yes, as a matter of fact, we had lunch with Price. It was strange to sit with
this man who had a huge art collection, and the ability to discuss practically
*any*thing that you could think of—and know that the public perception of
him was as an evil monster *[laughs]*! They couldn't have been more dissimilar,
the screen man and the real man, who was a pleasure to be with.

I had another experience like that on *Witchcraft*. I wasn't in England
when *Witchcraft* was being made, but I went over subsequently on something
else, and stayed for two or three days at the Thames Court, which was a big
house that had been turned into a hotel. It was run by a man and wife, and
when she found out I was connected with the movies, we started talking—
"Bob Hope stayed here once," things like that. She said, "The one I remember
the best was Lon Chaney, Jr. He was here making a picture *[Witchcraft]*, and
you know the terrible people he plays in the movies"—she admitted that she
was a little worried, having him going up and down the halls in her hotel!
And, she said, the first time she met him, he *was* coming down the hall: "He
spread his arms wide and said, 'Let's dance!'" She said he was the most lovely
man *[laughs]*!

*Once the Regal setup came to an end, Lippert called his company Associated
Producers.*

This was around nineteen fifty-nine, and television was a factor. As I understood it, Lippert and Skouras had the thought that they would make a
bunch of pictures for one hundred thousand dollars or less apiece. At the time,
film companies tended to sell features to TV in blocs of thirteen. A bloc from
Fox would include a big picture, half a dozen medium-sized pictures—and then
they wanted to sneak a few of these Lippert cheapies in at the bottom, and it
would be profitable in the long run! The market soon changed and the TV people lost interest in the smaller pictures, but it worked for a while.

Anyhow, when that was decided, we knew that we couldn't continue to
operate on the old basis, so it became a house operation. Maury Dexter was
the production manager for the company; he'd been an actor, and was anxious

to direct. I had been story editor, and I was anxious to write. So we were both there, and we became the nucleus of the thing, because the organization wasn't in a position to go out and bid in the open market for writers and so forth. We didn't have the money to pay 'em; then also, as in the case of (let's say) *The Day Mars Invaded Earth,* we used practical sets. In other words, we didn't go onto stages, and therefore we didn't have to pay any studio costs. When we had an idea for a picture, Maury and I would look over the situations, and see what could and couldn't be used. For *Day Mars Invaded Earth,* the script was written to the Doheny Mansion, to get the maximum out of the thing once we had rented it. Except for the opening office sequence — which was shot in one of our company offices — the entire film was shot at Greystone, built by the Doheny oil family in nineteen twenty-eight for what was then a staggering price for a residence, three million dollars. It had a pool, greenhouse, stables, movie theater and bowling alley. We rented it for around two thousand dollars a day and tried to use everything.

And we were doing six pictures a year, don't forget, so that meant a fresh, original script every two months. Now, that doesn't mean that you had two months *to write* the script: You had to come up with the idea, then you had to get it approved. Fortunately, Maury was a very talented guy and he knew production thoroughly. He was imaginative, he got along very well with crews, and he was unflappable. He'd run into things that would absolutely *destroy* the average director, and to him it was business as usual! He was, and is, a very, very capable guy. He later became a right-hand man to Michael Landon — directing for him, production-managing for him — and had a very successful career with him.

Was The Day Mars Invaded Earth *your first script?*

It was the second script I ever wrote and the first in the sci-fi genre. There was quite a lot of talk about Mars at that time — little green men and that sort of thing! I thought to myself, "Well, nothing that *we* know could live on Mars, if what they say about it is correct. If there's any life on Mars, then it's an abstract kind of life." And from that, I developed the idea of the "abstract life" coming down the beam to Earth, creating duplicates of human beings and so on. Of course, it had all *kinds* of advantages: It could all be done at the one place, and all the main characters play two parts!

Now, you have to understand that, for *me,* this was an absolutely fabulous opportunity. Not that the pictures were that great, but who ever gives you a chance to sit down and write scripts, and see every single one of them made, and find out where you went wrong and where things worked out? Of course, with pictures like these, you're very restricted: You can't shoot at night, you can't have snow, you can't have rain, you have to be able to "work" the location, and you have to be able to shoot the film in seven days. That's the most we'd have. The scripts would run around one hundred, one hundred five pages, and in seven days, that's a lot of pages a day to do. Also, one of Lippert's favorite sayings was, "Talk is cheap, action's expensive." So you'd get characters in a room and have 'em do twenty pages of dialogue; that's an awful lot easier than car-chasing and violence, which we couldn't really afford in those days.

The girl playing Kent Taylor's teenage daughter [Betty Beall] had a lookalike stand-in, didn't she?

We *did* use identical twins, which caused quite a stir on the set. They were a couple of nice youngsters with little or no experience. Mostly they worked in TV commercials. Casting them certainly made life a little easier for Maury Dexter.

The downbeat ending of Day Mars Invaded Earth *comes as a surprise.*

Everybody loved that. The picture still shows up on TV now and then, and gets mentioned in articles, which always pleases me. I always liked that one; I saw it again recently, and I was surprised how well it still plays. Kent Taylor loved it. He came up to me one day and said he'd given the script to his daughter the night before and asked her to read it, and she thought it was great. On the set, he would do *any*thing for us, in addition to acting, because he loved that particular story.

Part of Lippert's formula was using stars who were well past their prime.

Lippert — or Fox, as the case may be — would *always* say, "We have to have a recognizable 'name' in here, not just a bunch of guys named Joe." But the Recognizable Names didn't necessarily fit the script. That was the big problem with *Curse of the Fly*: Claude Rains was who I had in mind when I wrote it, not expecting to get him. It should have had a Claude Rains or a Herbert Marshall, and what we got was Brian Donlevy, who was a tough New York–type. He's the best Brian Donlevy–type around, but he's probably the poorest Claude Rains that ever walked *[laughs]*! That used to happen quite often. We had to use actors for their *one-time* name value, regardless of how badly they were miscast. At this stage of the game, many really didn't care, and a lot of 'em would just "phone it in." Kent Taylor was not that way, he liked to work, he enjoyed it. But a lot of those pictures could have been greatly helped with better casting, regardless of "name value."

How did House of the Damned *come about?*

Somebody quite high up in the business told me once that he would have given a lot for that script; not necessarily to shoot it exactly as written, but he loved the whole idea of the old circus owner taking in these sideshow freaks in their dying days. Here's how it came about: I was talking to somebody about Tod Browning's *Freaks,* and whoever I was talking to said, "You couldn't make that now because they don't have freak shows anymore." I took that little thought home with me and I wondered, "Well, if they don't have freak shows anymore, where *are* all these people?" That thought turned into *House of the Damned*. We got hold of a house up in the Hollywood Hills, a place that once had a lurid reputation. You went down a two-lane little concrete road to a *cul de sac*—not very big. And there this building was, tall and narrow. With *a* door. You opened the door, and there you were in a little foyer with an elevator. That was it. In the Prohibition days, it was a speakeasy—with all the stuff that went with the speakeasy business. And the way it was set up, they had absolute control of everybody coming in *and* going out. The man who was renting it at the time was a great collector of antiques. He had this place full of things he'd bought from the William Randolph Hearst estate, stuff that Hearst had picked up all over the world. And he was quite pleased and fascinated: Not only did he have all this Hearst stuff in his very strange house, but now he had a whole houseful of freaks working in there!

Tod Browning's old-time circus melodrama *Freaks* provided the inspiration for Spalding's creepy *House of the Damned*.

House, *I thought, was one of the better Lipperts.*

It's the one I would like to have done all over again. It had a nice ominous "feel," but it was a picture that you couldn't shoot properly in seven days, it was something you really had to work on. Especially *after* making a picture, you begin to see opportunities that you hadn't thought about before. The third act didn't look bad on paper but sorely lacked conflict and climactic action in actual fact. The freaks should have been used much more and been more integrated into the story. However, since they are basically handicapped people and not actors, this would have been almost impossible for Maury on a seven-day shooting schedule.

Did you know what kind of "freaks" you'd be using before you wrote the script?

No, no. In Hollywood, it doesn't matter *what* you want, there's an agent representing it. And there was a guy that represented freaks—I guess there *were* still some carnivals and freak shows around. I met them all at the time, of course, but the only one I remember is Richard Kiel, who later played Jaws in the James Bond films. He was a very soft-spoken, very mild sort of man.

Some of the later Lippert pictures were made in England.

In England, he could get Eady Plan money, and he could get *rid* of a good deal of the responsibilities, because the English producers were basically in charge of shooting. Lippert met a fellow named Jack Parsons, who was in the theater business over there; Jack was dying to get into pictures. So they got together. *Witchcraft* was the first one of those I was involved in.

Where did the idea for that come from?

When I was in San Francisco, there was a graveyard that dated back to before the Fire. It was full—no new bodies had been buried there for years. Somebody decided it would make a fantastic real estate development, so they offered to move all the bodies to another cemetery. Of course, great-grandchildren came out of the woodwork *[laughs]*, and it was a big news story in San Francisco. And it always stuck in my mind; thinking in terms of horror, I wondered, "If you ran a bulldozer through here, what might you run across?" I had that on the back burner for a long time—there was nothing I could do with the idea under the old Lippert program. But for an English horror film, it was perfect, because they did have that whole witch business back in Cromwell's time.

That's another one that came out particularly well.

I had more time, and they got a good director, Don Sharp. I met Don later, and he said he thoroughly enjoyed it. He realized the thing very well—they had about fifteen days to shoot in England, as compared to the seven here. And it got some very good reviews in England; *Sight and Sound* compared it to the Val Lewton pictures. So it helped Don quite a bit. The big ending was the scene of the house burning, which goes back to the burning of the witches in the first place. Instead of having "phony" flames coming out of a set, they found a suitable house that was going to be destroyed and made a

Yvette Rees as the witch in the Spalding-scripted *Witchcraft.*

deal. They burned the actual house to the ground! It made a very effective ending for a small picture.

Any memory of Spaceflight IC-1?

That one was made in England, too. Like a lot of movies, that was based on ideas that came out of the newspapers. There was talk back then that if people were ever going to fly to Mars, they'd have to be frozen for the trip and revived once they got there.

Recollections of Lippert's Hand of Death?

That script originated with an Eastern company which was a good customer of Fox. Wishing to accommodate him without involving the parent company, Fox passed the project on to us. They did this now and then with relatives or friends who wanted to get into the movie business. Gene Nelson had done some acting for us and very much wanted to direct. Bob decided to give him a chance with *Hand of Death,* which got Gene into the Directors Guild. It was his first directing assignment and led to many, many more. I had almost nothing to do with that one.

Were you involved at all on The Cabinet of Caligari?

[Laughs.] Steven Scheuer in his movies-on-TV book gave *The Cabinet of*

Caligari one half a star and characterized it as an "aberration." The perfect word!

One of the major agencies in Hollywood represented the remake rights to the all-time internationally famous film masterpiece *The Cabinet of Dr. Caligari*. They shopped it all over town with no takers and finally brought it to Bob Lippert. Everyone in our organization hated the whole idea, but Bob decided to take a chance. The next thing we knew, he'd hired a European director no one had heard of and installed him at the Goldwyn Studios.

It certainly was an odd sort of film for Lippert to try to do.

Bob got out of his depth very quickly in this thing—all his friends said, "Bob, for Christ's sake, don't start remaking the classic motion pictures of all time!" But Bob got stubborn, as he sometimes did, and he decided he was going to go ahead and do it no matter what *any*body said. He then found out that they were probably right *[laughs]*! I inherited the job of sort of unofficial liaison. The director hired Robert Bloch, who had just written *Psycho*, but soon had a falling-out with him. He then wrote a script himself, interesting in a Freudian way, but completely uncommercial. The "aberration" continued, including a fistfight at a cast meeting, because by now Lippert was in too deep to drop it. I wrote a report which fortunately ended my usefulness as liaison and someone else got stuck with the job. When the picture was finished, the Fox sales and publicity staffs had no idea what to do with it. The reviews generally were scathing. It was as if Roger Corman had decided to remake *Citizen Kane*.

My pleasantest personal memory of a very *un*pleasant project was of opening a door to go onto a Goldwyn stage and running into a young man coming out. He stepped back and politely held the door for me. It was Elvis Presley, who was shooting *Kid Galahad* [1962] on an adjoining stage. My teenage daughters were delighted.

Wasn't Lippert involved with The Last Man on Earth?

I was involved on *several* last-man-on-Earth-*type* pictures. When I first came down here to Hollywood, Charles Marquis Warren and Robert Stabler had an option on a book by George Stewart called *Earth Abides,* which was a last-man-on-Earth story. It would have been a bit expensive to make at the time, but nevertheless it was a good story. Unfortunately, before much happened, Metro made another last-man story, *The World, the Flesh, and the Devil,* so that pretty much killed *Earth Abides*. Then later on, I went through the old cliché of finding a book in a second-hand bookstore, a paperback of *I Am Legend* by Richard Matheson—another last-man-on-Earth story, several years old. I talked to Bob Lippert about it, and he liked the idea. (Last-man-on-Earth stories have very small casts, which makes 'em quite reasonable *[laughs]*!) So I got in touch with Dick Matheson, who is a very nice man, very

Alien robots *and* the living dead walk our streets in *The Earth Dies Screaming.* Left-right: David Spenser, Virginia Field and (reacting to a gunshot) zombie Vanda Godsell.

talented. He had an idea which I love to this day: Make one of the major scenes the last man on Earth trying to make friends with the terrified last *dog* on Earth. It typified the whole story.

    Meanwhile, a deal was made to shoot it in Italy, so it got out of our hands altogether. I had to go back to Matheson and tell him that, which didn't make him too happy. Didn't make *me* too happy, either. American International made it as *The Last Man on Earth,* with Vincent Price, and they had their own approach. Matheson was talking along the lines of *Cat People*—using the audience's imagination. American International had the attitude of putting as many vampires at the window as they could afford!

You later wrote an English picture for Lippert that was half-alike, The Earth Dies Screaming.

    That, I thought, was the worst title in the world. Somebody said that as a joke, and somehow it just *stuck*! That's the way things sometimes worked in those days. It had a good director, Terence Fisher, but apparently they had a lot of trouble on the set. What the problem was, I really couldn't say, because I wasn't there. And I've always wished that picture would kind of go away, because I hate that title so much *[laughs]*!

A menagerie of mutants — but no Fly — furnished the horror in the English-made *Curse of the Fly*. (Pictured above: Mary Manson, Carole Gray.)

Lippert went to the well once too often with Curse of the Fly.

Lippert was co-producing these ninety thousand dollar wonders, and *he* came up with this one: He said, "Why don't we do another Fly? We have the rights." I said, "Bob, how can we do a third Fly? We were lucky to be able to do a *second* one!" He said, "Well, you can handle it, kid!" Actually, considering the basic problem, it wasn't all that bad a script. As a matter of fact, Don Sharp said that the opening ten pages, where the girl [Carole Gray] is coming out of the insane asylum, was the best opening he'd ever had on a film.

So what was "the basic problem"?

The problem was that you really needed a Claude Rains kind of guy to play that main part — remember I told you that I had Rains in mind when I wrote it. And from the word *go,* you didn't believe Brian Donlevy, who ended up in that role. This threw a pall over the whole thing. I gathered that Don Sharp felt it wasn't working, and that he had lost confidence, or felt depressed by what he was getting. And he had rather *liked* the script, originally.

Who put Donlevy in there? Lippert?

Right. Bob tended to do what had worked before; he was a very practical guy. Donlevy had worked fine for *Creeping Unknown*; Lippert was about to do this similar picture *[Curse of the Fly]* in England; and the two things went together in Bob's head. Donlevy was getting very little work at that time. I saw the picture, and I don't remember liking it very much; I might like it better now than I did then. But it was very difficult writing a script here in Los Angeles for a production in England. It goes out of your hands, and they go ahead and make it. It's supposed to be a collaborative medium, but there was no collaboration there. You didn't get a chance to sit down with the director — or with *any*body — to discuss things, to pick *their* brains. So I was kind of uncomfortable with those, except for *Witchcraft,* which came out better than I had expected.

Did you worry that the audience might feel gypped by a Fly movie with no Fly?

I don't remember whether I worried about that or not. I *do* remember Donlevy complaining bitterly that he'd spent his whole life in movies, and the only thing anybody ever remembered was *The Great McGinty* [1940]!

Did they do any rewriting on these English pictures?

Not much, no. But it would have been all right with me if somebody had wanted to, under those circumstances. (On one of 'em, I forget which one, they shot the first draft with no revisions, and I objected a bit on *that!*) *They* [the English filmmakers] felt uncomfortable with it, too, I think. They didn't know quite what my relationship with Lippert was, they didn't want to hurt my feelings, things like that.

Why did you use the "Henry Cross" pseudonym on some of these pictures?

That was very simple. I wrote eighteen original scripts in three years, and I didn't want people to start thinking that the only writer in Hollywood was Harry Spalding! So there were maybe nine Harry Spaldings and nine Henry Crosses. That was the primary reason.

Why did you leave Lippert?

He closed down his production company and moved back to the Bay Area. I sat down with Bob and talked with him about it, and said, "I think I'd like to stay here." He said, "Great, kid, fine." I used to see him after that, up in San Francisco, from time to time. Then I went to Europe for a couple of years, and eventually wound up at Disney.

While at Disney, you co-wrote The Watcher in the Woods.

My wife Jean is a great mystery story reader, and one day she said to me, "I think this novel *Watcher in the Woods* would be pretty good for Disney." So I read it, and she was right. I took it over to a producer at Disney, and *he* took it to Ron Miller, Disney's son-in-law, who was in charge of motion picture

Filmmakers line up a low-angle shot of Bette Davis in this glimpse behind the scenes from *The Watcher in the Woods*.

production. They bought it, and I did the first draft. Disney at that time had a policy of doing a certain number of pictures in England, for various reasons; and this, they figured, was ideal for England. They turned it over to an English director [John Hough] who had done several things for them; and English directors always use English writers, in my experience. So I was *out* and they were *in*.

Did they retain what you had written?

Basically, there wasn't that much changed. *My* feeling was that you couldn't show the audience the Watcher, you had to let them imagine it. They got caught in the trap of trying to show it. That was the major difference. After all, we were all working from the same novel, the same material. I wound up with a co-credit on it, which was fine. I also kidded them that the least they could do was give my wife a finder's fee—which they laughed heartily about, and changed the subject!

Given all the limitations you've had to work with, have you enjoyed writing science fiction and horror films?

The thing I remember most about writing them was how much fun it was. I've always felt that way. They're really fairy tales for adults, and in a sense they take me back to my childhood when I loved *The Phantom of the Opera* and those things. It's an interesting kind of writing because you don't use much of your own life and experience in it; it's out of your head, it's fantasy, it's imagining. I was very fortunate that so much of what I wrote got on the screen, and gave me a chance to (hopefully) improve as time went on. It was just a lot of fun all the way along the line, and I have no regrets.

I feel I've had a career. Maybe not a great career, but what the hell. I won't retire, I'll just be found one morning, dead, with one shoe on and one shoe off. And with a script clutched in my hand!

Kenneth Tobey

WHAT DO THE MONSTERS FROM 20,000 Fathoms, from Another World and from Beneath the Sea have in common? Apart from the fact that they were nameless horrors threatening mankind in the Fabulous Fifties, the one other thing they share is that all were vanquished by movie and TV veteran Kenneth Tobey.

Born in Oakland, California, Tobey was headed for a law career when he first dabbled in acting at the University of California Little Theatre. That experience led to a year and a half of study at New York's Neighborhood Playhouse, where his classmates included Gregory Peck, Eli Wallach and Tony Randall. Throughout the 1940s, Tobey acted on Broadway and in stock, and in the late 1940s he made his Hollywood film debut in a Hopalong Cassidy Western. Since then he has appeared in 75 (or more) features and on countless TV series (including one of his own, the high-flying adventure series *The Whirlybirds*), but the monster-busting days when he took on vampires, dinosaurs and Martians remain his most enduring on-screen accomplishments.

Let's start out with me telling you how glad your fans are that you're so busy again lately.

It seems to *you* like I'm busy, but it seems to *me* that I haven't worked this year *[laughs]*! But last year [1991] was the best year I ever had.

Financially?

Yes, financially, *and* as far as doing some pretty good work. The last one that came out is *Honey, I Blew Up the Kid* and I played a walk-on in it, practically — an extra — and I got one of the best notices of anybody in the picture! "They were lucky to get Ken Tobey, the old tried-and-true..." — you know, all that crap *[laughs]*. I was a security guard in that. Then, in *Single White Female*, I have even *less* to do: I played a night clerk in a hotel. I ad-libbed quite a few lines, but I had only one written line. Also I did a two-parter on *L.A. Law* and I did a picture called *Desire and Hell at Sunset Motel* — hell, I'm pickin' up the crumbs now! (Actually, I had a pretty big part in that.)

Would you say that some of these roles you're getting lately in movies by young directors are thanks to The Thing?

Most of 'em. It's a golden oldie now and it's still got a lot of fans, and I don't have to tell you that that's very gratifying.

Even though The Thing *was a popular movie, in general it didn't do too much for the careers of the people in the cast.*

No, it didn't shoot me to stardom, you're right about that!

Previous page: They axed for it — the Things, Beasts and Its that threatened mankind in the 1950s, only to be beaten back by Kenneth Tobey. (Photo from *The Thing from Another World*.)

Did you have to compete with other actors to get the role? Did you have to test for it?

No. I did do a lot of testing, but I did it with people that were cast *around* me, Dewey Martin and so forth. I'd done a picture for Howard Hawks called *I Was a Male War Bride* [1949] that was supposed to be a daily job, but Cary Grant and Ann Sheridan laughed so hard at what I did (I have no idea *what* I did!) that Hawks kept writing in new scenes for me. And at the end of the picture he said to me, "You know, I'm gonna star you in a picture someday." Nothing more was said. So I kept my eyes and ears open as far as his next picture, and when I read about *The Thing* in a paper, I called him and he said, "I was just gonna call you. Come on in and see me." So I don't know if there were any other people up for it. I know a lot of people *hated* me 'cause I got it.

Other actors who would have liked the role?

Scores. I'm not gonna name 'em because that wouldn't be nice. I think Margaret Sheridan and I were the only two that didn't have to test [for leading parts]. I'm sure that some of the old character actors that Hawks knew didn't have to test, either.

When I first talked to Hawks about *The Thing*, he said, "Why don't you come in today?" I came in and Hawks was talking to a little short guy. And I had my brains blown when the secretary or somebody called this guy "Mr. Faulkner." I realized right away that's who it was, William Faulkner, because he looked exactly like his picture on the cover of books. I'd been a student of Faulkner's, but I never got a chance to talk too much to him because he was hurrying off to his first drink of the day *[laughs]*. He drank quite a bit, he was depressed out here. But Hawks loved great writers and did everything he could for them.

And Faulkner had a hand in The Thing, *you believe.*

Oh, yes. I know he was asked to write a treatment, but I'm not sure if he did, or if it just wasn't what they wanted. I realized then that even great writers are not always accepted on the first draft, either.

Margaret Sheridan had been under contract to Hawks since nineteen forty-five, and yet The Thing *was her first picture.*

And almost her *last*, as far as I remember. She wasn't aggressive about pursuing her [acting] career. She made quite a bit of money hair modeling and stuff like that. Margaret was a wonderful girl; she died a few years back. Robert Cornthwaite [who played Dr. Carrington] was a lovely man and a good actor, *still* working, still doing nice things. Douglas Spencer ["Scotty"] was Ray Milland's stand-in for years and years, and *The Thing* was his big chance. I know he did a Western after *The Thing* — I didn't see this, I only heard about it — and he had the reins tied around his fingers. And the goddamn horse lurched so quickly forward that it tore his finger out—literally tore his finger right out of his hand.

Was he good to work with on The Thing?

I had a little trouble with him, but otherwise he was fine. Somebody had taught him how to get upstage and all that crap. I don't do it and I don't want anybody else to do it to me.

Do you think The Thing *would have worked as well if Hawks had put established stars into it?*

No, I don't, I think he had the right idea. I mean *[laughs],* Tyrone Power could have played my part pretty easily, but I don't think it would have had the same impact. It was more believable with*out* name actors. At least, that's the story I'm getting now when they won't cast me in some of these new pictures—"No, no, you're too well-known!"

Was James Arness really *as embarrassed about* The Thing *as people say?*

[Emphatically.] Yes, he *was.* He was so embarrassed about all the makeup, he never came and had lunch in the RKO commissary with us! (I have no idea where he did eat; maybe he brought his lunch.) But he was a *very,* very nice man. I was down on my uppers at one time and I got a small part on an episode of his TV show *Gunsmoke,* and he *knew* I was having trouble. And, doggone it, he called an end to shooting that day at six o'clock just so I'd have to come back the next day and do (maybe) one line or something. So I got two days' pay instead of one. That was wonderful of him, and I'll never forget him for that.

Whenever you worked with Arness subsequent to The Thing, *did you feel free to mention the film, or did you think it was a sore subject?*

It didn't come up. *I* would have mentioned it, but I just never thought of it. I had nothing to ask him or tell him.

What did you think of Arness' makeup?

I was a touch disappointed. I think they should never have shown a closeup of what it looked like. Showing that detracted from the mystery and the scariness. The makeup itself—well, to me it looked like a big guy with a green face! Look, both the Greenway boys [makeup men Lee and Dan] have passed on, and they did a lot of good work, so I don't have to worry about them.

Did you ever meet Howard Hughes?

Oh, yeah. This was quite a bit before making *The Thing.* I met him at about three-thirty in the morning! He had an aide call me at about two-thirty in the morning, and I'd come home a little . . . inebriated. I told the aide, "I

More-than-heroic he-man, less-than-helpless heroine: Tobey and Margaret Sheridan in a nostalgically sexist posed shot from *The Thing*.

can't meet a man like Hughes at *this* hour" — I told the guy I'd been out playing and so forth. He said, "He just wants to look at you." I told him, "Oh, I look *awful*!" — I'd just been awakened from sleep. The aide said, "He just wants to *meet* you." So I thought, well, I'd better go or he might say *no* [to casting Tobey in *The Thing*]. So I went over there and he took a look at me, and said, "Okay." That was *it [laughs]*! This was at Hughes' little office across the street from RKO, a terrible little office — he probably *owned* the whole block! I walked in and he stared at me, looked me up and down, and said, "Okay." That was my Howard Hughes experience.

All the time that you were up in Cut Bank, Montana, waiting for snow, how did you pass the time?

We played poker, and I went for long walks; we entertained each other. Sometimes we'd go through a scene, under Hawks' direction; we'd see how it started and see if it played. There were two guys up there, radio personalities who were pretty clever, George Fenneman and Paul Frees—they played two of the scientists. Paul Frees entertained us quite a bit, he was a very funny man.

You stayed at a hotel up there?

[Laughs.] Well, up *there* it was called a hotel; down here, it would be called a rooming house! You didn't have too many of the comforts of home, that's for sure. We flew up there on a chartered plane, one of Howard Hughes' own planes. He owned TWA then, and they had all Constellations. He took an old, tired Constellation and gave it to us to go up and back. And the Indians up there made me an honorary Blackfoot when I got off the plane! They gave me all sorts of stuff—Indian mementos which I later gave to some kids down here. Things like declarations written on leather. I forget what my Indian name was now, it was something like Running Star or some other ... idiot name *[laughs]*. We ended up shooting the snow scenes at the RKO Ranch down here, with phony snow, and we all got pretty overheated. It was a hundred degrees when we shot it and we had on all that crap—fur coats and hats and so on. What they used for ice was photographic solution; photographic solution, when it hits the air, freezes, almost like dry ice. It was a very, very tough few days. That was towards the end of the shooting.

You also blew up the "saucer" in that scene.

And when that blast went off, we were *really* ducking! When I yelled, "Hit the deck!", it wasn't a written line, I wanted everybody to get down!

In scenes where your breath is showing because of the "cold," Robert Cornthwaite says you were actually blowing out cigarette smoke.

No, that's not true; maybe he was thinking of someone else. We worked in the Ice House in downtown Los Angeles, which is where ice was made. It was very old then; it's forty years older *now*, *if* it's still standing. The only reason we worked there was because Hawks wanted to see our breath coming out of our mouths, but it was kind of tough to do that. The Ice House was about thirty degrees, so naturally our breath *was* showing, but all of our bodies warmed it up in there to like thirty-eight or forty degrees, so our breath *stopped* showing. So what we'd have to do was take a gulp of hot soup or hot coffee on "Action!", take a second to get ready, and *then* blow it out. That produced the foggy air.

Was the scene of the Thing on fire also shot there?

No, that was shot on a stage at RKO—on a stage that I just worked on when I recently did Bob Newhart's new show. That fire scene was kind of scary, really. I was trying to protect Margaret Sheridan—then that damn mattress caught on fire, and I disappeared in a hurry! And so did *she,* I guess *[laughs]*! That shows how brave us actors are! The stuntman that was put on fire had a little tank of oxygen under all that crap he had on, and he had a tube going into his mouth. But he only had one minute of oxygen in it, 'cause otherwise it would take too big a tank. So we shot the scene in about seven or eight takes, because he kept running out of oxygen. That stuntman's name was Tom Steele, he was a real good man.

Did you ever read the original short story?
Yeah—*Who Goes There?* by John Campbell. And I was very impressed by that story, although our show is nothing like it. It was a terrifying story.

How long were you on The Thing*?*
Nineteen weeks—that was my first *g-o-o-d* run. I wasn't making enough money to save a lot, but I lived for quite a while on it.

Where did you see The Thing *for the first time?*
I saw it in Pasadena, with Hawks' family—his mother and father were very old and they lived in Pasadena. I sat in the balcony with a couple of friends of mine, and I almost fell *out* of the balcony at the scene where the airmen open the door and the Thing is right there on the other side of it. I'd forgotten all about it, and the scene scared *me!*

Talk about John Carpenter's newer version of The Thing.
I saw it. I didn't care much for it. To me it was kind of *phallic*—all those tentacles or arms or whatever you want to call 'em. And I never could recognize any actors at all; except for Kurt Russell, I can't tell you who was in it.

What made Hawks such a great director?
He *listened.* And he had impeccable taste, and a wonderful sense of humor. He got sick fairly closely after that, and he didn't make all that many more pictures. I was supposed to be cast in *The Big Sky* [1952], which was a pioneer-type picture with Kirk Douglas that Hawks did next. I don't know what happened, but *some*thing happened and Dewey Martin played the part I was supposed to play in that. Hawks and Howard Hughes had multiple ownership of my stupid contract, but I never made a picture for Howard Hawks again.

But you were *in a few other RKO movies for Howard Hughes.*

Bill Self and director Christian Nyby give Tobey a hand at the 1982 reunion of key personnel from *The Thing from Another World*. (Photo courtesy Ed Mangus.)

And at about four times the money I made in *The Thing*. One was directed by Otto Preminger [*Angel Face*, 1952] and I got that part with no trouble at all, he just said, "Fine!" But during the picture he was kind of a stinker, in a way. I did something in one scene that made him laugh, and he spoiled the take. The next time I did the scene, Robert Mitchum did something funny, and *I* laughed. Mitchum was singing under his breath, "*Don't kick the actors in the balls, Mr. Preminger, don't kick the actors in the balls...*" [*Laughs.*] Well, I bust out laughing. And Preminger said, "What are you trying to do, ruin my picture?" I was never sure if he was serious or not, but he did have kind of a short fuse.

Christian Nyby still gives interviews where he takes credit for directing The Thing.

Chris has to sell himself, too. I've told the truth in about fifteen newspapers, magazines, etc., and on the air, so I don't mind telling you what I told them: Howard Hawks directed it, all except one scene. Chris Nyby directed us coming through a door, and it's the worst scene in the picture. I've worked with Chris on television and he was very nice to me. (And *I* was very nice to *him*.) He was an editor prior to *The Thing,* and he was learning how to direct from Hawks. But Hawks didn't let him learn by *doing [laughs]*! [Nyby died in 1993.]

Do you ever watch The Thing *any more these days? Or any of your science fiction films?*

Yeah, I watched *The Thing* recently in color—I didn't even know it *had* been colorized. I don't think it harmed it that much, *although* the black-and-white photography was really more conducive to the mood. (Whoever colorized it couldn't decide whether I had red hair or black hair, so they made it kind of reddish-black *[laughs]*!) I love to collect my movies [on video] because I let my folks see 'em, and show 'em to kids on Saturday afternoons. I don't have that many.

Why did you get out of your contract with Howard Hawks and Howard Hughes?

'Cause I wasn't being used. It may not have been a smart thing to do—I got a little hungry after that!—but career-wise I don't think it made a damn bit of difference. And I don't know if they'd have renewed me or not anyway.

What can you recall about The Beast from 20,000 Fathoms?

It was produced by a fellow that was originally a Dead End Kid, Hal E. Chester—nice guy—and they had a short schedule. I got along fine with everybody *except* a second assistant director who accused me of drinking, which I hadn't been doing. (I never drink while I'm working, I have my drinks *after* work *[laughs]*)! He spread the rumor that I was a drinker, and that kind of thing is anathema to your career. But I got along fine with everybody else: Paul Christian was the star and the girl was Paula Raymond, who became a friend of mine later. She was in a horrible automobile accident after the picture, but she was able to get back into pictures and she's still around.

That was Eugene Lourie's first film as director. Did he do much directing of the actors?

Well, he put us in position and then kind of let *us* work it out. He was a designer of special effects and art direction and things like that, an extremely talented man. He was another wonderful guy. I also met Ray Harryhausen on *Beast from 20,000 Fathoms,* and I'm very, very proud of that moment. He was extremely witty and very well trained in his profession. I enjoyed that whole picture very much.

You were in the next Harryhausen picture as well, It Came from Beneath the Sea, *for producer Sam Katzman.*

[Laughs.] Sam Katzman was a character, oh, my God. *It Came from Beneath the Sea* was a six- or seven-day picture: We had five days up in San Francisco and two days down here at the Columbia Ranch. Katzman comes over during the last day of shooting and says to the director, "How much more do you have to do?" The director, whose name was Robert Gordon, says, "We

only have three pages here"—it was my whole love scene with Faith Domergue. Katzman says, "Show me what you have to shoot," and Gordon shows him the script and says, "Just these three pages here." Katzman tears out the three pages and says, "*Now* how much do you have to shoot?" Gordon says, "Now we don't have *any*thing left." And Katzman says, "*G-o-o-d...*!" There went my whole love scene *[laughs]*!

Faith Domergue was another Howard Hughes "discovery." What was she like?
     She was a very nice lady. I didn't get to know her too well: I was married to a gal that was very jealous, so I didn't get to know *any* of my leading ladies too well. But we got along very nicely and she was a splendid girl. I remember we had a scene on a beach which we shot on a stage on the Columbia back lot; they had a truckload of sand brought in. And I weighing more than Faith, I kept sinking through the sand, down to the stage floor, and then I'd be looking *up* at her! I kept scraping the sand together at the beginning of the scene, packing it as hard as I could, and I'd start out looking over her head. But, by God, I'd sink down through that sand *during* the scene, and she looked like she was two feet taller than I was! I couldn't lick it, I just had to swallow my pride and look short.

What were you actually looking at when you were supposedly looking at the monsters in Beast *and* Beneath the Sea?
     The assistant director would walk around with something at the end of a stick, and you would follow *that* with your eyes. I tried to visualize what the monster might look like; we'd never even seen the giant octopus up till then.

The submarine scenes were shot on a real sub, correct?
     Absolutely. In fact, the fellow that played my executive officer *was* the commander of the sub. (I thought *his* acting was better than *mine!*) We went down under the ocean, so forth and so on, and it's pretty remarkable—the quality of the picture—considering it was done in seven days, and going on location to San Francisco!

Some scenes were photographed while the sub was actually submerged?
     Oh, yeah. They're lacking in room, submarines, so there were handheld cameras, [shortcuts] like that.

Did you stay with your folks while making that picture up in your old stamping grounds?
     No, I stayed in the hotel—the St. Francis, a great old hotel.

You were on Broadway in the nineteen forties, working with people like Ingrid Bergman—do you ever wish that people would ask you about things like that

Donald Curtis, Faith Domergue and Tobey, ready(?) for action in Sam Katzman's *It Came from Beneath the Sea.*

once in a while, and not just about The Thing *and the giant octopus and all this other nonsense?*

I hadn't thought of it. I did twenty-nine Broadway shows—don't ask me to name 'em *[laughs]*!—and a lot of people *do* remember me from Broadway. It's just nice that people remember you at *all*, it doesn't matter from *what!*

When you were on Broadway, were you earning a living by acting only?

When I was working, I never worked on the outside. Between jobs, I had several different jobs temporarily—I worked as a bartender, for instance, at the Commodore Hotel. There'd be periods of two or three months between jobs; if you didn't get something in the fall, you had to wait for summer theater.

You also went back to Broadway in nineteen sixty-four, for Golden Boy.

Oh, sure, with Sammy Davis. I was coming out of a jazz spot called Shelly's Manne-Hole in L.A. one night as Sammy was just going in, with his business manager, I think. The guy said, "There's your Tom Moody," and Sammy liked me ever since he saw *The Thing*. So they auditioned me—I had to sing a song, and I didn't do too well *[laughs]*. Then they had me come to

New York and audition again, and then they had me work with [conductor] Elliott Lawrence for an afternoon on one of the songs I had to sing in the show. I got the job.

You were also in one of the first reincarnation films of the nineteen fifties, The Search for Bridey Murphy.

I enjoyed it very much. I worked with Teresa Wright and Louis Hayward—I *loved* Louis Hayward, I worked with him several times in little tiny small-budget TV things at Ziv. I worked with a lot of wonderful people there at Ziv, people on their way down—like *I* am now *[laughs]*!

Reincarnation was a fad of sorts in the mid-nineteen fifties. Was the picture taken seriously by the people involved?

We *tried* to take it seriously. I went to one of the technical guys on it, a guy who knew all about hypnotism and stuff like that, and had him try to hypnotize me. Which he couldn't. I *pretended* he did—I didn't want to disappoint him too much. He said, "You're now starting to drool," so I pushed a bunch of spit out the side of my mouth to make it look right *[laughs]*! We had a real nice, big party at the director's house afterwards.

Any recollections of The Vampire *with John Beal?*

Yes, I enjoyed it very much. That was another six-day wonder, and we were at locations all over Hollywood. Most of the outdoor stuff was shot at an undeveloped lot, and all I remember is *running.* I'd run out one end of the lot, then we'd have to go back and set up at the *other* end of the lot, and shoot me running out the other end! What I also remember is John Beal, who is a very, very nice man; we've been friends ever since, although we don't see each other too much since he moved to New York. Coleen Gray was nice, too; she tried to get me into selling skin products and things like that door to door. I told her, "I may be unemployed, but I'm not *unintelligent*!" *[Laughs.]*

Was there any difference between working in these low-budget movies and working in TV?

W-e-l-l, not really. But I really did enjoy having my own series, *The Whirlybirds,* that was fun. In doing that series, I learned to fly, became a commercial pilot—I should say, I got a commercial *license.* All I needed was to take one flight test and I could have been a commercial helicopter pilot. But I didn't pursue it because it was so expensive; I hit a low spot about then and really couldn't afford to go that route.

Around the time of Psycho *you were the hero in a cheap thriller that tried to pass itself off as* Psycho-*ish,* Stark Fear.

Is that what it's called? I never knew the name of it! On that one, the director pooped out—the director was a drama teacher at the University of Oklahoma. He was inexperienced, he couldn't hold it, couldn't keep it together. The kid who was playing the villain, Skip Homeier, took over the direction. Oh, that was a miserable thing! They housed us in the hotel in Oklahoma City and we shot the film in Norman, Oklahoma, where the university is. We shot in sorority houses *[laughs]*—I don't know why, but we did. They built little sets or used the rooms that they had and so forth. And several times driving back from there, back to the hotel, I had to drive through thunderstorms. And, let me tell you, they were *wicked*! Tornadoes and stuff like that! I'd see cars *all over*—in the ditches beside the highway, *on* the highway—oh, it was awful. I got scared several times.

That's one film I'd like to see again, and show to people—show 'em I did some *bad* things, too *[laughs]*. Which I *did*—I've done some *awful* performances in this business. But in fifty years, you're allowed to have a few, you know.

In the nineteen seventies you had small parts in the Willard *sequel* Ben *and in a thriller called* Homebodies.

Oh, Jesus, *Ben*! I played a city engineer in that in a scene with Joe Campanella, and we shot that on one of the streets at Paramount at night, *all* night. And I want to tell you, it was the *coldest* night that Hollywood had ever seen—it set a record, it was below zero. Cold, wind—*awful*! I *hated* it. *Homebodies* was about a bunch of old people who don't want to be evicted from the tenement where they're living, so they start killing everyone who's trying to get 'em out. One of the old ladies was a gal named Paula Trueman; strangely enough, I went overseas with her doing a play with Moss Hart during the War, nineteen forty-four or forty-five, and *Homebodies* was the first time I'd seen her since. It was fun—she's a bird-like little thing, a little bit "tetched" here and there! I played a construction boss, and we shot that on a construction site in downtown L.A. And I hated that location, because the air was always full of cement dust.

You've played a number of sci-fi roles in the nineteen eighties, like Strange Invaders *and several Joe Dante pictures.*

I went to Toronto, Canada, for *Strange Invaders* and I enjoyed that very much. I don't think I was very *good* in it, but the director seemed to like it; I played the head cricket, and I was working as a little hotel keeper. I had a big part in that, I was on that for about five weeks.

And working with Joe Dante?

I enjoy Joe very much, but I really don't "work" with him, actually. He assigns me a part and he says, "Write a five-minute scene" when I show up— and writing's something I'm not too good at *[laughs]*! So I'm not sure I've ever really gotten to do my best, working for him. But I certainly don't mean that critically; he's one of my favorite directors, and very loyal to old actors. He hires the same ones all the time.

You worked with him for the first time on The Howling.

I played a policeman in that, a very, very tiny part. We were in the police car and they were taking shots of us traveling up and down the street. Three or four "custodians" of that street (if I can call 'em that) stopped us — prostitutes and bag ladies, drunks, all sorts of people. I almost ran over 'em — you can't see very well at night down Western Avenue. They came out into the street and flagged us down — either they needed help, or somebody was gonna shoot them, or some terrifying story, and they wanted our help! I was nonplussed — I didn't like to let 'em down, but I told 'em, "Well, we can't help you now, we're on a call!" *[Laughs.]*

I was also on Joe's *Innerspace*, which was a very funny movie — I had a famous scene in that. And it was only one tiny scene, just one line. Marty Short and I were in a men's room in a railway station; he's takin' a leak in a urinal and I'm coming out from takin' a crap. I'm putting on my coat and washing my hands, and it looks like he's talking to his dong 'cause he's looking right down there. He's had miniaturized people injected into his bloodstream and he's talking to them, but *I* don't know that. I say to him, "It's all right to play with it, but don't *talk* to it!" That got the biggest laugh in the show.

Any closing comment? Has it been a good career? Has it been everything you might have wanted or hoped for?

Yes, yes, no, no *[laughs]*. I've loved being an actor — that's what I do, that's what I enjoy doing. It's hard work — most people think it's a cushy job, but it's really not. I've been in it for fifty-three years or something close to that, and I've enjoyed . . . most of it. The long waits *between* jobs sometimes are not much fun, and the long waits on the set waiting for a scene to come up are not enjoyable, either. But I've become accustomed to the way it works and I feel I've had a career. Maybe not a *great* career, but what the hell. I won't retire, I'll just be found one morning, dead, with one shoe on and one shoe off. And with a script clutched in my hand!

KENNETH TOBEY FILMOGRAPHY

The Man on the Ferry (Soundies Short, 1943)
Dangerous Venture (United Artists, 1947)
This Time for Keeps (MGM, 1947)
Beyond Glory (Paramount, 1948)
He Walked by Night (Eagle-Lion, 1948)
I Was a Male War Bride (20th Century–Fox, 1949)

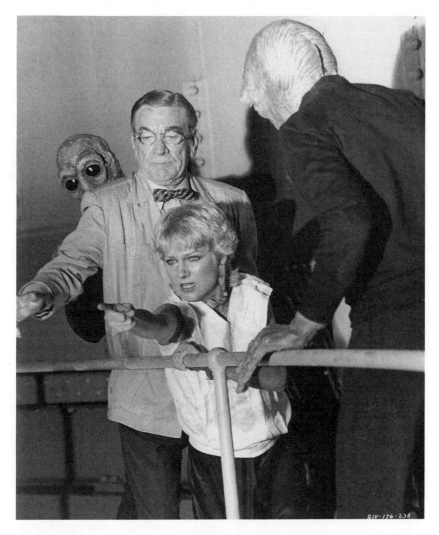

After fighting an alien threat in *The Thing,* Tobey was the humanoid leader of bug-like *Strange Invaders,* here contending with Diana Scarwid.

Task Force (Warners, 1949)
The File on Thelma Jordon (Thelma Jordon) (Paramount, 1949)
Free for All (Universal, 1949)
The Stratton Story (MGM, 1949)
Twelve O'Clock High (20th Century–Fox, 1949)
The Doctor and the Girl (MGM, 1949)
The Great Sinner (MGM, 1949)
Illegal Entry (Universal, 1949)
Love That Brute (20th Century–Fox, 1950)

Three Secrets (Warners, 1950)
When Willie Comes Marching Home (20th Century–Fox, 1950)
The Gunfighter (20th Century–Fox, 1950)
My Friend Irma Goes West (Paramount, 1950)
Kiss Tomorrow Goodbye (Warners, 1950)
Right Cross (MGM, 1950)
The Flying Missile (Columbia, 1950)
Up Front (Universal, 1951)
The Company She Keeps (The Wall Outside) (RKO, 1951)
The Thing from Another World (The Thing) (RKO, 1951)
Rawhide (Desperate Siege) (20th Century–Fox, 1951)
Angel Face (RKO, 1952)
The Beast from 20,000 Fathoms (Warners, 1953)
Fighter Attack (Allied Artists, 1953)
The Bigamist (Filmmakers, 1953)
Ring of Fear (Warners, 1954)
Down Three Dark Streets (United Artists, 1954)
The Steel Cage (United Artists, 1954)
Rage at Dawn (RKO, 1955)
Davy Crockett, King of the Wild Frontier (Buena Vista, 1955)
It Came from Beneath the Sea (Columbia, 1955)
The Steel Jungle (Warners, 1956)
The Man in the Gray Flannel Suit (20th Century–Fox, 1956)
The Great Locomotive Chase (Andrews' Raiders) (Buena Vista, 1956)
Davy Crockett and the River Pirates (Buena Vista, 1956)
The Search for Bridey Murphy (Paramount, 1956)
Jet Pilot (Universal, 1957)
Gunfight at the O.K. Corral (Paramount, 1957)
The Vampire (Mark of the Vampire) (United Artists, 1957)
The Wings of Eagles (MGM, 1957)
Cry Terror! (MGM, 1958)
Seven Ways from Sundown (Universal, 1960)
X-15 (United Artists, 1961)
Stark Fear (Ellis, 1962)
A Man Called Adam (Embassy, 1966)
40 Guns to Apache Pass (Columbia, 1967)
A Time for Killing (The Long Ride Home) (Columbia, 1967)
Marlowe (MGM, 1969)
Billy Jack (Warners, 1971)
The Candidate (Warners, 1972)
Ben (CRC, 1972)
Rage (Warners, 1972)
Walking Tall (CRC, 1973)
Dirty Mary, Crazy Larry (20th Century–Fox, 1974)
Homebodies (Avco Embassy, 1974)
Baby Blue Marine (Columbia, 1976)
W.C. Fields and Me (Universal, 1976)
MacArthur (Universal, 1977)
Goodbye Franklin High (Cal-Am, 1978)
Hero at Large (MGM, 1980)
Airplane! (Paramount, 1980)

The Howling (Avco Embassy, 1981)
The Creature Wasn't Nice (Creatures Features, 1981)
Strange Invaders (Orion, 1983)
Gremlins (Warners, 1984)
The Lost Empire (JGM Enterprises, 1985)
Innerspace (Warners, 1987)
Big Top Pee-wee (Paramount, 1988)
Freeway (New World, 1988)
Gremlins 2 The New Batch (Warners, 1990)
Honey, I Blew Up the Kid (Disney/Buena Vista, 1992)
Single White Female (Columbia, 1992)
Desire and Hell at Sunset Motel (Two Moon Releasing, 1992)

Halloween (Compass International, 1978) features clips with Tobey from *The Thing*. *Mr. Mom* (1983) features clips with Tobey from *I Was a Male War Bride*.

I *didn't think that I was
sexy [in* Dracula]*, but my youngest
grandson, when he finally saw the film,
said, "Grandma, I know now why Grandpa
married you!"*

Lupita Tovar

THE YEAR 1992 MAY GO DOWN IN THE Big Book of Horror History as the Year of the Vampire, and not just by virtue of the many new vampire films which invaded theaters that year. As fans of modern horror geared up for the unveiling of Francis Ford Coppola's eagerly awaited (and ultimately lousy) *Bram Stoker's Dracula*, followers of the classic chillers found cause to celebrate early: MCA Universal Home Video released the ultra-rare Spanish-language version of the 1931 horror milestone *Dracula*. Made in the days before the dubbing of Hollywood movies into foreign languages became commonplace, the Spanish *Dracula* was shot at Universal at night, on the same sets and locations where director Tod Browning put Bela Lugosi and the rest of his English-speaking cast through their paces during the day. Sparsely released (in the States) and seldom revived during the years since its original run, the film is being acknowledged by some fans as a more creative and cinematic rendition of Stoker's classic tale than Browning's stuffy museum piece; and one of the movie's only survivors, co-star Lupita Tovar, is still around to share 60-year-old memories of 1992's most notable horror release.

Born in Oaxaca, Mexico, Tovar appeared first in silent Fox films before making the move to Universal and co-starring in the Spanish-language version of 1930's *The Cat Creeps (La Voluntad del Muerto)*. For the same producer, Czech-born Paul Kohner, she also appeared as Eva (the Spanish-language counterpart of Helen Chandler's Mina) in the Spanish *Dracula*; in 1932 she married Kohner, who later became one of the top agents in Hollywood. (Their daughter Susan Kohner was Oscar-nominated for her performance in Universal's 1959 *Imitation of Life*.) Widowed since 1988, still sharp-witted, always friendly, Lupita Tovar Kohner remembers vividly falling under the spell of Dracula (Carlos Villarias), the undead *conde* who never drank ... *vino*.

Were the people involved on the Spanish Dracula *looking to "outdo" the Tod Browning* Dracula *that was shooting during the day?*

Yes, we were, and many of the critics say that we did. We were using the exact same sets, and we even had the same "marks" as the English cast, so that we would stand in the same spots.

Do you remember whether you ever bumped into Bela Lugosi or Tod Browning?

Oh, yes, Lugosi, he was terribly nice. I used to see him, usually on weekends. All the Europeans used to get together for a koffeeklatsch—they'd have coffee and pastries, and talk. And then sometimes they'd get together at small dinner parties, like at [actor] Victor Varconi's house—his wife was a wonderful cook. All the Hungarians would get together at places like that, and I was always invited because at that time Paul Kohner was sort of courting me; he was part of that group, and so whenever he was invited, he would bring me along. Even though they spoke German, and I hardly spoke English *[laughs]*!

Previous page: **Mexican actress Lupita Tovar brought a surprising level of sexy appeal to the Spanish-language version of Universal's** *Dracula.*

Paul Kohner was very romantic. Always there were flowers in my dressing room, and Sunday there were flowers at my house and boxes of candy. I started putting on weight, which I was not supposed to do *[laughs]*!

The cast of Dracula *knew that he had his eye on you?*
He was very, very careful, but of course everybody knew it. Everybody except me—I didn't realize it for a while because I was so worried about being good in the picture. When he came by, he said hello to everybody and he had dinner with us and sat next to me, but it was all business-like. I lived with my grandmother, so on Sundays he would take me out for coffee at Ernst Lubitsch's house or Mike Curtiz's—all of these Europeans. But he always came and asked my grandmother's permission, and he brought my *grandmother* flowers. You'd think he was courting my grandmother *[laughs]*! He had a very wonderful manner and he was quite a gentleman.

And Tod Browning?
No, I don't remember much about him. Naturally I met him afterwards, when we did publicity and all that. But not during work.

How about Carlos Villarias, "your" Dracula?
Villarias was a *wonderful* person. He was trying very hard to be as good as Lugosi. When you see the two versions, I think there's very, very little difference. They were both good actors—Villarias was really a good actor. The difference between the two was how they worked with their hands. Lugosi's fingers were very long, and Carlos Villarias had short fingers.

Did you have any inkling how Helen Chandler was playing her role in the English-language Dracula*?*
No, none of us had any opportunity to see the performances of the English actors. There *were* some movies I did where they'd have a moviola on the set and run the English-language versions, and we'd see what we were supposed to do. But on *Dracula,* we just didn't do that—it was a completely different interpretation. We didn't even see our own *Spanish* rushes, we never saw *any*thing.

Did Villarias stay "in character" between takes, the way Lugosi supposedly did?
He *was* concentrated on his performance and he kept to himself. He was determined not to get out of character. He was very serious. The only one that was always joking was young Barry Norton, who played my fiancé [Juan Harker]—he was always kidding and telling stories. Well, he was very young, and full of beans *[laughs]*! And Pablo Alvarez Rubio [Renfield] was wonderful. He was always very, very lively—and he had a *tough* role, very strenuous,

Cast photo from the Spanish *Dracula* with (left-right) Soriano Viosca, Carlos Villarias (Dracula), Carmen Guerrero, Tovar, Senorita Peza, Enrique Avalos, Barry Norton, Eduardo Arozamena (Van Helsing) and Pablo Alvarez Rubio (Renfield).

very demanding. I have wonderful memories of the making of this film. In between scenes, when there was a change of camera settings, all of these people used to tell stories about the theater and the plays they did, mostly in Spain. It was *fascinating*. They told different stories about actors and actresses and things that happened in the theater. I remember thinking that I had to "come up" to the other actors in the film, it was important to me that I didn't let them all down.

Looking back, do you think it was a good idea not *to show you Helen Chandler's performance?*

I think so, because I would have been very worried about copying her. I probably would have tried to imitate her performance, and we were two entirely different personalities. The way we did it, I was myself. I tried to understand George Melford, who was a wonderful director. We used to call him "Uncle George." Even though he did not speak Spanish, he somehow communicated with us what he wanted. There *was* an interpreter, but I tried to follow Melford, tried to understand what he wanted.

You see, I had no dramatic training. I came here to Hollywood from school; [director] Robert Flaherty came to Mexico City looking for talent, he went to my school and saw me doing gymnastics. Apparently he thought I had possibilities, because he had me make a test; Mr. Flaherty directed the test, *with* an interpreter. And a few weeks later, [Fox Films] came to me with a contract—which my father very quickly refused. He just would have no part of it. So they sent a second contract, and he still refused. No way could I go to Hollywood alone. So what happened was that I came to Hollywood with my grandmother, and I had a [Fox] contract which was supposed to be for seven years, with six-month options.

And so I had no [acting] training. At Fox, I did a couple of silent films where I didn't have to worry about dialogue or anything. But then when the "talkies" came along, everything changed. There was complete chaos at all the studios. They decided to bring in actors from New York, from the stage. And many of the big silent stars lost their careers because of the talkies. That was when I went to Universal, where I did first the Spanish version of *The Cat Creeps* [1930] and then *Dracula.* So there I was in *Dracula,* acting with wonderful actors, some of them stage actors very well known in their own countries for their theater work. I was still just a young girl, still very green, I still knew nothing. So I had to try very hard.

Helen Chandler is very prim in her Dracula, *and you're very sexy in yours.*

[Laughs.] I didn't even realize that! As we were doing it, I had no idea! For one thing, we had different wardrobes, Helen Chandler and I. Entirely different wardrobes—mine *was* very sexy. *I* didn't think that I was sexy or anything like that, but my youngest grandson, when he finally saw the film, said, "Grandma, I know now why Grandpa married you!" *[Laughs.]*

Was Kohner on the set of Spanish Dracula *most of the time?*

He was quite a bit. We were shooting at night, and naturally he worked there at Universal in the daytime, too. He used to come in as we got started, and then he'd go back to his office, I suppose to take a nap or something. We got a break about midnight for supper, and he used to come before that to see that everything was all right. Then about five o'clock in the morning he'd come around again and see how everything was going. He said he had a couch or something to nap on in between. So, yes, he came by every few hours. But, really, there was no need for him to come by because everything was going smoothly. We worked steadily until about seven-thirty in the morning, and then the English cast came in at eight.

So he was there at Universal twenty-four hours a day?

He was a very ambitious young man, very conscientious.

Did the people who made the Spanish Dracula *earn as much as the English* Dracula *people?*

No, no—we got a small salary. But that was the whole idea. The idea was to make the Spanish version for as little money as possible. So they used the same sets and everything. And these [Spanish-speaking actors] were not demanding big salaries. We didn't know any better, and everybody was very happy to get a job. Most of them had been having little parts in silent films, and many of them had even played extras, even though they had a name in Spain and in Mexico. When Universal said, "The role pays so-much," you didn't argue, you said, "Fine!"

Also, I was always there almost an hour early, so that I would feel "at home" in the set, so that I would feel that I was secure. Many times I went in and the crew hadn't arrived yet, so I would sit there in the dark until they came and started lighting the place up. And it was very scary, the whole feeling of being in there alone! If someone had come up behind me, I would have let out a scream *[laughs]*!

Was there ever any concern about all the different accents in Spanish Dracula?

No. For their Spanish films, the Fox studio employed only people from Spain, because [Fox] thought they were the only ones that spoke proper Spanish. Universal didn't care. If we fit the role, it didn't matter where we were from — Mexico, Spain, Argentina — nobody worried. It was the same way at Columbia. I made a picture at Columbia with one Spaniard, one Cuban and myself, a Mexican. And it was a beautiful film.

What do you remember about the public appearances you made in connection with Dracula?

I made some appearances here in California when the picture opened, and then I went to Mexico to different states with the film. It was a terrific success and it made a lot of money.

Do you remember where you saw it for the first time?

I saw it at the studio. There was a screening for the whole cast — none of us had seen anything. So they had the special screening, and afterwards a little party at the commissary. We got a lot of compliments, and we were very excited about seeing the film.

When did you see the Lugosi Dracula?

I didn't see it right after the Spanish; I was busy and doing publicity things for the film, and I was concentrated in my job. But years later I saw it, and then I saw it again on television not long ago. I think the Spanish is better! The other one is a little *dull*, it's too passive. And the Spanish keeps you interested in it, it has a little more excitement in it.

If you could have picked your own roles in those days, what would you have played?

Oh, I liked very dramatic roles. I made the first talking pictures in Mexico.

Tovar and actor Barry Norton (playing "Juan Harker") between takes on *Dracula*.

I did a picture called *Santa*—it means "The Saint"—and that's still playing on television in Mexico. It's the story of a young, innocent girl that is seduced by an officer, and then becomes the most famous prostitute in town. (That was *my* role!) It's been remade twice, but the version that I made is the one that is still going on. Last November [1991] was the sixtieth anniversary and I was invited down there. I went to Mexico City, right to the spot where our first scene was shot. They had actors coming in on horses and a girl dressed like I was dressed in the film—they had the whole thing reenacted. It was very moving. And I received a gold medal for it. There were only two other survivors: One was the sound engineer and the other one was an extra in the film, they brought him in a wheelchair. There again, I thought to myself, "My

God—sixty years!" An awful lot went through my mind, my whole *life*, I think. I mean, I'm no spring chicken, I'm an old lady, with grown-up grand-children. And all of these fantastic things keep happening.

Did you enjoy your acting days?

Oh, I loved to work. I did many Westerns, and for things like that I had to get up very early, like three in the morning. In those days, you had calls at four for makeup, and then you'd go on location. Paul [Kohner] used to drive me there, and then they'd bring me back to the studio and he'd pick me up in the afternoon. But his career was important, and we had to enter-tain. Many a time I'd come home and quickly take off my makeup, dead tired—and then be a hostess! Finally he said, "Look, this just won't work. I want a wife. You don't have to work." I said, "If that's what you want, fine." So I just completely ignored my career. I was interested always in what was going on when he stopped producing and became an agent; he was always with people who were in the business, so I didn't feel "out of it." Then I had my children, and that's a career in itself, to be a mother and raise two children and be a wife. I wanted my family to be happy, that was the most important thing to me. Once I gave up acting, I just lived for my husband, and I never thought about acting anymore.

Lately you've done some public appearances in connection with the Spanish Dracula.

I was asked to go to Dallas about a year ago, to go to the nineteen ninety-one USA Film Festival—Mr. [David] Skal's book *Hollywood Gothic* had come out, and the festival organizer Richard Peterson wanted to show the Spanish *Dracula*. They invited me, so I went with my son Pancho and two of my grand-children. And I felt very peculiar, I can tell you, especially when I arrived at the [Lakewood Theater] and got out of the car, and people came toward me — people wanting autographs. Then we went in and it was a wonderful theater, a theater that was built in the thirties. They showed the movie — no subtitles, and with one reel missing. And you could hear a pin drop. Nobody walked out. I was a little nervous—in fact, let me tell you, I was very, *very* nervous. Then when it was over, they asked me to come up on the stage and my knees were shaking! I sat there thinking, "Oh, dear, what am I doing here?", you know? But after a little while I was able to control myself and answer ques-tions, and it was all very, very exciting. It was like a *dream*. You don't expect that something you did sixty years before could ever catch up with you!

You did a special introduction for MCA's home video release of Spanish Dracula.

I hope that came out all right. I don't have any idea how I'll look on TV. You know, vanity. No matter how old you are, you still like to look good *[laughs]*.

And you are *enjoying the attention the film is now getting?*

Oh, my goodness, *yes!* The University of Madrid invited me to go for a seminar; when they called, I thought somebody was fooling me! I thought somebody was pulling my leg, making fun of me! So I was very, very cagey; I told them that, yes, I would be interested, but would you be so kind as to talk to my son? I told them to arrange it with him. Then I called *him* and told him I thought somebody was playing a joke on me. Well, after about a half an hour he called me back and said, "Mama, it's no joke!" They wanted me to come and talk about my movies from twenty-seven to thirty-five, to make a speech, to talk to the students. I thought, "My Lord, I'm not sure I can do this, but—why *not?*" And so I did it, last July [1992]. To do things like this is a *challenge.* And instead of becoming a vegetable *[laughs],* I can do *some*thing!

LUPITA TOVAR FILMOGRAPHY

The Veiled Woman (Fox, 1929)
La Voluntad del Muerto (Spanish-language version of *The Cat Creeps*) (Universal, 1930)
King of Jazz (Spanish-language version) (Universal, 1930)
Serenata de Hollywood (Hollywood Serenade) (Universal, 1930)
Dracula (Spanish-language version) (Universal, 1931)
Un Sueño Fue Tu Amor (Just a Dream; Only a Dream) (Universal, 1931)
El Tenorio del Harem (Universal, 1931)
Carne de Cabaret (Spanish-language version of *Ten Cents a Dance*) (Columbia, 1931)
Border Law (Columbia, 1931)
East of Borneo (Universal, 1931)
Yankee Don (Daredevil Dick) (Capitol/Mercury, 1931)
Santa (Compania Nacional Productora de Peliculas/Rafael Calderon [Mexican], 1932)
Alas Sobre el Chaco (Spanish-language version of *Storm Over the Andes*) (Universal, 1935)
Vidas Rotas (Broken Lives) (Inca, 1935)
El Capitán Tormenta (Spanish-language version of *Captain Calamity*) (Regal/Grand
    National, 1936)
An Old Spanish Custom (The Invader) (J.H. Hoffberg, 1936)
Blockade (United Artists, 1938)
El Traidor (The Traitor) (Duquesa Olga release, 1938)
The Fighting Gringo (RKO, 1939)
Maria (PISA, 1939)
South of the Border (Republic, 1939)
Tropic Fury (Universal, 1939)
Green Hell (Universal, 1940)
The Westerner (United Artists, 1940)
Two Gun Sheriff (Republic, 1941)
Gun to Gun (Warners short, 1944)
The Crime Doctor's Courage (Columbia, 1945)

Tovar's 1931 credit *El Tenorio del Harem* was edited together from the unreleased shorts *Caballeros Árabes* (Arabian Knights) and *Let's Play.*

Index

Numbers in **boldface** refer to pages with photographs.